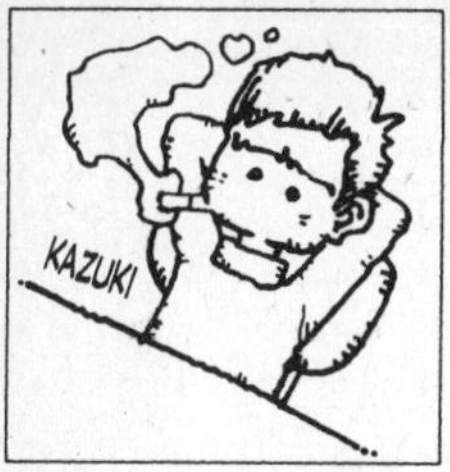
KAZUKI

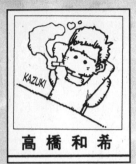

高橋和希

KAZUKI TAKAHA

I HADN'T SEEN JADEN IN A WHILE, SO WHEN I CAME FACE-TO-FACE WITH HIM WHEN HE APPEARED IN THE THEATRICAL *YU-GI-OH!* ANIME, I WAS MOVED BY HOW MUCH HE'D GROWN AS A CHARACTER AND HOW RELIABLE HE SEEMED! I'M REALLY LOOKING FORWARD TO SEEING HOW THE MANGA JADEN GROWS AS WELL!

KAZUKI TAKAHASHI

Artist/author Kazuki Takahashi first tried to break into the manga business in 1982, but success eluded him until *Yu-Gi-Oh!* debuted in the Japanese *Weekly Shonen Jump* magazine in 1996. *Yu-Gi-Oh!*'s themes of friendship and fighting, together with Takahashi's weird and imaginative monsters, soon became enormously successful, spawning a real-world card game, video games, and four anime series (two Japanese *Yu-Gi-Oh!* series, *Yu-Gi-Oh! GX* and *Yu-Gi-Oh! 5D's*). A lifelong gamer, Takahashi enjoys Shogi (Japanese chess), Mahjong, card games, and tabletop RPGs, among other games.

NAOYUKI KAGEYAMA

Naoyuki Kageyama was born April 12, 1969, which makes him an Aries, and is originally from Tokyo, Japan. He is the recipient of an honorable mention for the 1990 *Weekly Shonen Jump* Hop Step Award for his work *Mahou No Trump* (Magic Trump) and started drawing *Yu-Gi-Oh! GX* for *Monthly V Jump* in February 2006. Kageyama is a baseball fan and his favorite team is the Seibu Lions.

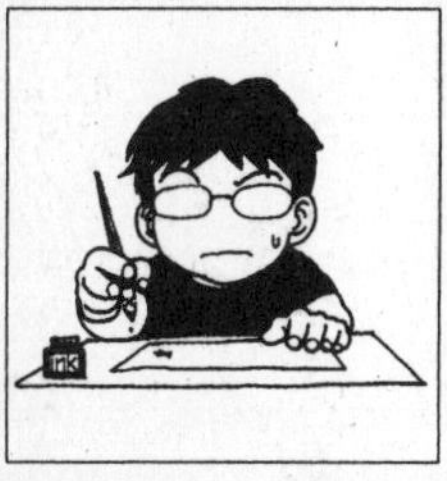
ink

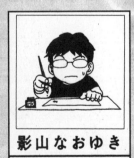

影山なおゆき

NAOYUKI KAGEYAMA

IT'S ALREADY BEEN FIVE YEARS SINCE I STARTED WORK ON THIS SERIAL. THAT SAID, IT'S GONE BY QUICKLY. IN THAT TIME, ALL SORTS OF THINGS AROUND ME HAVE CHANGED, AND OF COURSE I'VE CHANGED AS WELL. I SUPPOSE THAT WILL KEEP HAPPENING.

YU-GI-OH! GX Volume 8
SHONEN JUMP Manga Edition

ORIGINAL CONCEPT/SUPERVISED BY
KAZUKI TAKAHASHI

STORY AND ART BY
NAOYUKI KAGEYAMA

Translation & English Adaptation/Taylor Engel and Ian Reid, HC Language Solutions
Touch-up Art & Lettering/John Hunt
Designer/Ronnie Casson
Editor/Mike Montesa

Printed in the U.S.A.

Published by VIZ Media, LLC
P.O. Box 77010
San Francisco, CA 94107

10 9 8 7 6 5 4 3 2 1
First printing, January 2012

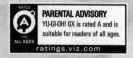

www.viz.com

RATED A FOR ALL AGES
PARENTAL ADVISORY
YU-GI-OH! GX is rated A and is suitable for readers of all ages.
ratings.viz.com

THE WORLD'S MOST POPULAR MANGA
www.shonenjump.com

VOLUME 8
Masked Hero vs. Vision Hero!!

Story & Art by
NAOYUKI
KAGEYAMA

Original Concept/
Supervised by
KAZUKI
TAKAHASHI

THE STORY SO FAR

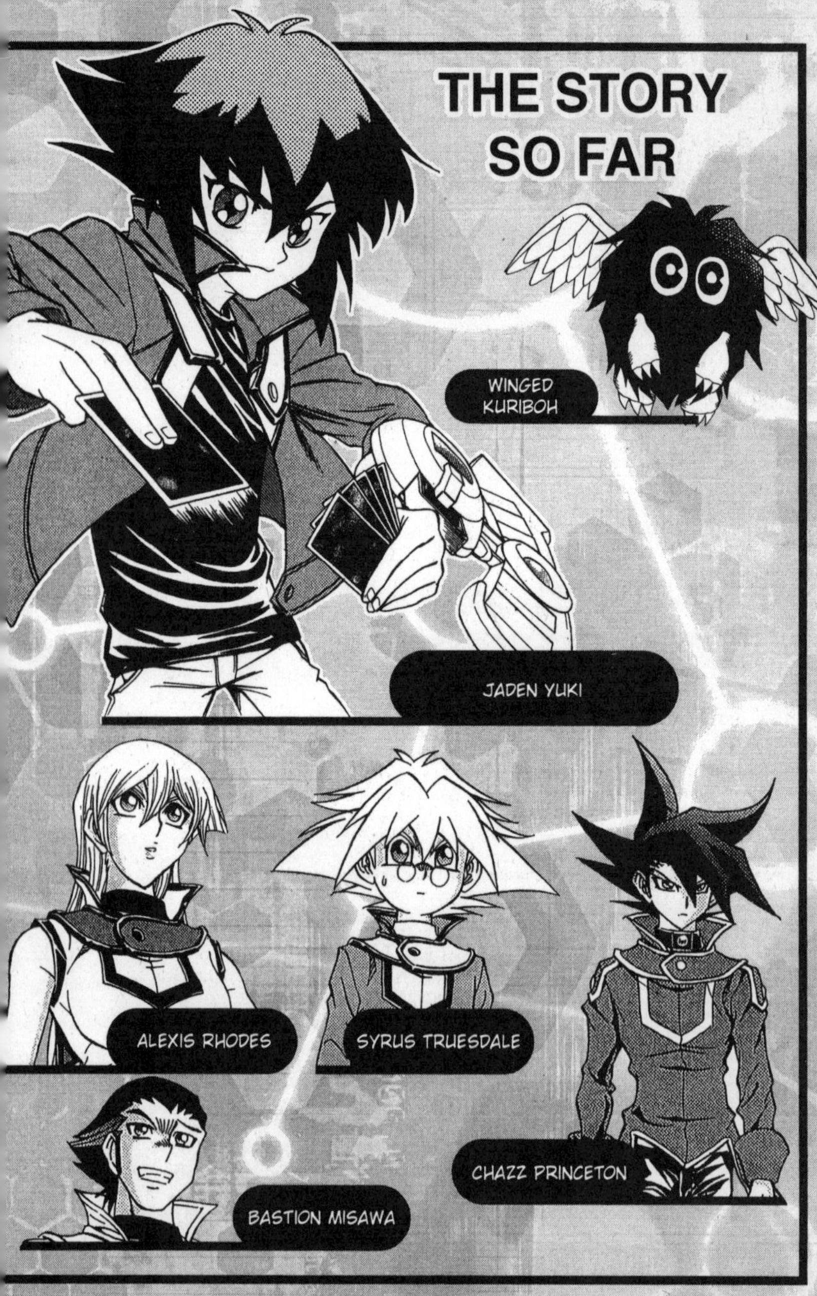
WINGED KURIBOH
JADEN YUKI
CHAZZ PRINCETON
SYRUS TRUESDALE
ALEXIS RHODES
BASTION MISAWA

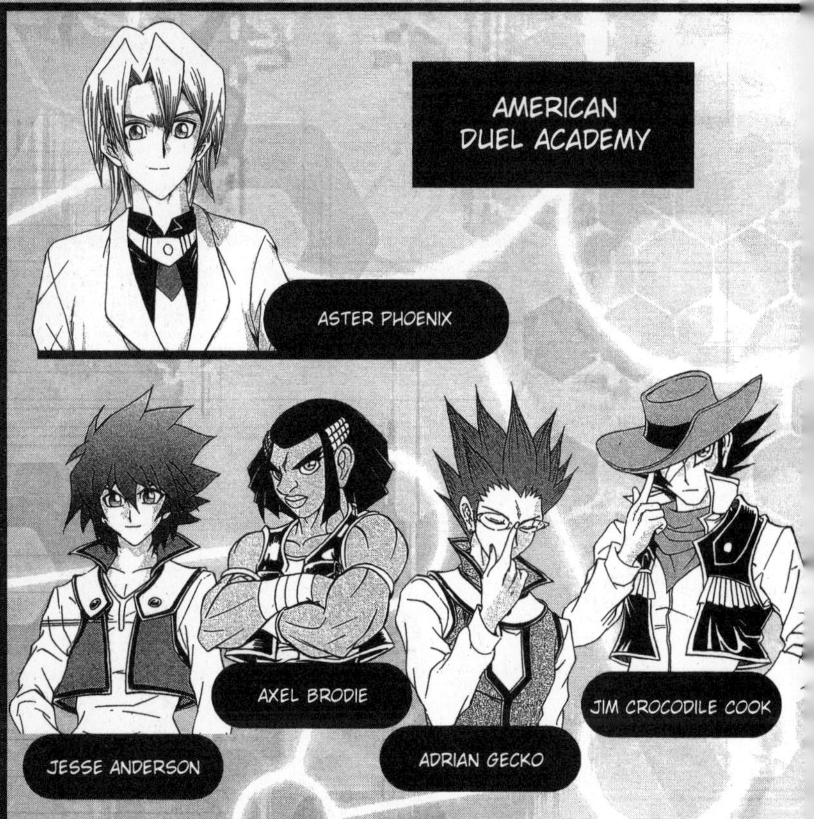
AMERICAN
DUEL ACADEMY
ASTER PHOENIX
JIM CROCODILE COOK
ADRIAN GECKO
AXEL BRODIE
JESSE ANDERSON

ON AN ISLAND IN THE SOUTHERN SEA STANDS AN ACADEMY WHERE THE NEXT GENERATION OF DUELISTS IS TRAINED. IT IS CALLED DUEL ACADEMY!

JADEN YUKI LEARNED ABOUT THE EXCITEMENT OF DUELING THROUGH AN ENCOUNTER WITH DUEL WORLD CHAMPION, KOYO HIBIKI. ENTRUSTED WITH HIBIKI'S DECK, JADEN TAKES ON ALL CHALLENGERS AT THE ACADEMY IN ORDER TO BECOME A TRUE DUELIST!

HAVING LEARNED OF THE BLACK SHADOW THAT'S AFTER THE SPIRIT CARDS, JADEN RESOLVED TO DUEL WITH A NEW DECK OF HIS OWN! THEN, SEVERAL AMERICAN DUELISTS ARRIVED FOR AN EXCHANGE BATTLE. ALEXIS AND BASTION'S TEAM WON THEIR TAG DUEL, AND SYRUS'S AND CHAZZ'S VICTORY PUT DUEL ACADEMY AHEAD 2-0. NOW ONLY JADEN IS LEFT, AND HIS OPPONENT IS ASTER PHOENIX, ANOTHER HEROES USER. HOW WILL JADEN MANAGE AGAINST A PRO DUELIST?!

Volume 8:
Masked Hero vs. Vision Hero!!

CONTENTS

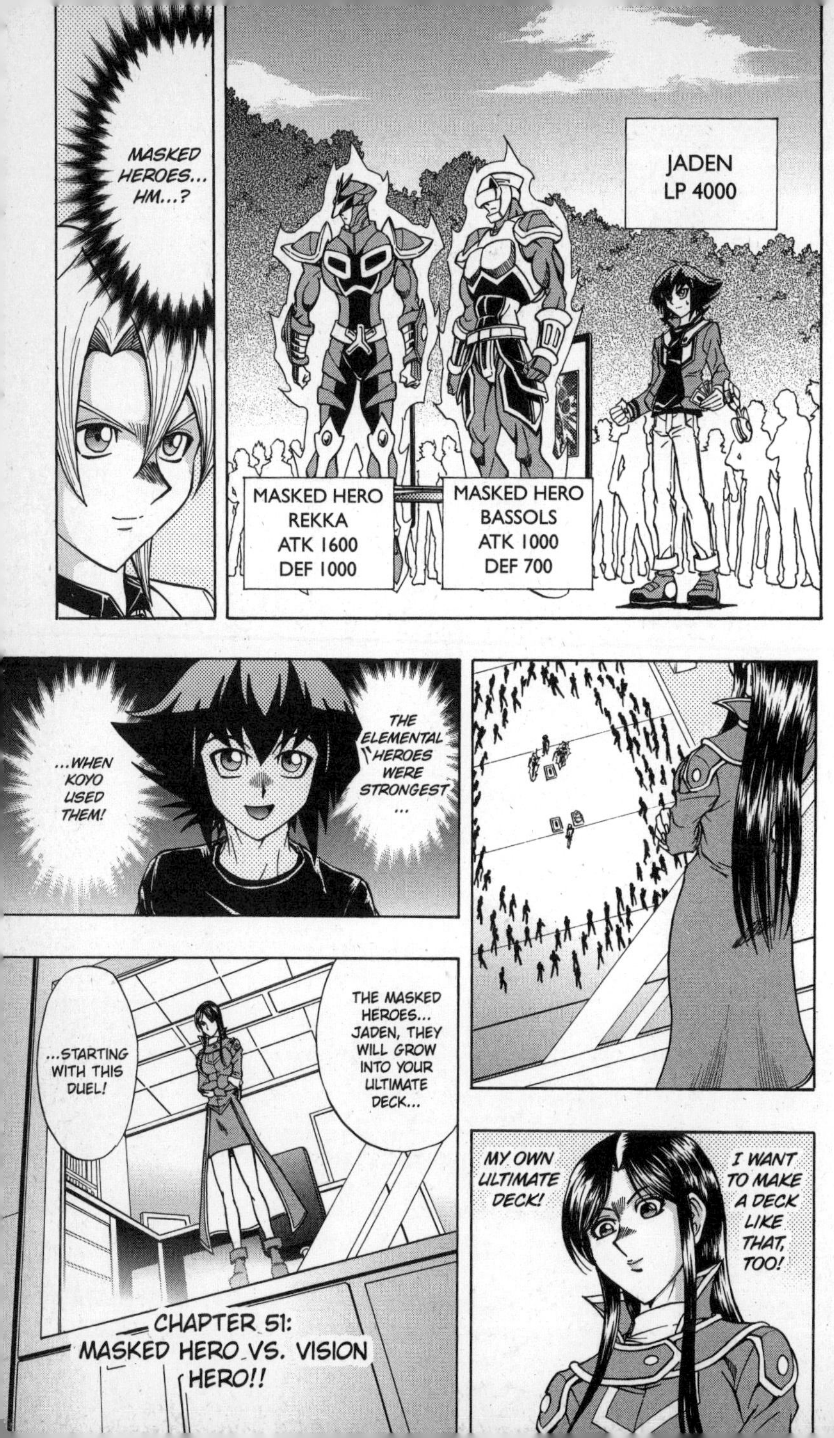

JADEN
LP 4000
MASKED HERO
BASSOLS
ATK 1000
DEF 700
MASKED HERO
REKKA
ATK 1600
DEF 1000
MASKED HEROES... HM...?
THE ELEMENTAL HEROES WERE STRONGEST...
...WHEN KOYO USED THEM!
THE MASKED HEROES... JADEN, THEY WILL GROW INTO YOUR ULTIMATE DECK...
...STARTING WITH THIS DUEL!
CHAPTER 51:
MASKED HERO VS. VISION HERO!!
I WANT TO MAKE A DECK LIKE THAT, TOO!
MY OWN ULTIMATE DECK!

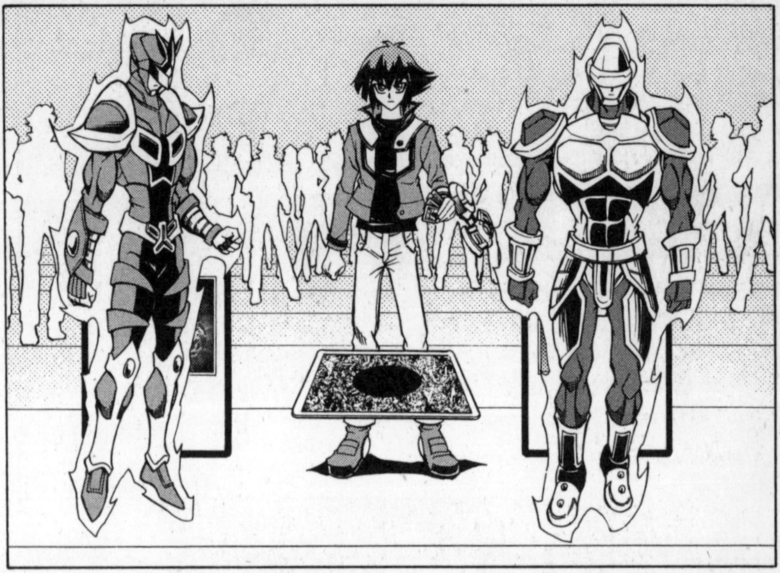

CHAPTER 51: MASKED HERO VS. VISION HERO!!

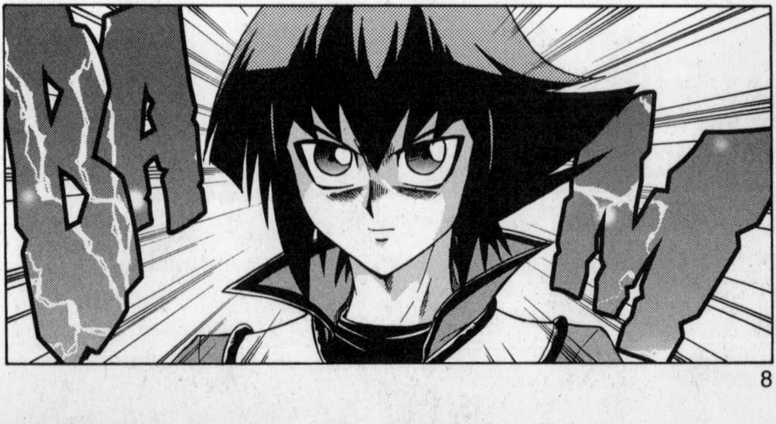
BAM

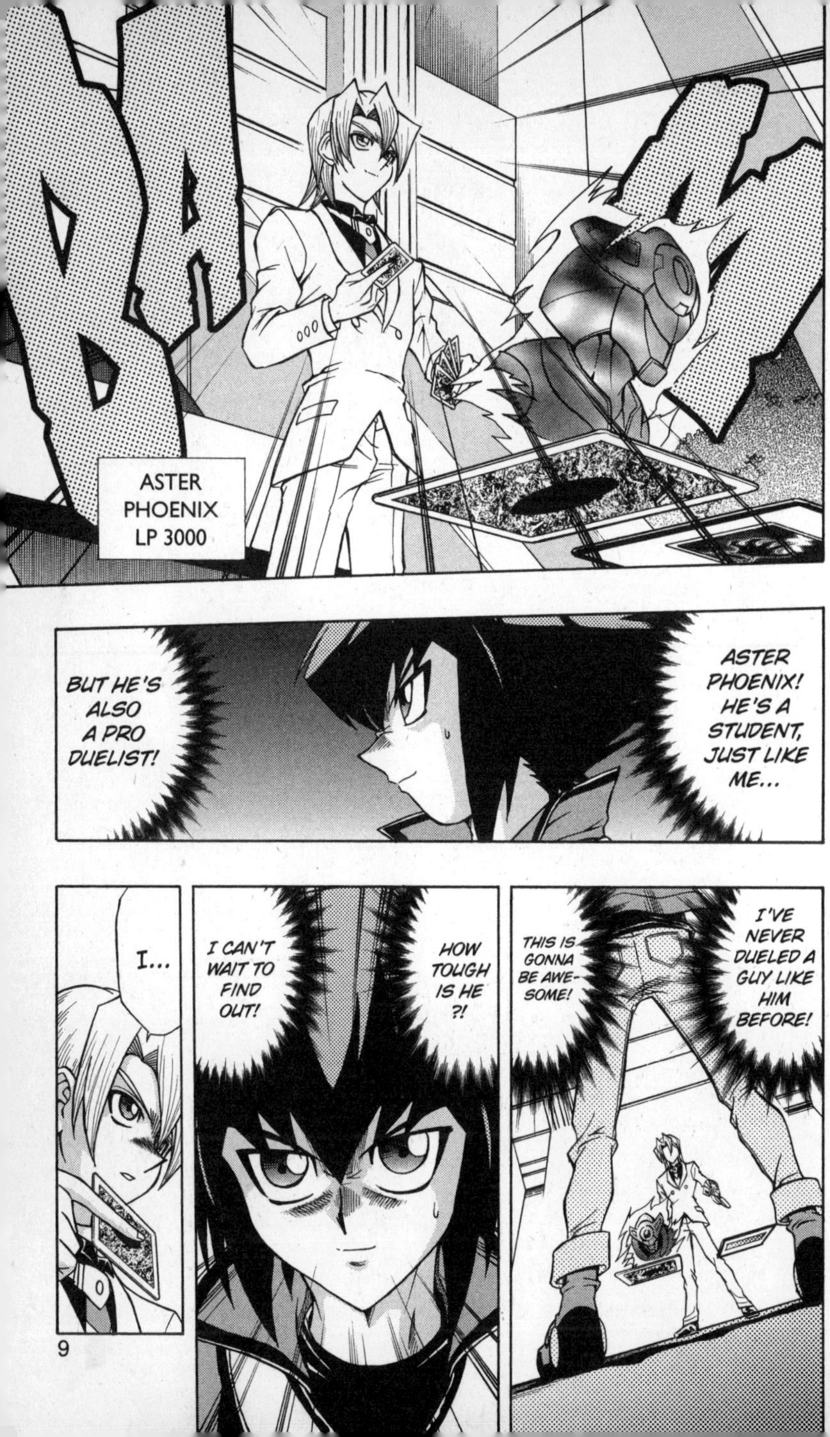
ASTER PHOENIX LP 3000
ASTER PHOENIX! HE'S A STUDENT, JUST LIKE ME...
BUT HE'S ALSO A PRO DUELIST!
I'VE NEVER DUELED A GUY LIKE HIM BEFORE!
THIS IS GONNA BE AWESOME!
HOW TOUGH IS HE?!
I CAN'T WAIT TO FIND OUT!
I...

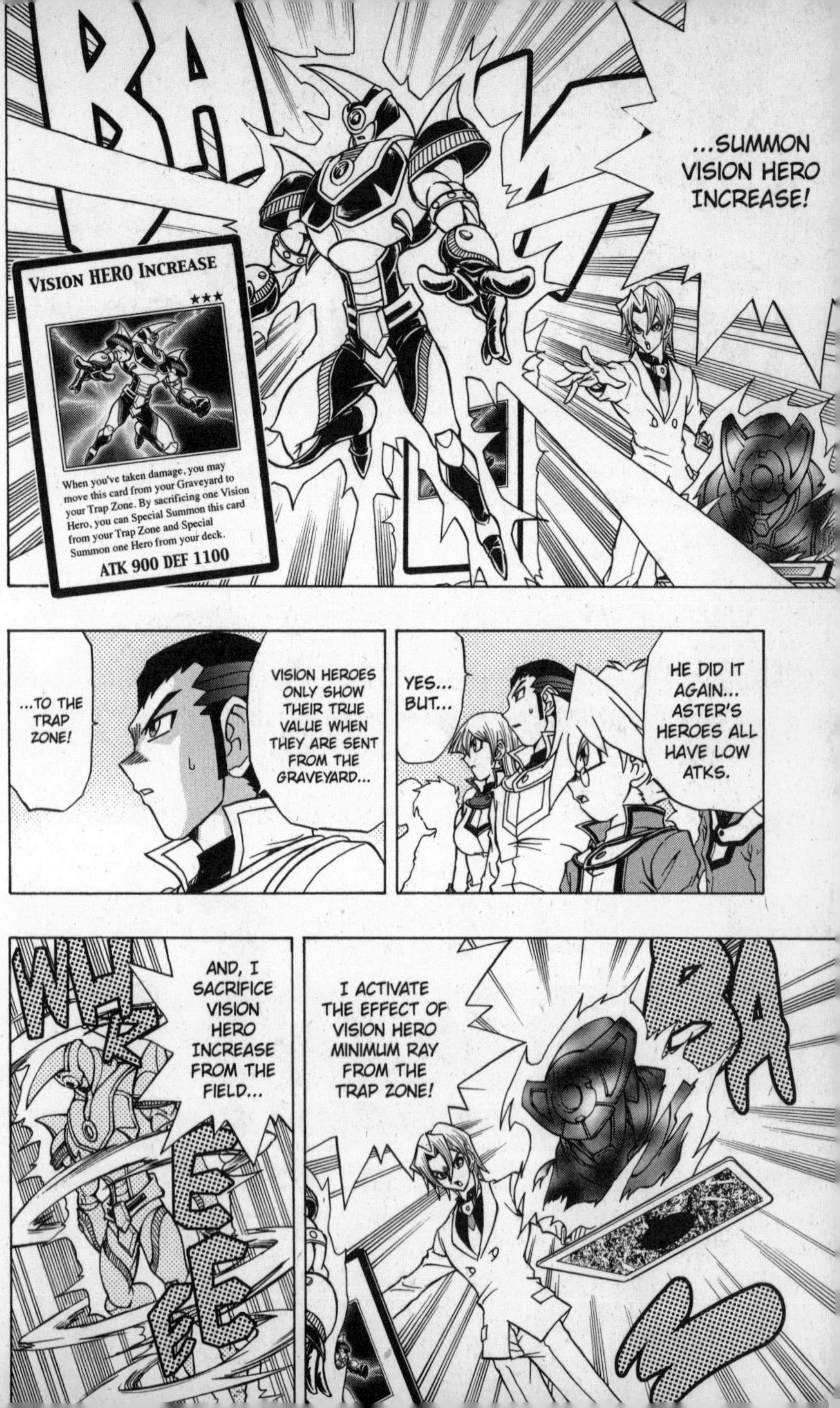
...SUMMON VISION HERO INCREASE!
VISION HERO INCREASE
★★★
When you've taken damage, you may move this card from your Graveyard to your Trap Zone. By sacrificing one Vision Hero, you can Special Summon this card from your Trap Zone and Special Summon one Hero from your deck.
ATK 900 DEF 1100
HE DID IT AGAIN... ASTER'S HEROES ALL HAVE LOW ATKS.
YES... BUT...
VISION HEROES ONLY SHOW THEIR TRUE VALUE WHEN THEY ARE SENT FROM THE GRAVEYARD...
...TO THE TRAP ZONE!
I ACTIVATE THE EFFECT OF VISION HERO MINIMUM RAY FROM THE TRAP ZONE!
AND, I SACRIFICE VISION HERO INCREASE FROM THE FIELD...

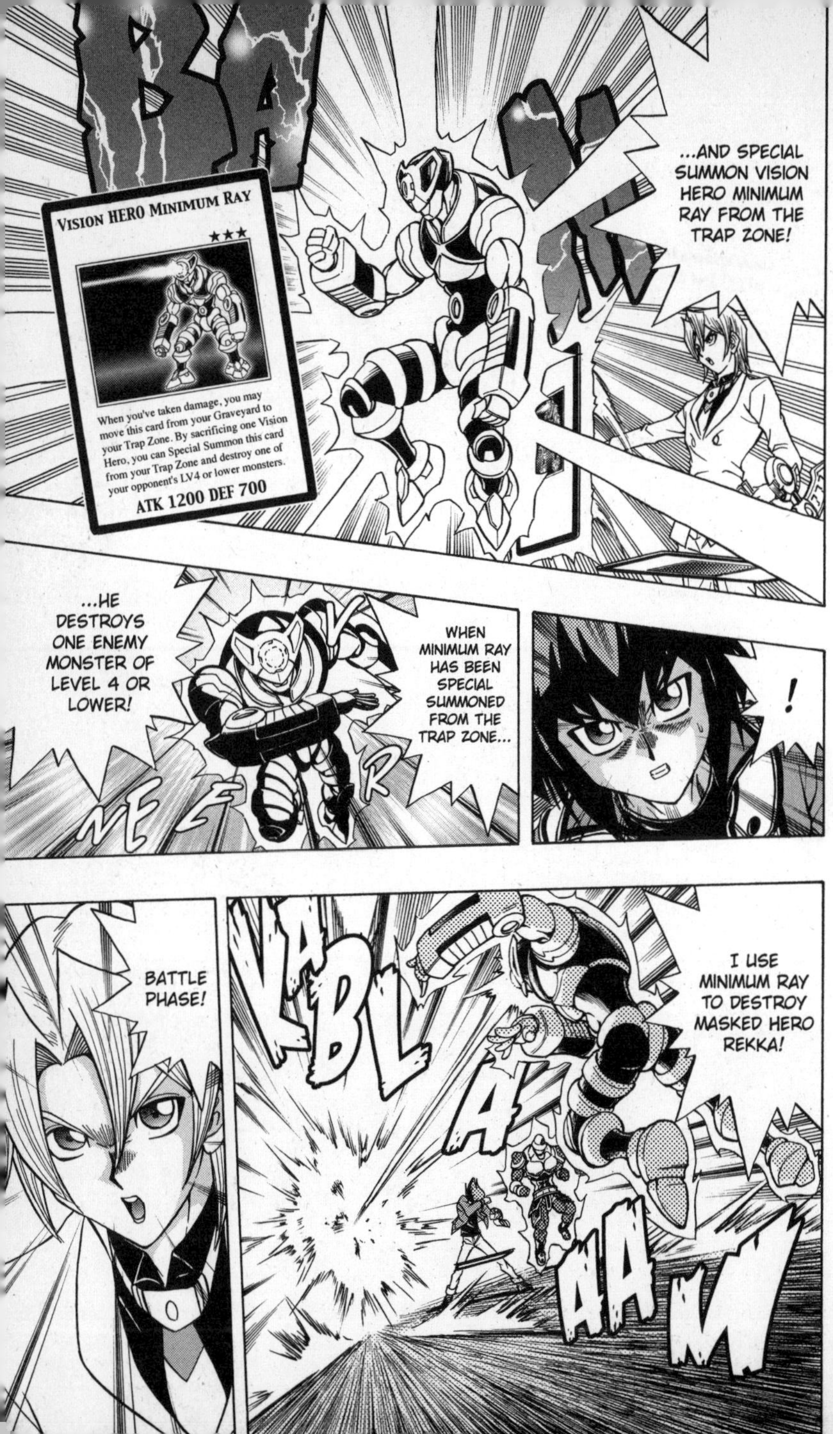

...AND SPECIAL SUMMON VISION HERO MINIMUM RAY FROM THE TRAP ZONE!
Vision HERO Minimum Ray
When you've taken damage, you may move this card from your Graveyard to your Trap Zone. By sacrificing one Vision Hero, you can Special Summon this card from your Trap Zone and destroy one of your opponent's LV4 or lower monsters.
ATK 1200 DEF 700
!
WHEN MINIMUM RAY HAS BEEN SPECIAL SUMMONED FROM THE TRAP ZONE...
...HE DESTROYS ONE ENEMY MONSTER OF LEVEL 4 OR LOWER!
I USE MINIMUM RAY TO DESTROY MASKED HERO REKKA!
BATTLE PHASE!

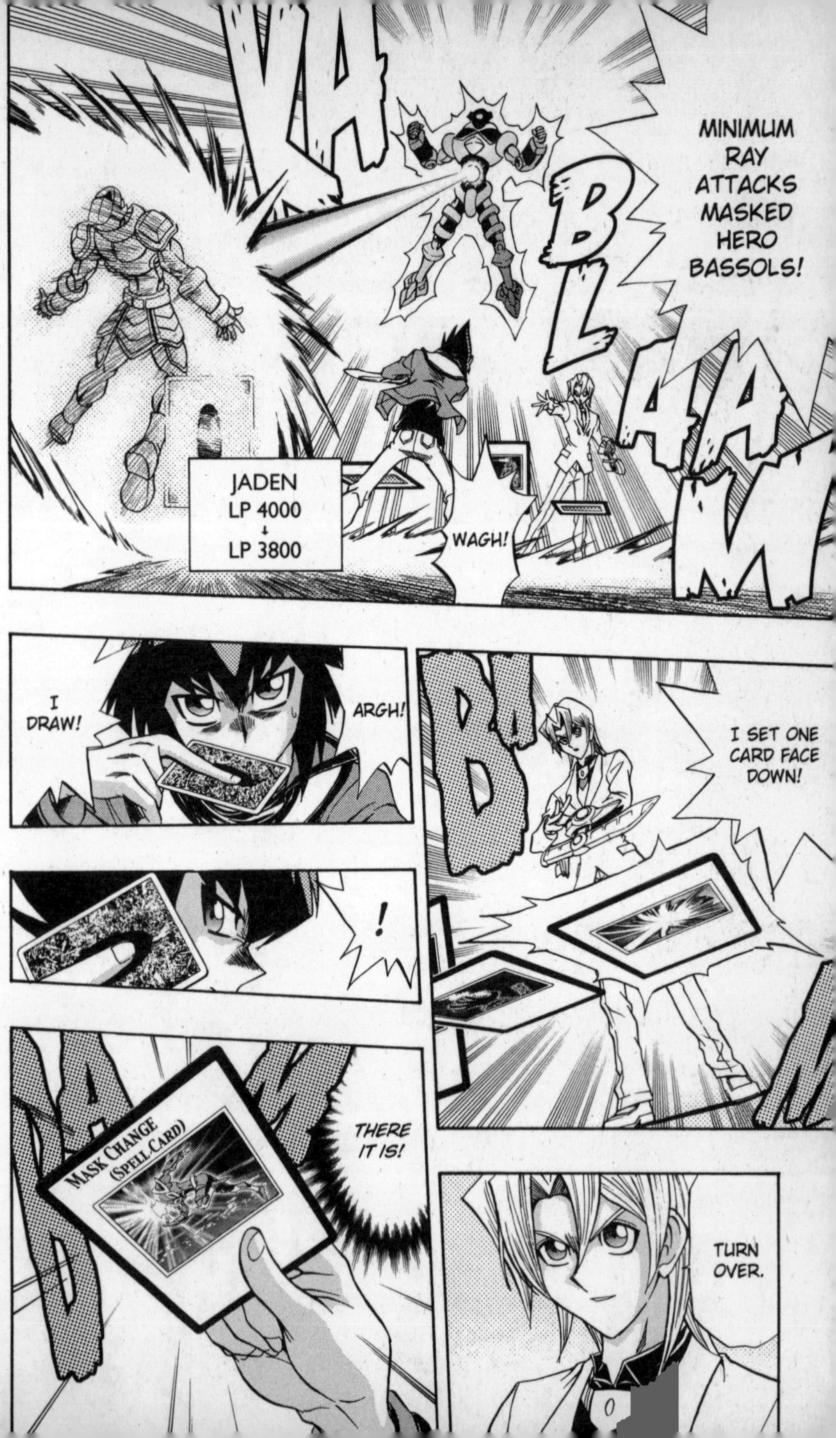
MINIMUM RAY ATTACKS MASKED HERO BASSOLS!
JADEN
LP 4000
↓
LP 3800
WAGH!
I SET ONE CARD FACE DOWN!
TURN OVER.
ARGH!
I DRAW!
!
THERE IT IS!
MASK CHANGE
(SPELL CARD)

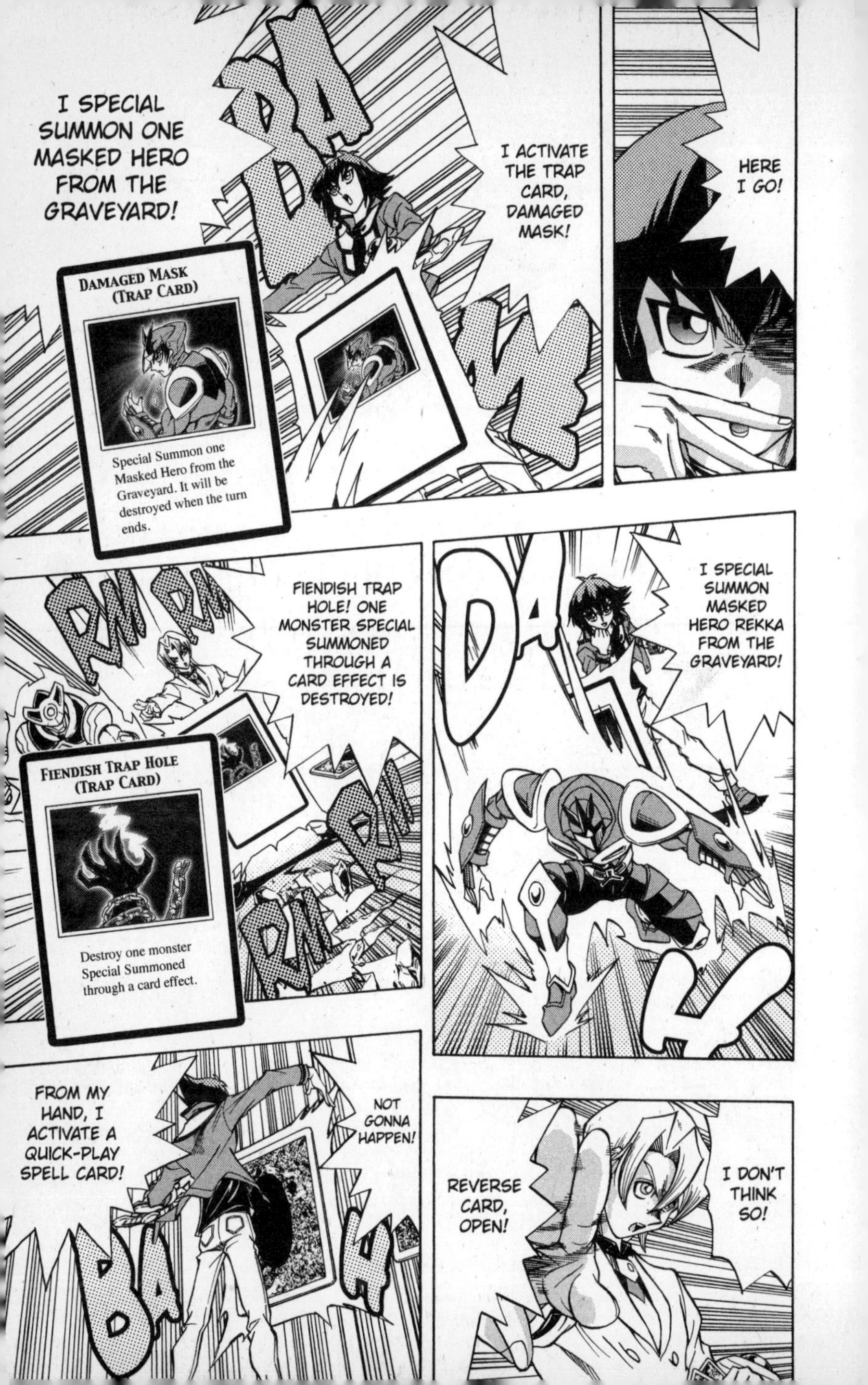
HERE I GO!
I ACTIVATE THE TRAP CARD, DAMAGED MASK!
BA
I SPECIAL SUMMON ONE MASKED HERO FROM THE GRAVEYARD!
DAMAGED MASK (TRAP CARD)
Special Summon one Masked Hero from the Graveyard. It will be destroyed when the turn ends.
DA
I SPECIAL SUMMON MASKED HERO REKKA FROM THE GRAVEYARD!
FIENDISH TRAP HOLE! ONE MONSTER SPECIAL SUMMONED THROUGH A CARD EFFECT IS DESTROYED!
FIENDISH TRAP HOLE (TRAP CARD)
Destroy one monster Special Summoned through a card effect.
I DON'T THINK SO!
REVERSE CARD, OPEN!
NOT GONNA HAPPEN!
FROM MY HAND, I ACTIVATE A QUICK-PLAY SPELL CARD!

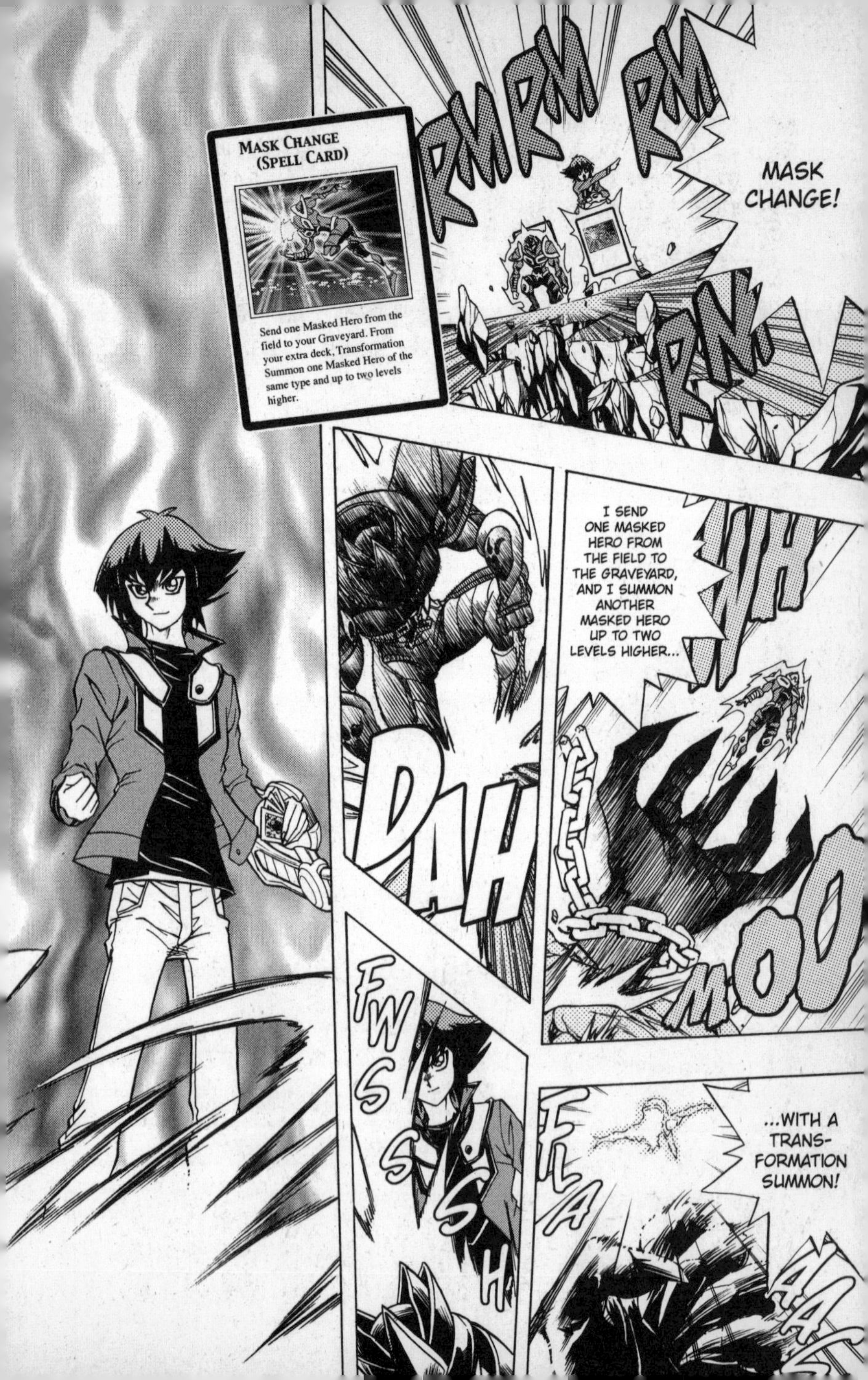
RMRM
RM
MASK CHANGE!
RN...
I SEND ONE MASKED HERO FROM THE FIELD TO THE GRAVEYARD, AND I SUMMON ANOTHER MASKED HERO UP TO TWO LEVELS HIGHER...
WH
MOO
DAH
...WITH A TRANS-FORMATION SUMMON!
MASK CHANGE
(SPELL CARD)
Send one Masked Hero from the field to your Graveyard. From your extra deck, Transformation Summon one Masked Hero of the same type and up to two levels higher.

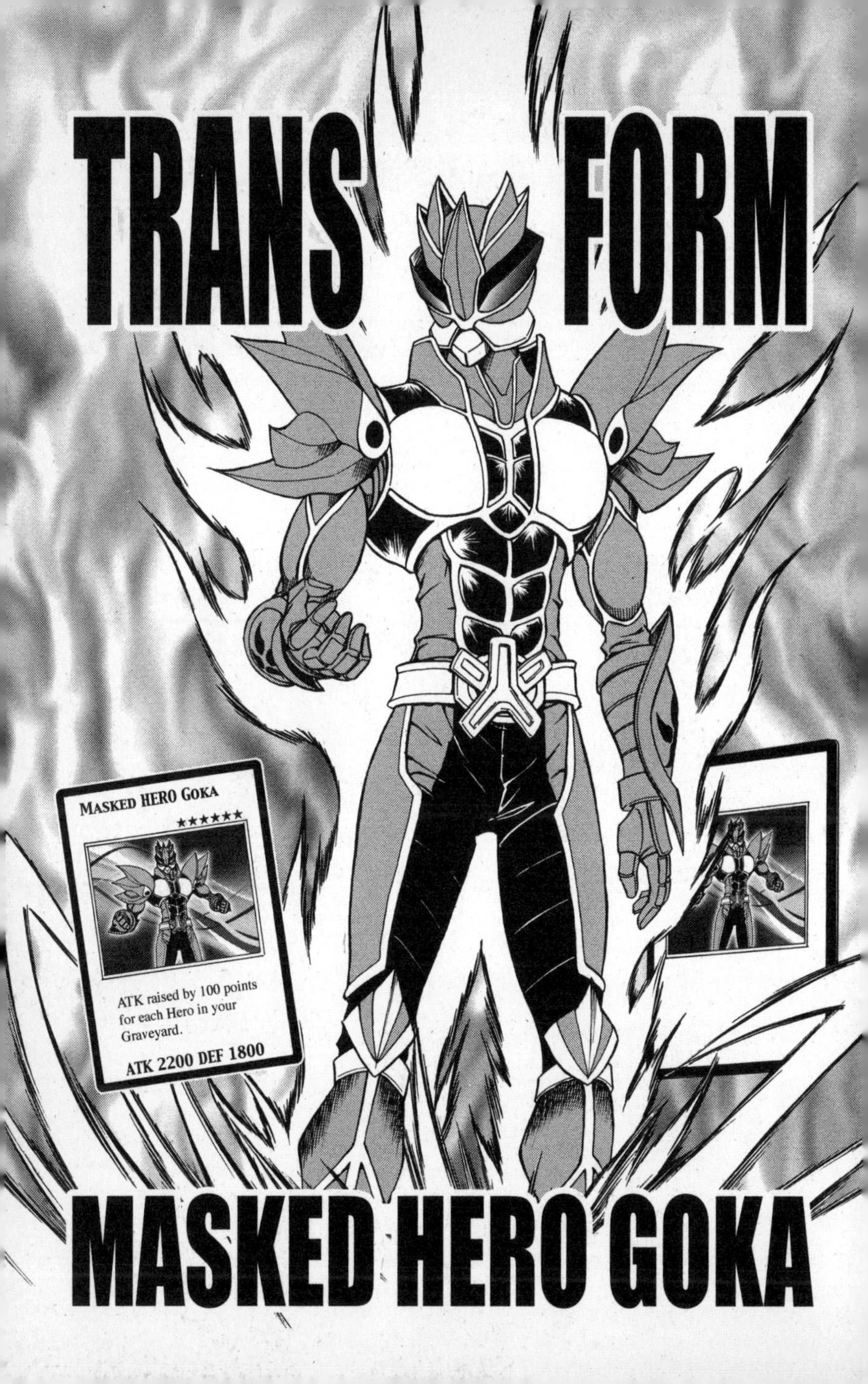
TRANS FORM
MASKED HERO GOKA
★★★★★★
ATK raised by 100 points for each Hero in your Graveyard.
ATK 2200 DEF 1800
MASKED HERO GOKA

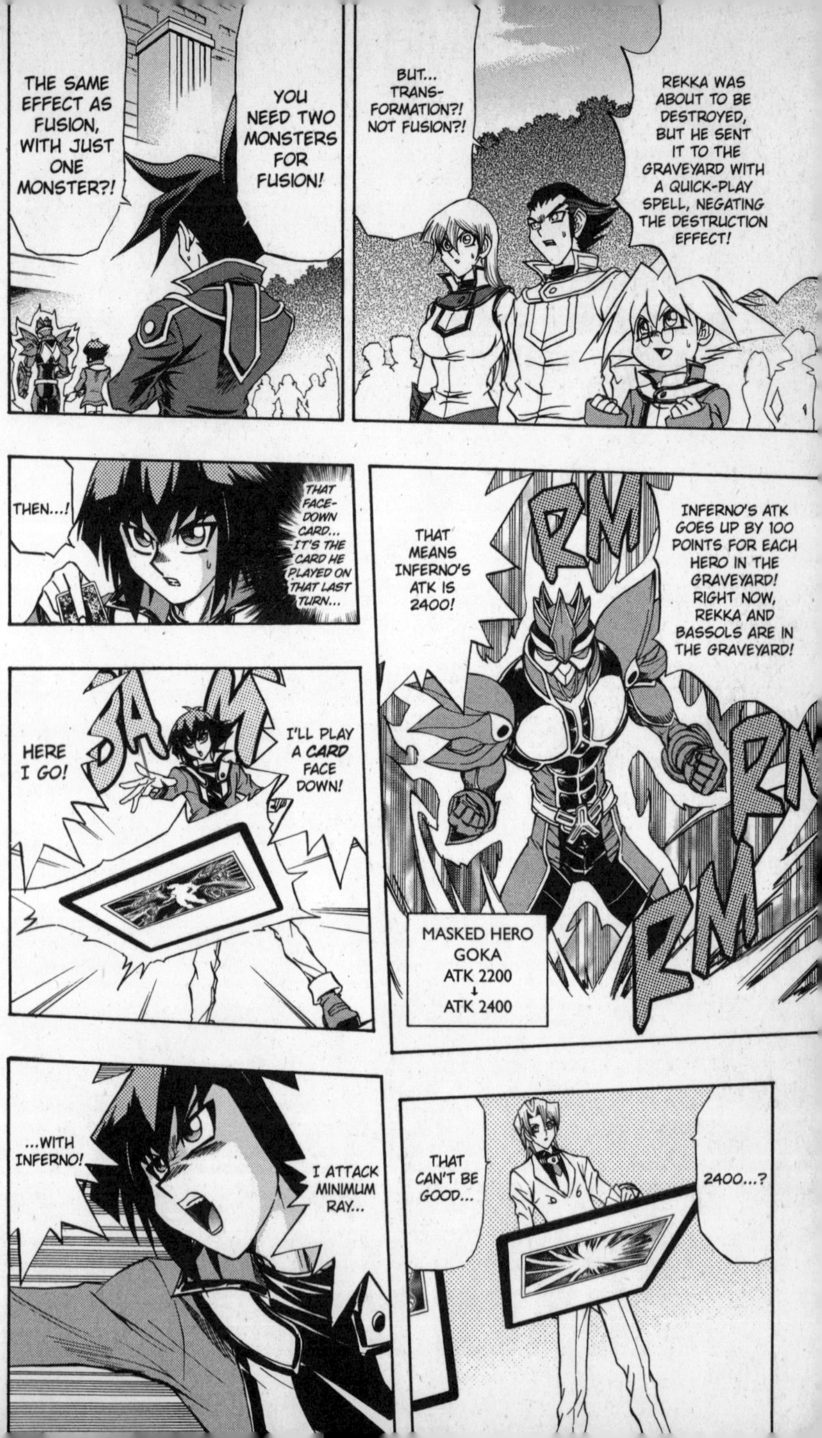
REKKA WAS ABOUT TO BE DESTROYED, BUT HE SENT IT TO THE GRAVEYARD WITH A QUICK-PLAY SPELL, NEGATING THE DESTRUCTION EFFECT!
BUT... TRANS-FORMATION?! NOT FUSION?!
YOU NEED TWO MONSTERS FOR FUSION!
THE SAME EFFECT AS FUSION, WITH JUST ONE MONSTER?!
INFERNO'S ATK GOES UP BY 100 POINTS FOR EACH HERO IN THE GRAVEYARD! RIGHT NOW, REKKA AND BASSOLS ARE IN THE GRAVEYARD!
THAT MEANS INFERNO'S ATK IS 2400!
RM
RM
RM
MASKED HERO GOKA ATK 2200 ↓ ATK 2400
THAT FACE-DOWN CARD... IT'S THE CARD HE PLAYED ON THAT LAST TURN...
THEN...!
I'LL PLAY A CARD FACE DOWN!
JAM
HERE I GO!
2400...?
THAT CAN'T BE GOOD...
I ATTACK MINIMUM RAY...
...WITH INFERNO!

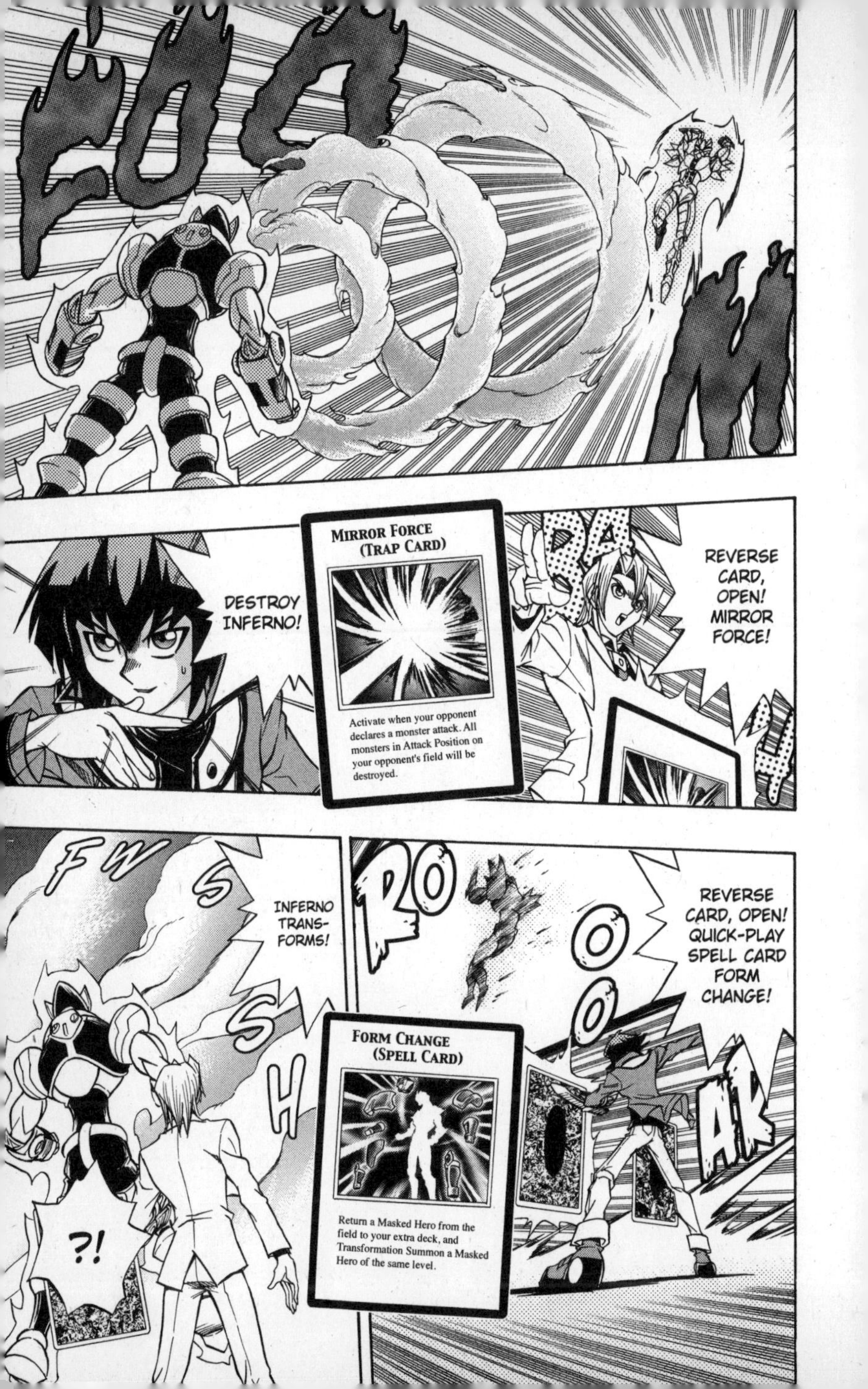
FOOM
PA
REVERSE CARD, OPEN! MIRROR FORCE!
MIRROR FORCE (TRAP CARD)
Activate when your opponent declares a monster attack. All monsters in Attack Position on your opponent's field will be destroyed.
DESTROY INFERNO!
ROOOAR
REVERSE CARD, OPEN! QUICK-PLAY SPELL CARD FORM CHANGE!
FORM CHANGE (SPELL CARD)
Return a Masked Hero from the field to your extra deck, and Transformation Summon a Masked Hero of the same level.
FWSSH
INFERNO TRANS-FORMS!
?!

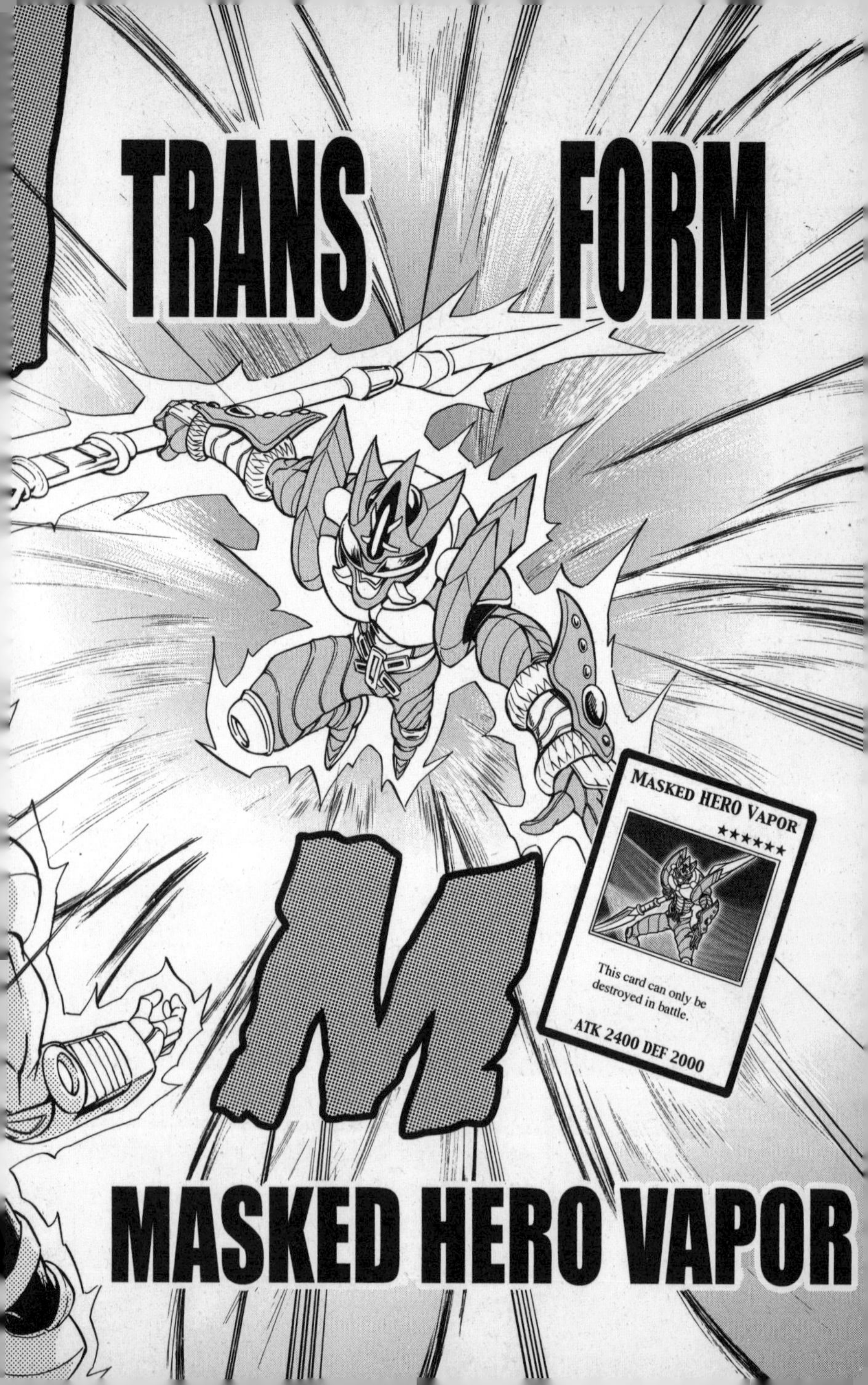
TRANS FORM
M
MASKED HERO VAPOR
MASKED HERO VAPOR
★★★★★★
This card can only be destroyed in battle.
ATK 2400 DEF 2000
MASKED HERO VAPOR

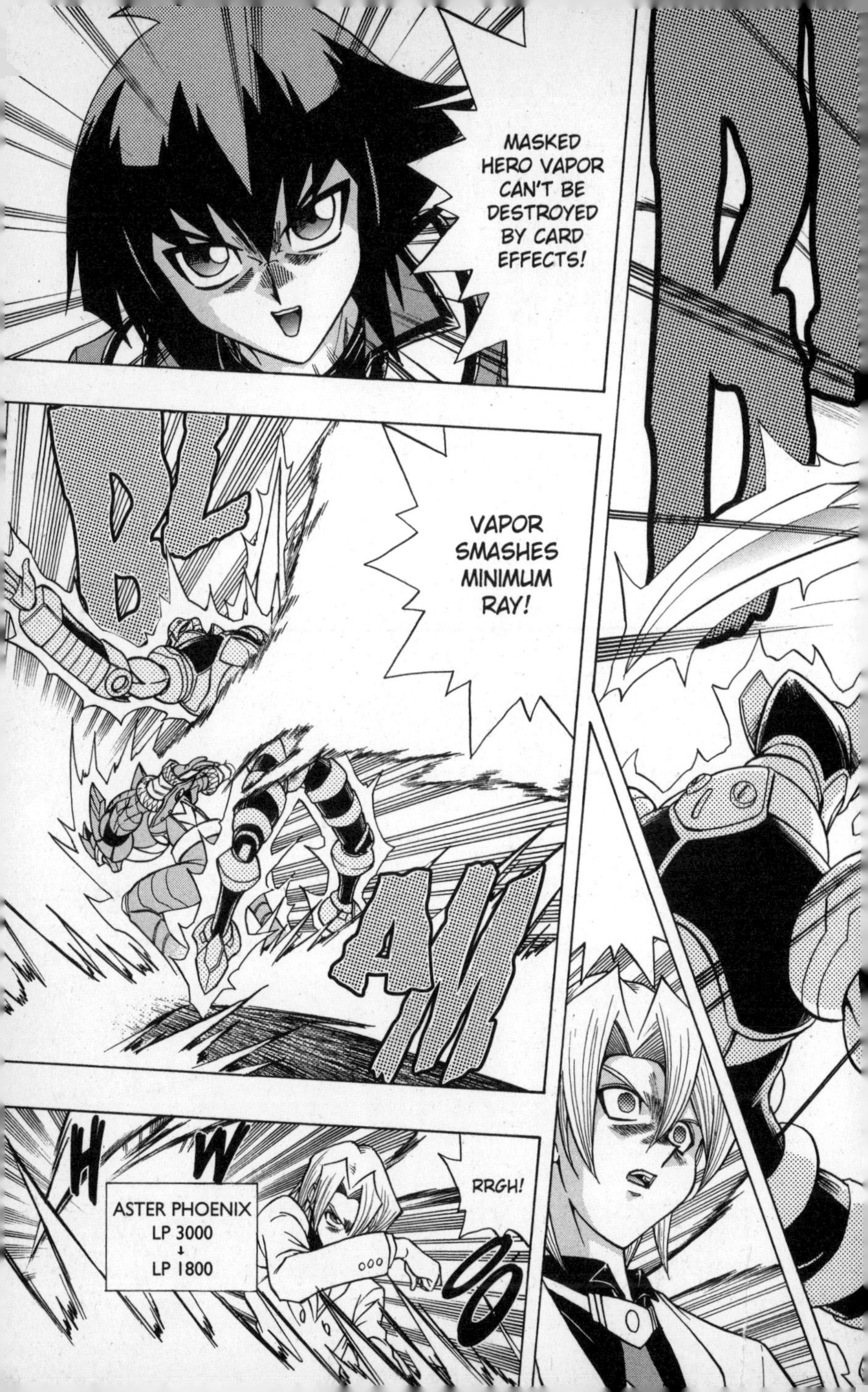
RRGH!
MASKED HERO VAPOR CAN'T BE DESTROYED BY CARD EFFECTS!
VAPOR SMASHES MINIMUM RAY!
ASTER PHOENIX
LP 3000
↓
LP 1800

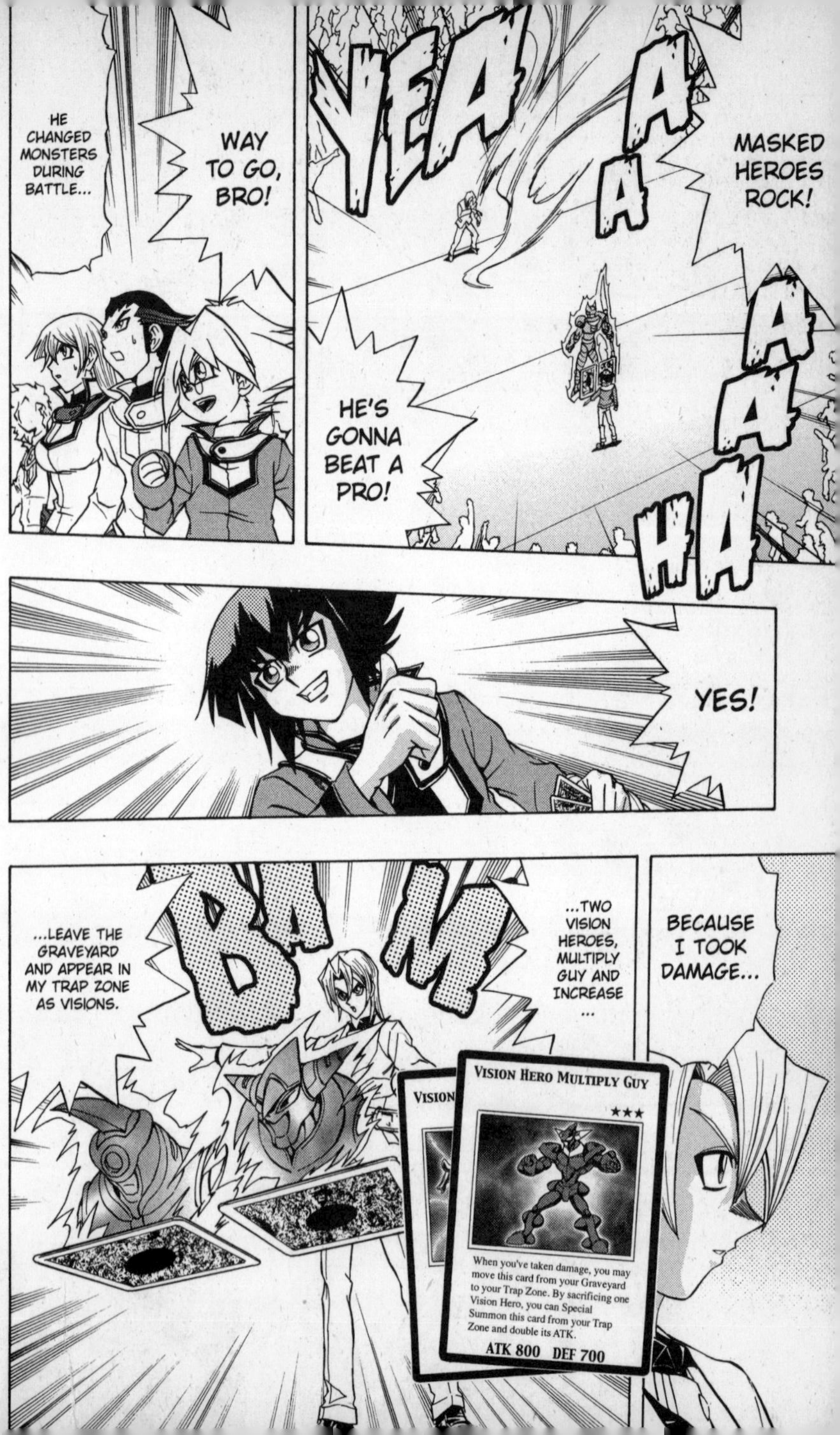
YEAAAAAAHA
MASKED HEROES ROCK!
HE'S GONNA BEAT A PRO!
WAY TO GO, BRO!
HE CHANGED MONSTERS DURING BATTLE...
YES!
BECAUSE I TOOK DAMAGE...
...TWO VISION HEROES, MULTIPLY GUY AND INCREASE ...
BAM
...LEAVE THE GRAVEYARD AND APPEAR IN MY TRAP ZONE AS VISIONS.
VISION
VISION HERO MULTIPLY GUY
★★★
When you've taken damage, you may move this card from your Graveyard to your Trap Zone. By sacrificing one Vision Hero, you can Special Summon this card from your Trap Zone and double its ATK.
ATK 800 DEF 700

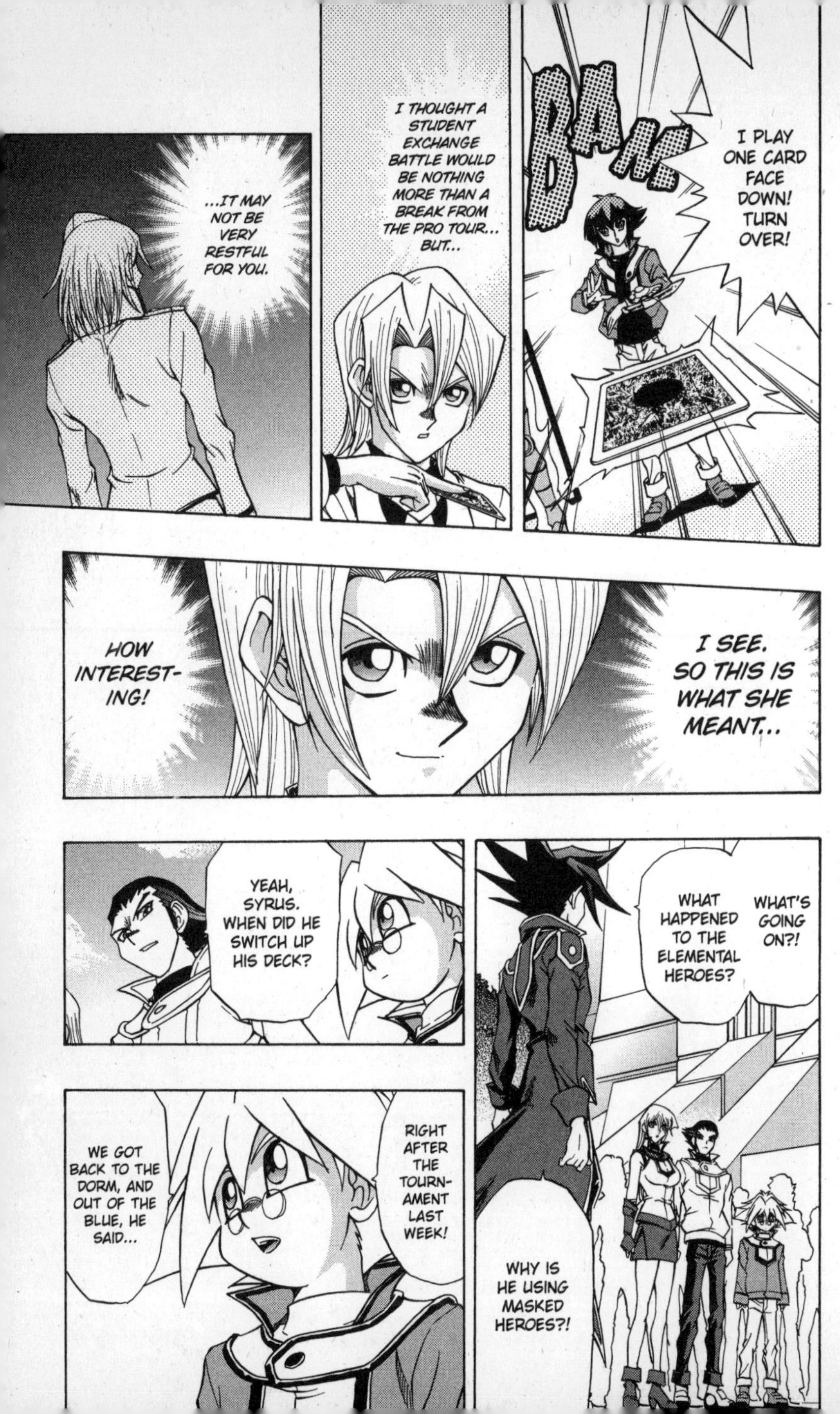
BAM
I PLAY ONE CARD FACE DOWN! TURN OVER!
I THOUGHT A STUDENT EXCHANGE BATTLE WOULD BE NOTHING MORE THAN A BREAK FROM THE PRO TOUR... BUT...
...IT MAY NOT BE VERY RESTFUL FOR YOU.
I SEE. SO THIS IS WHAT SHE MEANT...
HOW INTEREST-ING!
WHAT'S GOING ON?!
WHAT HAPPENED TO THE ELEMENTAL HEROES?
WHY IS HE USING MASKED HEROES?!
YEAH, SYRUS. WHEN DID HE SWITCH UP HIS DECK?
RIGHT AFTER THE TOURNAMENT LAST WEEK!
WE GOT BACK TO THE DORM, AND OUT OF THE BLUE, HE SAID...

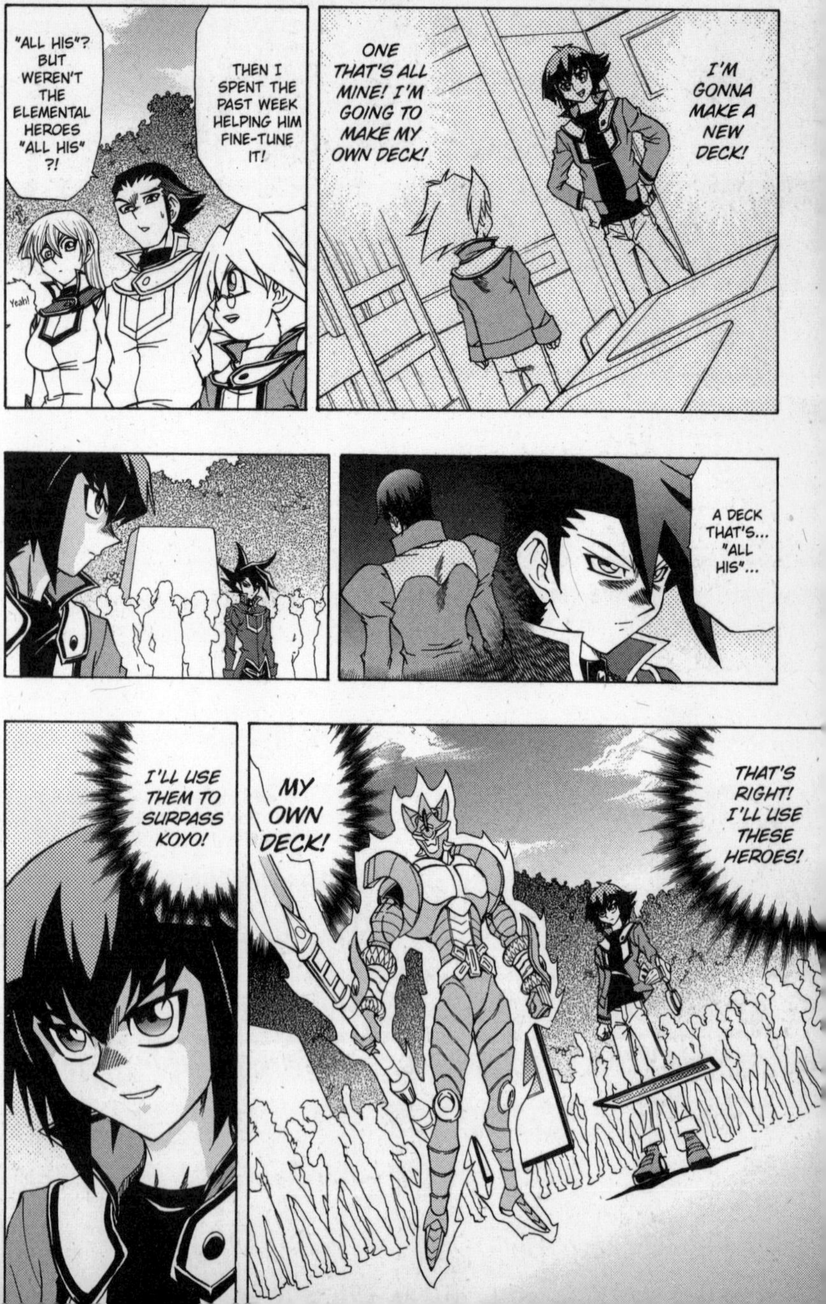
I'M GONNA MAKE A NEW DECK!
ONE THAT'S ALL MINE! I'M GOING TO MAKE MY OWN DECK!
THEN I SPENT THE PAST WEEK HELPING HIM FINE-TUNE IT!
"ALL HIS"? BUT WEREN'T THE ELEMENTAL HEROES "ALL HIS"?!
Yeah!
A DECK THAT'S... "ALL HIS"...
THAT'S RIGHT! I'LL USE THESE HEROES!
MY OWN DECK!
I'LL USE THEM TO SURPASS KOYO!

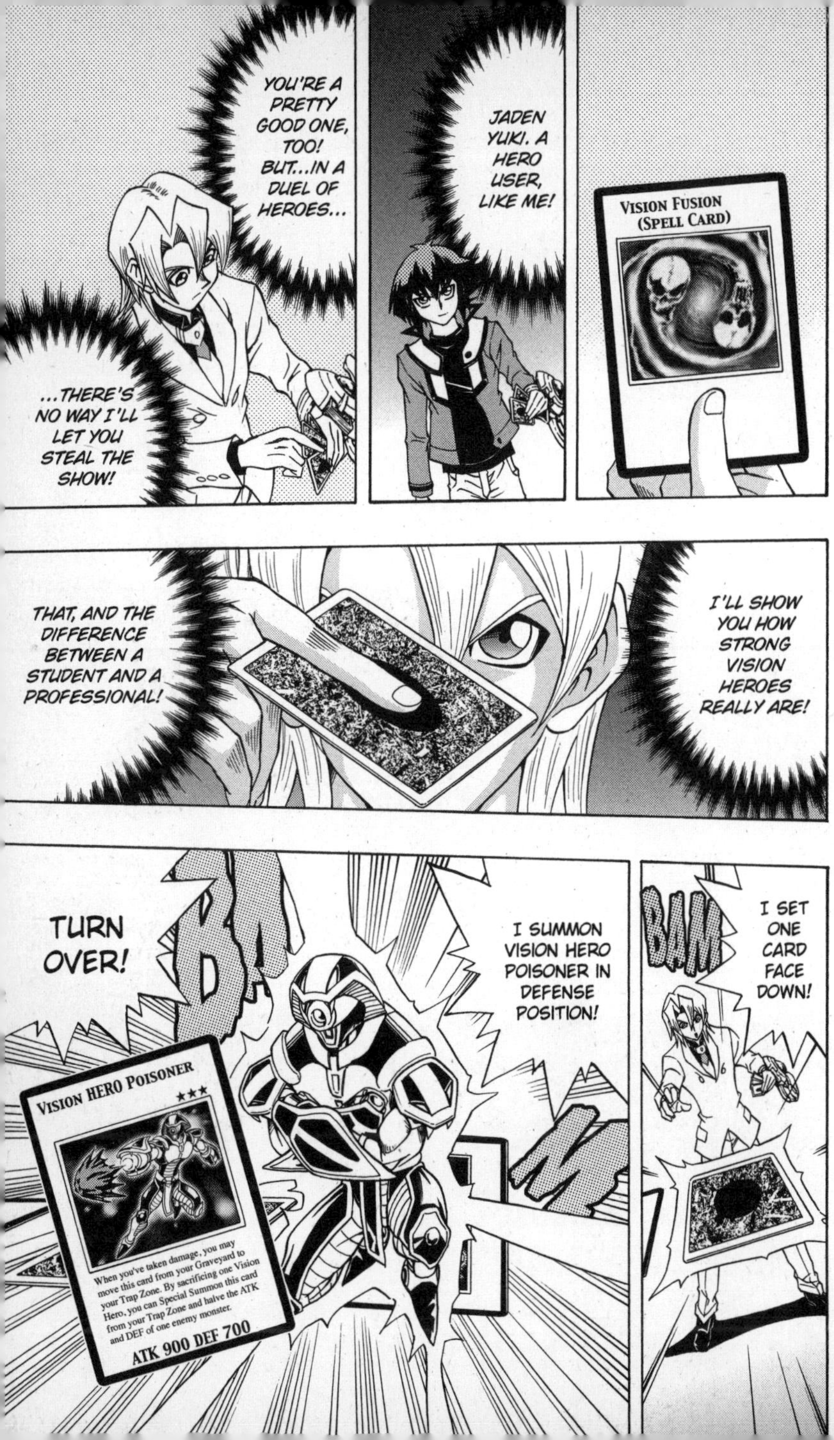
VISION FUSION (SPELL CARD)
JADEN YUKI. A HERO USER, LIKE ME!
YOU'RE A PRETTY GOOD ONE, TOO! BUT...IN A DUEL OF HEROES...
...THERE'S NO WAY I'LL LET YOU STEAL THE SHOW!
I'LL SHOW YOU HOW STRONG VISION HEROES REALLY ARE!
THAT, AND THE DIFFERENCE BETWEEN A STUDENT AND A PROFESSIONAL!
BAM
I SET ONE CARD FACE DOWN!
I SUMMON VISION HERO POISONER IN DEFENSE POSITION!
TURN OVER!
VISION HERO POISONER
When you've taken damage, you may move this card from your Graveyard to your Trap Zone. By sacrificing one Vision Hero, you can Special Summon this card from your Trap Zone and halve the ATK and DEF of one enemy monster.
ATK 900 DEF 700

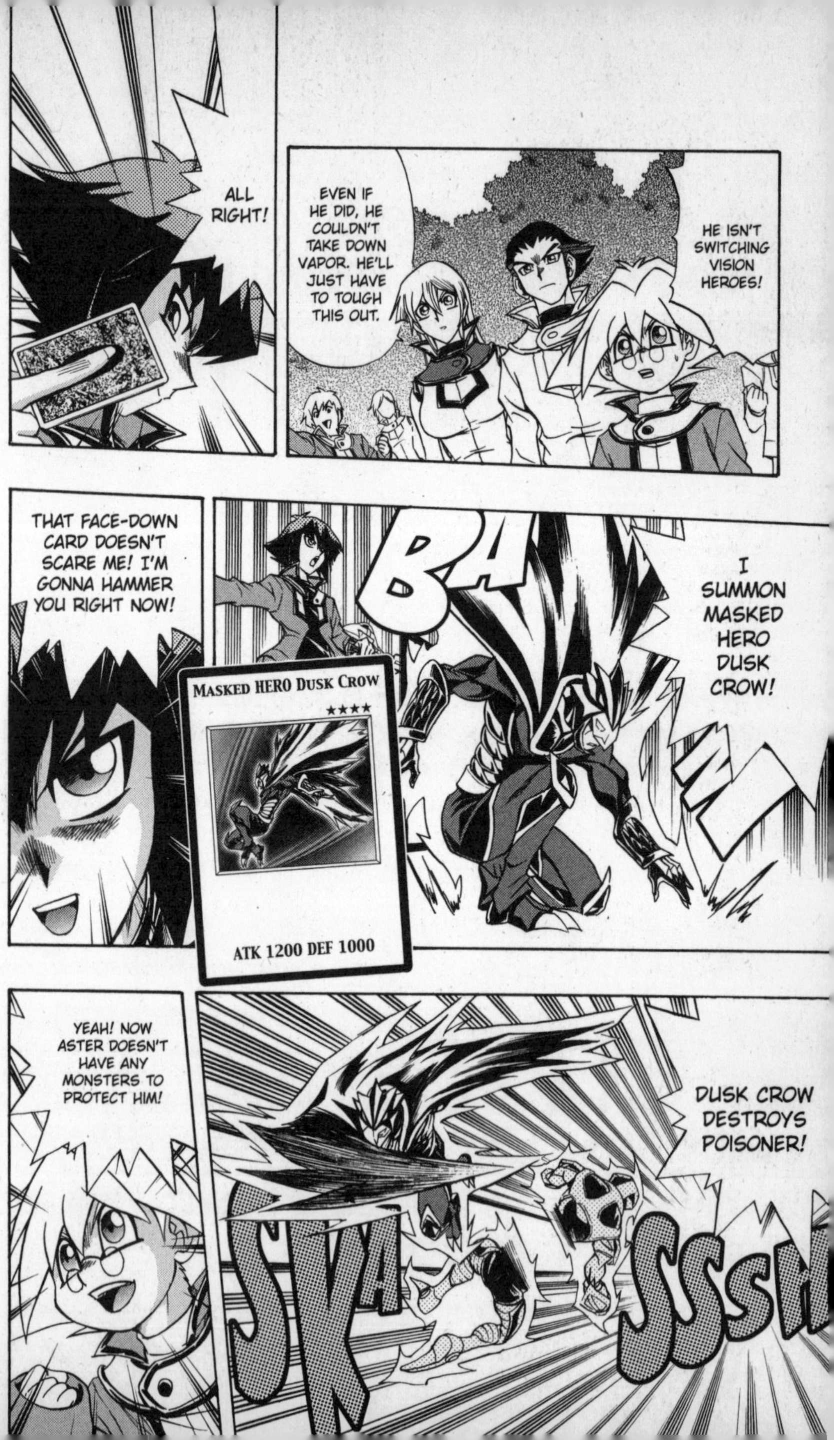
HE ISN'T SWITCHING VISION HEROES!
EVEN IF HE DID, HE COULDN'T TAKE DOWN VAPOR. HE'LL JUST HAVE TO TOUGH THIS OUT.
ALL RIGHT!
BA
I SUMMON MASKED HERO DUSK CROW!
MASKED HERO DUSK CROW
ATK 1200 DEF 1000
THAT FACE-DOWN CARD DOESN'T SCARE ME! I'M GONNA HAMMER YOU RIGHT NOW!
DUSK CROW DESTROYS POISONER!
SSSH
SKA
YEAH! NOW ASTER DOESN'T HAVE ANY MONSTERS TO PROTECT HIM!

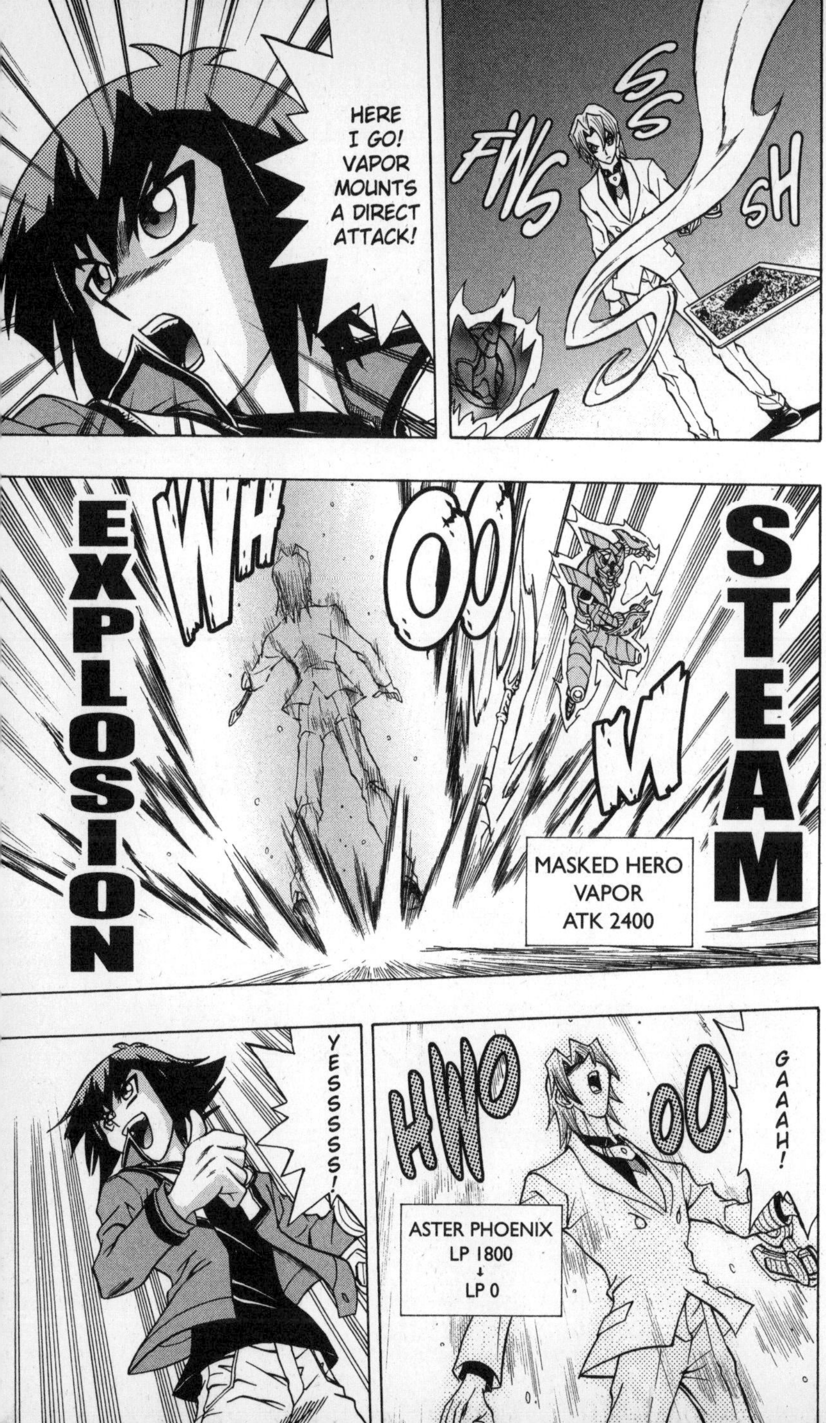
FWS
SSS
SH
HERE I GO! VAPOR MOUNTS A DIRECT ATTACK!
STEAM
WH
OO
M
EXPLOSION
MASKED HERO
VAPOR
ATK 2400
GAAAH!
HWO
OO
ASTER PHOENIX
LP 1800
↓
LP 0
YESSSSS!

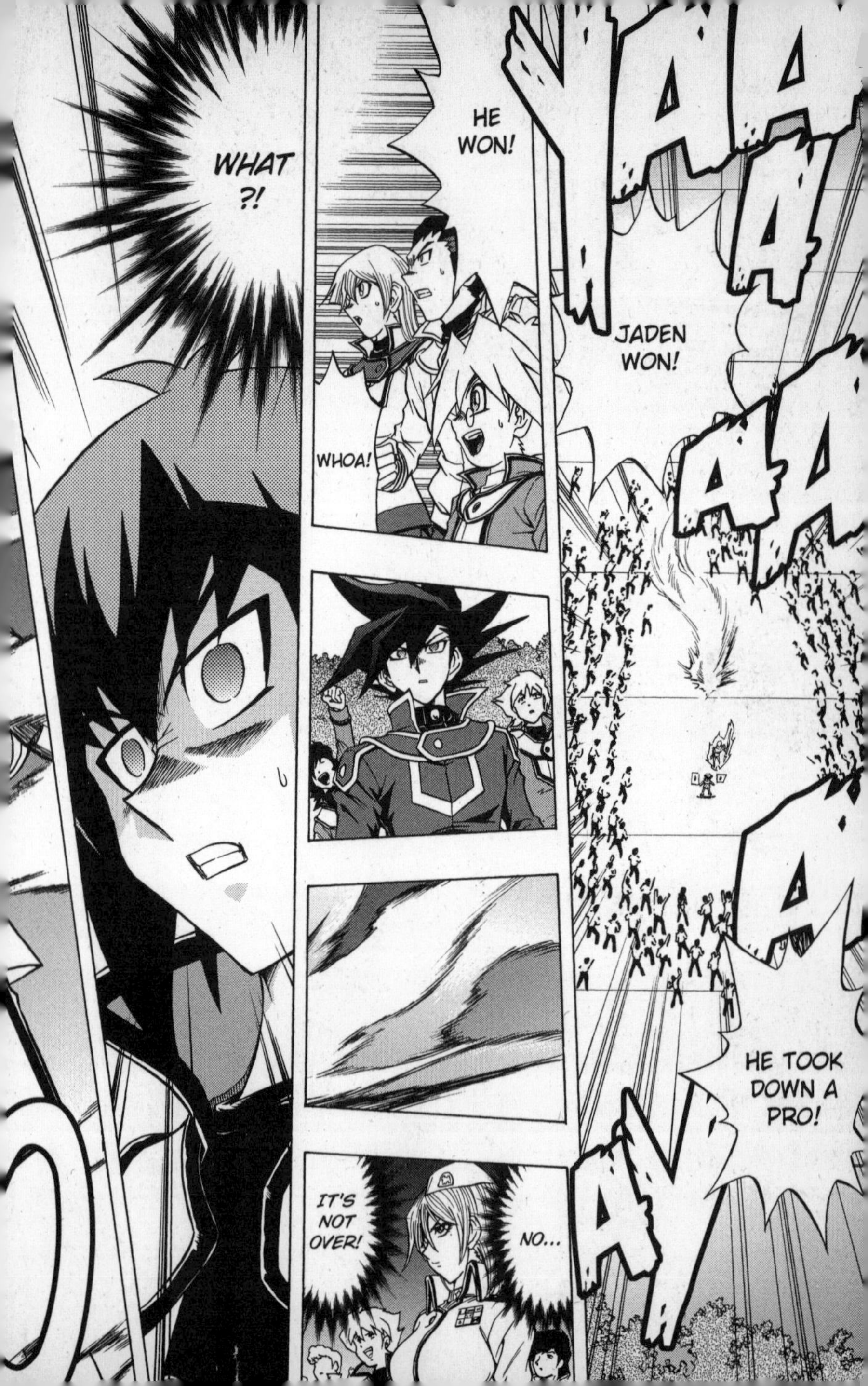
JADEN WON!
HE TOOK DOWN A PRO!
HE WON!
WHOA!
NO...
IT'S NOT OVER!
WHAT ?!

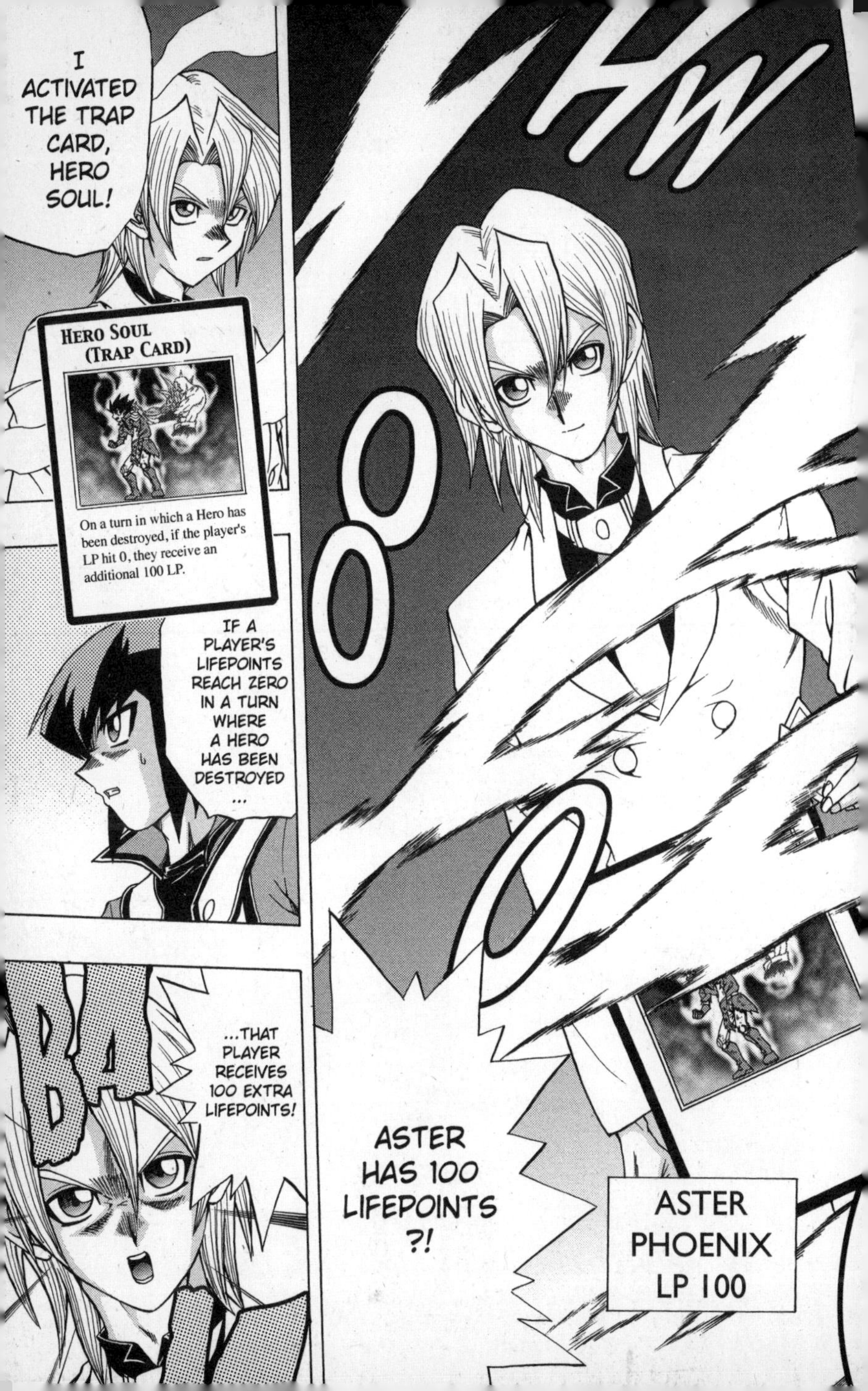
HW
ASTER HAS 100 LIFEPOINTS ?!
ASTER PHOENIX LP 100
I ACTIVATED THE TRAP CARD, HERO SOUL!
HERO SOUL (TRAP CARD)
On a turn in which a Hero has been destroyed, if the player's LP hit 0, they receive an additional 100 LP.
IF A PLAYER'S LIFEPOINTS REACH ZERO IN A TURN WHERE A HERO HAS BEEN DESTROYED ...
BA
...THAT PLAYER RECEIVES 100 EXTRA LIFEPOINTS!

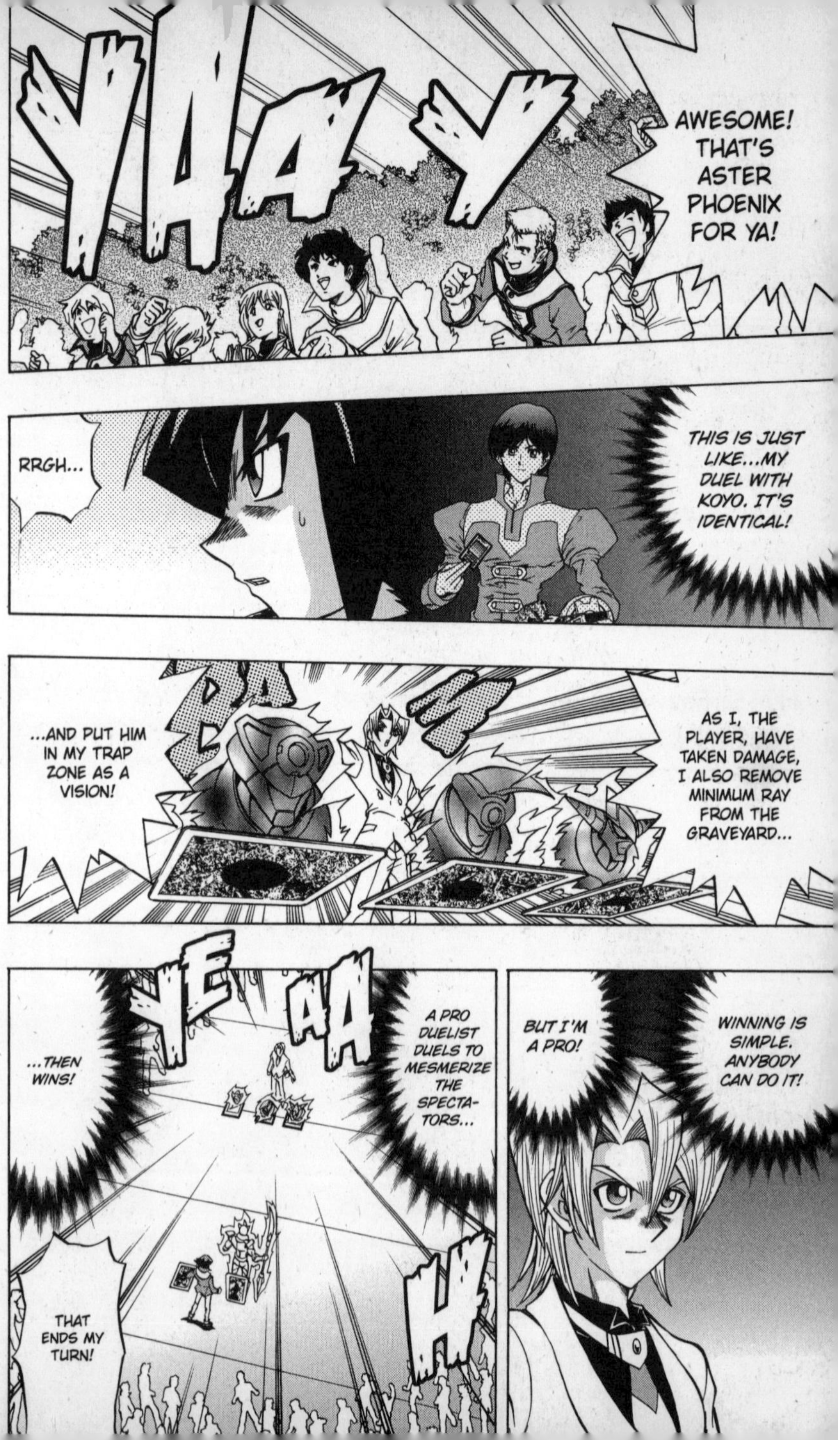
YAAY
AWESOME! THAT'S ASTER PHOENIX FOR YA!
THIS IS JUST LIKE...MY DUEL WITH KOYO. IT'S IDENTICAL!
RRGH...
AS I, THE PLAYER, HAVE TAKEN DAMAGE, I ALSO REMOVE MINIMUM RAY FROM THE GRAVEYARD...
...AND PUT HIM IN MY TRAP ZONE AS A VISION!
WINNING IS SIMPLE. ANYBODY CAN DO IT!
BUT I'M A PRO!
A PRO DUELIST DUELS TO MESMERIZE THE SPECTATORS...
...THEN WINS!
YEAAH
THAT ENDS MY TURN!

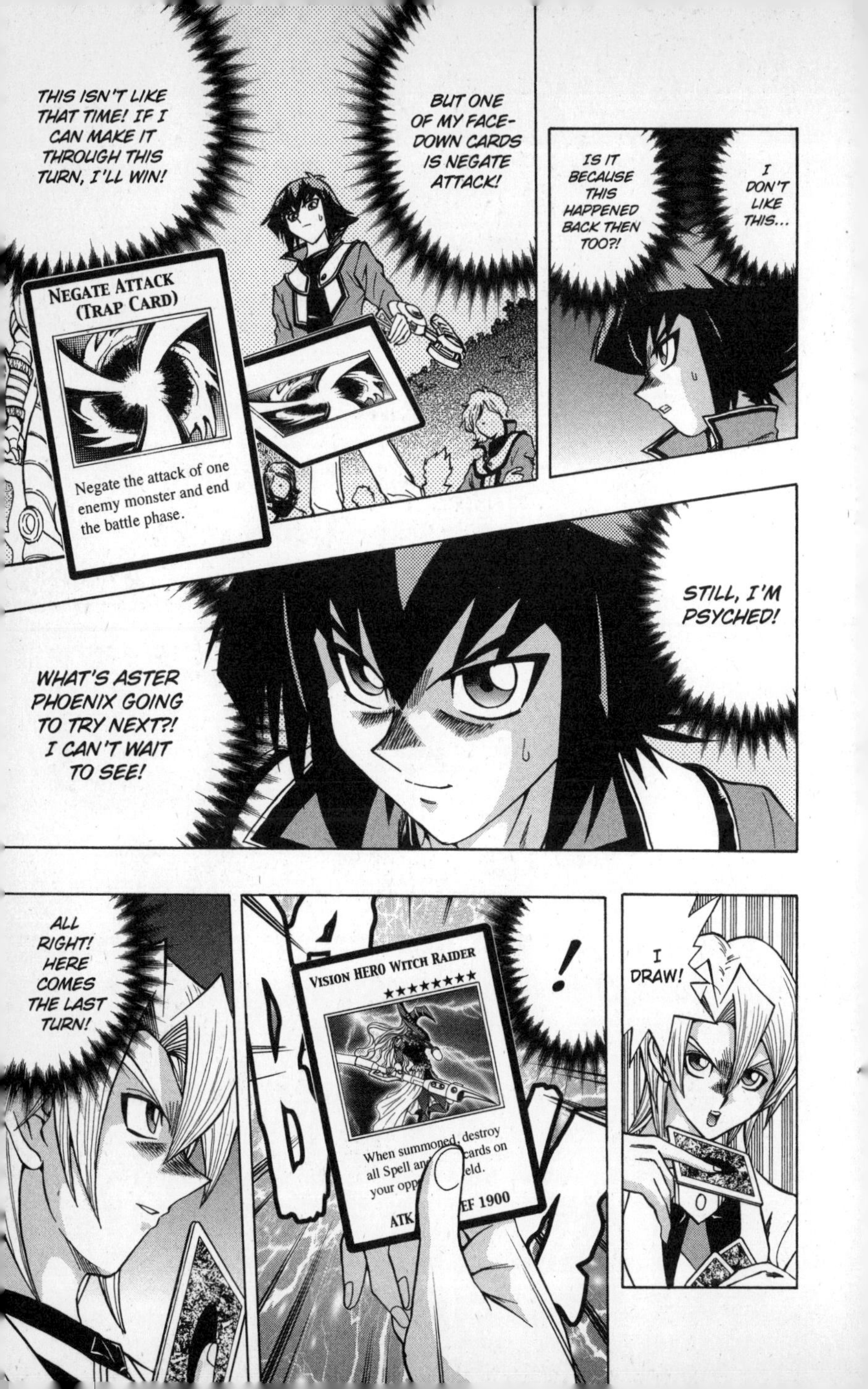
I DON'T LIKE THIS...
IS IT BECAUSE THIS HAPPENED BACK THEN TOO?!
BUT ONE OF MY FACE-DOWN CARDS IS NEGATE ATTACK!
THIS ISN'T LIKE THAT TIME! IF I CAN MAKE IT THROUGH THIS TURN, I'LL WIN!
NEGATE ATTACK (TRAP CARD)
Negate the attack of one enemy monster and end the battle phase.
STILL, I'M PSYCHED!
WHAT'S ASTER PHOENIX GOING TO TRY NEXT?! I CAN'T WAIT TO SEE!
I DRAW!
!
VISION HERO WITCH RAIDER
When summoned, destroy
cards on
all Spell an
your opp
eld.
ATK
EF 1900
ALL RIGHT! HERE COMES THE LAST TURN!

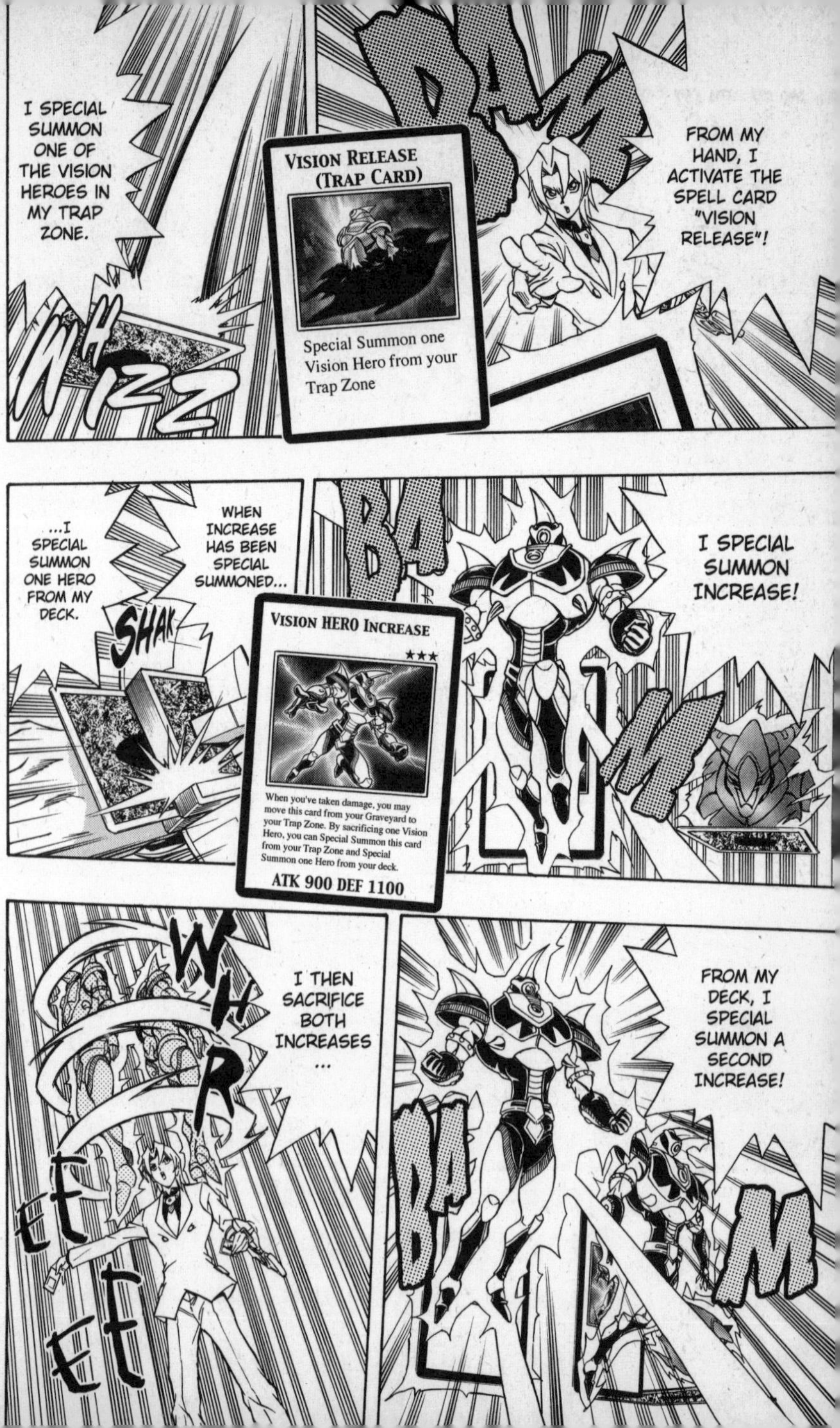
BAM
FROM MY HAND, I ACTIVATE THE SPELL CARD "VISION RELEASE"!
VISION RELEASE (TRAP CARD)
Special Summon one Vision Hero from your Trap Zone
I SPECIAL SUMMON ONE OF THE VISION HEROES IN MY TRAP ZONE.
WHIZZ
BAM
I SPECIAL SUMMON INCREASE!
VISION HERO INCREASE
When you've taken damage, you may move this card from your Graveyard to your Trap Zone. By sacrificing one Vision Hero, you can Special Summon this card from your Trap Zone and Special Summon one Hero from your deck.
ATK 900 DEF 1100
WHEN INCREASE HAS BEEN SPECIAL SUMMONED...
...I SPECIAL SUMMON ONE HERO FROM MY DECK.
SHAK
FROM MY DECK, I SPECIAL SUMMON A SECOND INCREASE!
BAM
I THEN SACRIFICE BOTH INCREASES ...
WHR

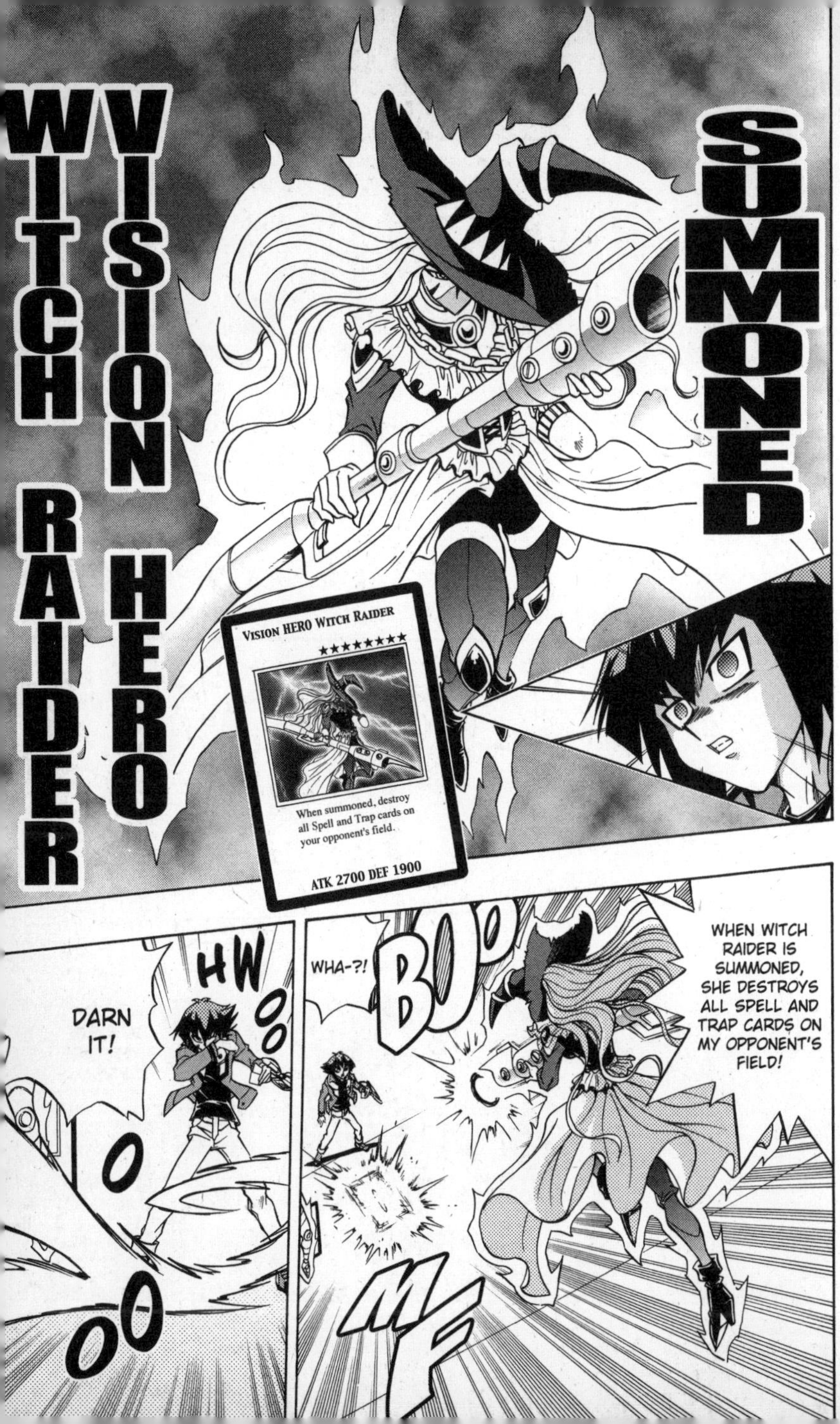
SUMMONED
VISION HERO
WITCH RAIDER
VISION HERO WITCH RAIDER
When summoned, destroy all Spell and Trap cards on your opponent's field.
ATK 2700 DEF 1900
WHEN WITCH RAIDER IS SUMMONED, SHE DESTROYS ALL SPELL AND TRAP CARDS ON MY OPPONENT'S FIELD!
WHA-?!
BOO
MF
HWOOOOOO
DARN IT!

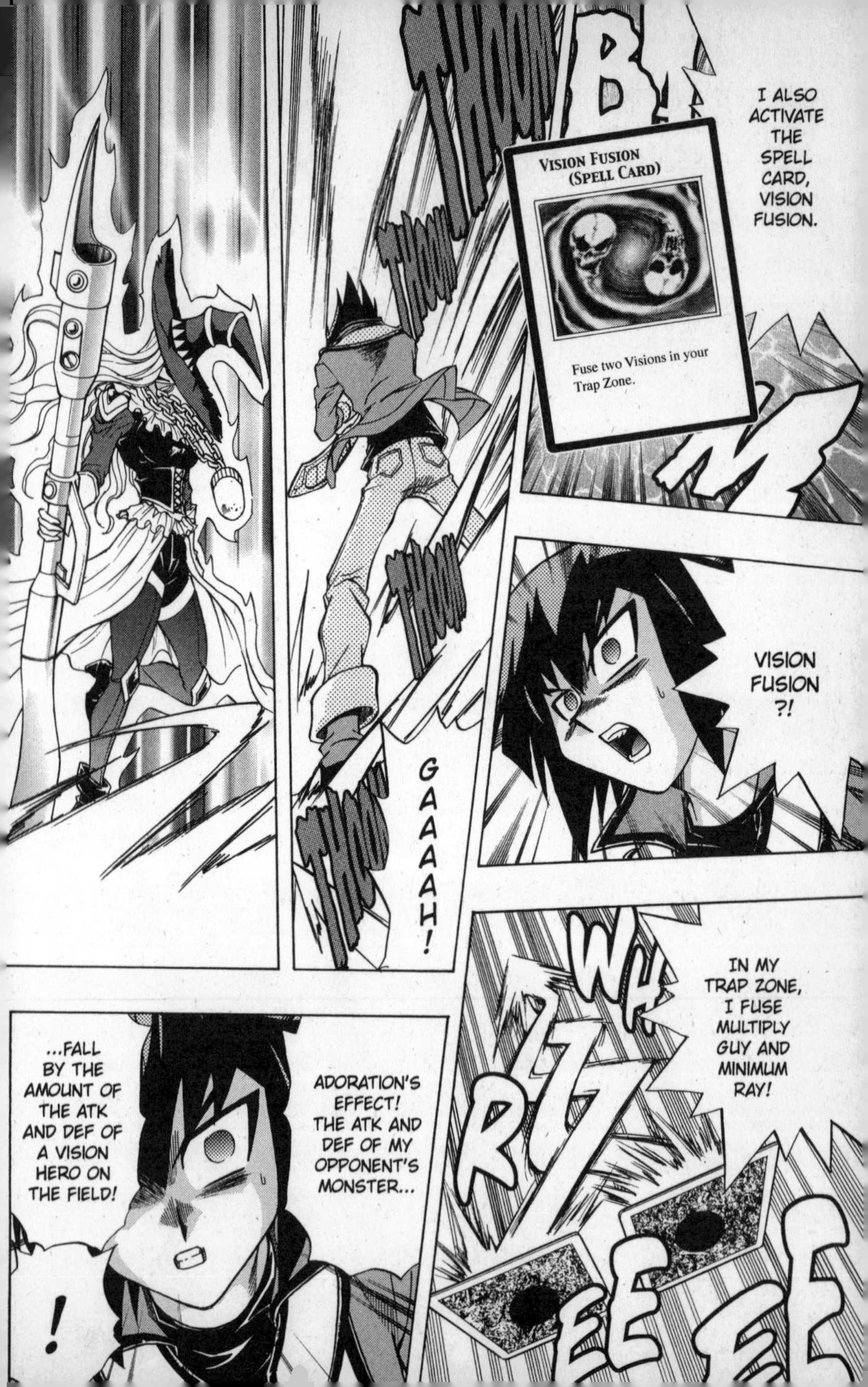
I ALSO ACTIVATE THE SPELL CARD, VISION FUSION.
VISION FUSION
(SPELL CARD)
Fuse two Visions in your Trap Zone.
VISION FUSION ?!
GAAAAAH!
IN MY TRAP ZONE, I FUSE MULTIPLY GUY AND MINIMUM RAY!
ADORATION'S EFFECT! THE ATK AND DEF OF MY OPPONENT'S MONSTER...
...FALL BY THE AMOUNT OF THE ATK AND DEF OF A VISION HERO ON THE FIELD!
!

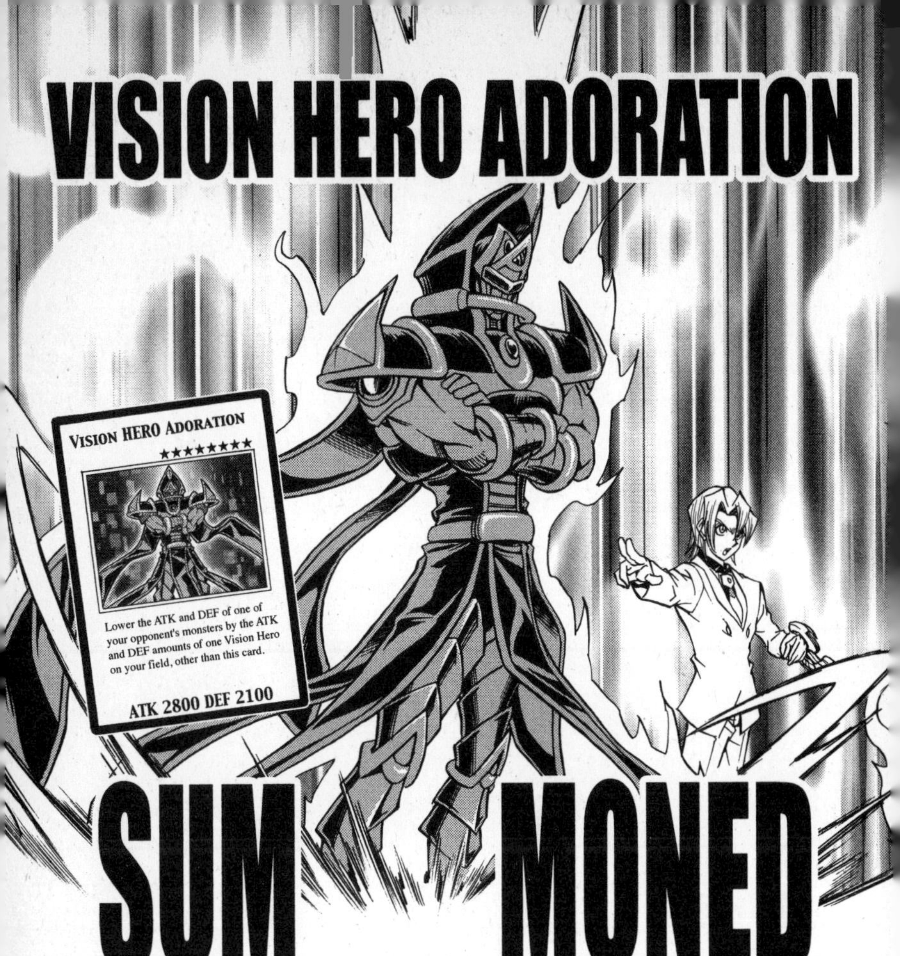
VISION HERO ADORATION
Vision HERO Adoration
★★★★★★★★
Lower the ATK and DEF of one of your opponent's monsters by the ATK and DEF amounts of one Vision Hero on your field, other than this card.
ATK 2800 DEF 2100
SUM MONED

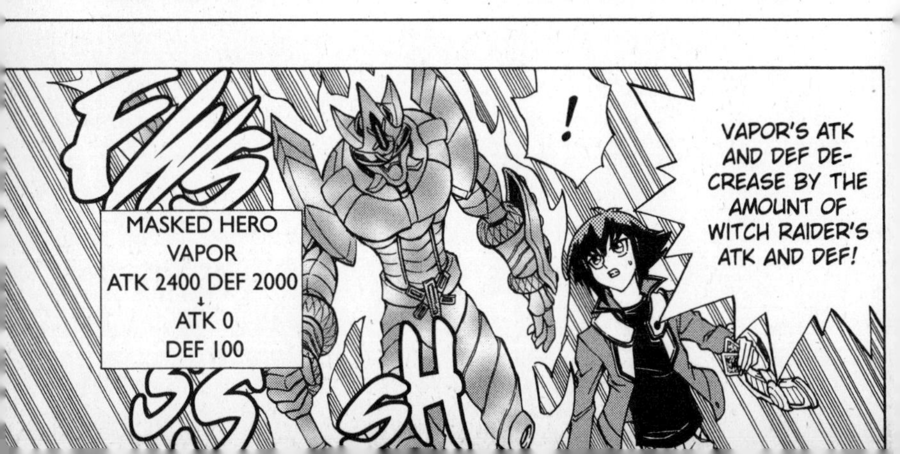
!
VAPOR'S ATK AND DEF DE-CREASE BY THE AMOUNT OF WITCH RAIDER'S ATK AND DEF!
MASKED HERO VAPOR
ATK 2400 DEF 2000
↓
ATK 0
DEF 100
SH

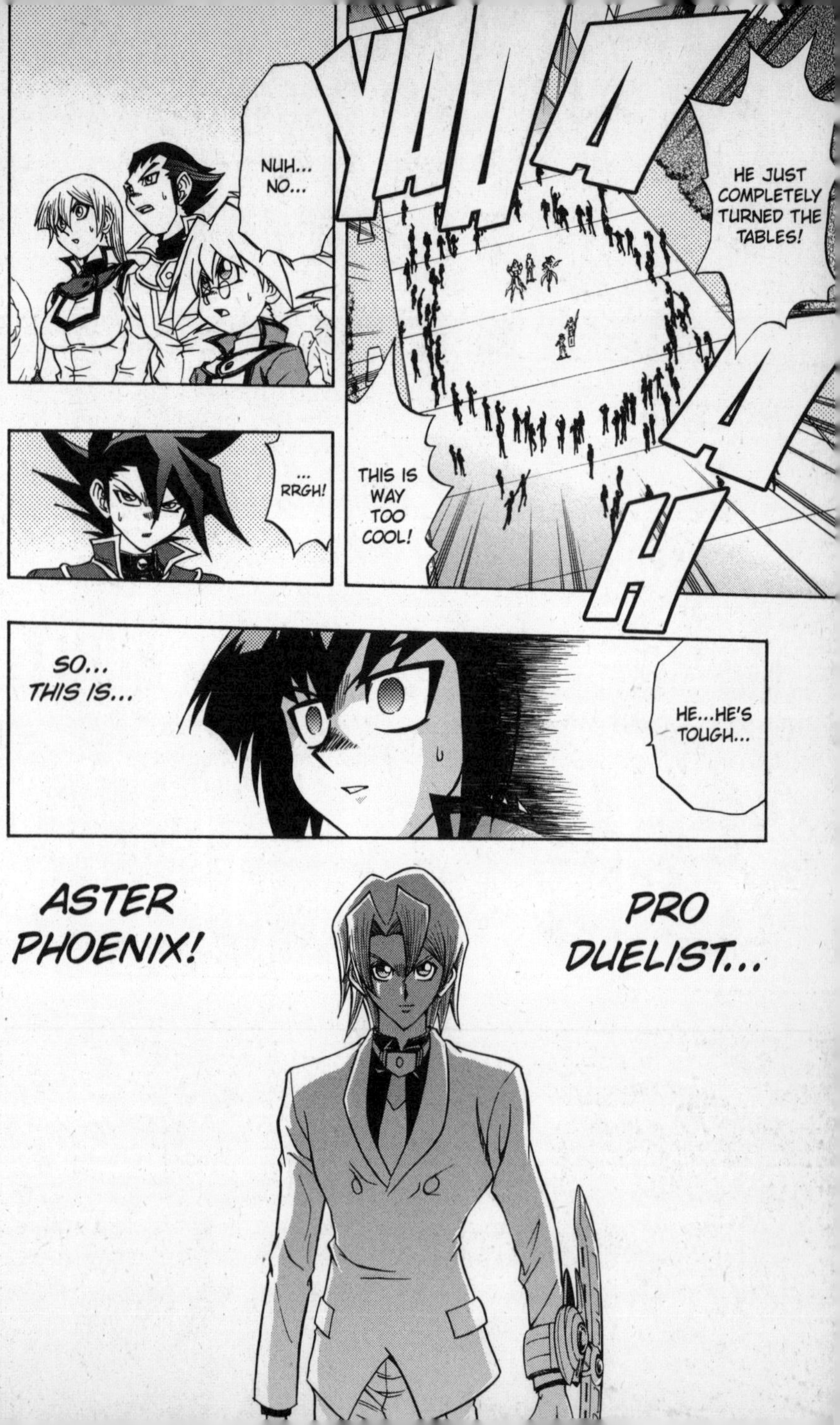
YAAAAH
HE JUST COMPLETELY TURNED THE TABLES!
THIS IS WAY TOO COOL!
NUH... NO...
...RRGH!
HE...HE'S TOUGH...
SO... THIS IS...
PRO DUELIST...
ASTER PHOENIX!

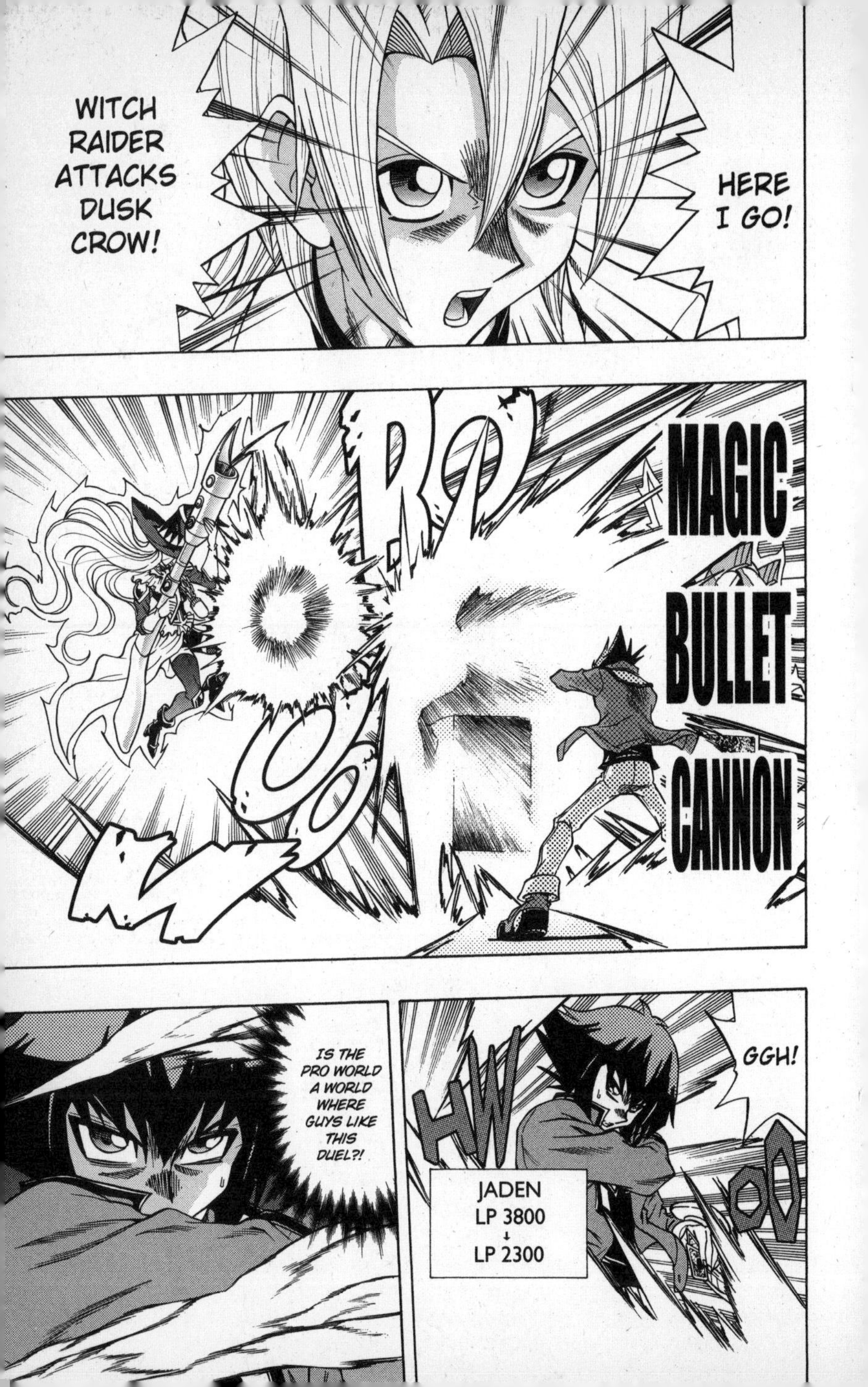
HERE I GO!
WITCH RAIDER ATTACKS DUSK CROW!
MAGIC BULLET CANNON
GGH!
JADEN
LP 3800
↓
LP 2300
IS THE PRO WORLD A WORLD WHERE GUYS LIKE THIS DUEL?!

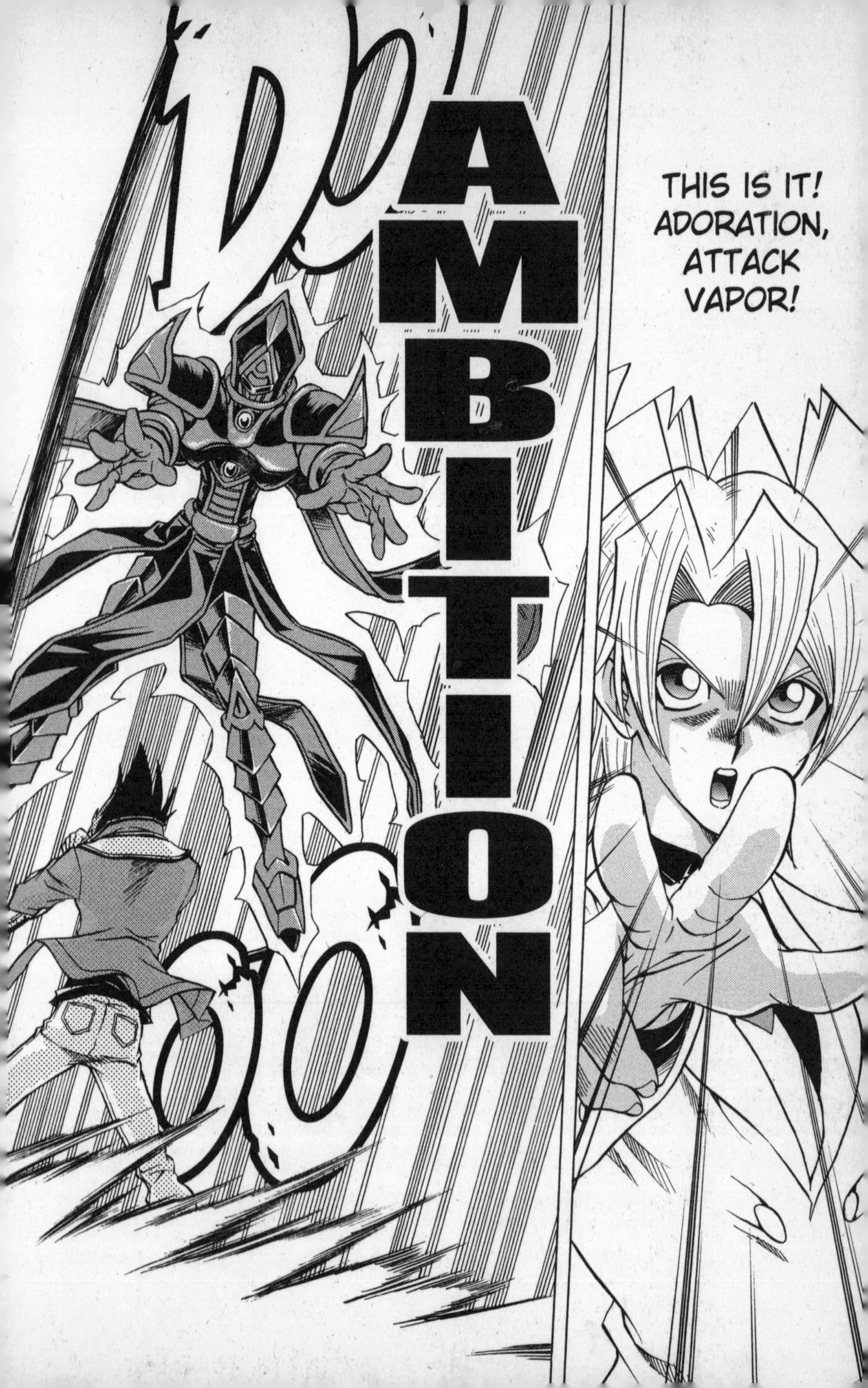
THIS IS IT! ADORATION, ATTACK VAPOR!
AMBITION

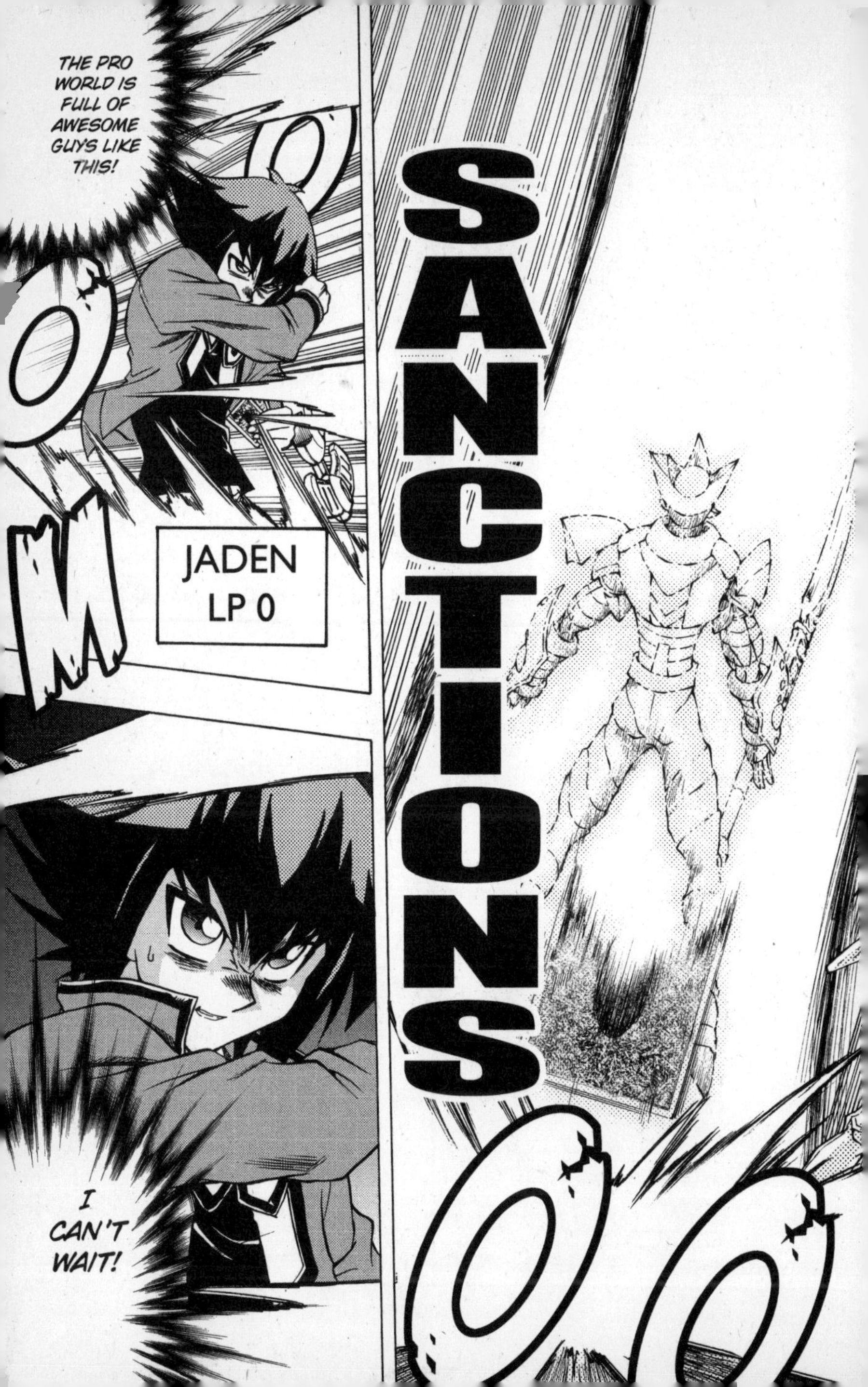
SANCTIONS
THE PRO WORLD IS FULL OF AWESOME GUYS LIKE THIS!
JADEN LP 0
I CAN'T WAIT!

COMRADE MURANO!

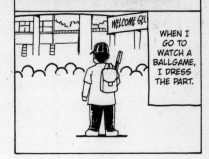

WELCOME SEI.
WHEN I GO TO WATCH A BALLGAME, I DRESS THE PART.
THIS REPLICA UNIFORM WAS A PRESENT FROM MR. MURANO, A VJ EDITOR.
Cap
Lions flag
Uniform
HE'S AN EVEN BIGGER LIONS FAN THAN I AM!
THE TOKYO DOME IS NEAR SHUEISHA, AND EVERY YEAR DURING THE CENTRAL-PACIFIC INTERLEAGUE TOURNAMENT, WE GO WATCH GAMES TOGETHER.
TOKYO'S DOME
GIANTS
LIONS
...SO THAT'S MR. MURANO FOR YOU. THEN MR. TERASHI GAVE HIM A PRESENT!
CLICK
LEO'S EARS!

LEO'S EARS!

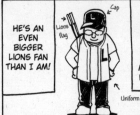

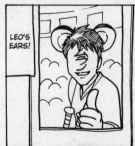

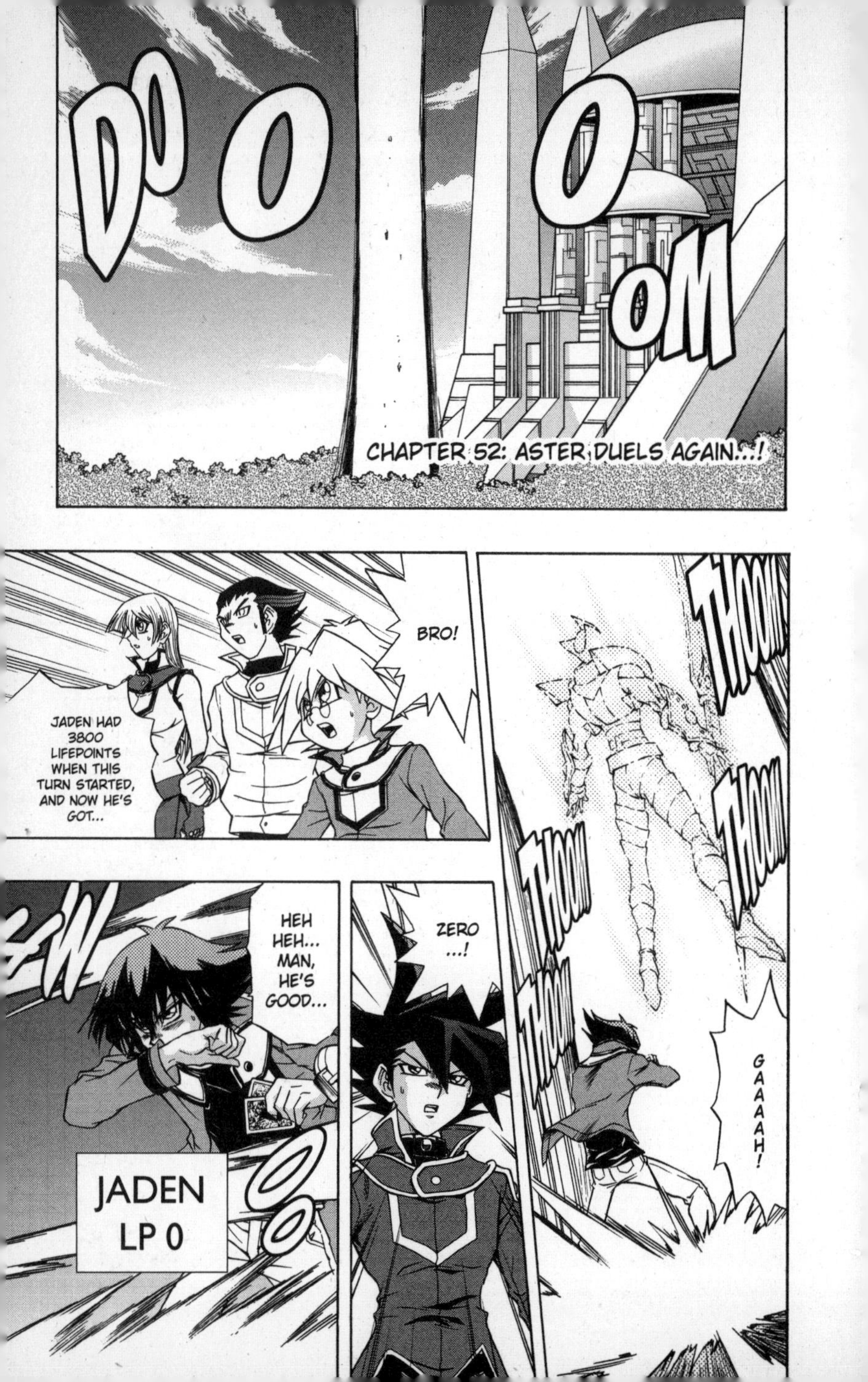
DOOOOM
CHAPTER 52: ASTER DUELS AGAIN...!
THOOM
THOOM
THOOM
THOOM
GAAAAAH!
BRO!
JADEN HAD 3800 LIFEPOINTS WHEN THIS TURN STARTED, AND NOW HE'S GOT...
ZERO ...!
HEH HEH... MAN, HE'S GOOD...
JADEN LP 0

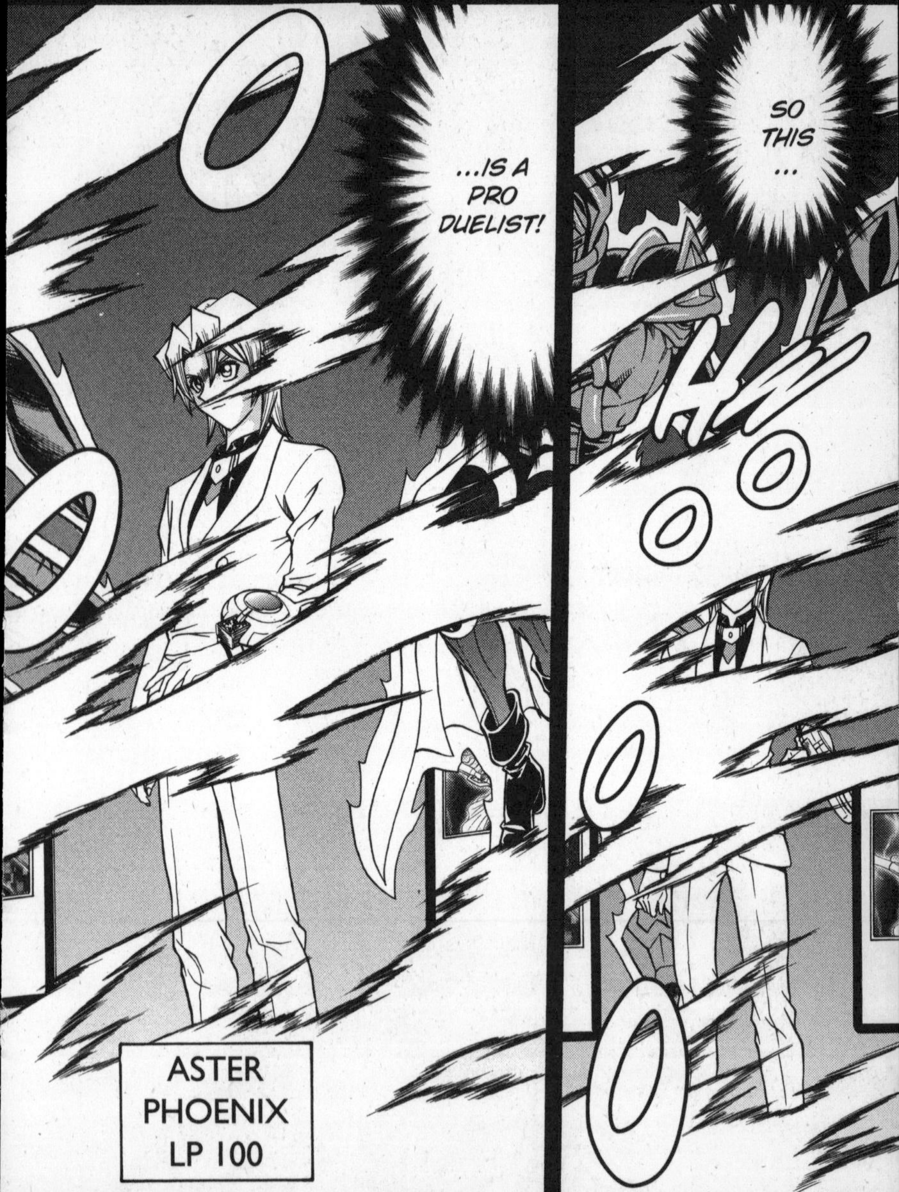
SO THIS ...
...IS A PRO DUELIST!
ASTER PHOENIX LP 100

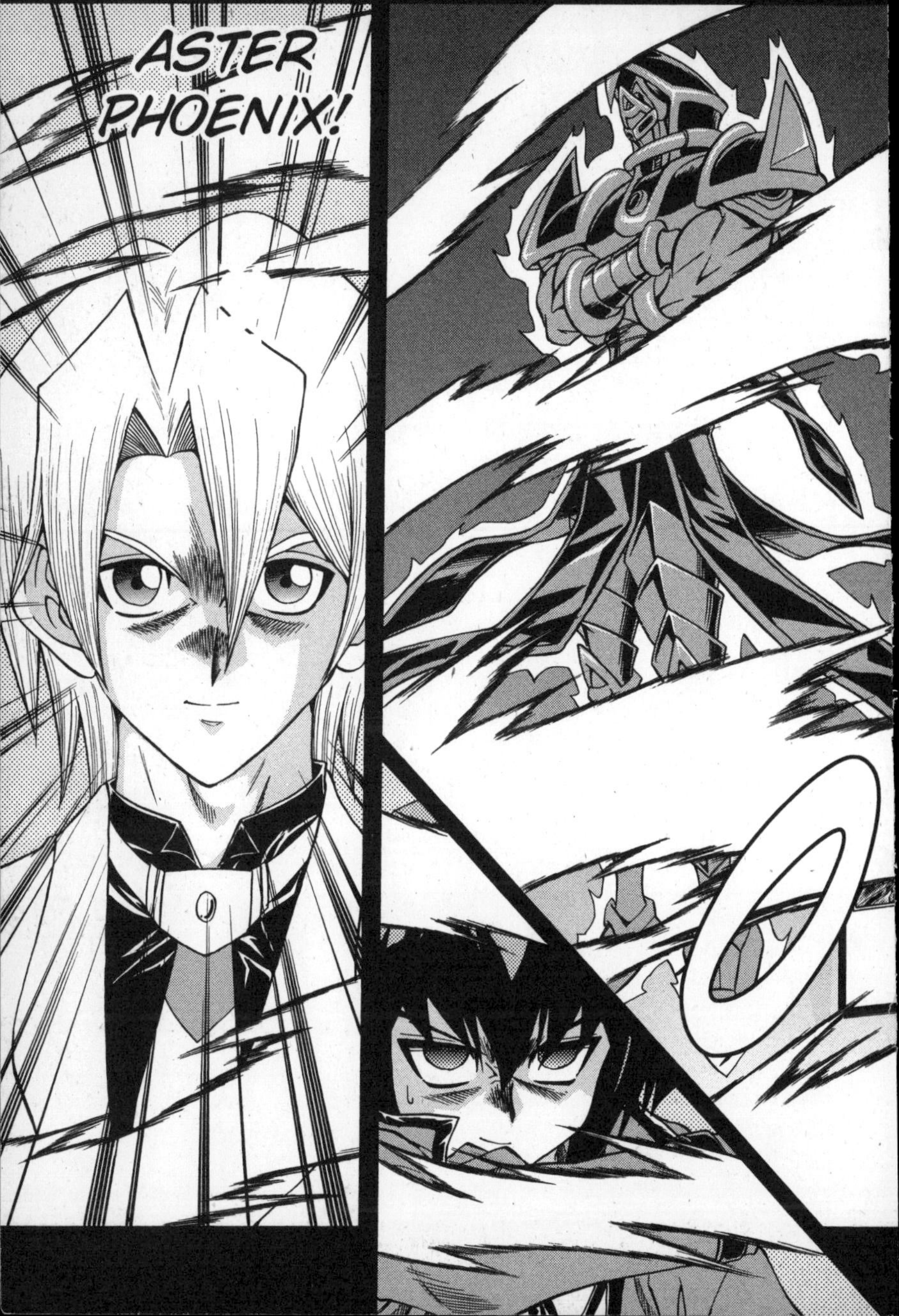
ASTER PHOENIX!

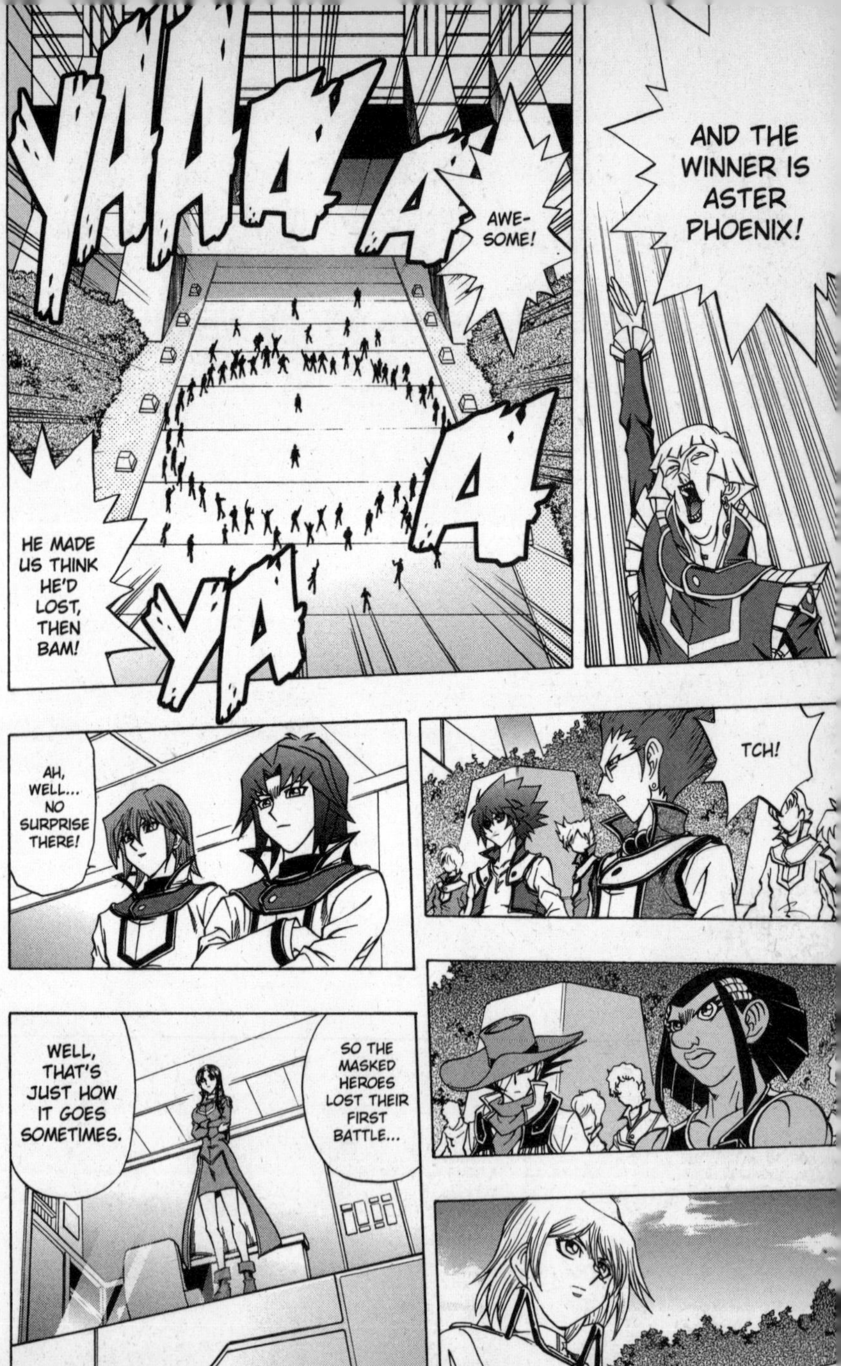
AND THE WINNER IS ASTER PHOENIX!
YAAAA
AWE-SOME!
A
HE MADE US THINK HE'D LOST, THEN BAM!
YA
TCH!
AH, WELL... NO SURPRISE THERE!
SO THE MASKED HEROES LOST THEIR FIRST BATTLE...
WELL, THAT'S JUST HOW IT GOES SOMETIMES.

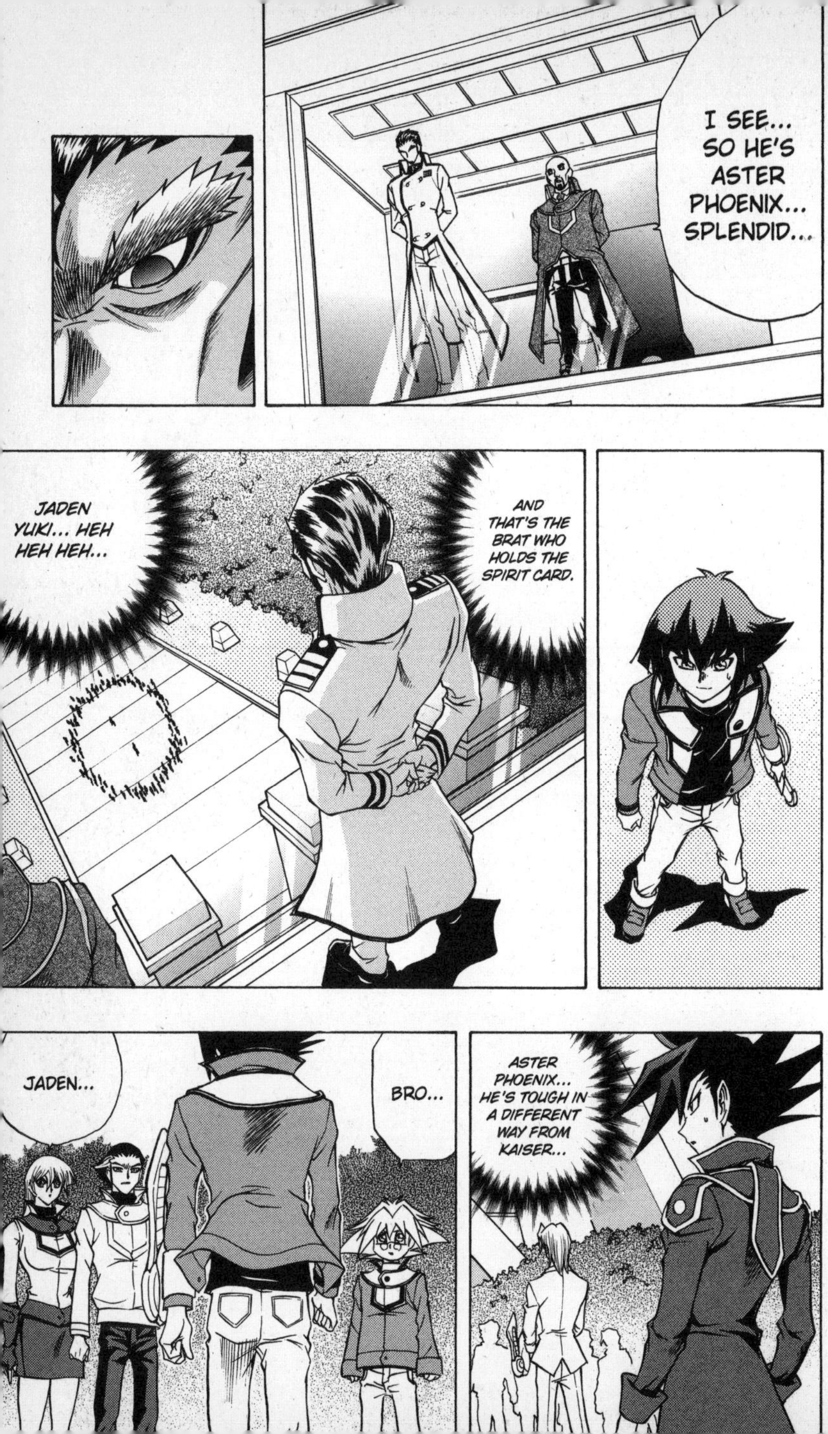
I SEE... SO HE'S ASTER PHOENIX... SPLENDID...
AND THAT'S THE BRAT WHO HOLDS THE SPIRIT CARD.
JADEN YUKI... HEH HEH HEH...
ASTER PHOENIX... HE'S TOUGH IN A DIFFERENT WAY FROM KAISER...
BRO...
JADEN...

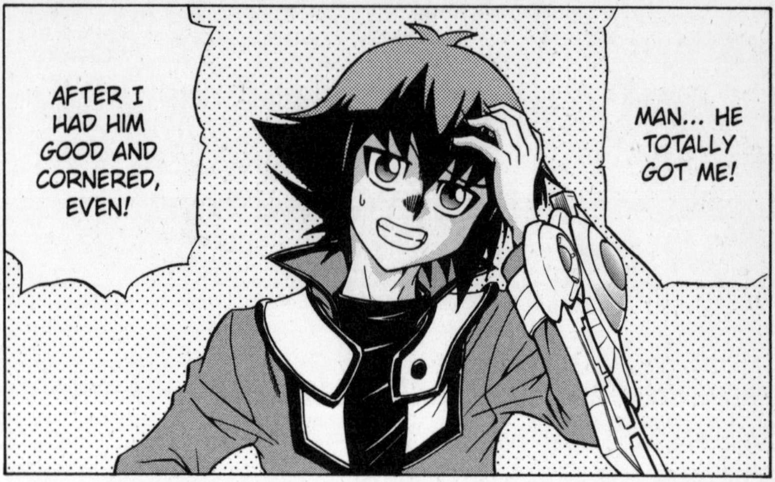
MAN... HE TOTALLY GOT ME!
AFTER I HAD HIM GOOD AND CORNERED, EVEN!

CHAPTER 52: ASTER DUELS AGAIN...!

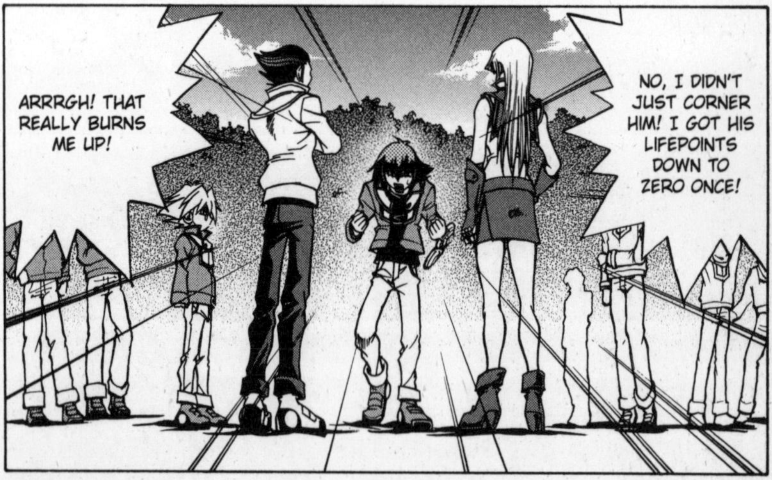
NO, I DIDN'T JUST CORNER HIM! I GOT HIS LIFEPOINTS DOWN TO ZERO ONCE!
ARRRGH! THAT REALLY BURNS ME UP!

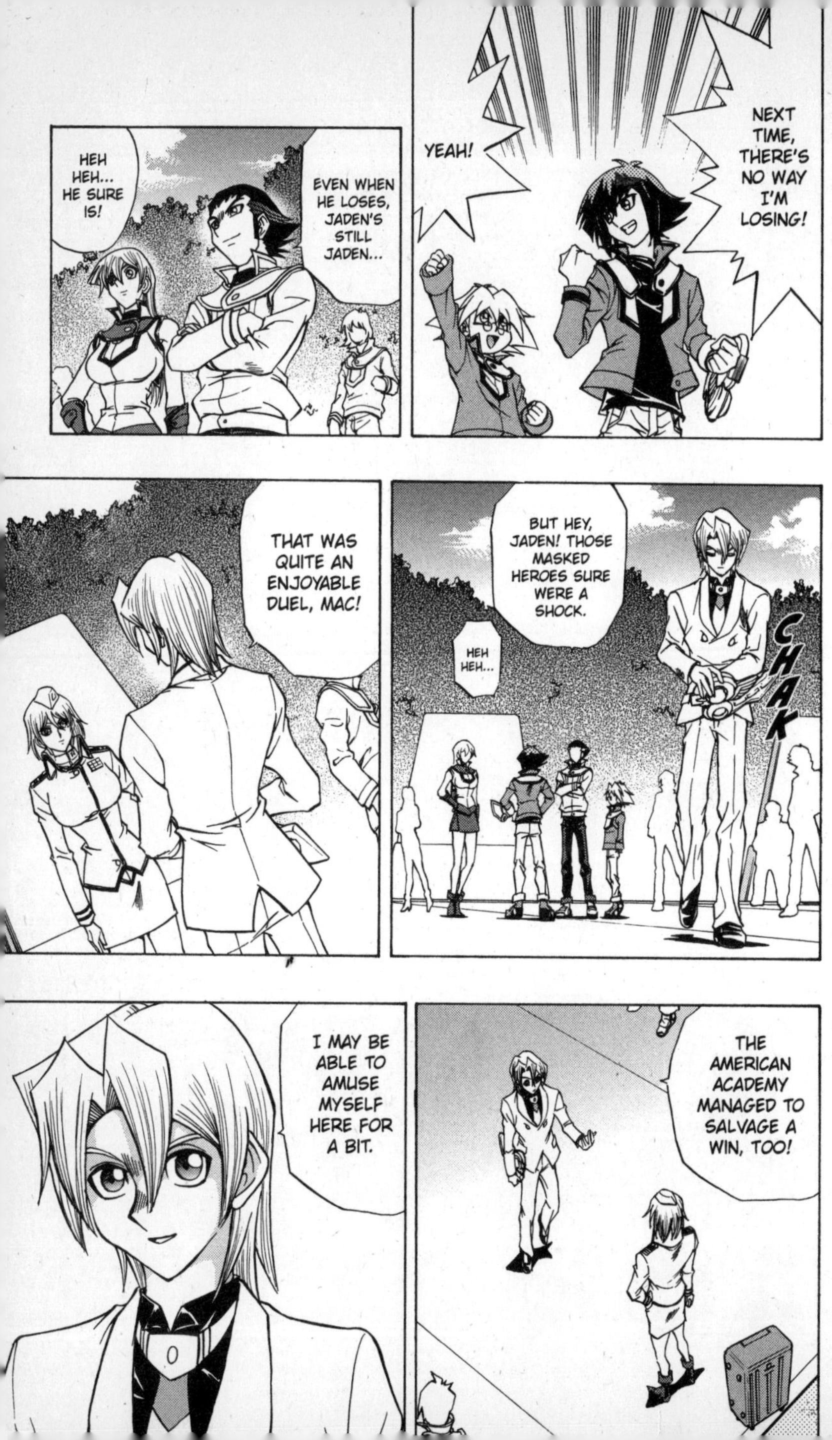
NEXT TIME, THERE'S NO WAY I'M LOSING!
YEAH!
EVEN WHEN HE LOSES, JADEN'S STILL JADEN...
HEH HEH... HE SURE IS!
BUT HEY, JADEN! THOSE MASKED HEROES SURE WERE A SHOCK.
HEH HEH...
CHAK
THAT WAS QUITE AN ENJOYABLE DUEL, MAC!
THE AMERICAN ACADEMY MANAGED TO SALVAGE A WIN, TOO!
I MAY BE ABLE TO AMUSE MYSELF HERE FOR A BIT.

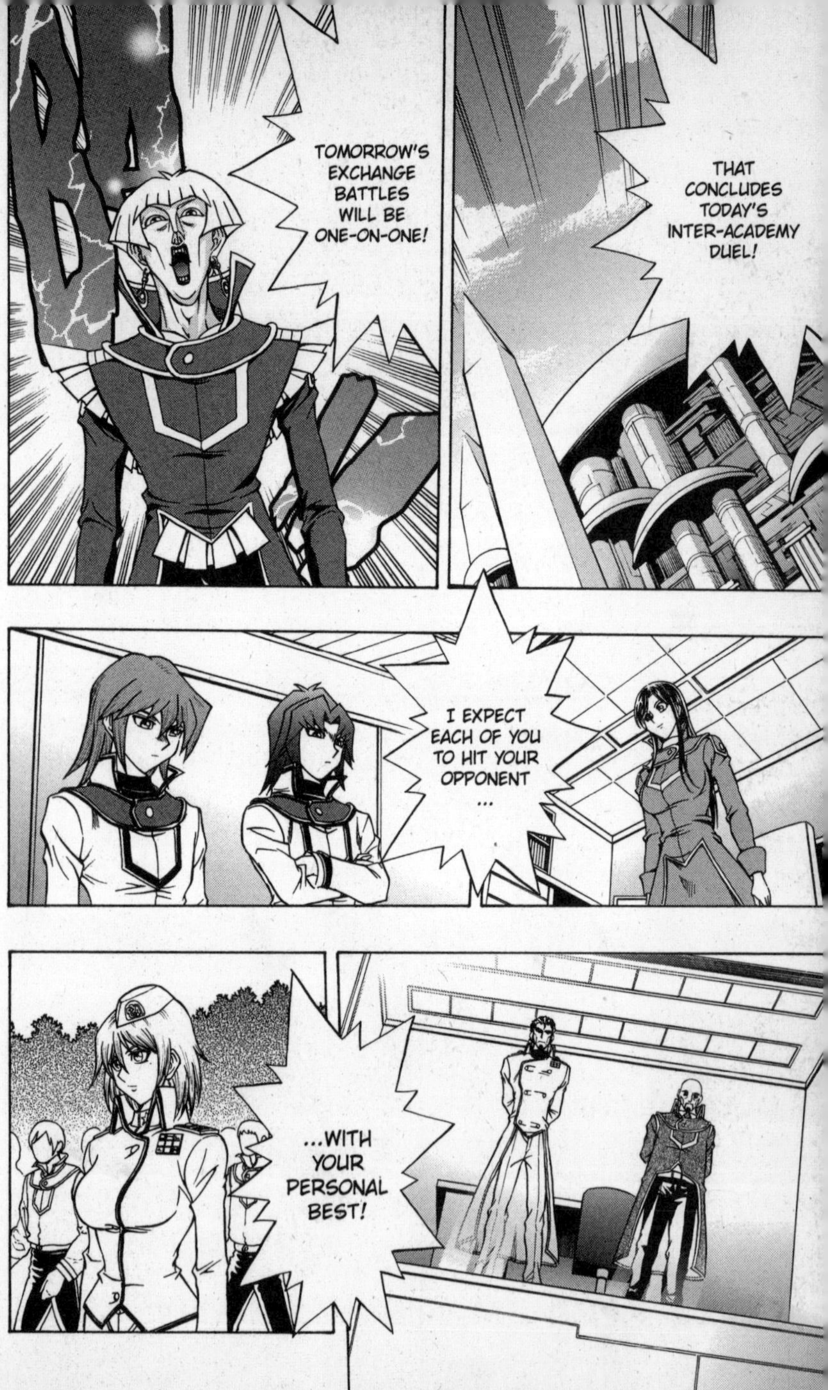
THAT CONCLUDES TODAY'S INTER-ACADEMY DUEL!
TOMORROW'S EXCHANGE BATTLES WILL BE ONE-ON-ONE!
I EXPECT EACH OF YOU TO HIT YOUR OPPONENT ...
...WITH YOUR PERSONAL BEST!

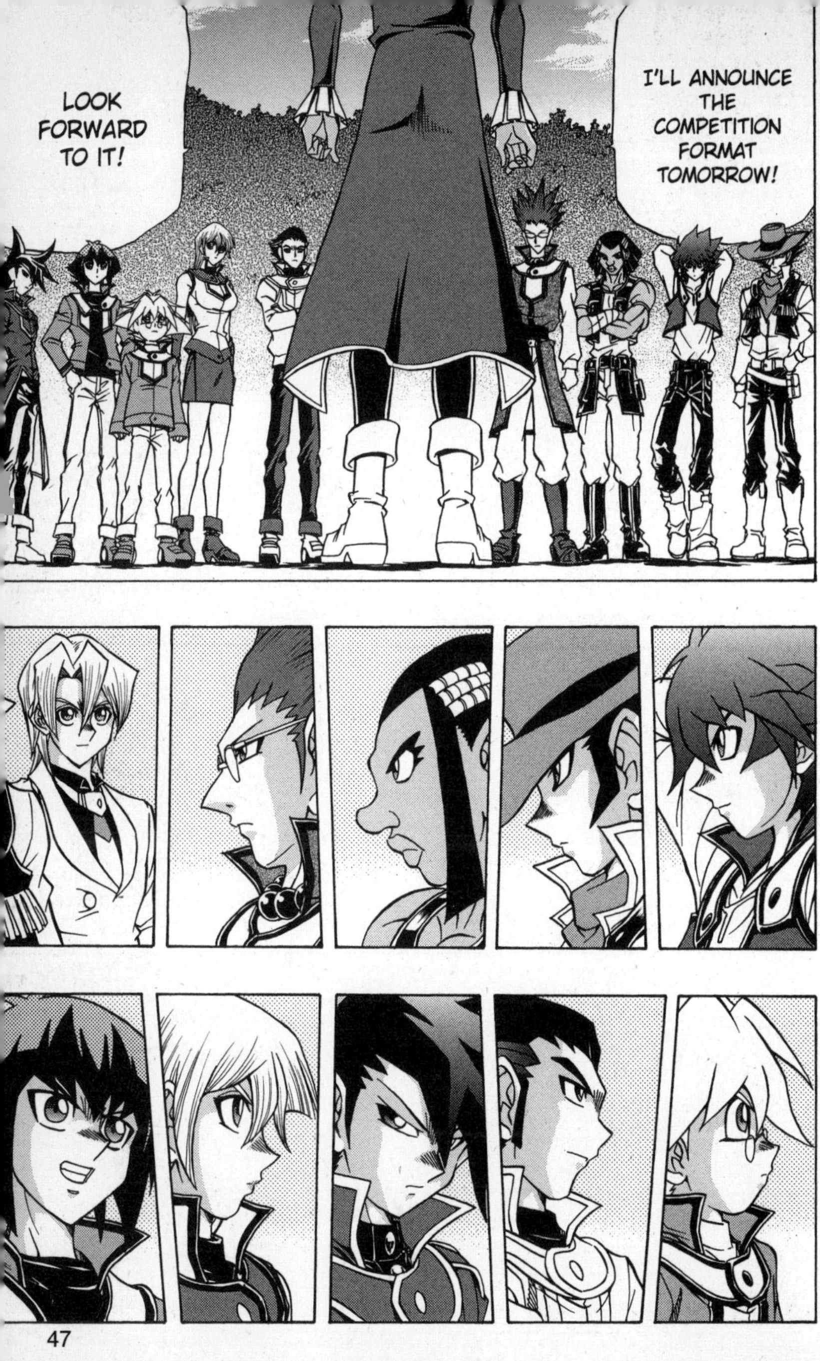
I'LL ANNOUNCE THE COMPETITION FORMAT TOMORROW!
LOOK FORWARD TO IT!

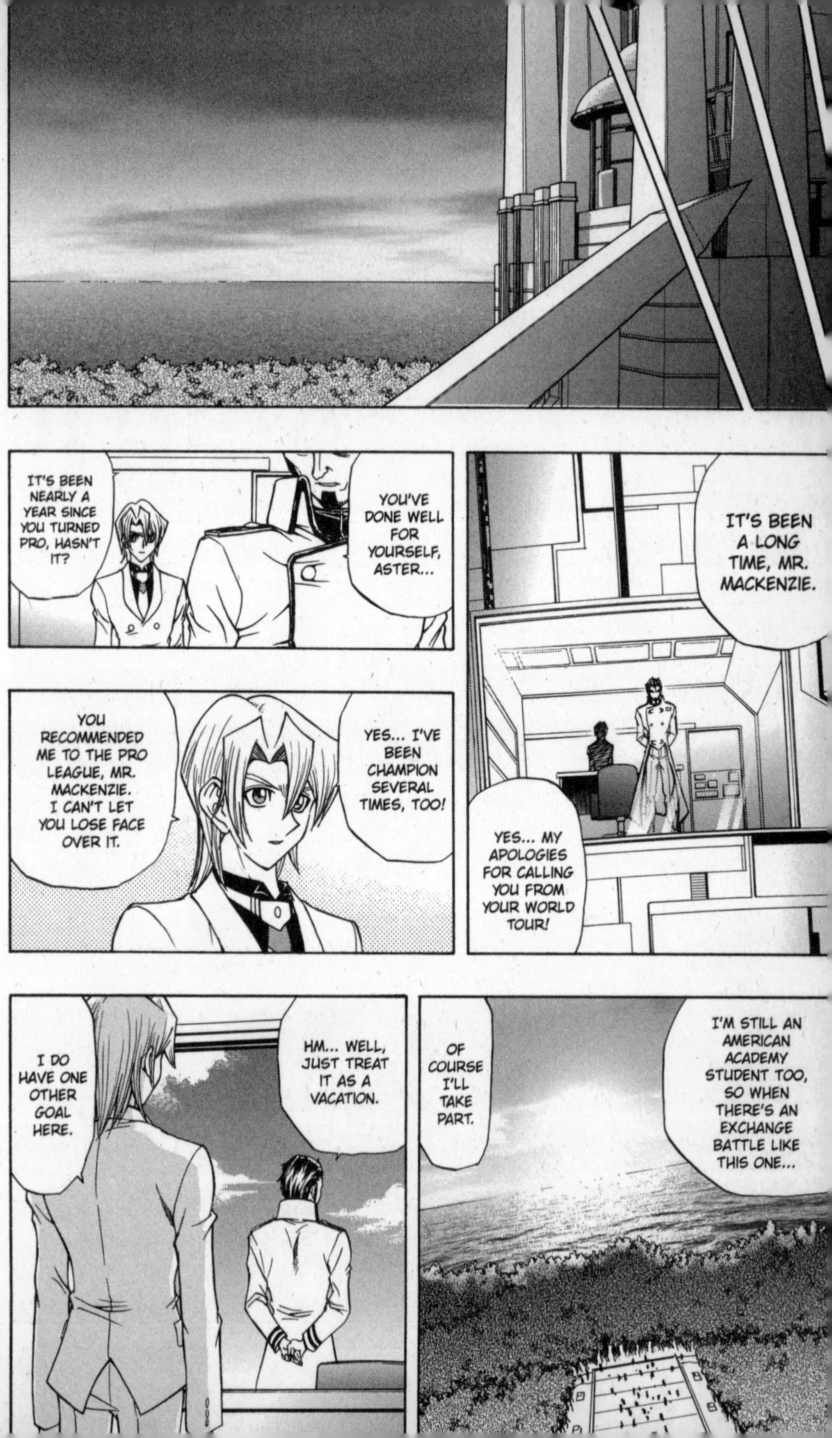
IT'S BEEN A LONG TIME, MR. MACKENZIE.
YES... MY APOLOGIES FOR CALLING YOU FROM YOUR WORLD TOUR!
YOU'VE DONE WELL FOR YOURSELF, ASTER...
IT'S BEEN NEARLY A YEAR SINCE YOU TURNED PRO, HASN'T IT?
YES... I'VE BEEN CHAMPION SEVERAL TIMES, TOO!
YOU RECOMMENDED ME TO THE PRO LEAGUE, MR. MACKENZIE. I CAN'T LET YOU LOSE FACE OVER IT.
I'M STILL AN AMERICAN ACADEMY STUDENT TOO, SO WHEN THERE'S AN EXCHANGE BATTLE LIKE THIS ONE...
OF COURSE I'LL TAKE PART.
HM... WELL, JUST TREAT IT AS A VACATION.
I DO HAVE ONE OTHER GOAL HERE.

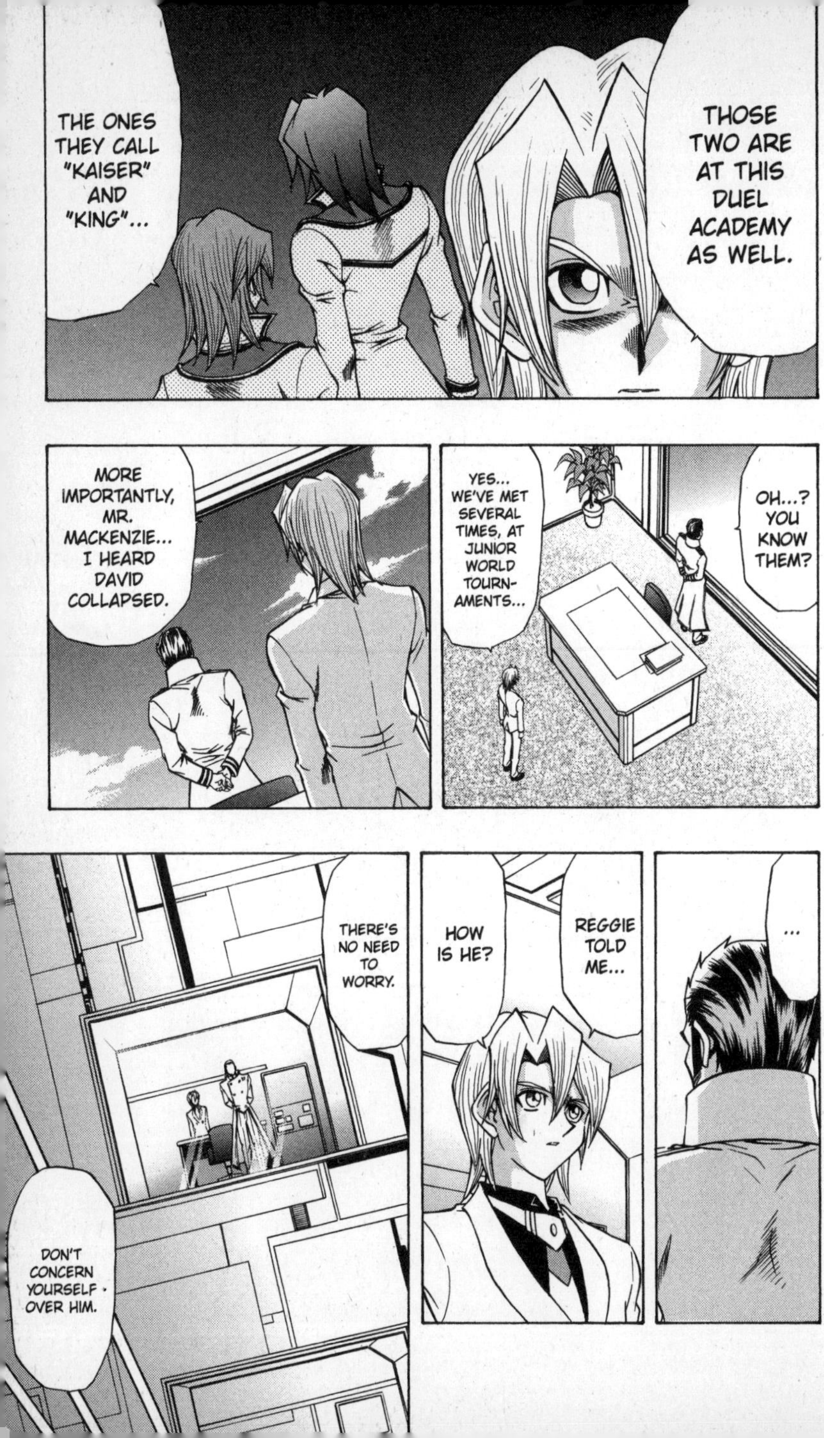
THOSE TWO ARE AT THIS DUEL ACADEMY AS WELL.
THE ONES THEY CALL "KAISER" AND "KING"...
OH...? YOU KNOW THEM?
YES... WE'VE MET SEVERAL TIMES, AT JUNIOR WORLD TOURN-AMENTS...
MORE IMPORTANTLY, MR. MACKENZIE... I HEARD DAVID COLLAPSED.
...
REGGIE TOLD ME...
HOW IS HE?
THERE'S NO NEED TO WORRY.
DON'T CONCERN YOURSELF OVER HIM.

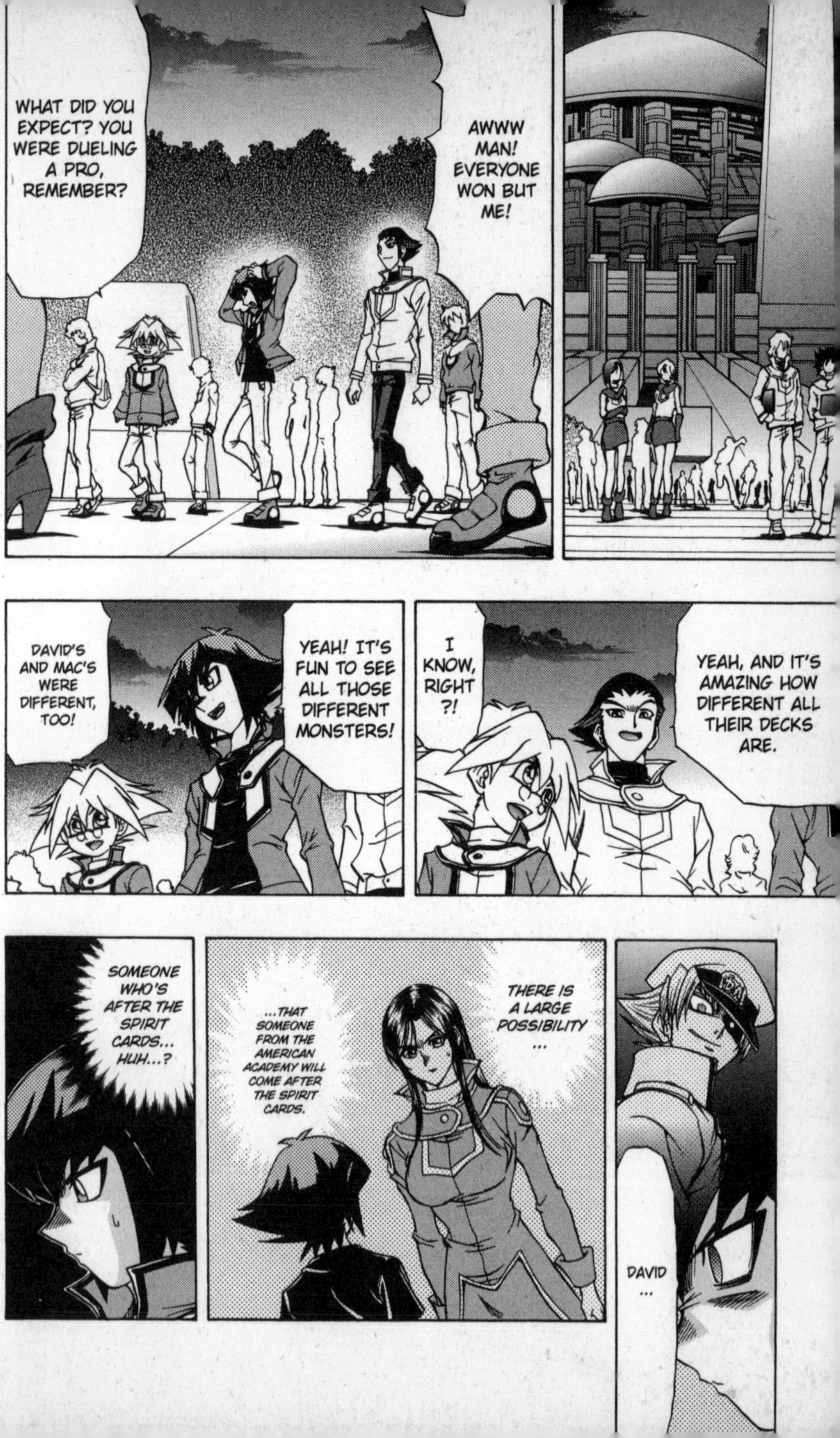
AWWW MAN! EVERYONE WON BUT ME!
WHAT DID YOU EXPECT? YOU WERE DUELING A PRO, REMEMBER?
YEAH, AND IT'S AMAZING HOW DIFFERENT ALL THEIR DECKS ARE.
I KNOW, RIGHT?!
YEAH! IT'S FUN TO SEE ALL THOSE DIFFERENT MONSTERS!
DAVID'S AND MAC'S WERE DIFFERENT, TOO!
DAVID...
THERE IS A LARGE POSSIBILITY...
...THAT SOMEONE FROM THE AMERICAN ACADEMY WILL COME AFTER THE SPIRIT CARDS.
SOMEONE WHO'S AFTER THE SPIRIT CARDS... HUH...?

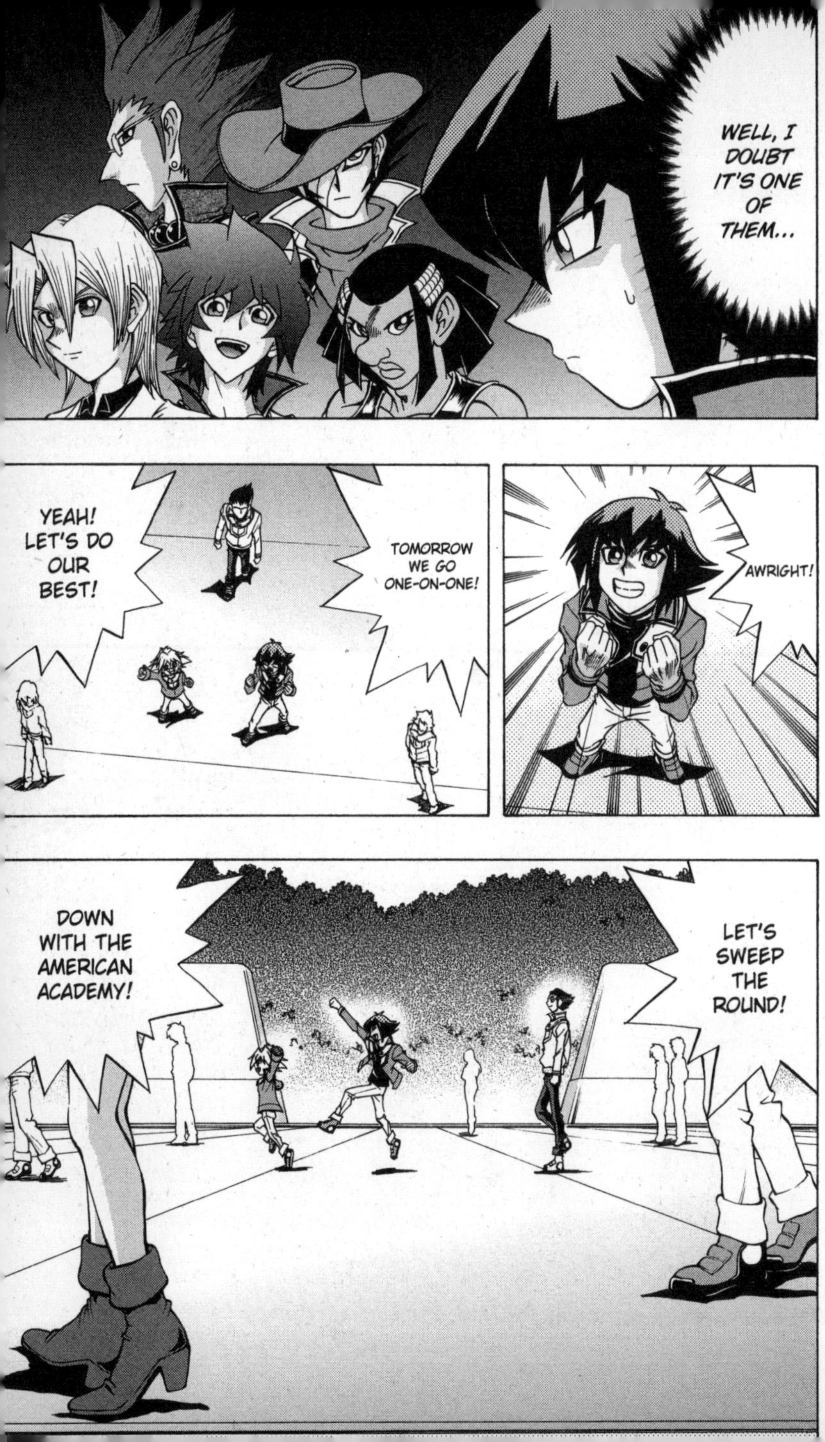
WELL, I DOUBT IT'S ONE OF THEM...
AWRIGHT!
TOMORROW WE GO ONE-ON-ONE!
YEAH! LET'S DO OUR BEST!
LET'S SWEEP THE ROUND!
DOWN WITH THE AMERICAN ACADEMY!

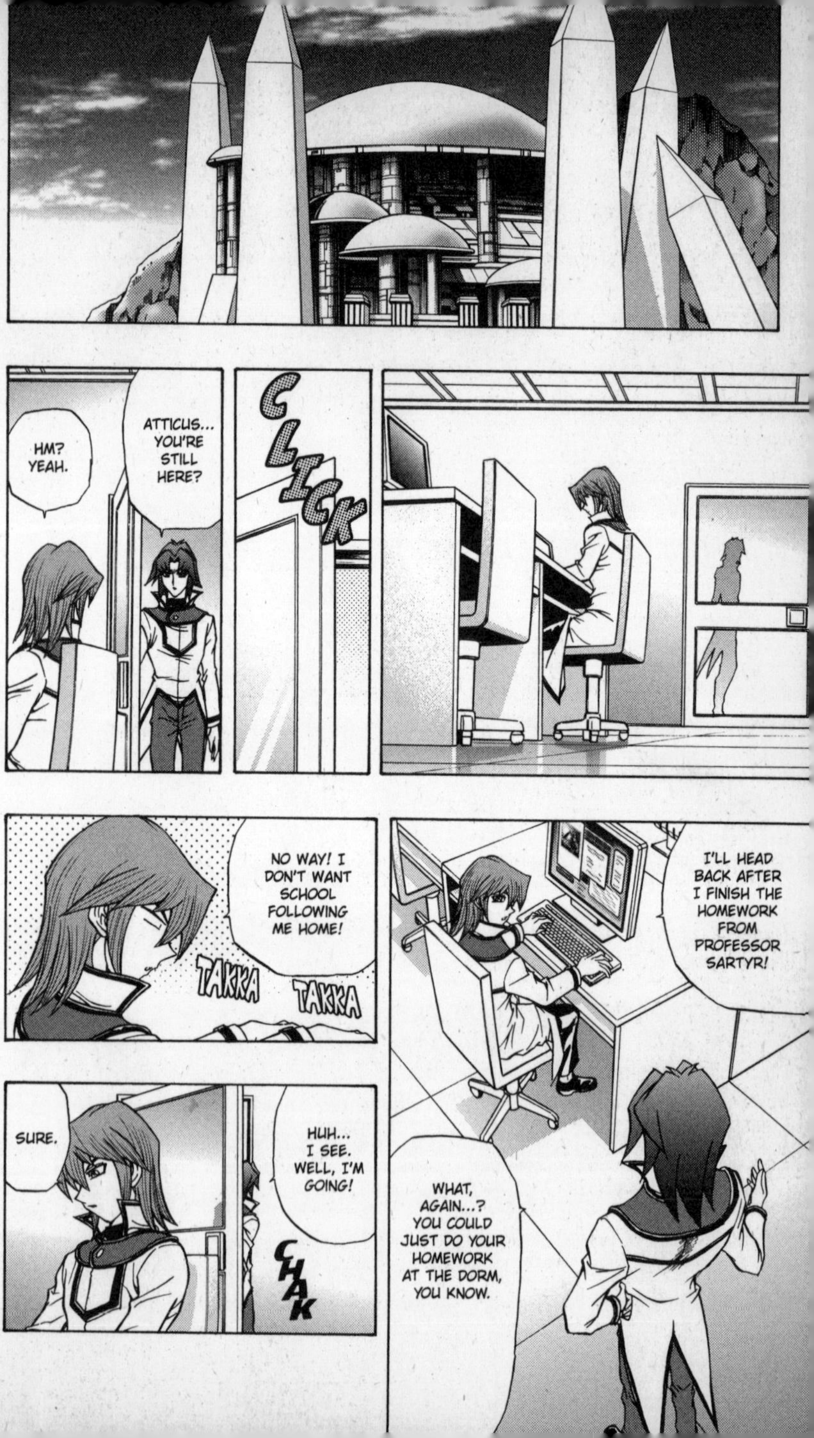
CLICK
ATTICUS... YOU'RE STILL HERE?
HM? YEAH.
I'LL HEAD BACK AFTER I FINISH THE HOMEWORK FROM PROFESSOR SARTYR!
WHAT, AGAIN...? YOU COULD JUST DO YOUR HOMEWORK AT THE DORM, YOU KNOW.
NO WAY! I DON'T WANT SCHOOL FOLLOWING ME HOME!
TAKKA
TAKKA
HUH... I SEE. WELL, I'M GOING!
SURE.
CHAK

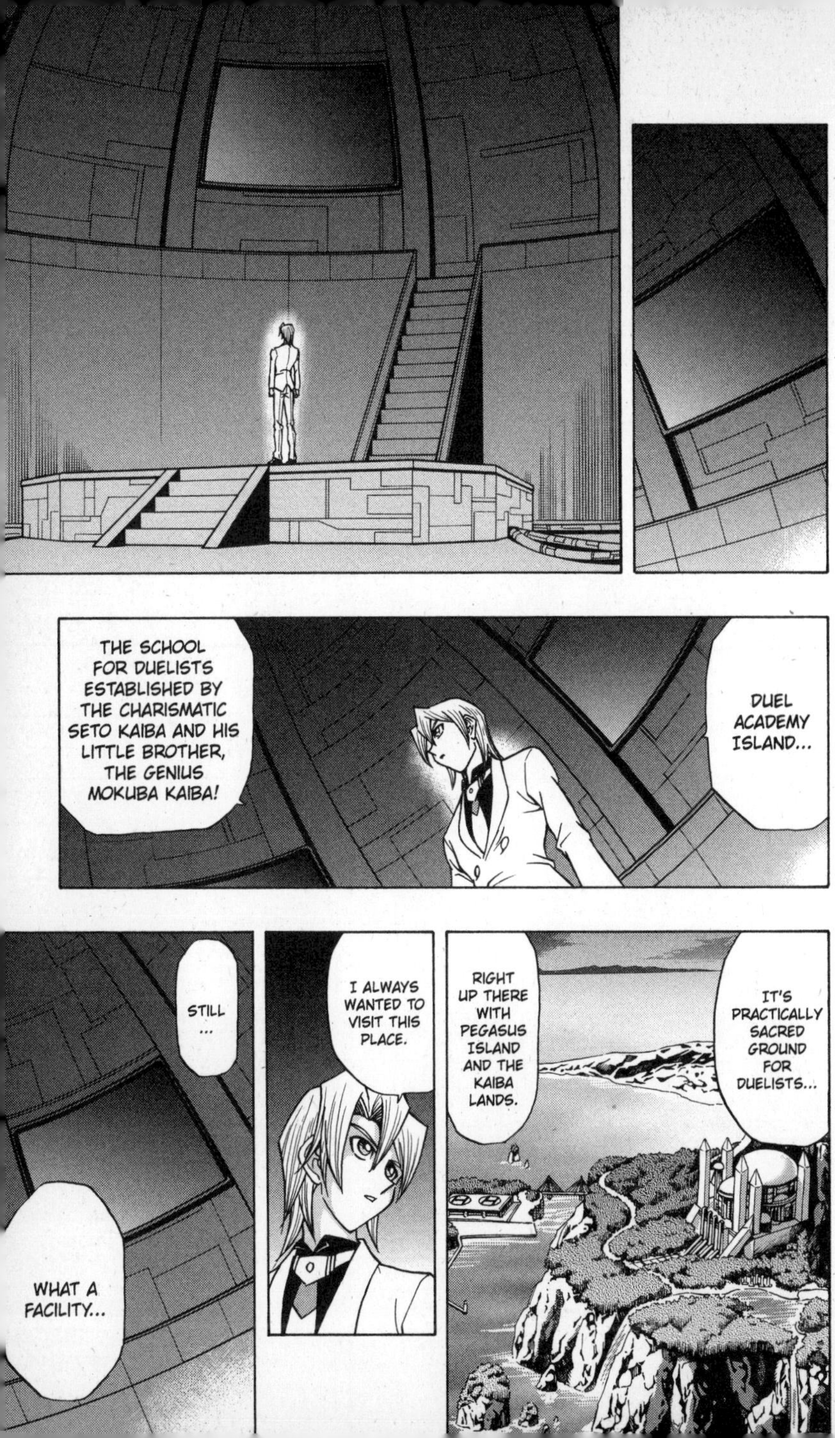
DUEL ACADEMY ISLAND...
THE SCHOOL FOR DUELISTS ESTABLISHED BY THE CHARISMATIC SETO KAIBA AND HIS LITTLE BROTHER, THE GENIUS MOKUBA KAIBA!
IT'S PRACTICALLY SACRED GROUND FOR DUELISTS...
RIGHT UP THERE WITH PEGASUS ISLAND AND THE KAIBA LANDS.
I ALWAYS WANTED TO VISIT THIS PLACE.
STILL...
WHAT A FACILITY...

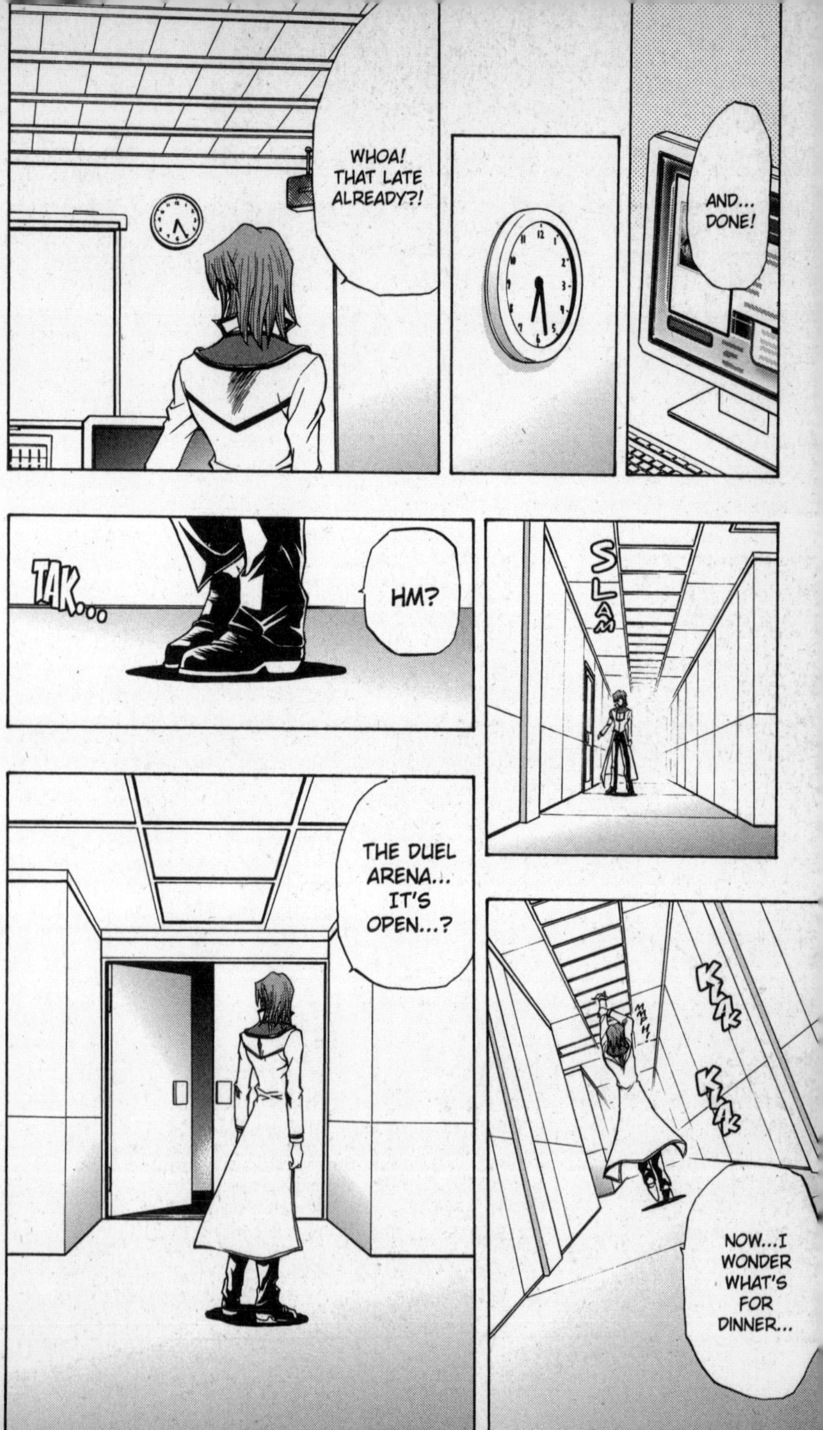
AND... DONE!
WHOA! THAT LATE ALREADY?!
SLAM
KLAK
KLAK
MMPH!
NOW...I WONDER WHAT'S FOR DINNER...
TAK...
HM?
THE DUEL ARENA... IT'S OPEN...?

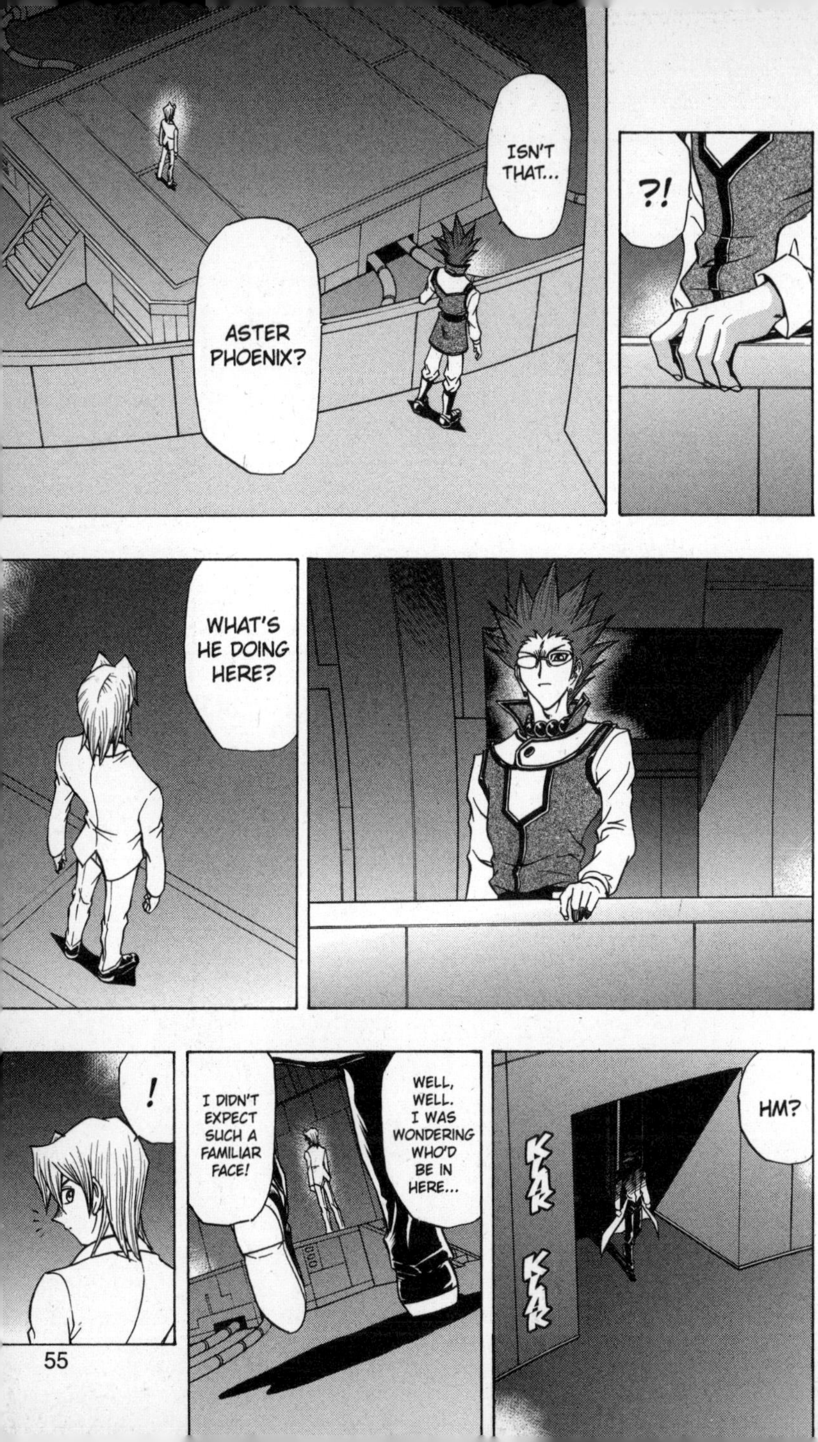
?!
ISN'T THAT...
ASTER PHOENIX?
WHAT'S HE DOING HERE?
HM?
KLAK KLAK
WELL, WELL. I WAS WONDERING WHO'D BE IN HERE...
I DIDN'T EXPECT SUCH A FAMILIAR FACE!
!

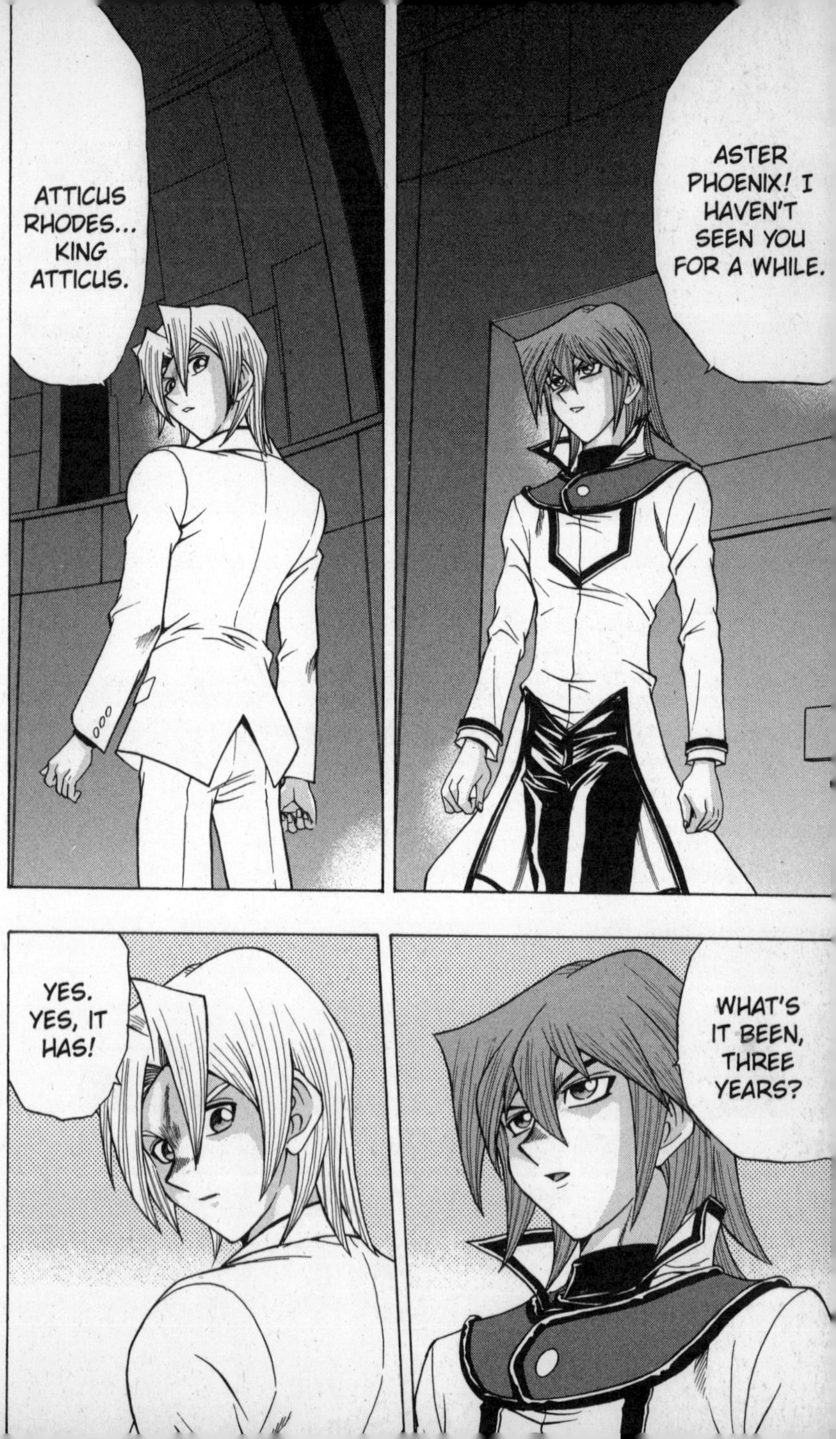
ASTER PHOENIX! I HAVEN'T SEEN YOU FOR A WHILE.
ATTICUS RHODES... KING ATTICUS.
WHAT'S IT BEEN, THREE YEARS?
YES. YES, IT HAS!

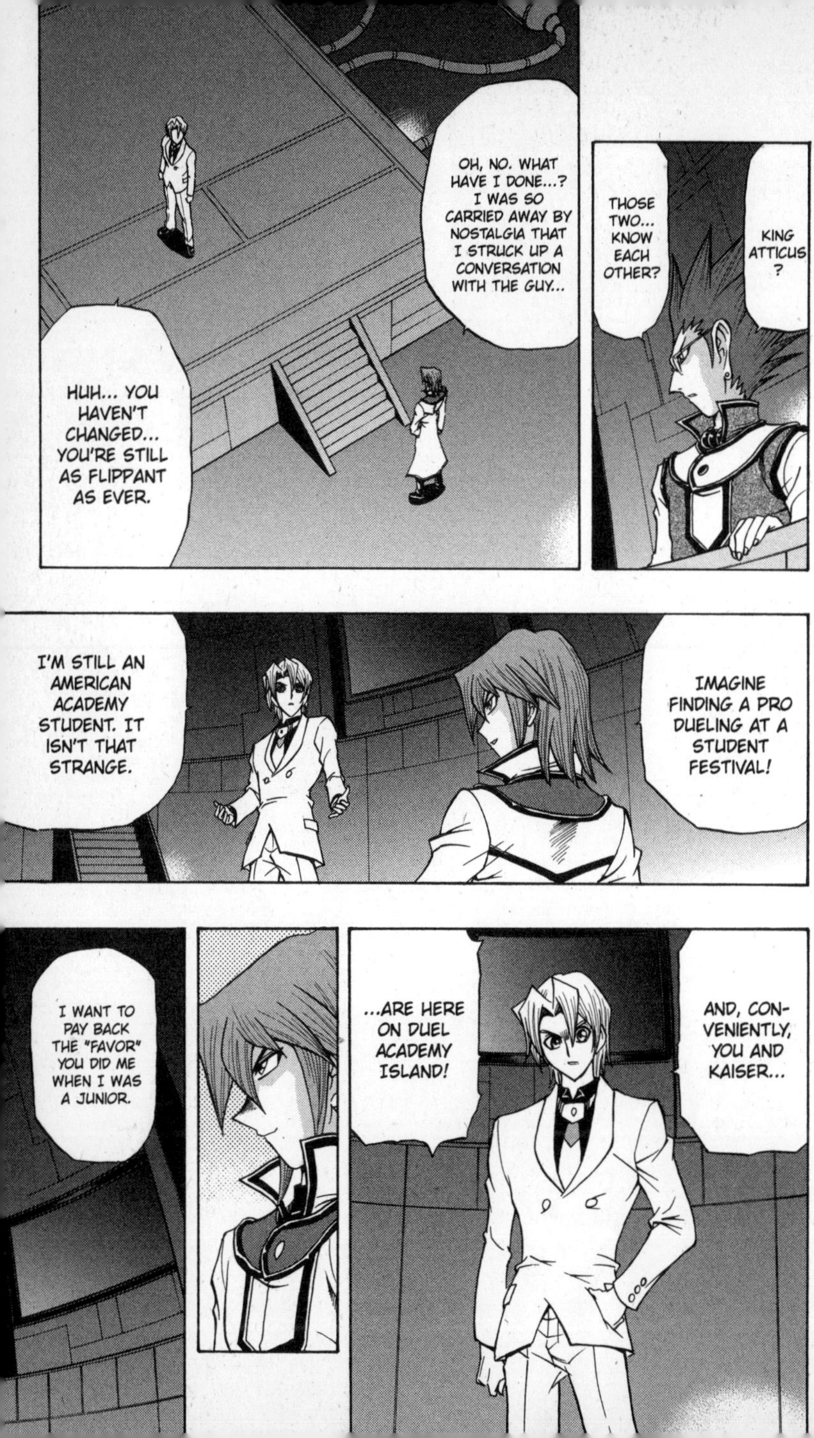
KING ATTICUS?
THOSE TWO... KNOW EACH OTHER?
OH, NO. WHAT HAVE I DONE...? I WAS SO CARRIED AWAY BY NOSTALGIA THAT I STRUCK UP A CONVERSATION WITH THE GUY...
HUH... YOU HAVEN'T CHANGED... YOU'RE STILL AS FLIPPANT AS EVER.
IMAGINE FINDING A PRO DUELING AT A STUDENT FESTIVAL!
I'M STILL AN AMERICAN ACADEMY STUDENT. IT ISN'T THAT STRANGE.
AND, CON-VENIENTLY, YOU AND KAISER...
...ARE HERE ON DUEL ACADEMY ISLAND!
I WANT TO PAY BACK THE "FAVOR" YOU DID ME WHEN I WAS A JUNIOR.

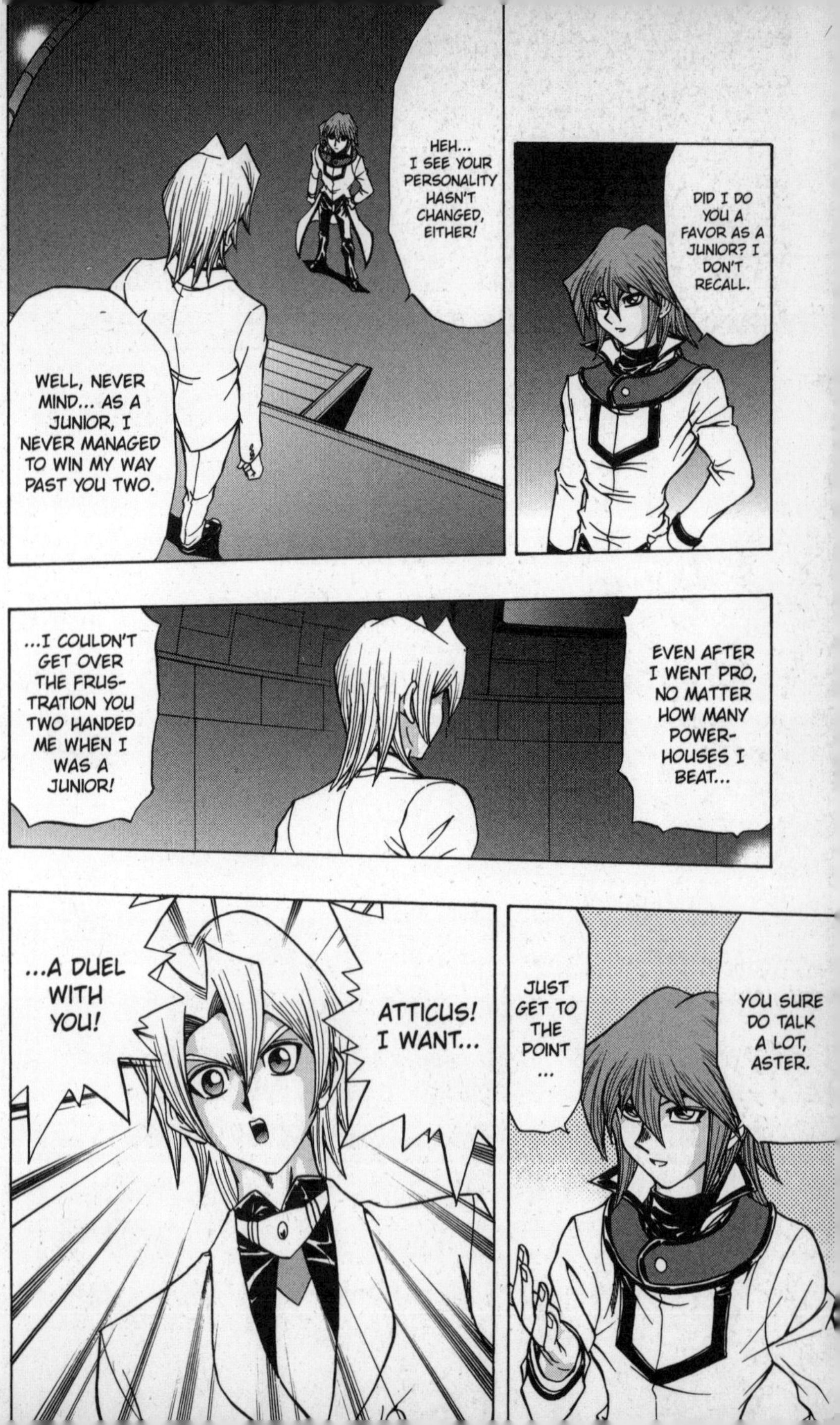
DID I DO YOU A FAVOR AS A JUNIOR? I DON'T RECALL.
HEH... I SEE YOUR PERSONALITY HASN'T CHANGED, EITHER!
WELL, NEVER MIND... AS A JUNIOR, I NEVER MANAGED TO WIN MY WAY PAST YOU TWO.
EVEN AFTER I WENT PRO, NO MATTER HOW MANY POWER-HOUSES I BEAT...
...I COULDN'T GET OVER THE FRUS-TRATION YOU TWO HANDED ME WHEN I WAS A JUNIOR!
YOU SURE DO TALK A LOT, ASTER.
JUST GET TO THE POINT ...
ATTICUS! I WANT...
...A DUEL WITH YOU!

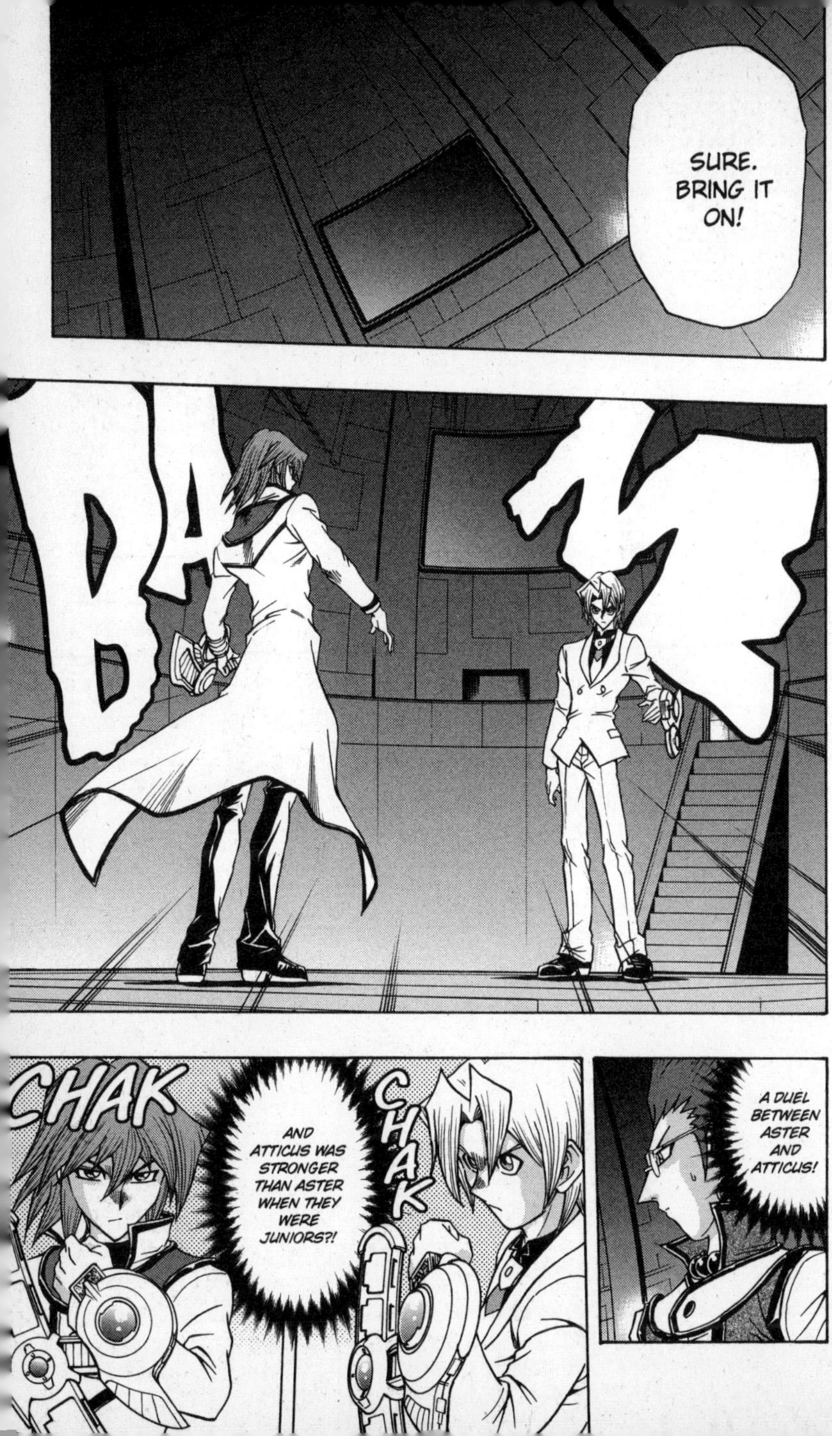
SURE. BRING IT ON!
BAM
A DUEL BETWEEN ASTER AND ATTICUS!
CHAK
CHAK
AND ATTICUS WAS STRONGER THAN ASTER WHEN THEY WERE JUNIORS?!

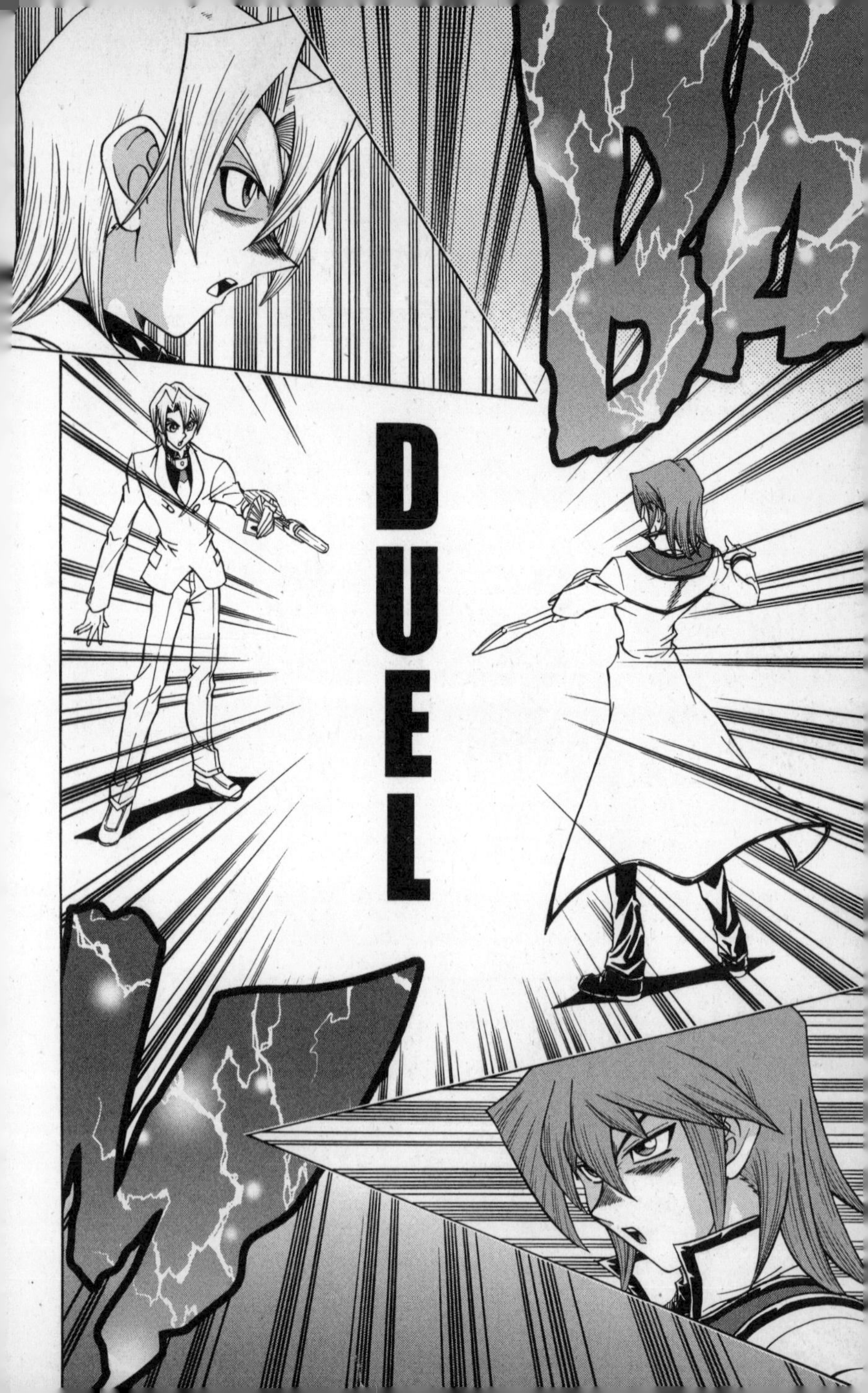
DUEL

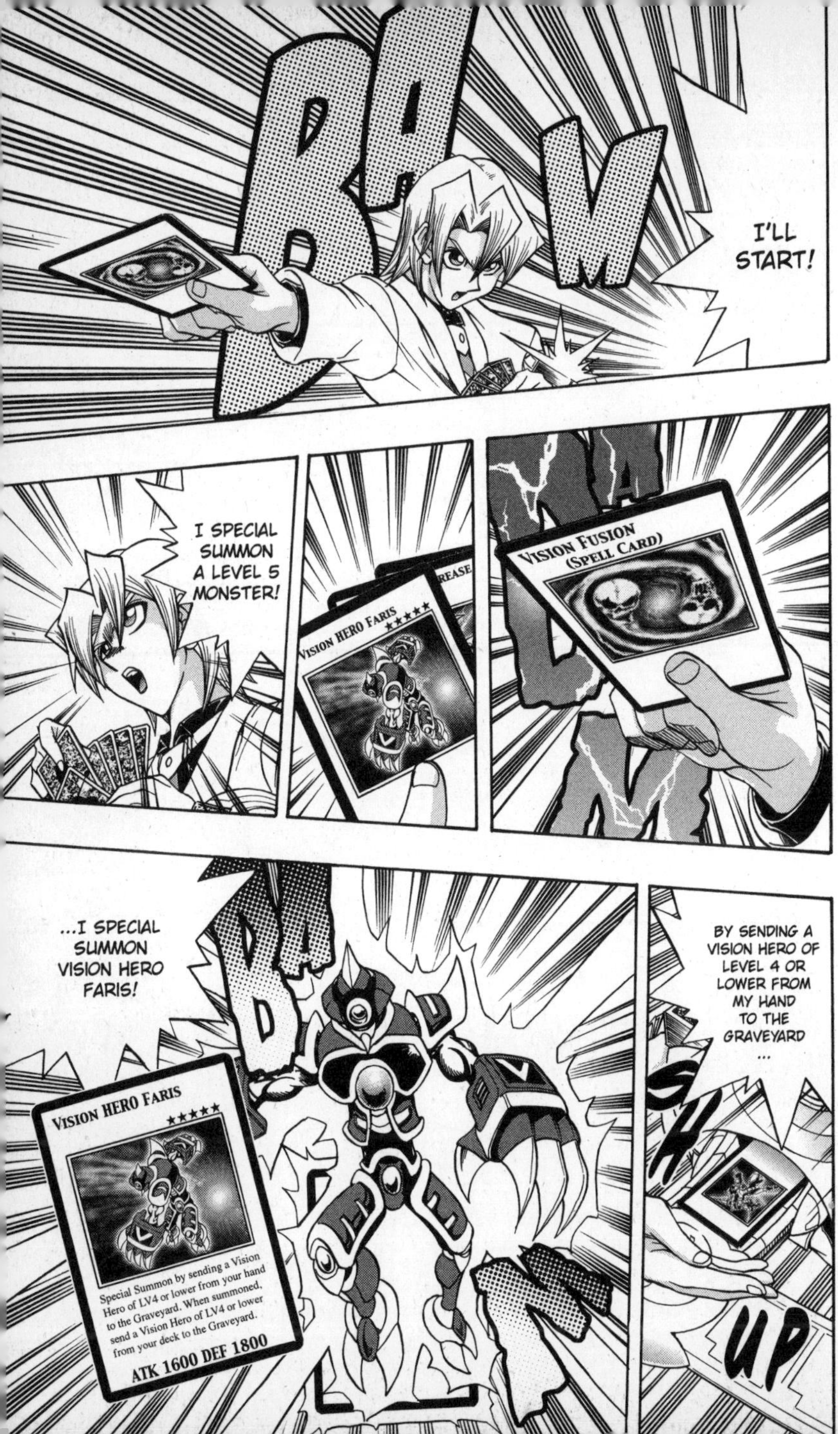
BAM
I'LL START!
VISION FUSION
(SPELL CARD)
VISION HERO FARIS
I SPECIAL SUMMON A LEVEL 5 MONSTER!
BY SENDING A VISION HERO OF LEVEL 4 OR LOWER FROM MY HAND TO THE GRAVEYARD ...
...I SPECIAL SUMMON VISION HERO FARIS!
VISION HERO FARIS
Special Summon by sending a Vision Hero of LV4 or lower from your hand to the Graveyard. When summoned, send a Vision Hero of LV4 or lower from your deck to the Graveyard.
ATK 1600 DEF 1800

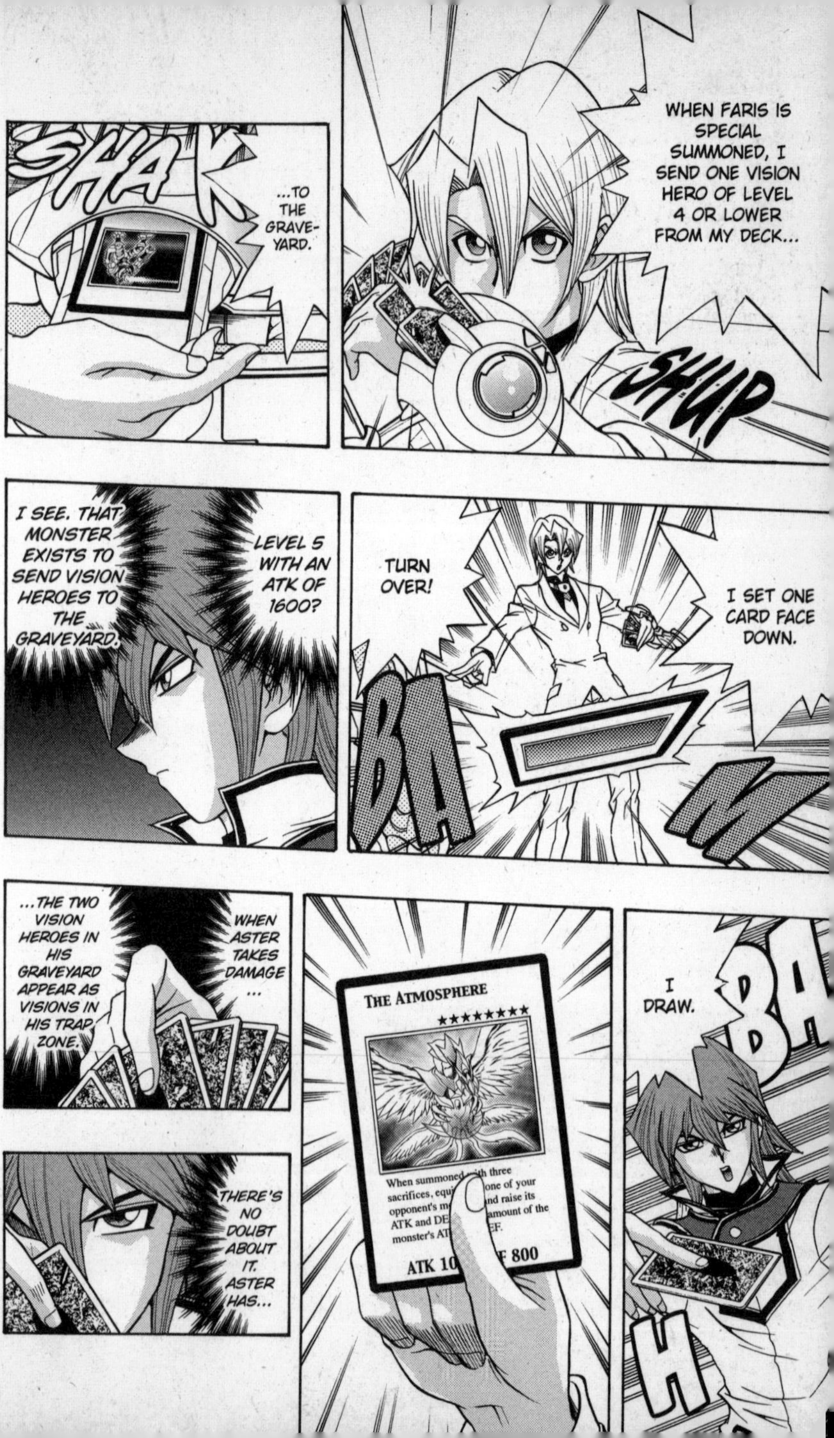
WHEN FARIS IS SPECIAL SUMMONED, I SEND ONE VISION HERO OF LEVEL 4 OR LOWER FROM MY DECK...
SHUP
SHAK
...TO THE GRAVEYARD.
I SET ONE CARD FACE DOWN.
TURN OVER!
BA
LEVEL 5 WITH AN ATK OF 1600?
I SEE. THAT MONSTER EXISTS TO SEND VISION HEROES TO THE GRAVEYARD.
I DRAW.
H
THE ATMOSPHERE
WHEN ASTER TAKES DAMAGE...
...THE TWO VISION HEROES IN HIS GRAVEYARD APPEAR AS VISIONS IN HIS TRAP ZONE.
THERE'S NO DOUBT ABOUT IT. ASTER HAS...

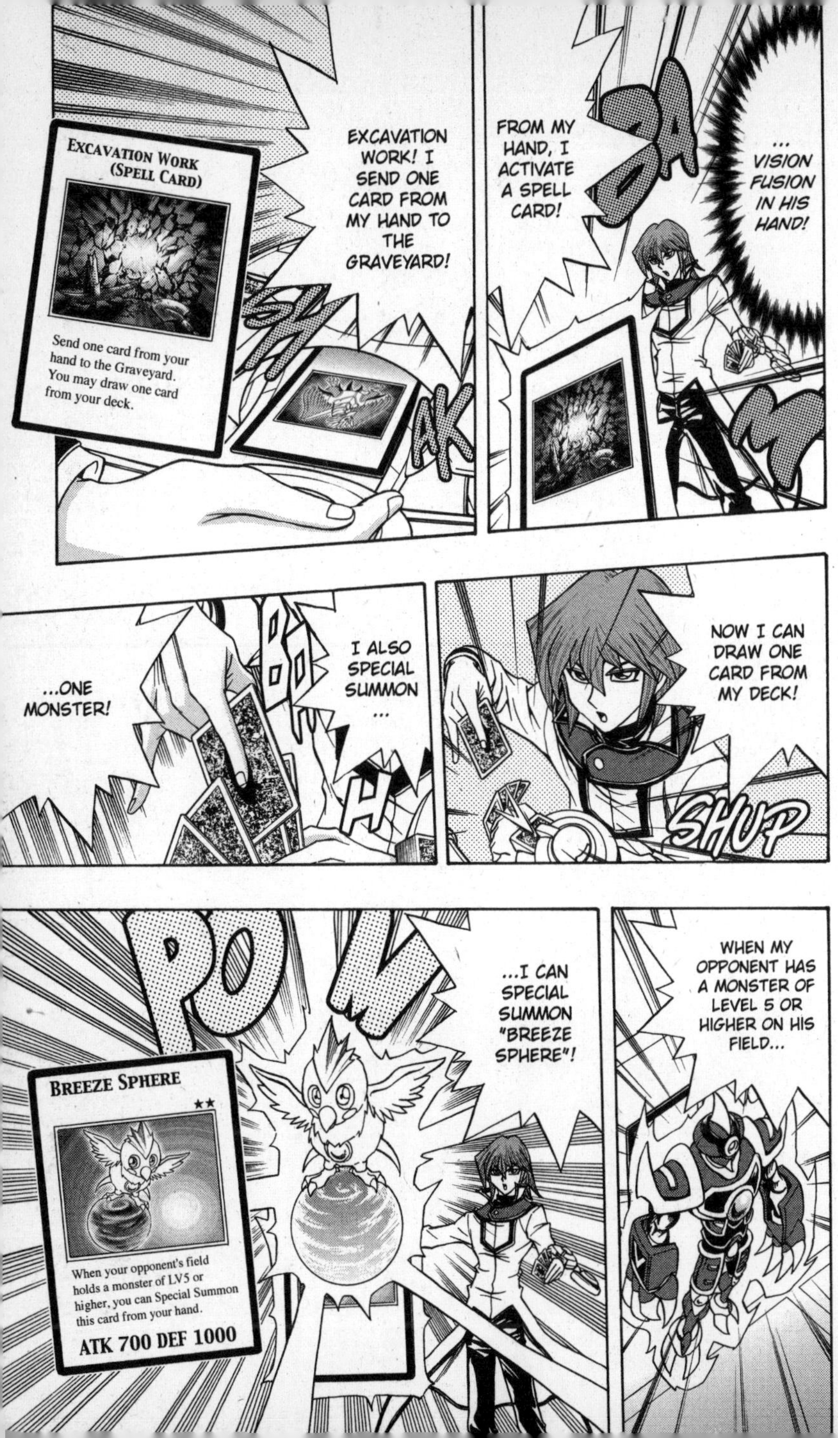
BA
...VISION FUSION IN HIS HAND!
FROM MY HAND, I ACTIVATE A SPELL CARD!
EXCAVATION WORK! I SEND ONE CARD FROM MY HAND TO THE GRAVEYARD!
EXCAVATION WORK (SPELL CARD)
Send one card from your hand to the Graveyard. You may draw one card from your deck.
NOW I CAN DRAW ONE CARD FROM MY DECK!
SHUP
I ALSO SPECIAL SUMMON...
...ONE MONSTER!
WHEN MY OPPONENT HAS A MONSTER OF LEVEL 5 OR HIGHER ON HIS FIELD...
...I CAN SPECIAL SUMMON "BREEZE SPHERE"!
POW
BREEZE SPHERE
When your opponent's field holds a monster of LV5 or higher, you can Special Summon this card from your hand.
ATK 700 DEF 1000

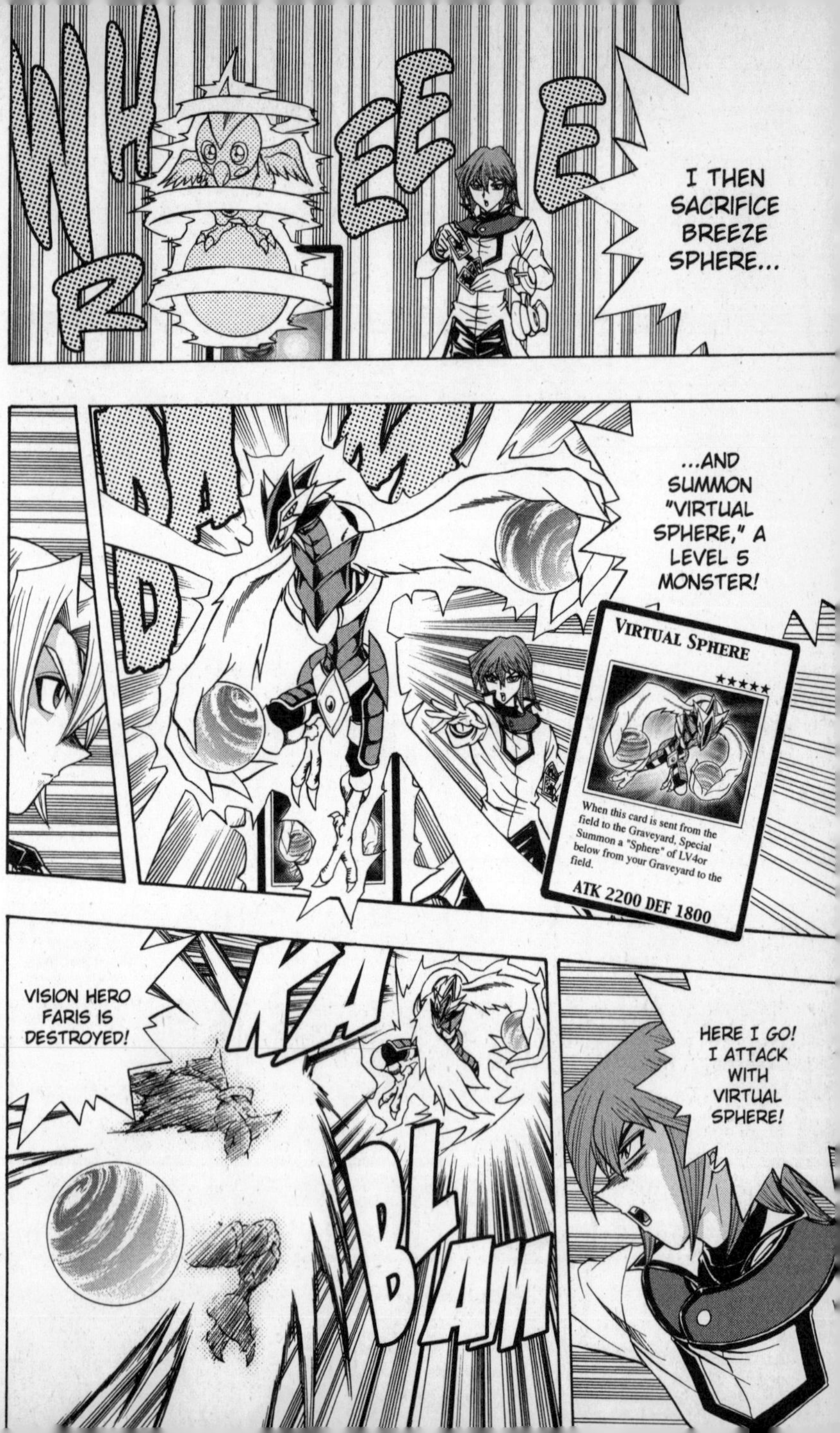
I THEN SACRIFICE BREEZE SPHERE...
...AND SUMMON "VIRTUAL SPHERE," A LEVEL 5 MONSTER!
VIRTUAL SPHERE
When this card is sent from the field to the Graveyard, Special Summon a "Sphere" of LV4or below from your Graveyard to the field.
ATK 2200 DEF 1800
HERE I GO! I ATTACK WITH VIRTUAL SPHERE!
KA
BLAM
VISION HERO FARIS IS DESTROYED!

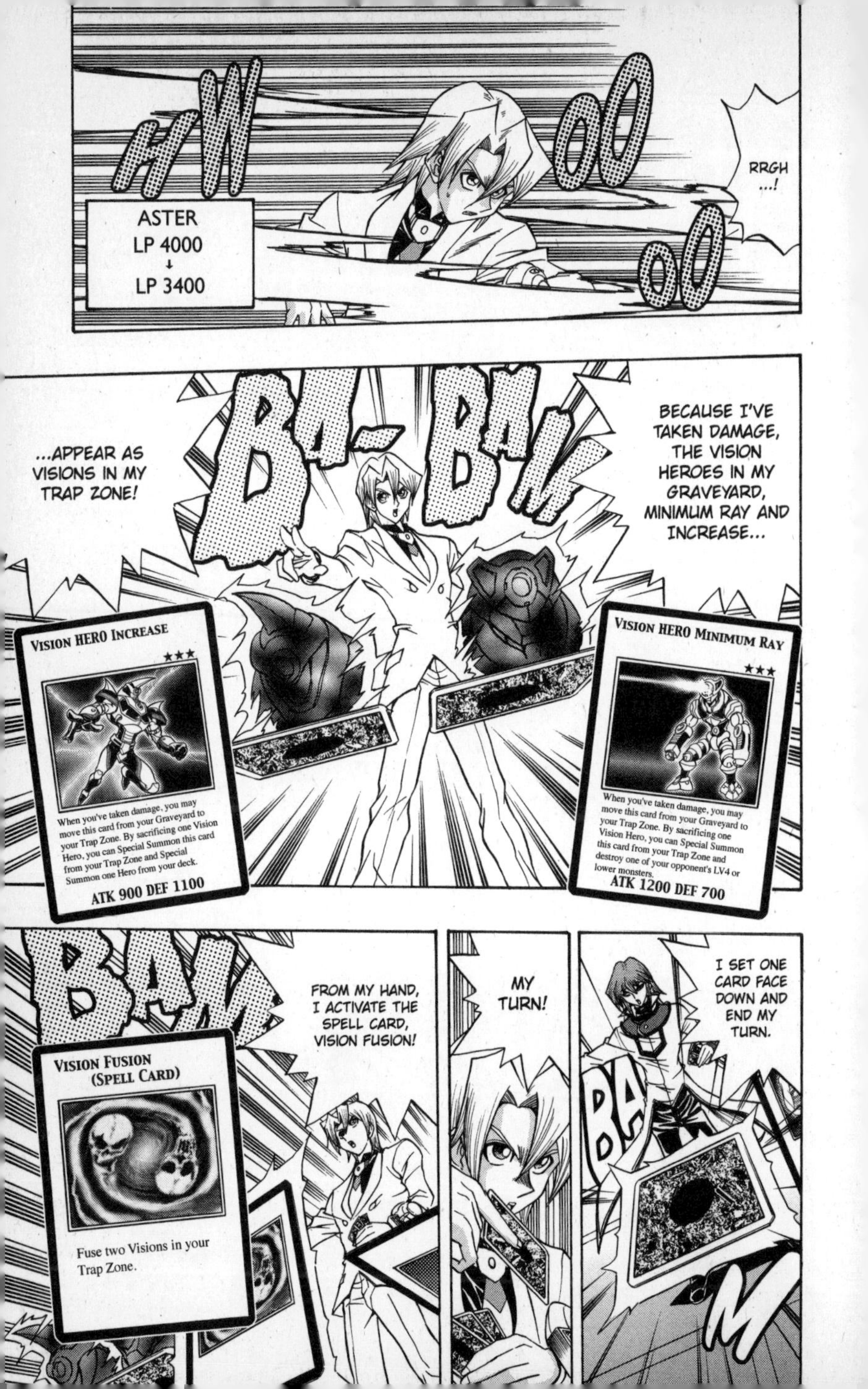
HWOOOO
RRGH ...!
ASTER
LP 4000
↓
LP 3400
BECAUSE I'VE TAKEN DAMAGE, THE VISION HEROES IN MY GRAVEYARD, MINIMUM RAY AND INCREASE...
BA-BAM
...APPEAR AS VISIONS IN MY TRAP ZONE!
VISION HERO MINIMUM RAY
When you've taken damage, you may move this card from your Graveyard to your Trap Zone. By sacrificing one Vision Hero, you can Special Summon this card from your Trap Zone and destroy one of your opponent's LV4 or lower monsters.
ATK 1200 DEF 700
VISION HERO INCREASE
When you've taken damage, you may move this card from your Graveyard to your Trap Zone. By sacrificing one Vision Hero, you can Special Summon this card from your Trap Zone and Special Summon one Hero from your deck.
ATK 900 DEF 1100
I SET ONE CARD FACE DOWN AND END MY TURN.
BAM
MY TURN!
FROM MY HAND, I ACTIVATE THE SPELL CARD, VISION FUSION!
BAM
VISION FUSION
(SPELL CARD)
Fuse two Visions in your Trap Zone.

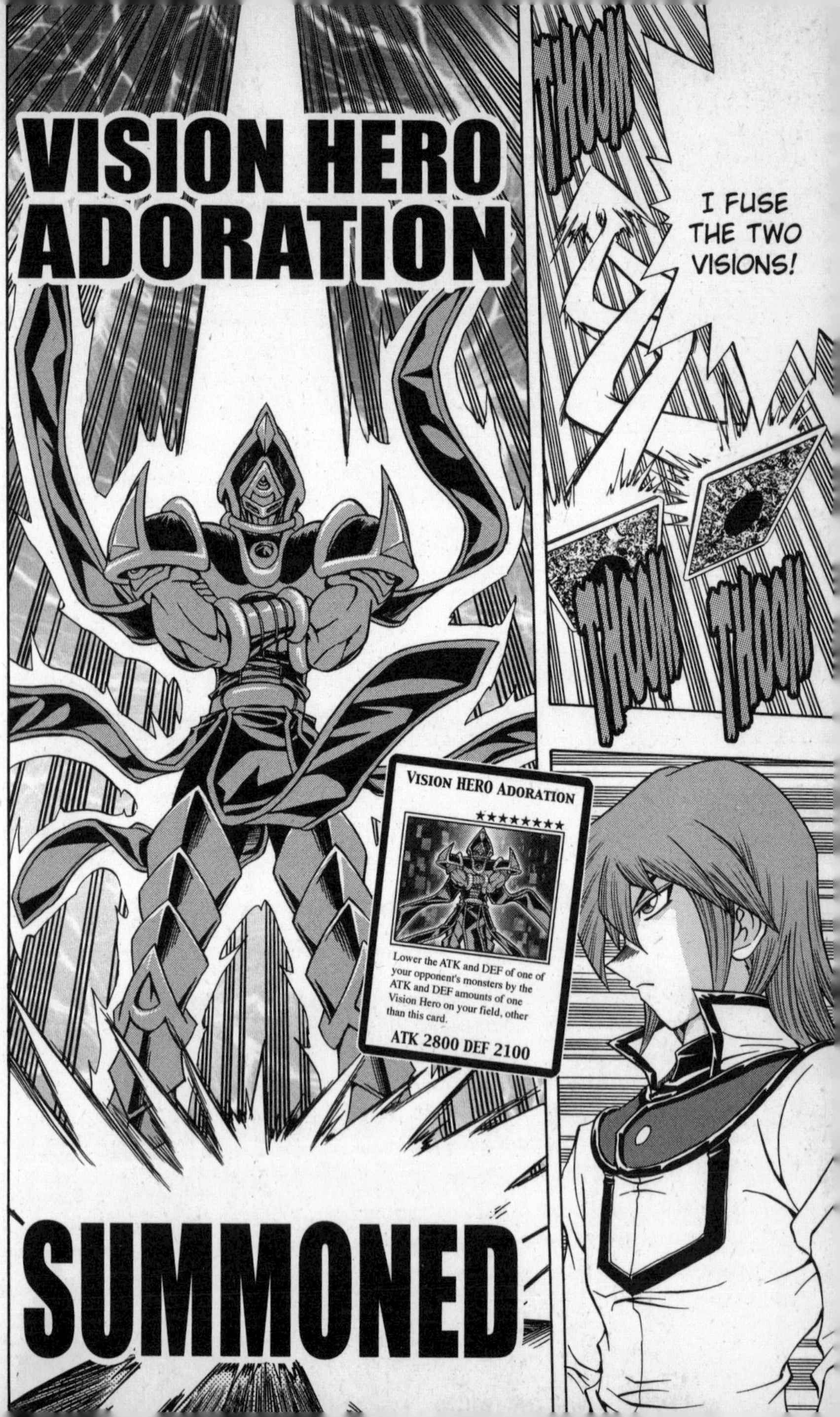
THOOM
I FUSE THE TWO VISIONS!
THOOM
THOOM
VISION HERO ADORATION
VISION HERO ADORATION
Lower the ATK and DEF of one of your opponent's monsters by the ATK and DEF amounts of one Vision Hero on your field, other than this card.
ATK 2800 DEF 2100
SUMMONED

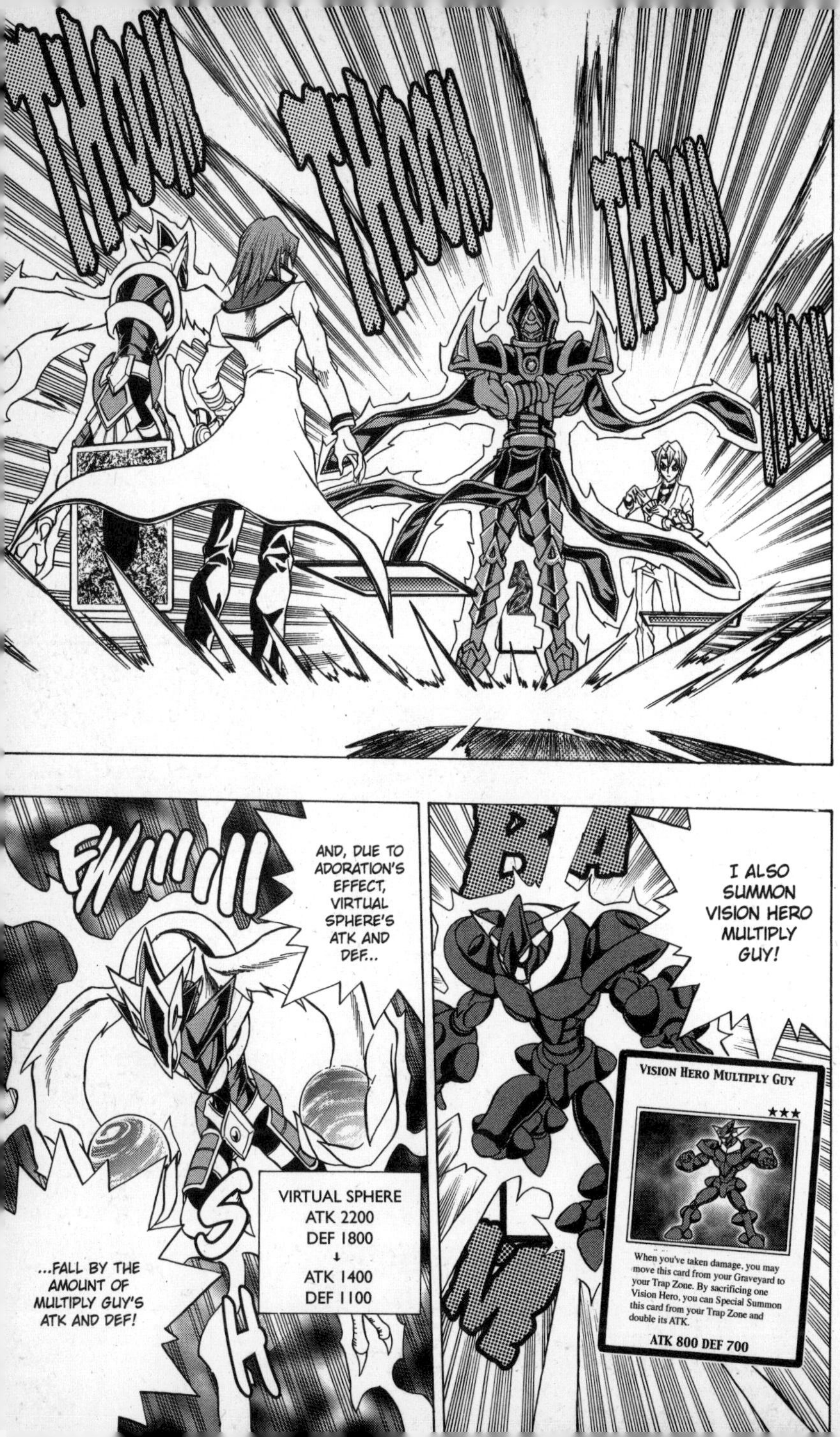
THOOM
THOOM
THOOM
I ALSO SUMMON VISION HERO MULTIPLY GUY!
VISION HERO MULTIPLY GUY
When you've taken damage, you may move this card from your Graveyard to your Trap Zone. By sacrificing one Vision Hero, you can Special Summon this card from your Trap Zone and double its ATK.
ATK 800 DEF 700
AND, DUE TO ADORATION'S EFFECT, VIRTUAL SPHERE'S ATK AND DEF...
VIRTUAL SPHERE
ATK 2200
DEF 1800
↓
ATK 1400
DEF 1100
...FALL BY THE AMOUNT OF MULTIPLY GUY'S ATK AND DEF!

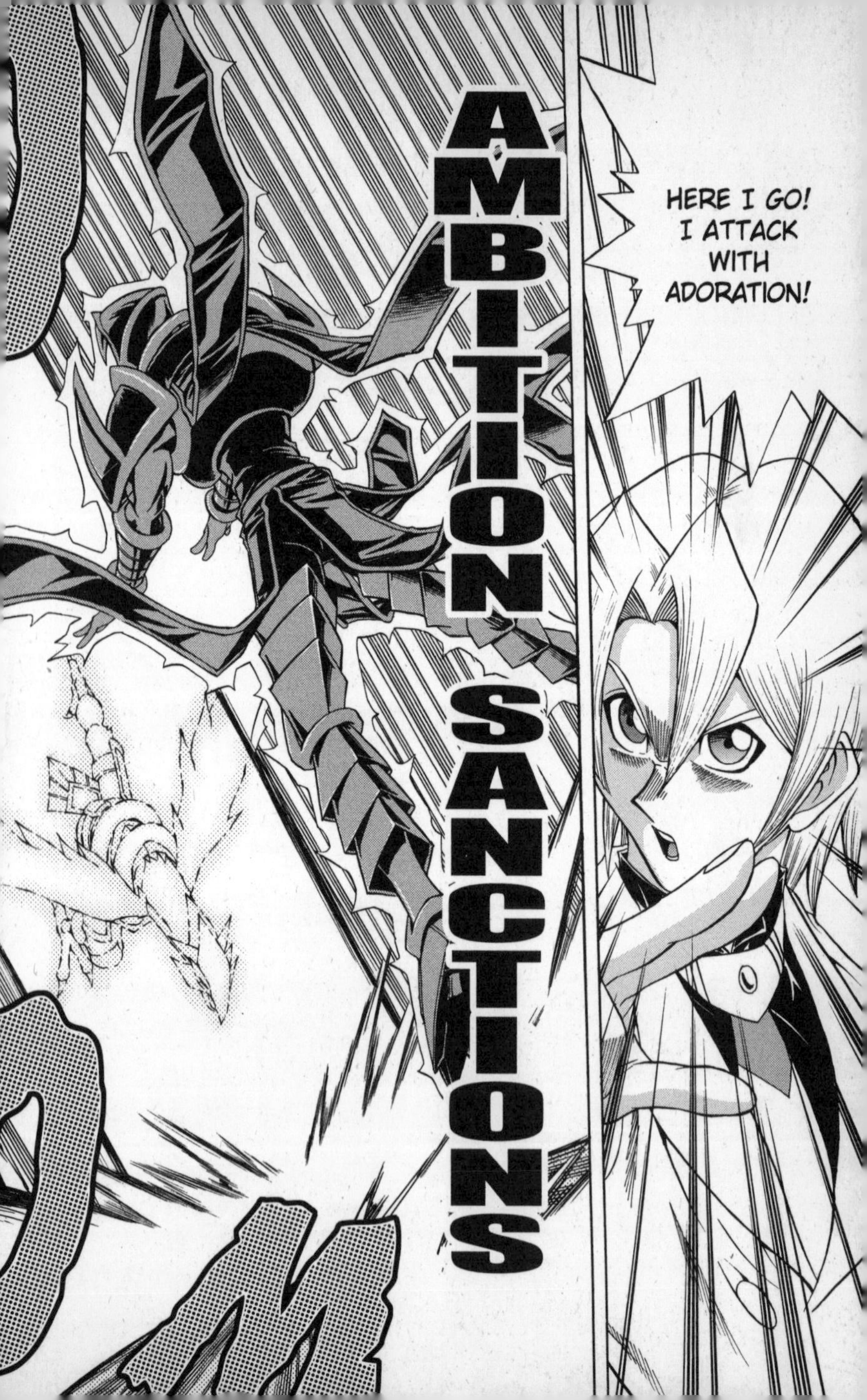
HERE I GO! I ATTACK WITH ADORATION!
AMBITION SANCTIONS

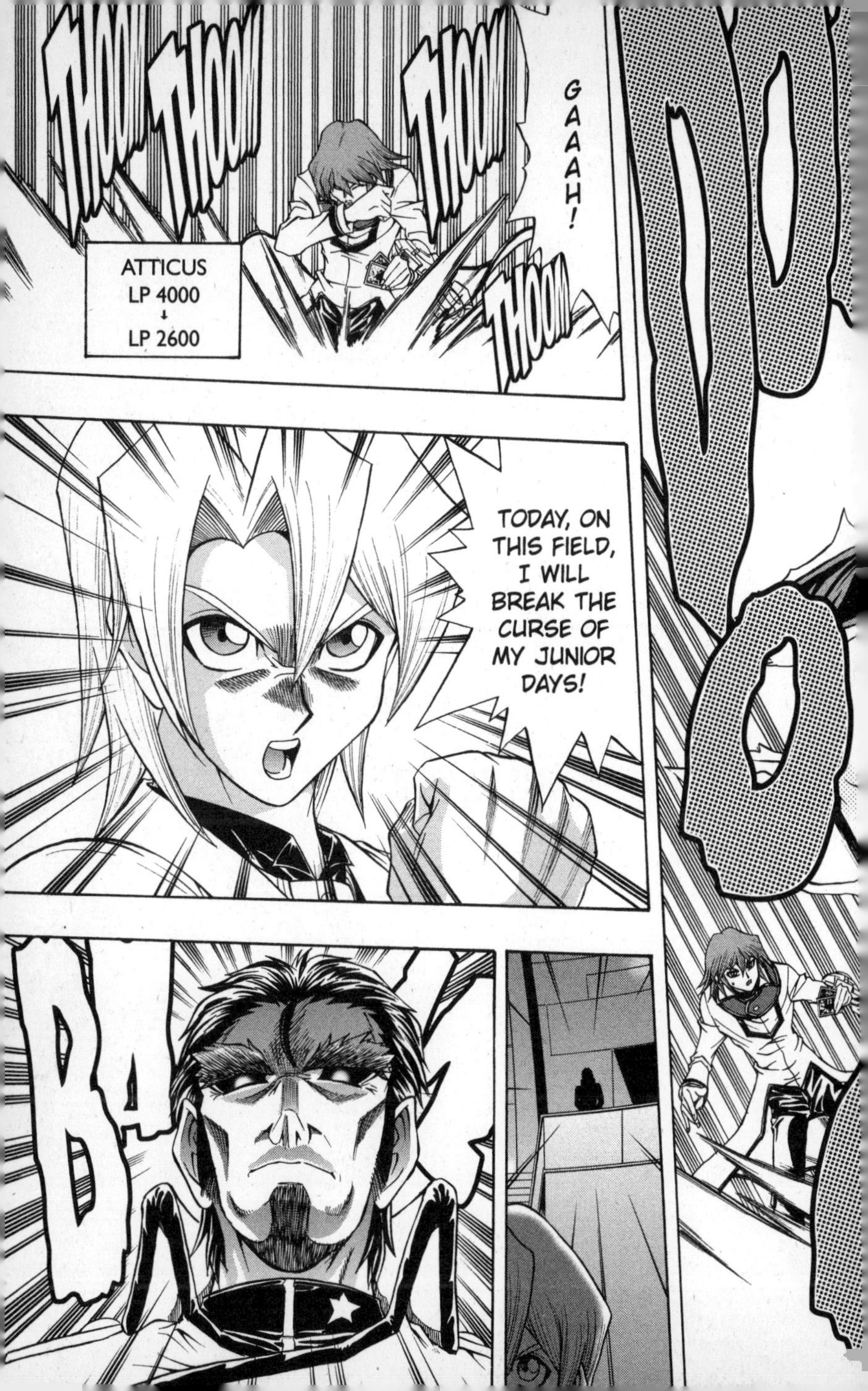
GAAAAH!
THOOM
THOOM
THOOM
ATTICUS
LP 4000
↓
LP 2600
THOOM
TODAY, ON THIS FIELD, I WILL BREAK THE CURSE OF MY JUNIOR DAYS!

THEY SELL ALL SORTS OF STUFF

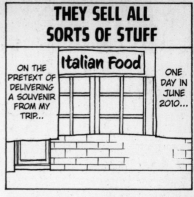

Italian Food
ONE DAY IN JUNE 2010...
ON THE PRETEXT OF DELIVERING A SOUVENIR FROM MY TRIP...
...I GOT TREATED TO A MEAL AT MR. TAKAHASHI'S FAVORITE ITALIAN RESTAURANT.
I WAS WORRIED WE'D BE WEARING THE SAME THING, KAGEYAMACCHI. LOOKS LIKE I'M SAFE.
HM? WHAT DO YOU MEAN?
HUH? WHAT'S WITH THAT T-SHIRT? THEY SELL THOSE?!
WHAT? YOU DON'T HAVE ONE?
DUEL
OSIRIS RED
ACADEMIA
NO I DON'T!

I CHECKED AROUND, AND THERE WERE ALL SORTS OF *YU-GI-OH!* T-SHIRTS FOR SALE...

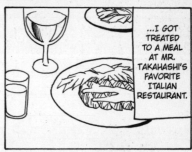

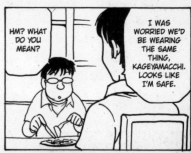

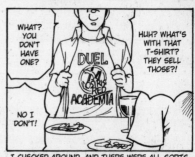

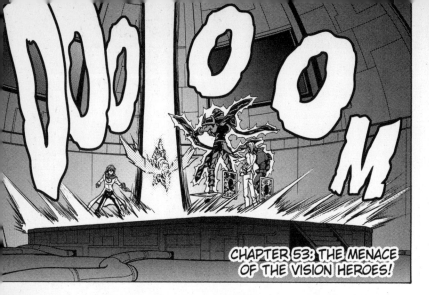

CHAPTER 53: THE MENACE OF THE VISION HEROES!

RRGH...

GAAAAH!

ATTICUS
LP 4000
↓
LP 2600

...

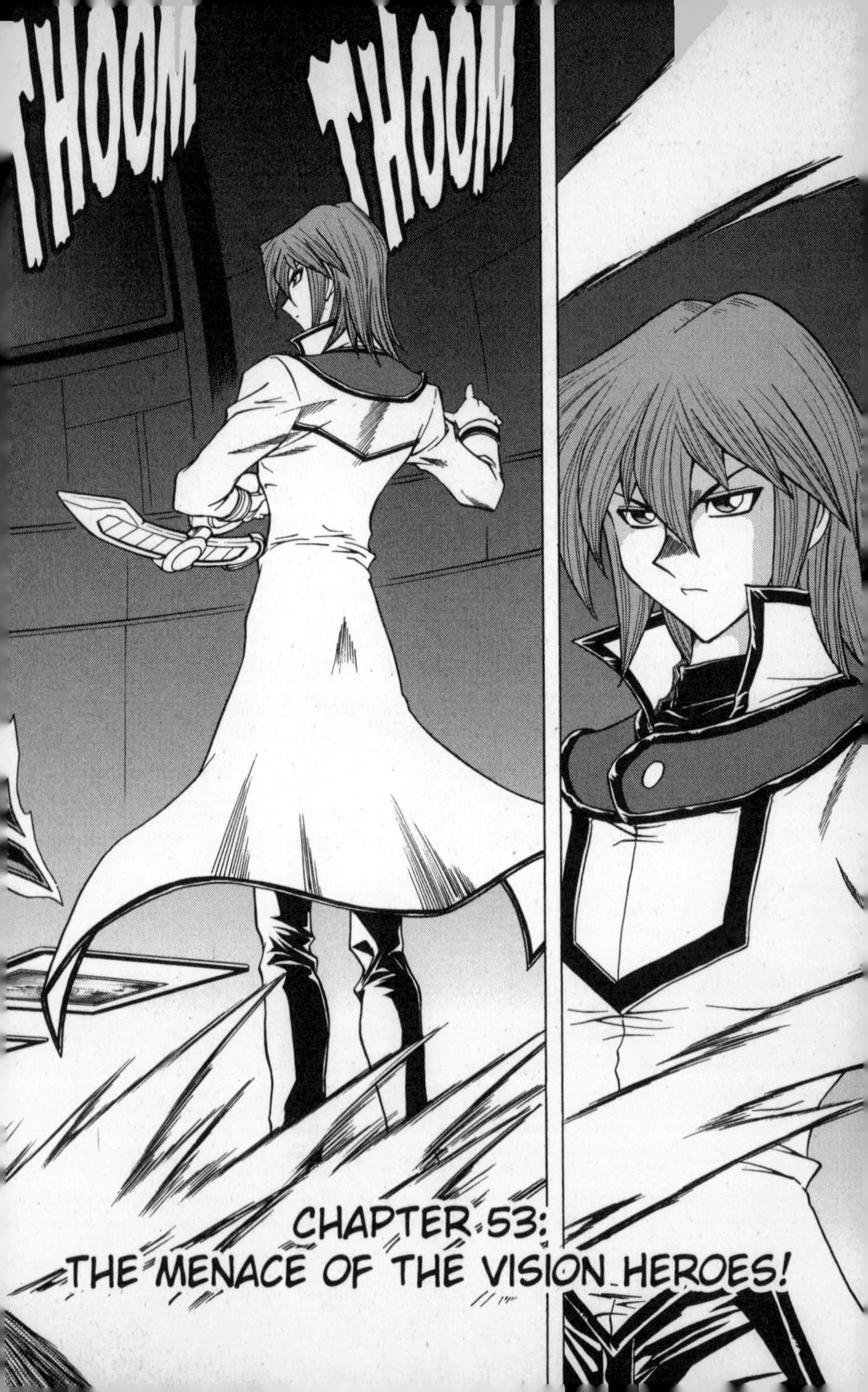
THOOM
THOOM
CHAPTER 53:
THE MENACE OF THE VISION HEROES!

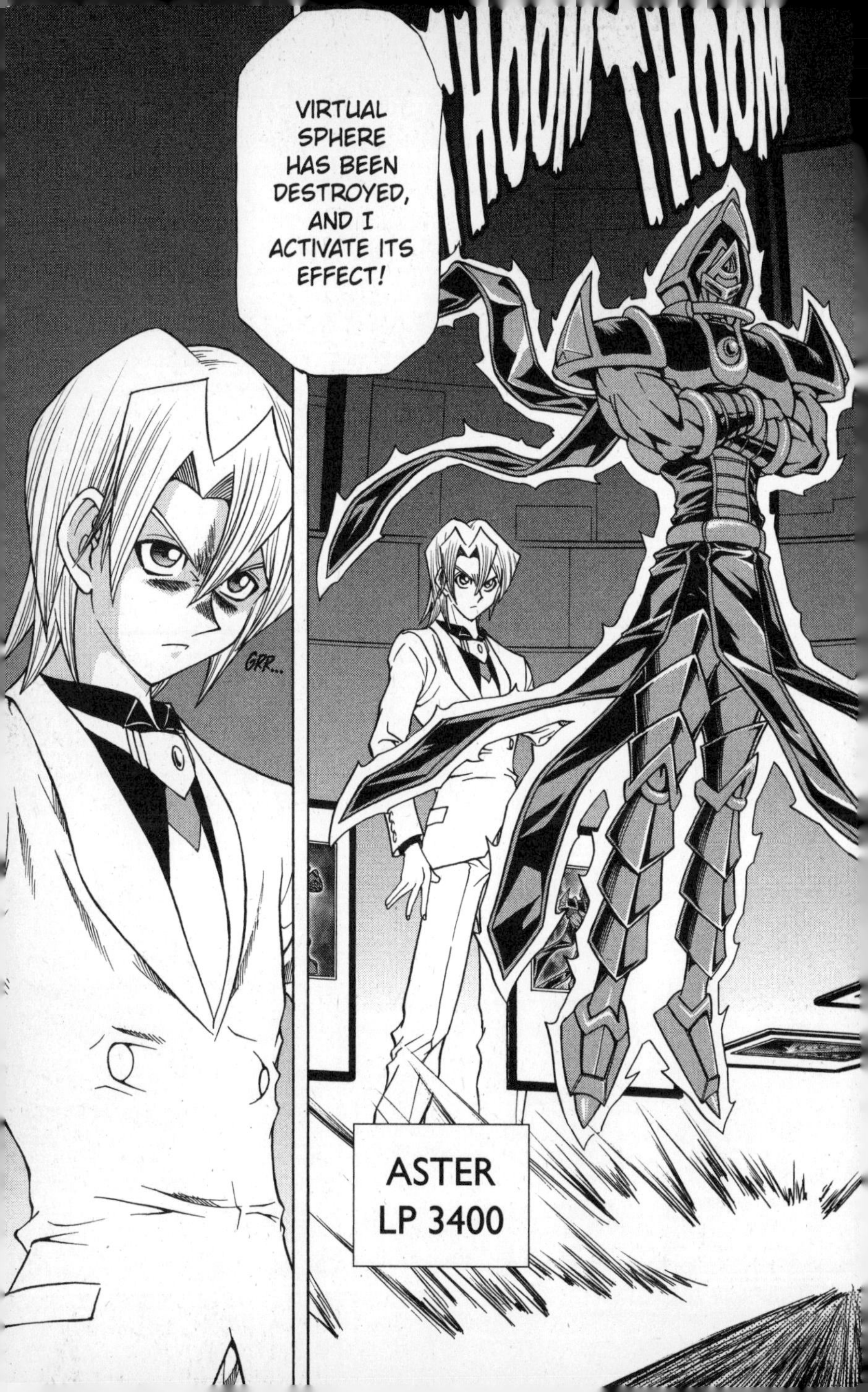
THOOM THOOM
VIRTUAL SPHERE HAS BEEN DESTROYED, AND I ACTIVATE ITS EFFECT!
ASTER LP 3400
GRR...

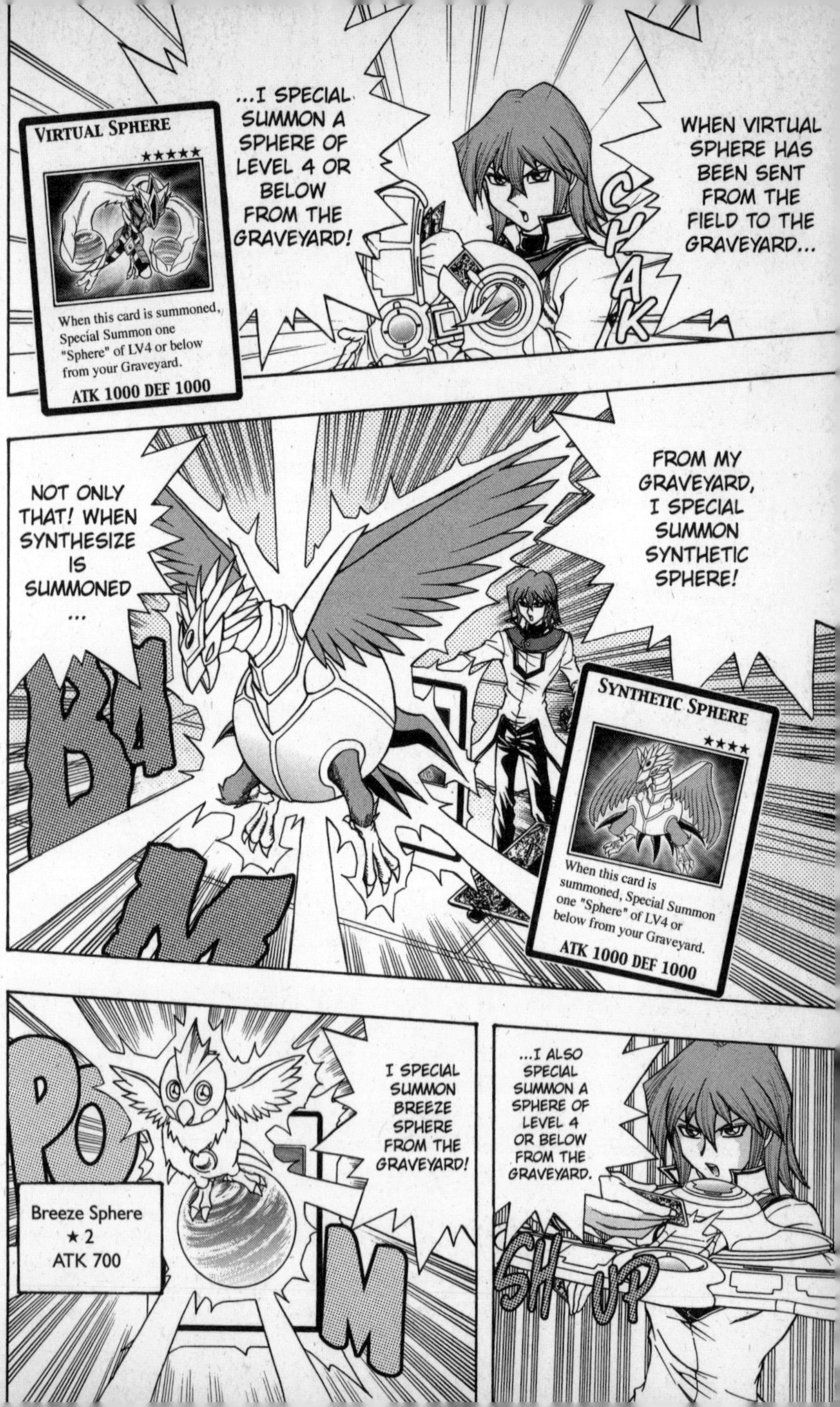
WHEN VIRTUAL SPHERE HAS BEEN SENT FROM THE FIELD TO THE GRAVEYARD...
CHAK
...I SPECIAL SUMMON A SPHERE OF LEVEL 4 OR BELOW FROM THE GRAVEYARD!
VIRTUAL SPHERE
★★★★★
When this card is summoned, Special Summon one "Sphere" of LV4 or below from your Graveyard.
ATK 1000 DEF 1000
FROM MY GRAVEYARD, I SPECIAL SUMMON SYNTHETIC SPHERE!
SYNTHETIC SPHERE
★★★★
When this card is summoned, Special Summon one "Sphere" of LV4 or below from your Graveyard.
ATK 1000 DEF 1000
NOT ONLY THAT! WHEN SYNTHESIZE IS SUMMONED...
...I ALSO SPECIAL SUMMON A SPHERE OF LEVEL 4 OR BELOW FROM THE GRAVEYARD.
SHUP
I SPECIAL SUMMON BREEZE SPHERE FROM THE GRAVEYARD!
Breeze Sphere
★2
ATK 700

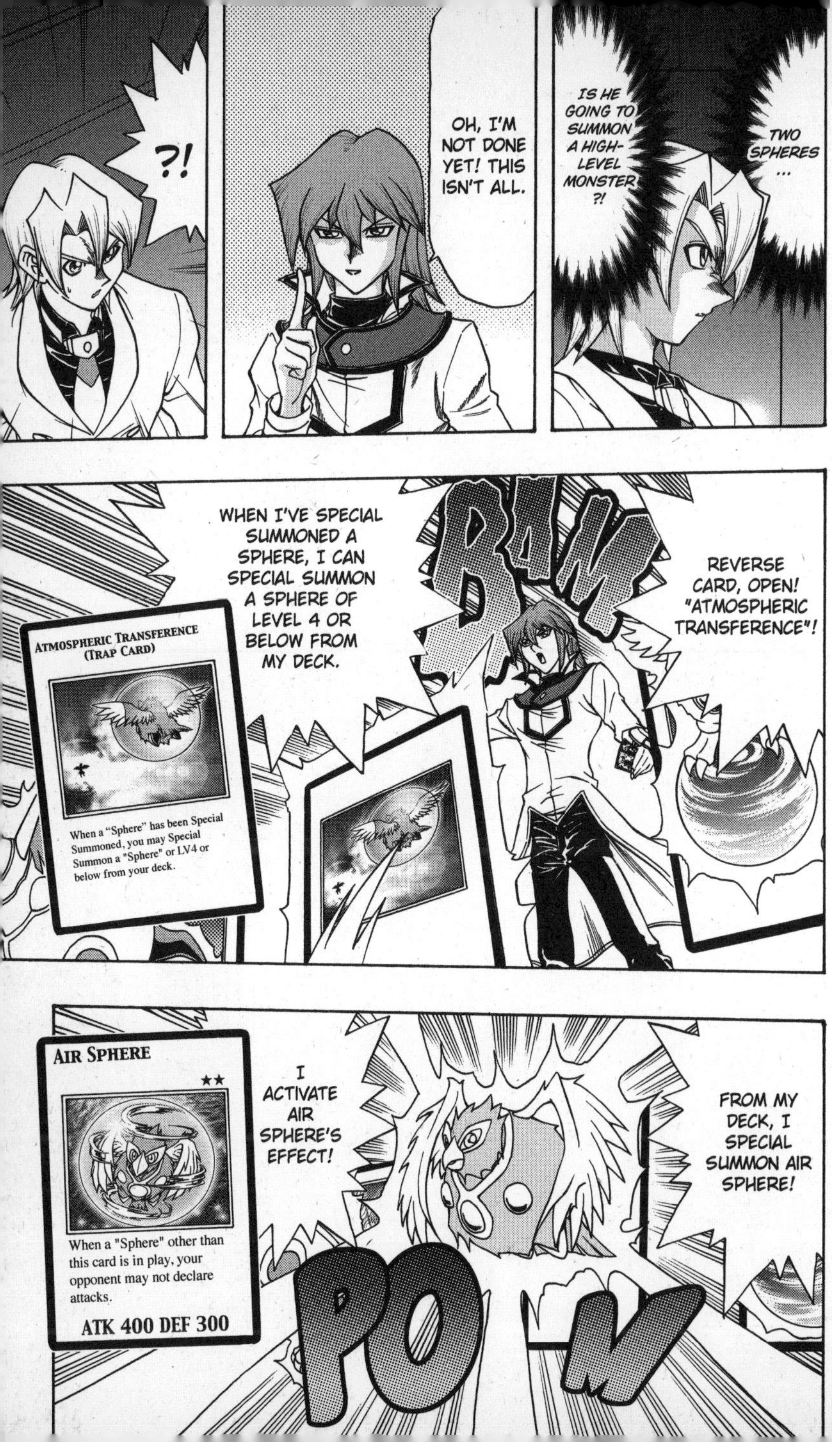

TWO SPHERES ...
IS HE GOING TO SUMMON A HIGH-LEVEL MONSTER ?!
OH, I'M NOT DONE YET! THIS ISN'T ALL.
?!
REVERSE CARD, OPEN! "ATMOSPHERIC TRANSFERENCE"!
BAM
WHEN I'VE SPECIAL SUMMONED A SPHERE, I CAN SPECIAL SUMMON A SPHERE OF LEVEL 4 OR BELOW FROM MY DECK.
ATMOSPHERIC TRANSFERENCE (TRAP CARD)
When a "Sphere" has been Special Summoned, you may Special Summon a "Sphere" or LV4 or below from your deck.
FROM MY DECK, I SPECIAL SUMMON AIR SPHERE!
I ACTIVATE AIR SPHERE'S EFFECT!
AIR SPHERE
★★
When a "Sphere" other than this card is in play, your opponent may not declare attacks.
ATK 400 DEF 300
POW

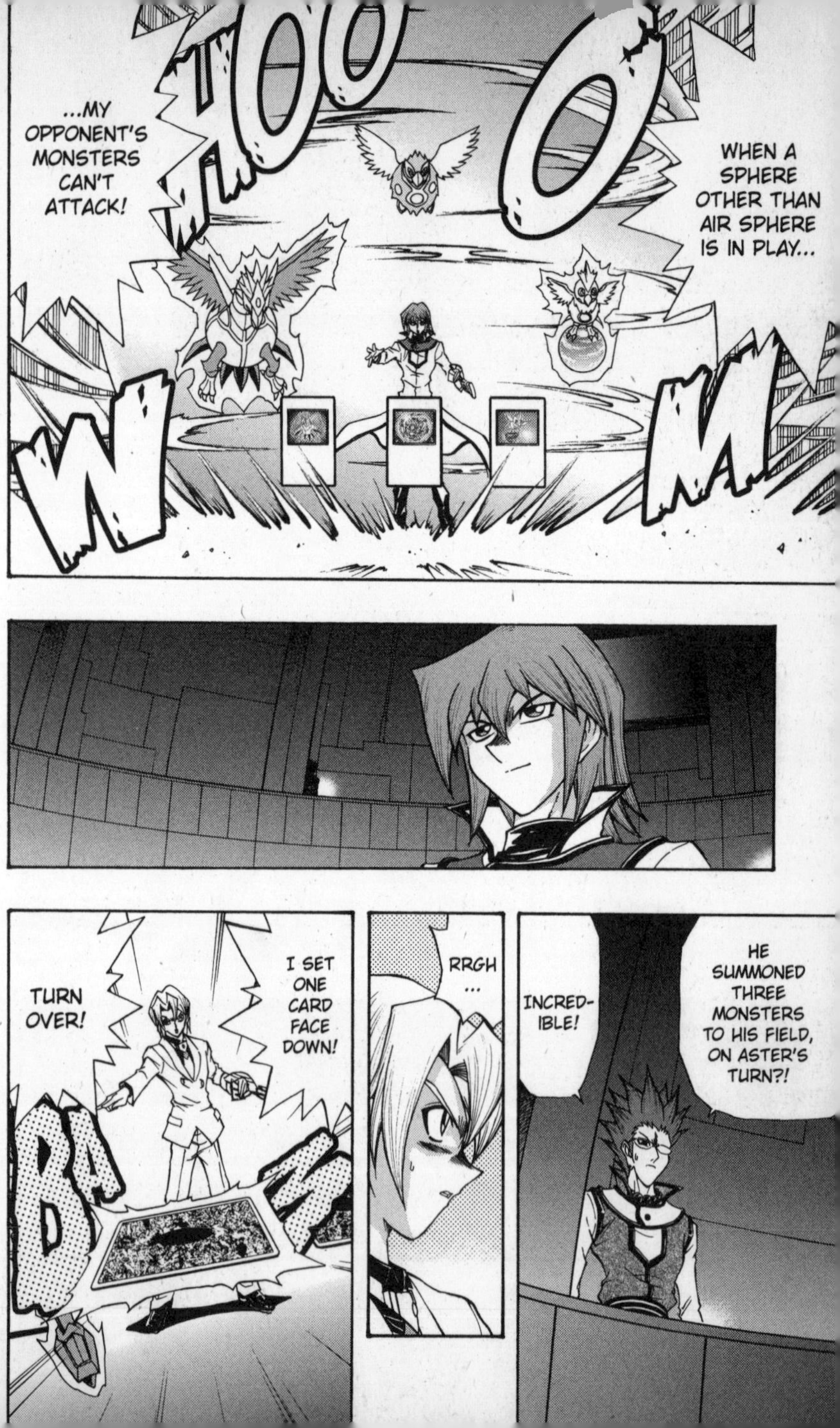
WHEN A SPHERE OTHER THAN AIR SPHERE IS IN PLAY...
...MY OPPONENT'S MONSTERS CAN'T ATTACK!
HE SUMMONED THREE MONSTERS TO HIS FIELD, ON ASTER'S TURN?!
INCRED-IBLE!
RRGH ...
I SET ONE CARD FACE DOWN!
TURN OVER!

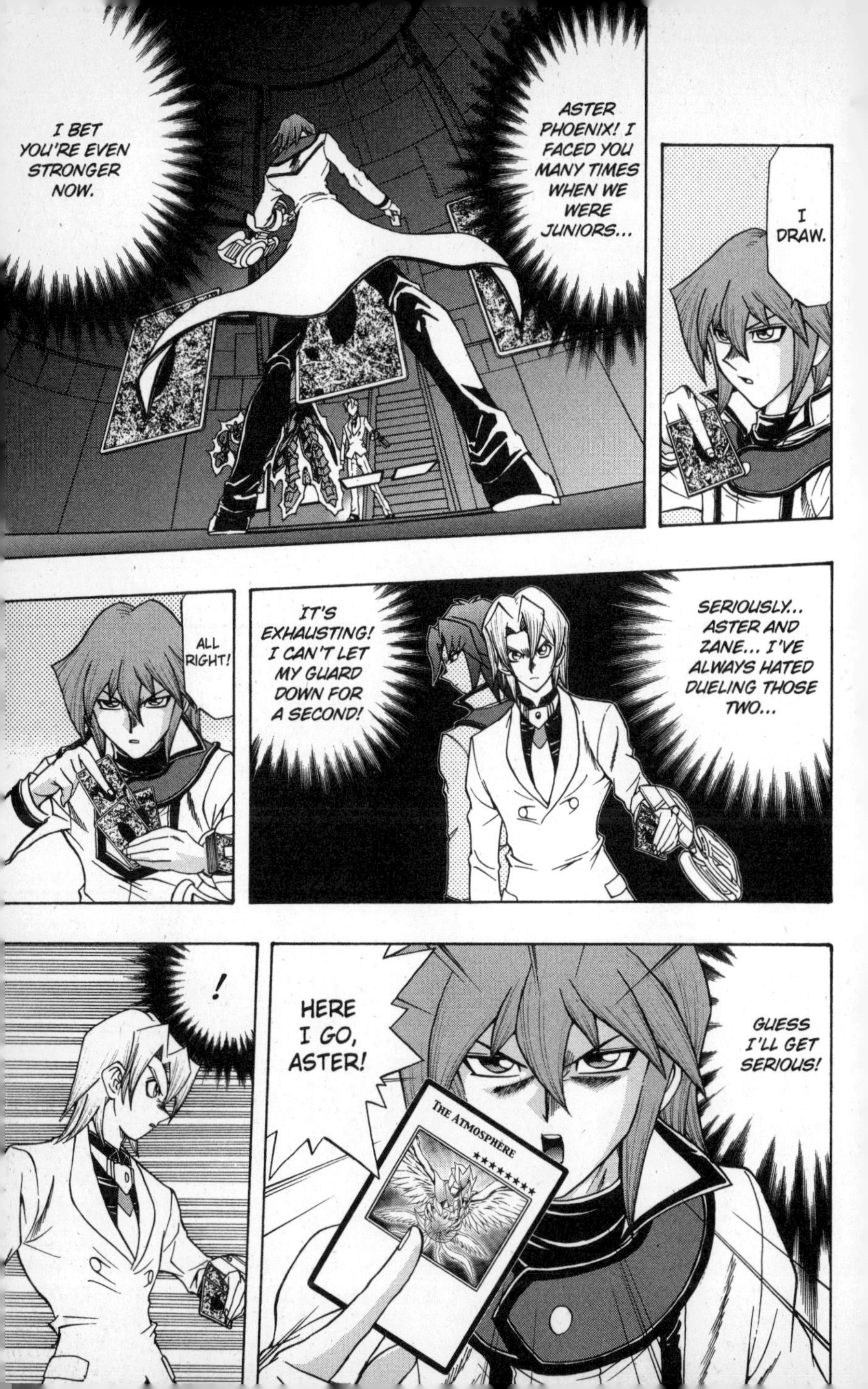
I DRAW.
ASTER PHOENIX! I FACED YOU MANY TIMES WHEN WE WERE JUNIORS...
I BET YOU'RE EVEN STRONGER NOW.
SERIOUSLY... ASTER AND ZANE... I'VE ALWAYS HATED DUELING THOSE TWO...
IT'S EXHAUSTING! I CAN'T LET MY GUARD DOWN FOR A SECOND!
ALL RIGHT!
GUESS I'LL GET SERIOUS!
HERE I GO, ASTER!
THE ATMOSPHERE
!

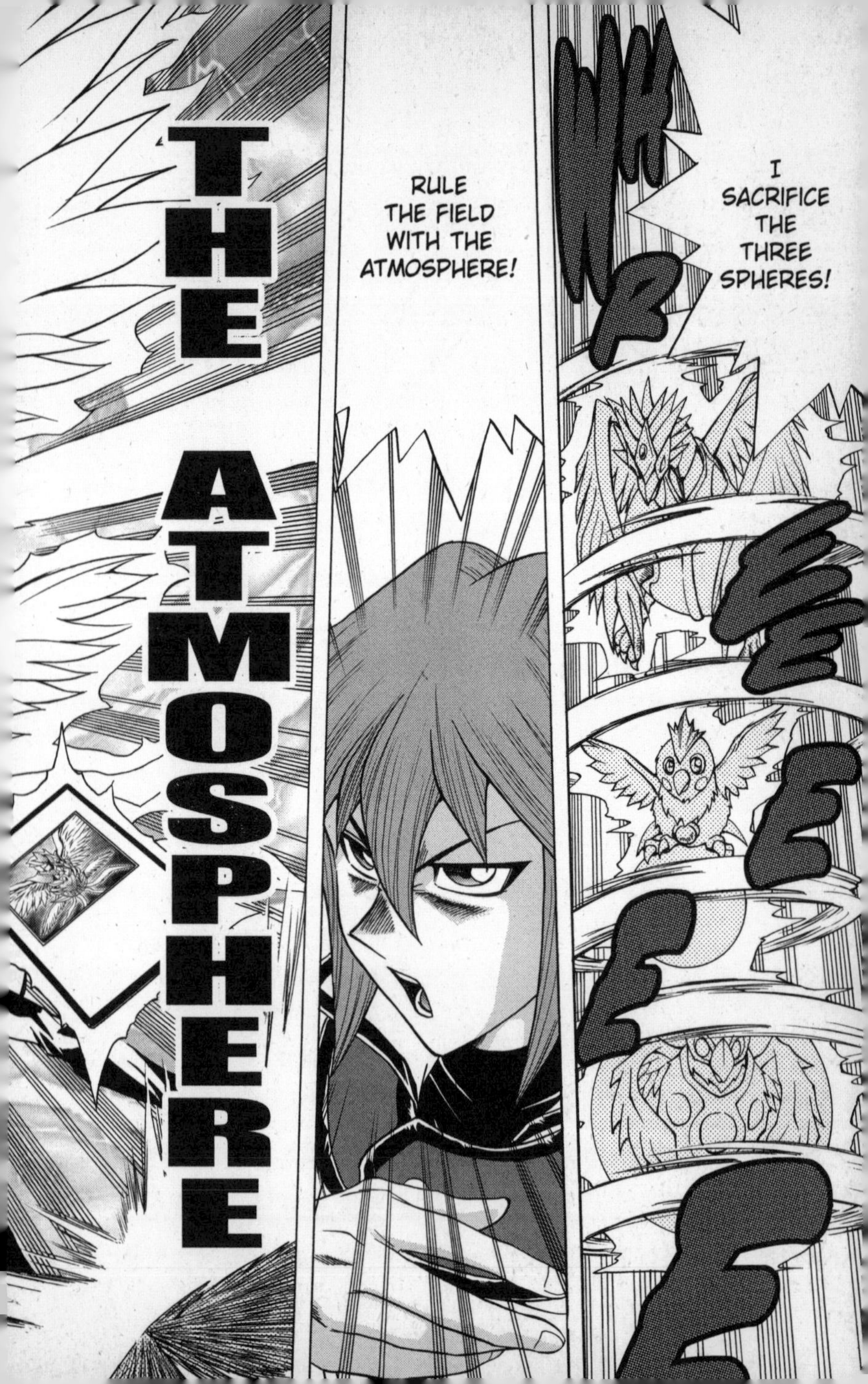
I SACRIFICE THE THREE SPHERES!
RULE THE FIELD WITH THE ATMOSPHERE!
THE ATMOSPHERE

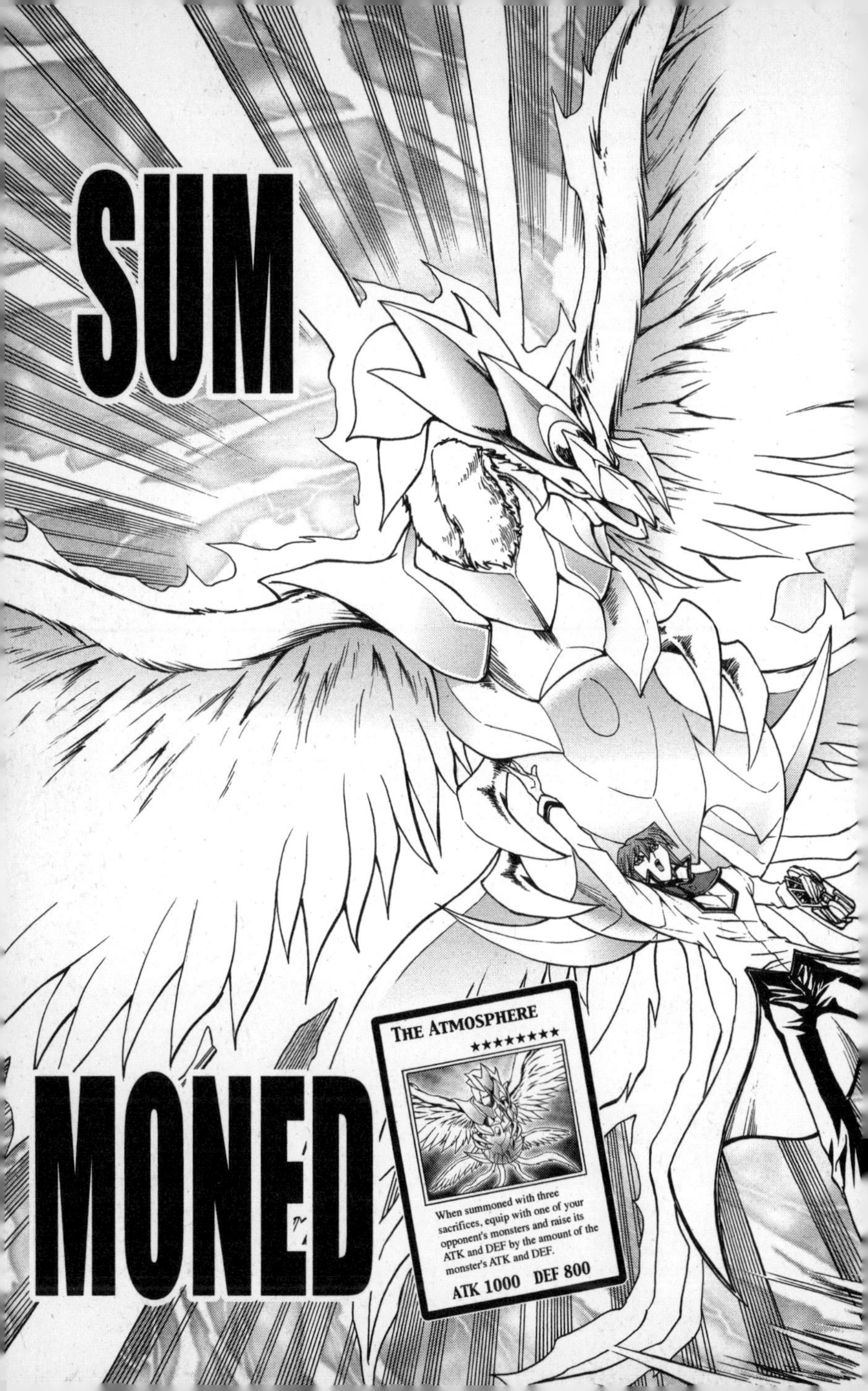
SUM
MONED
THE ATMOSPHERE
★★★★★★★★
When summoned with three sacrifices, equip with one of your opponent's monsters and raise its ATK and DEF by the amount of the monster's ATK and DEF.
ATK 1000 DEF 800

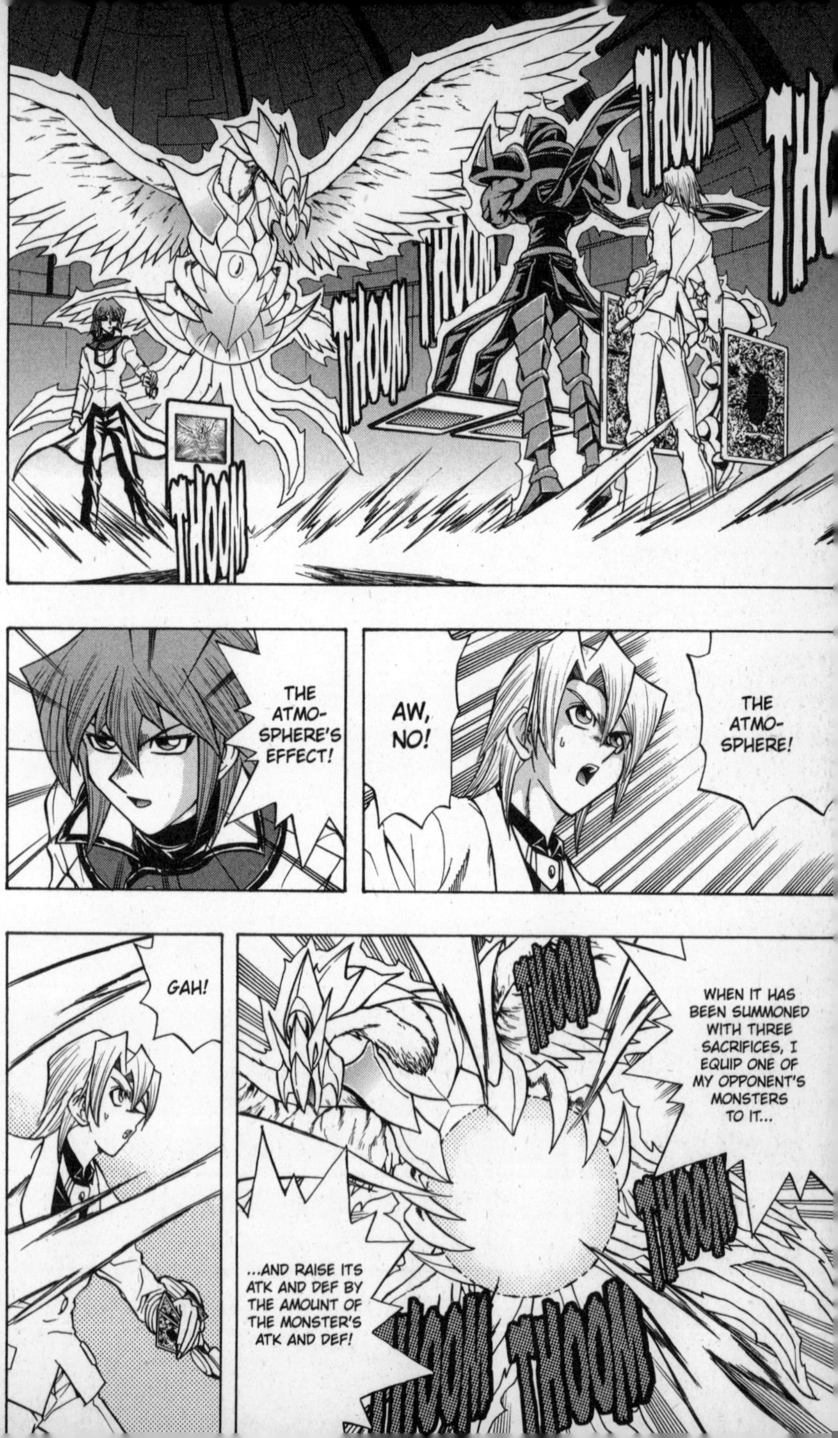
THOOM
THOOM
THOOM
THOOM
THOOM
THOOM
THE ATMOSPHERE!
AW, NO!
THE ATMOSPHERE'S EFFECT!
WHEN IT HAS BEEN SUMMONED WITH THREE SACRIFICES, I EQUIP ONE OF MY OPPONENT'S MONSTERS TO IT...
THOOM
THOOM
...AND RAISE ITS ATK AND DEF BY THE AMOUNT OF THE MONSTER'S ATK AND DEF!
THOOM
THOOM
GAH!

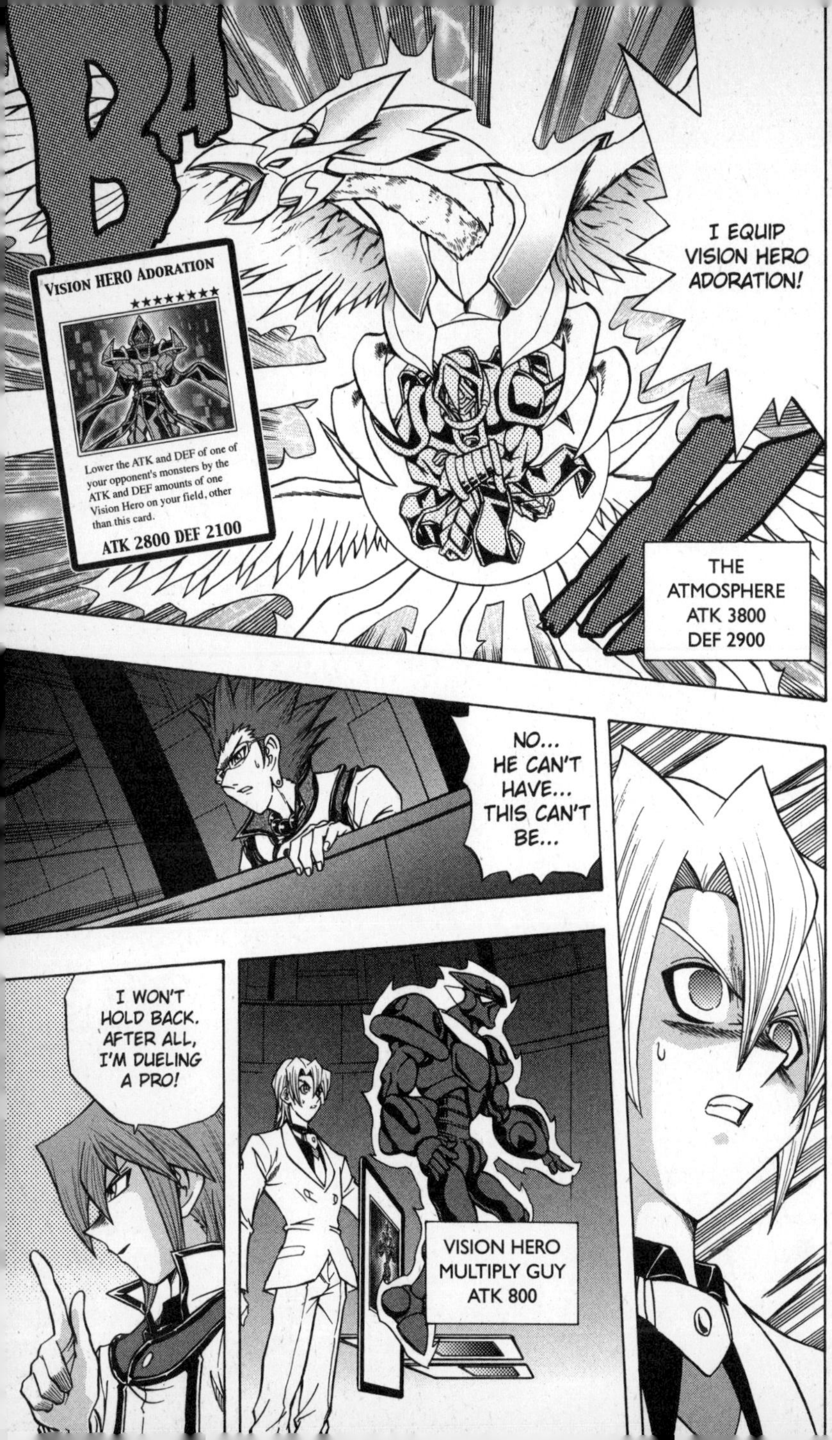
I EQUIP VISION HERO ADORATION!
BA
VISION HERO ADORATION
Lower the ATK and DEF of one of your opponent's monsters by the ATK and DEF amounts of one Vision Hero on your field, other than this card.
ATK 2800 DEF 2100
THE ATMOSPHERE ATK 3800 DEF 2900
NO... HE CAN'T HAVE... THIS CAN'T BE...
VISION HERO MULTIPLY GUY ATK 800
I WON'T HOLD BACK. AFTER ALL, I'M DUELING A PRO!

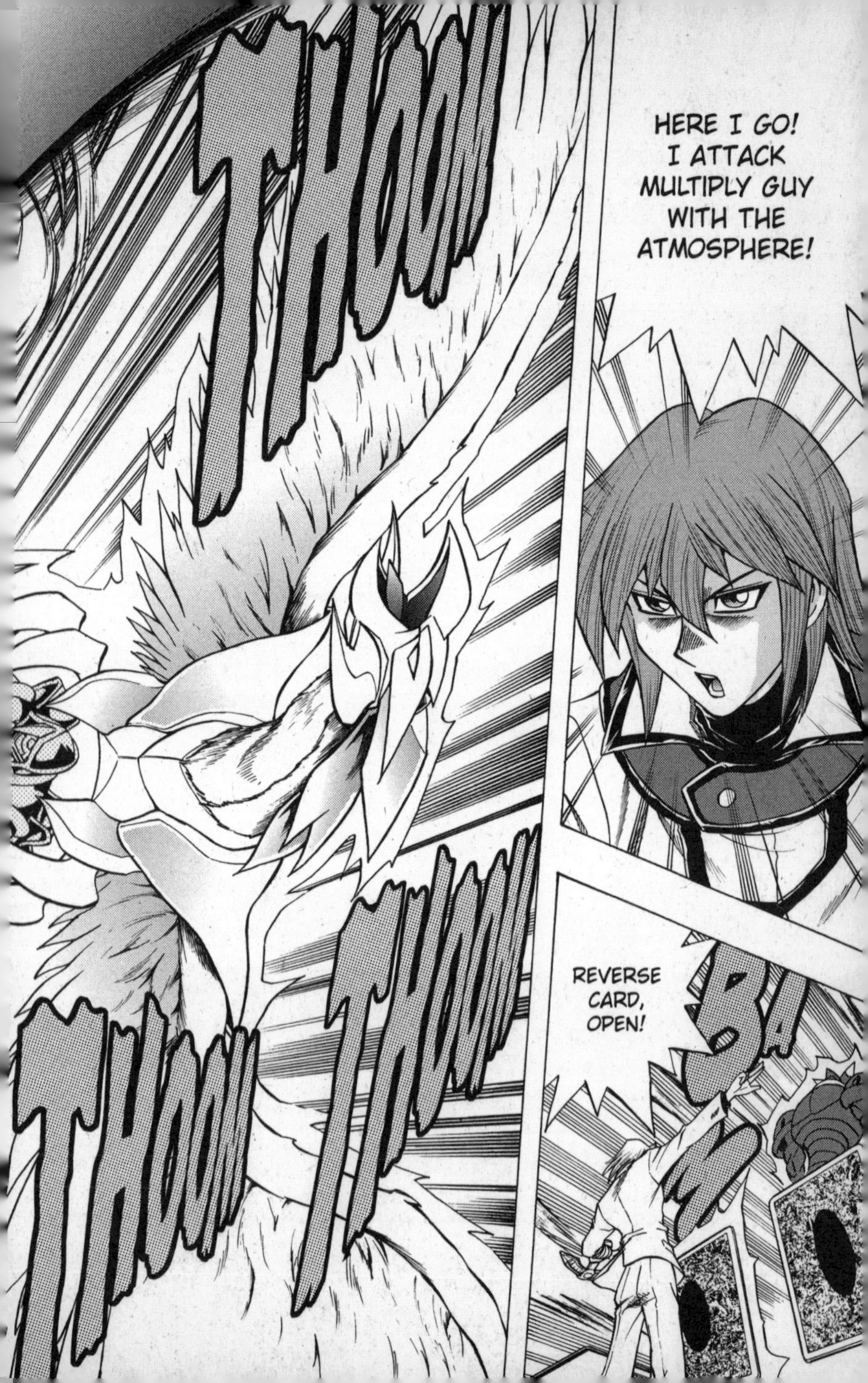
HERE I GO! I ATTACK MULTIPLY GUY WITH THE ATMOSPHERE!
THOOM
REVERSE CARD, OPEN!
BA
THOOM
THOOM

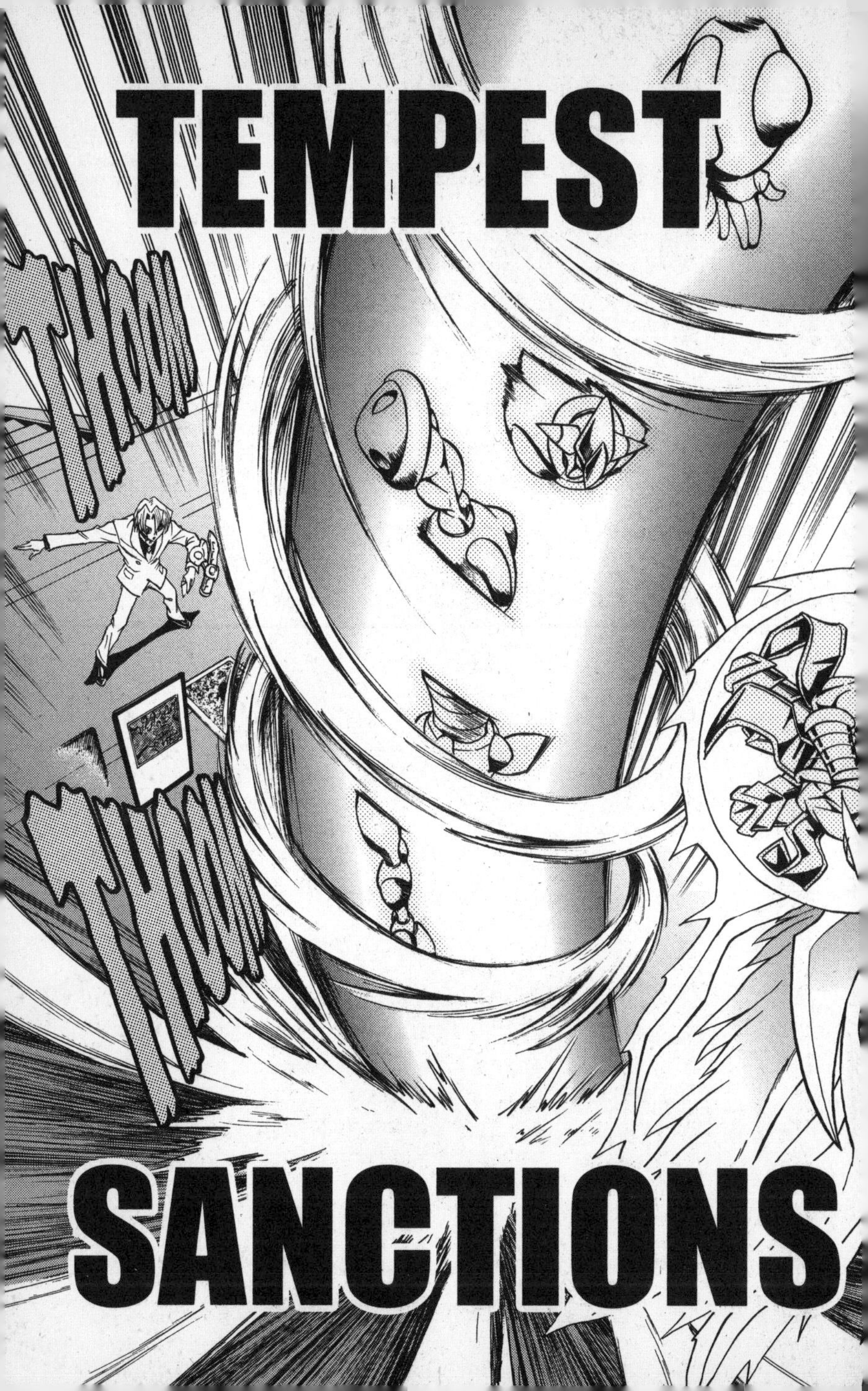
TEMPEST
THOOM
THOOM
SANCTIONS

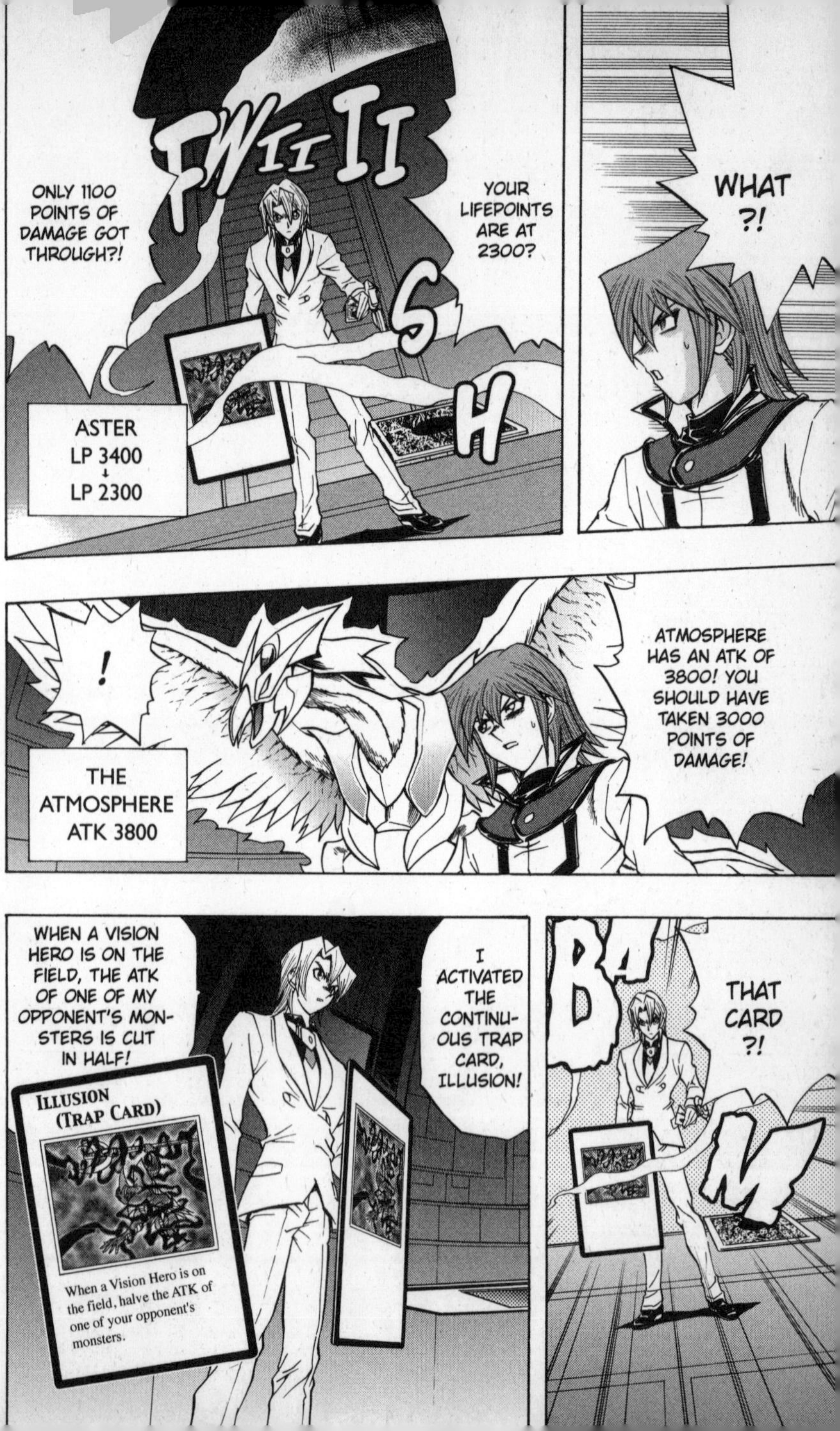
WHAT ?!
YOUR LIFEPOINTS ARE AT 2300?
FWIIIISH
ONLY 1100 POINTS OF DAMAGE GOT THROUGH?!
ASTER
LP 3400
↓
LP 2300
ATMOSPHERE HAS AN ATK OF 3800! YOU SHOULD HAVE TAKEN 3000 POINTS OF DAMAGE!
!
THE ATMOSPHERE
ATK 3800
BAM
THAT CARD ?!
I ACTIVATED THE CONTINUOUS TRAP CARD, ILLUSION!
WHEN A VISION HERO IS ON THE FIELD, THE ATK OF ONE OF MY OPPONENT'S MONSTERS IS CUT IN HALF!
ILLUSION (TRAP CARD)
When a Vision Hero is on the field, halve the ATK of one of your opponent's monsters.

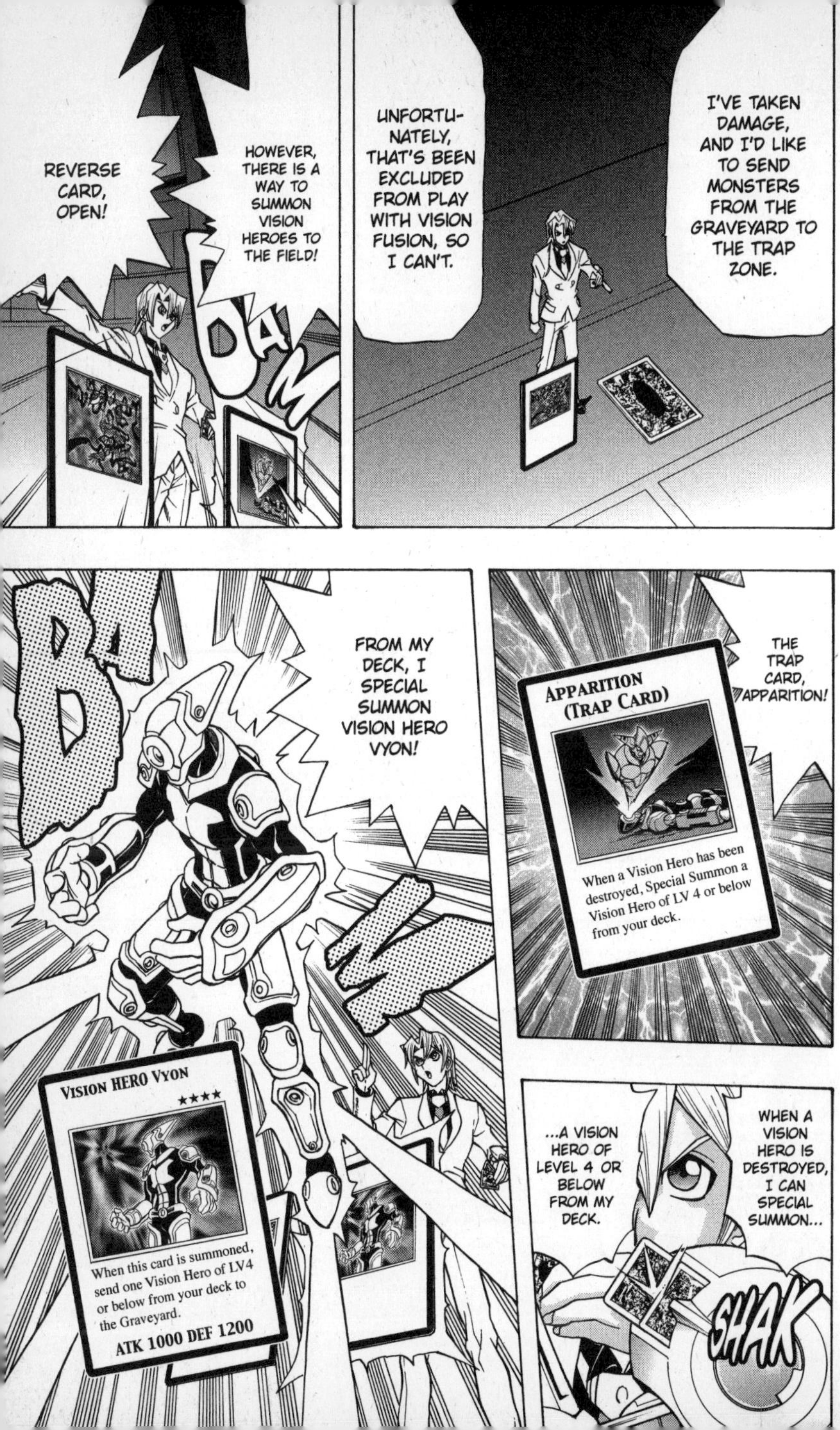
I'VE TAKEN DAMAGE, AND I'D LIKE TO SEND MONSTERS FROM THE GRAVEYARD TO THE TRAP ZONE.
UNFORTUNATELY, THAT'S BEEN EXCLUDED FROM PLAY WITH VISION FUSION, SO I CAN'T.
HOWEVER, THERE IS A WAY TO SUMMON VISION HEROES TO THE FIELD!
REVERSE CARD, OPEN!
THE TRAP CARD, APPARITION!
APPARITION (TRAP CARD)
When a Vision Hero has been destroyed, Special Summon a Vision Hero of LV 4 or below from your deck.
WHEN A VISION HERO IS DESTROYED, I CAN SPECIAL SUMMON...
...A VISION HERO OF LEVEL 4 OR BELOW FROM MY DECK.
SHAK
FROM MY DECK, I SPECIAL SUMMON VISION HERO VYON!
VISION HERO VYON
★★★★
When this card is summoned, send one Vision Hero of LV4 or below from your deck to the Graveyard.
ATK 1000 DEF 1200

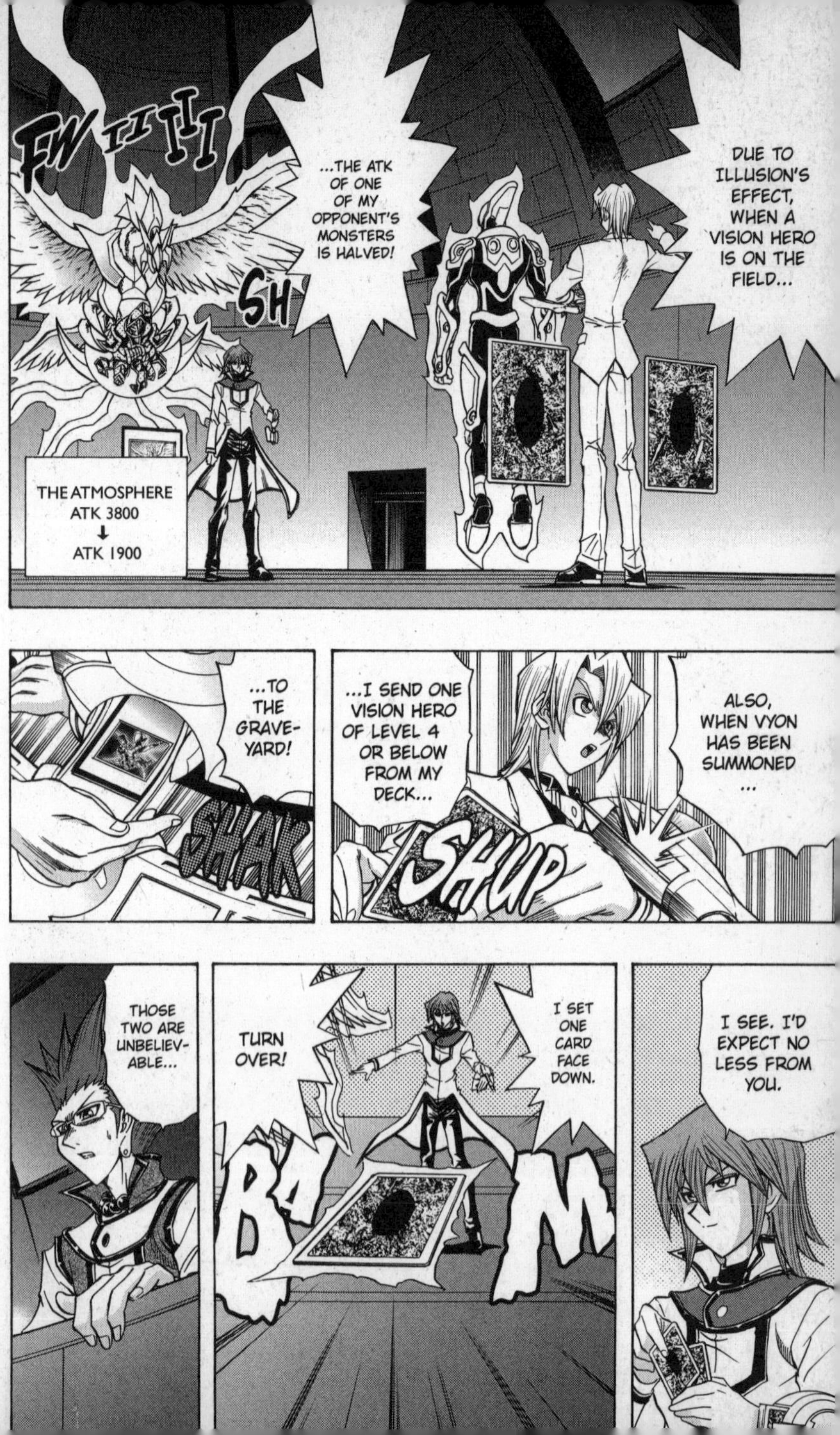

DUE TO ILLUSION'S EFFECT, WHEN A VISION HERO IS ON THE FIELD...
...THE ATK OF ONE OF MY OPPONENT'S MONSTERS IS HALVED!
FWIIIII
SH
THE ATMOSPHERE ATK 3800 ↓ ATK 1900
ALSO, WHEN VYON HAS BEEN SUMMONED...
...I SEND ONE VISION HERO OF LEVEL 4 OR BELOW FROM MY DECK...
SHUP
...TO THE GRAVE-YARD!
SHAK
I SEE. I'D EXPECT NO LESS FROM YOU.
I SET ONE CARD FACE DOWN.
TURN OVER!
BAM
THOSE TWO ARE UNBELIEVABLE...

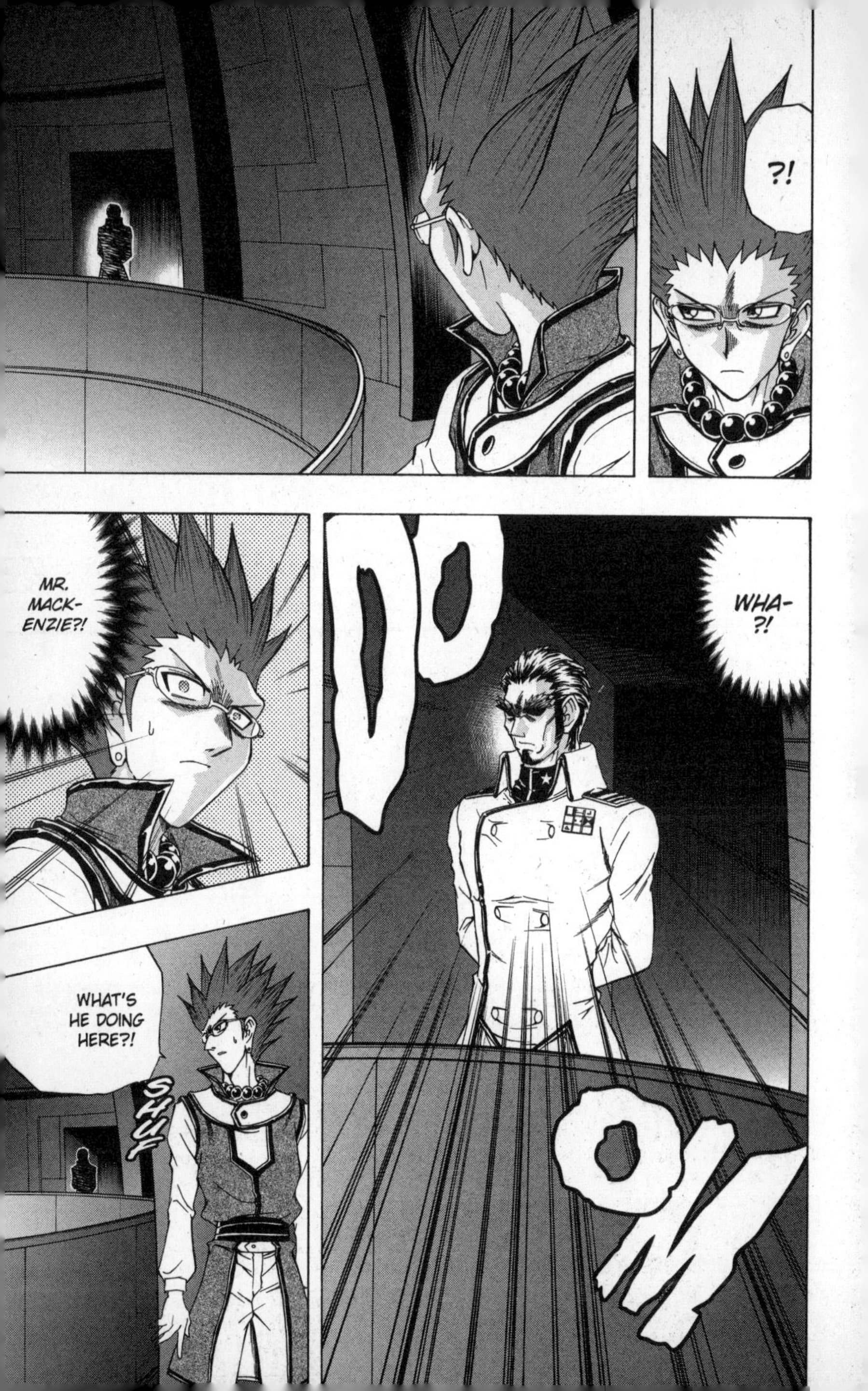
?!
WHA-?!
DOOM
MR. MACK-ENZIE?!
WHAT'S HE DOING HERE?!
SHUF

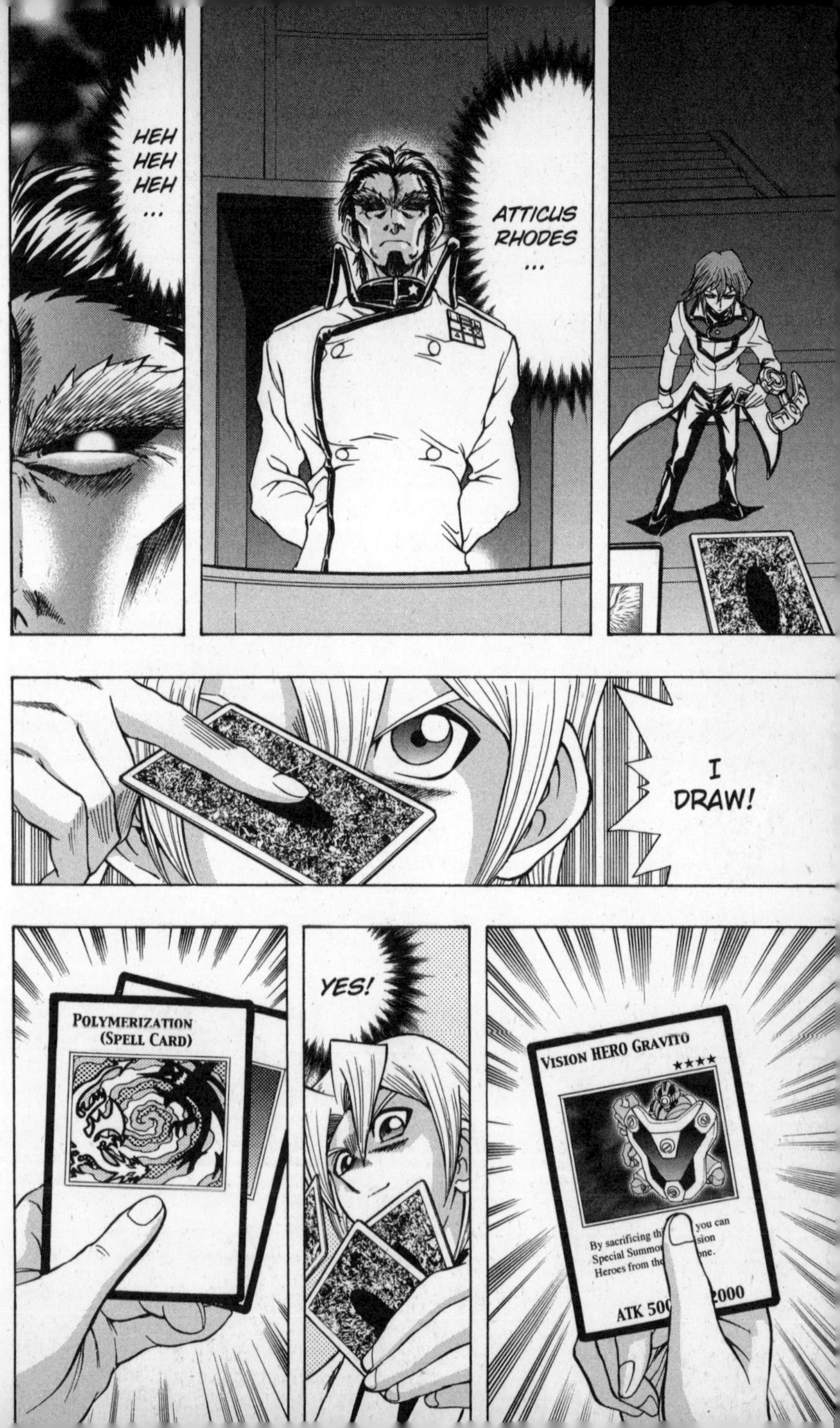
ATTICUS RHODES ...
HEH HEH HEH ...
I DRAW!
VISION HERO GRAVITO
YES!
POLYMERIZATION (SPELL CARD)

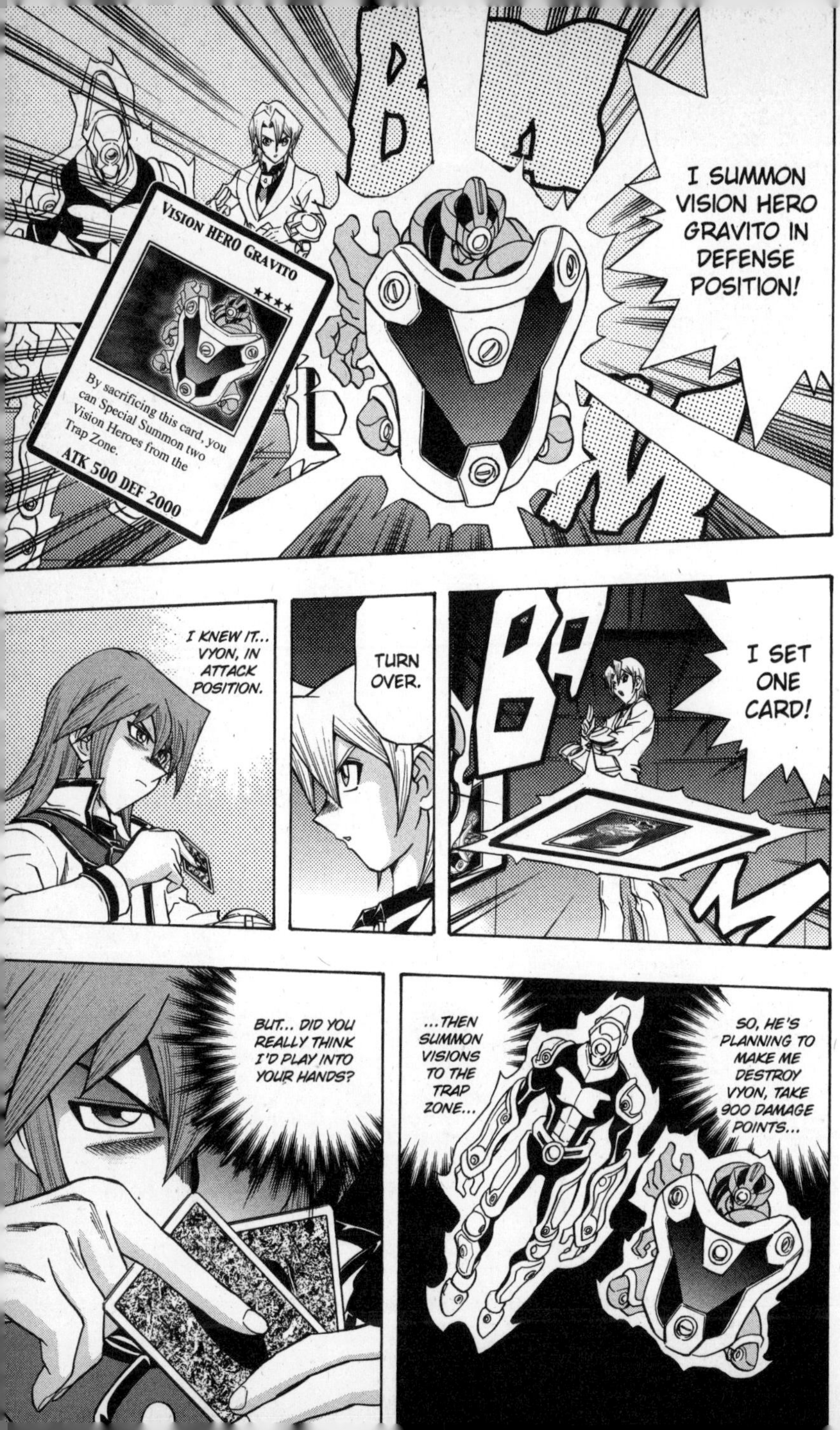
BAM
I SUMMON VISION HERO GRAVITO IN DEFENSE POSITION!
VISION HERO GRAVITO
By sacrificing this card, you can Special Summon two Vision Heroes from the Trap Zone.
ATK 500 DEF 2000
I SET ONE CARD!
BAM
TURN OVER.
I KNEW IT... VYON, IN ATTACK POSITION.
SO, HE'S PLANNING TO MAKE ME DESTROY VYON, TAKE 900 DAMAGE POINTS...
...THEN SUMMON VISIONS TO THE TRAP ZONE...
BUT... DID YOU REALLY THINK I'D PLAY INTO YOUR HANDS?

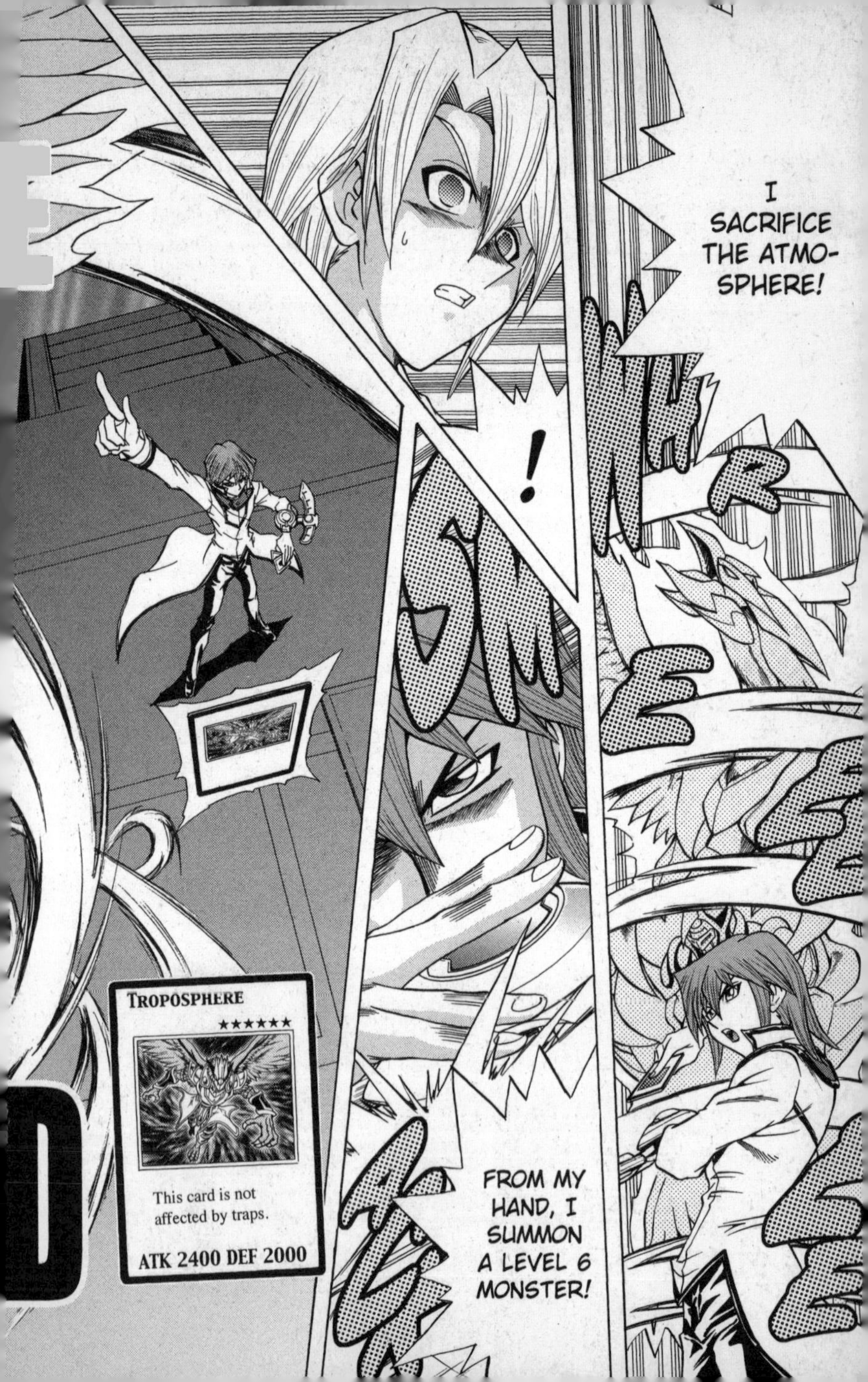
I SACRIFICE THE ATMO-SPHERE!
!
FROM MY HAND, I SUMMON A LEVEL 6 MONSTER!
TROPOSPHERE
★★★★★★
This card is not affected by traps.
ATK 2400 DEF 2000

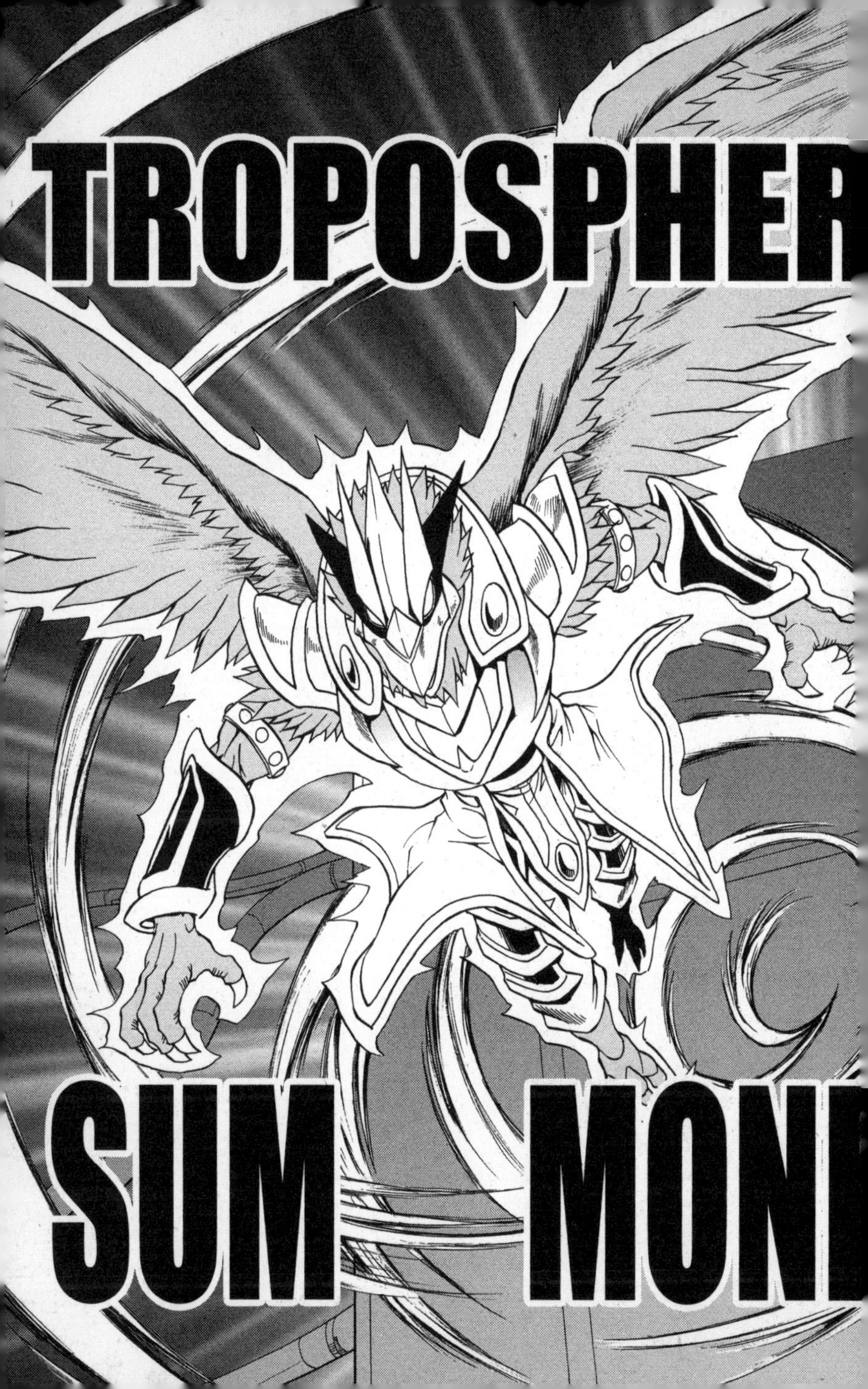
TROPOSPHER
SUM MONE

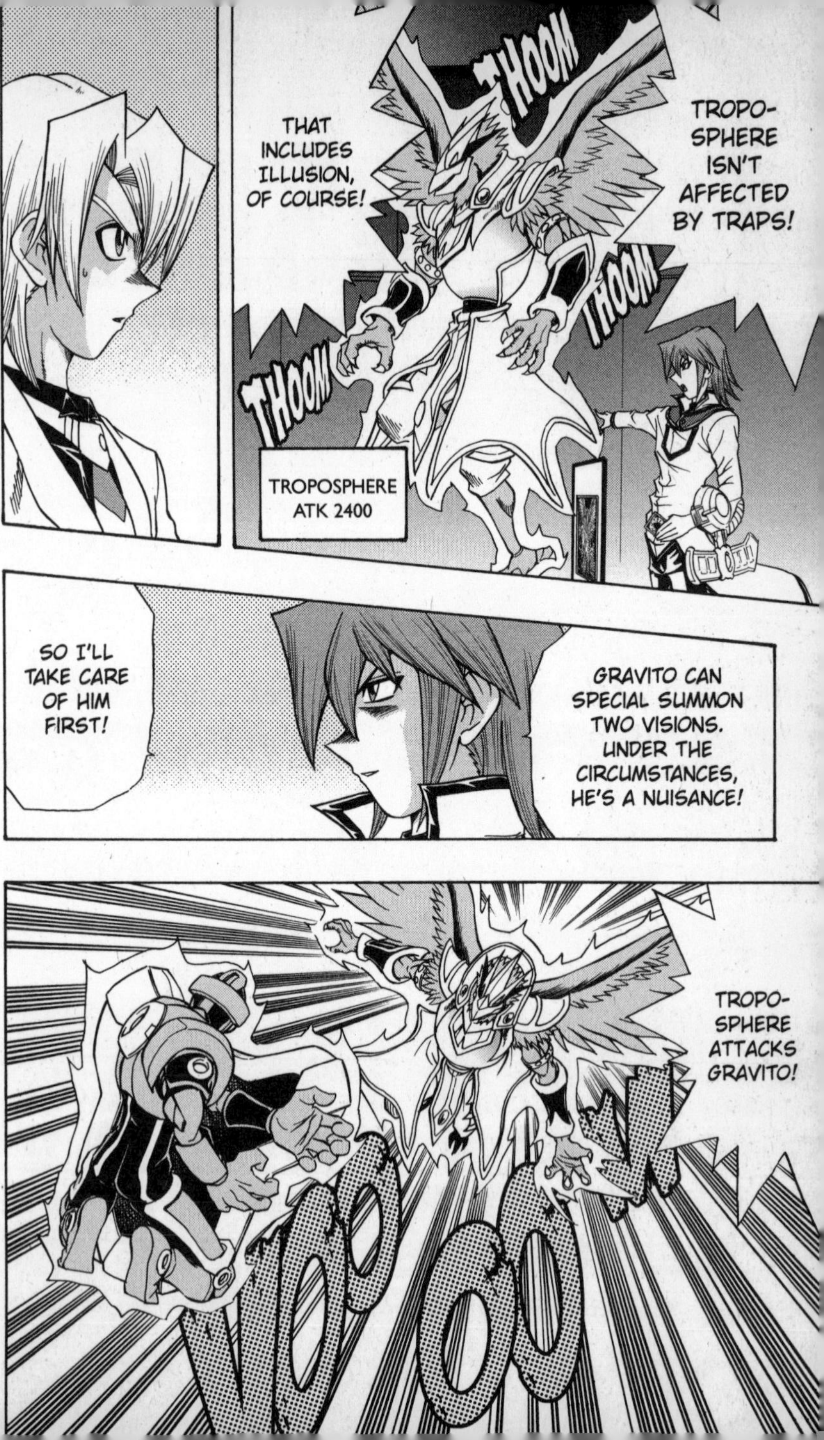
TROPO-SPHERE ISN'T AFFECTED BY TRAPS!
THOOM
THAT INCLUDES ILLUSION, OF COURSE!
THOOM
THOOM
TROPOSPHERE ATK 2400
GRAVITO CAN SPECIAL SUMMON TWO VISIONS. UNDER THE CIRCUMSTANCES, HE'S A NUISANCE!
SO I'LL TAKE CARE OF HIM FIRST!
TROPO-SPHERE ATTACKS GRAVITO!

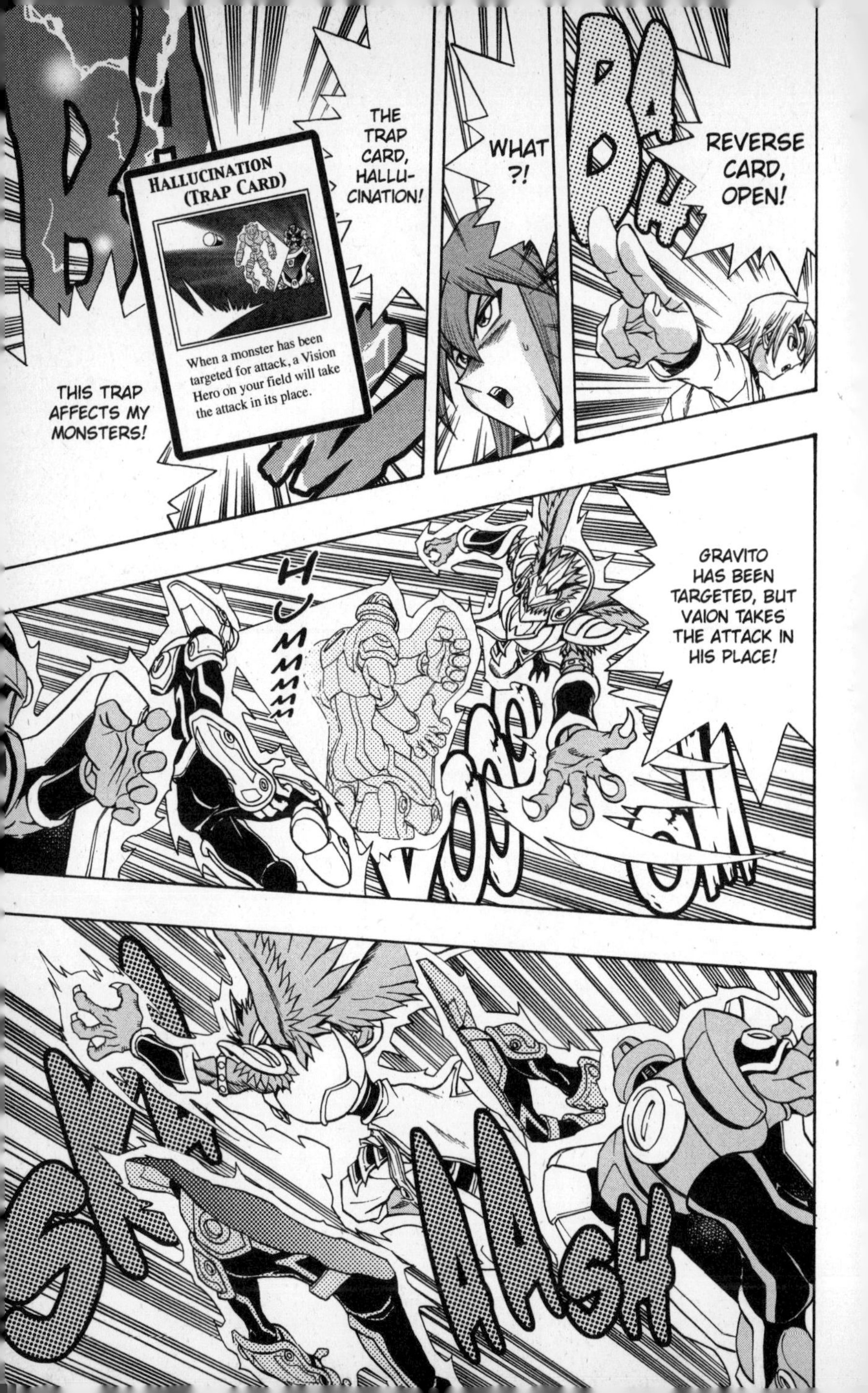
REVERSE CARD, OPEN!
WHAT?!
THE TRAP CARD, HALLUCINATION!
HALLUCINATION (TRAP CARD)
When a monster has been targeted for attack, a Vision Hero on your field will take the attack in its place.
THIS TRAP AFFECTS MY MONSTERS!
GRAVITO HAS BEEN TARGETED, BUT VAION TAKES THE ATTACK IN HIS PLACE!

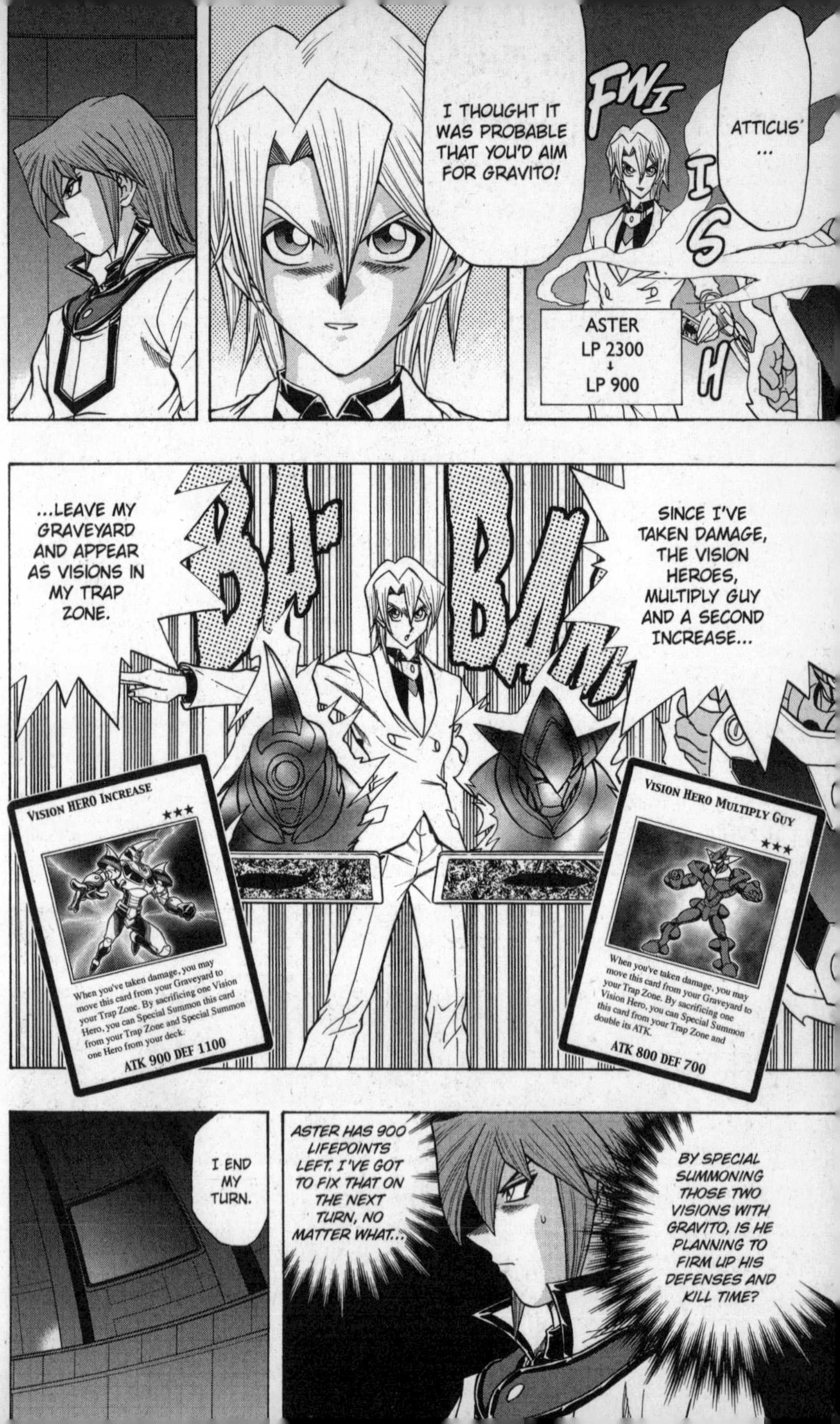
FWISH
ATTICUS' ...
ASTER
LP 2300
↓
LP 900
I THOUGHT IT WAS PROBABLE THAT YOU'D AIM FOR GRAVITO!
SINCE I'VE TAKEN DAMAGE, THE VISION HEROES, MULTIPLY GUY AND A SECOND INCREASE...
BAM
BAM
...LEAVE MY GRAVEYARD AND APPEAR AS VISIONS IN MY TRAP ZONE.
Vision HERO Multiply Guy
When you've taken damage, you may move this card from your Graveyard to your Trap Zone. By sacrificing one Vision Hero, you can Special Summon this card from your Trap Zone and double its ATK.
ATK 800 DEF 700
Vision HERO Increase
When you've taken damage, you may move this card from your Graveyard to your Trap Zone. By sacrificing one Vision Hero, you can Special Summon this card from your Trap Zone and Special Summon one Hero from your deck.
ATK 900 DEF 1100
BY SPECIAL SUMMONING THOSE TWO VISIONS WITH GRAVITO, IS HE PLANNING TO FIRM UP HIS DEFENSES AND KILL TIME?
ASTER HAS 900 LIFEPOINTS LEFT. I'VE GOT TO FIX THAT ON THE NEXT TURN, NO MATTER WHAT...
I END MY TURN.

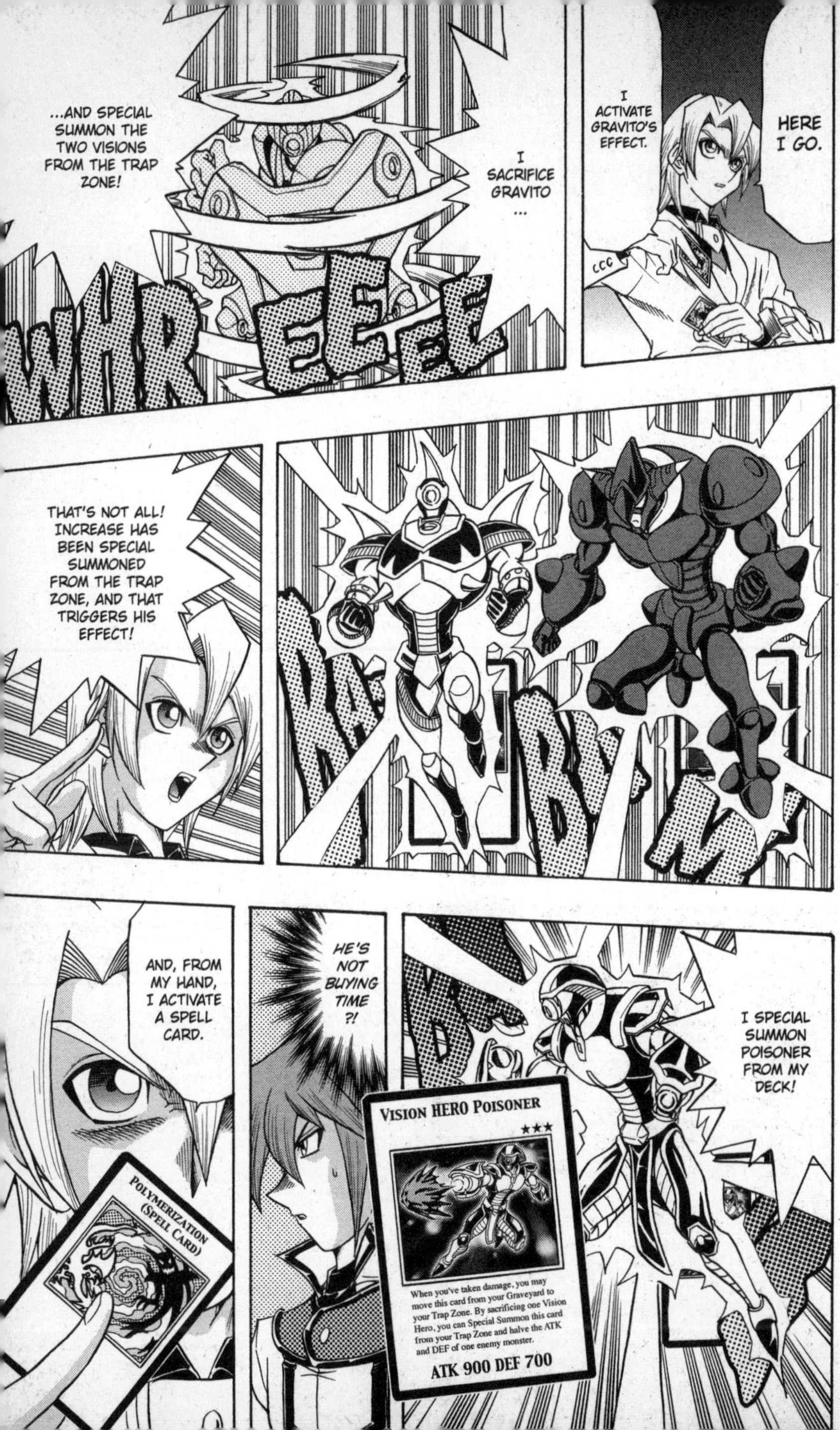
HERE I GO.
I ACTIVATE GRAVITO'S EFFECT.
I SACRIFICE GRAVITO ...
...AND SPECIAL SUMMON THE TWO VISIONS FROM THE TRAP ZONE!
THAT'S NOT ALL! INCREASE HAS BEEN SPECIAL SUMMONED FROM THE TRAP ZONE, AND THAT TRIGGERS HIS EFFECT!
I SPECIAL SUMMON POISONER FROM MY DECK!
VISION HERO POISONER
When you've taken damage, you may move this card from your Graveyard to your Trap Zone. By sacrificing one Vision Hero, you can Special Summon this card from your Trap Zone and halve the ATK and DEF of one enemy monster.
ATK 900 DEF 700
HE'S NOT BUYING TIME ?!
AND, FROM MY HAND, I ACTIVATE A SPELL CARD.
POLYMERIZATION (SPELL CARD)

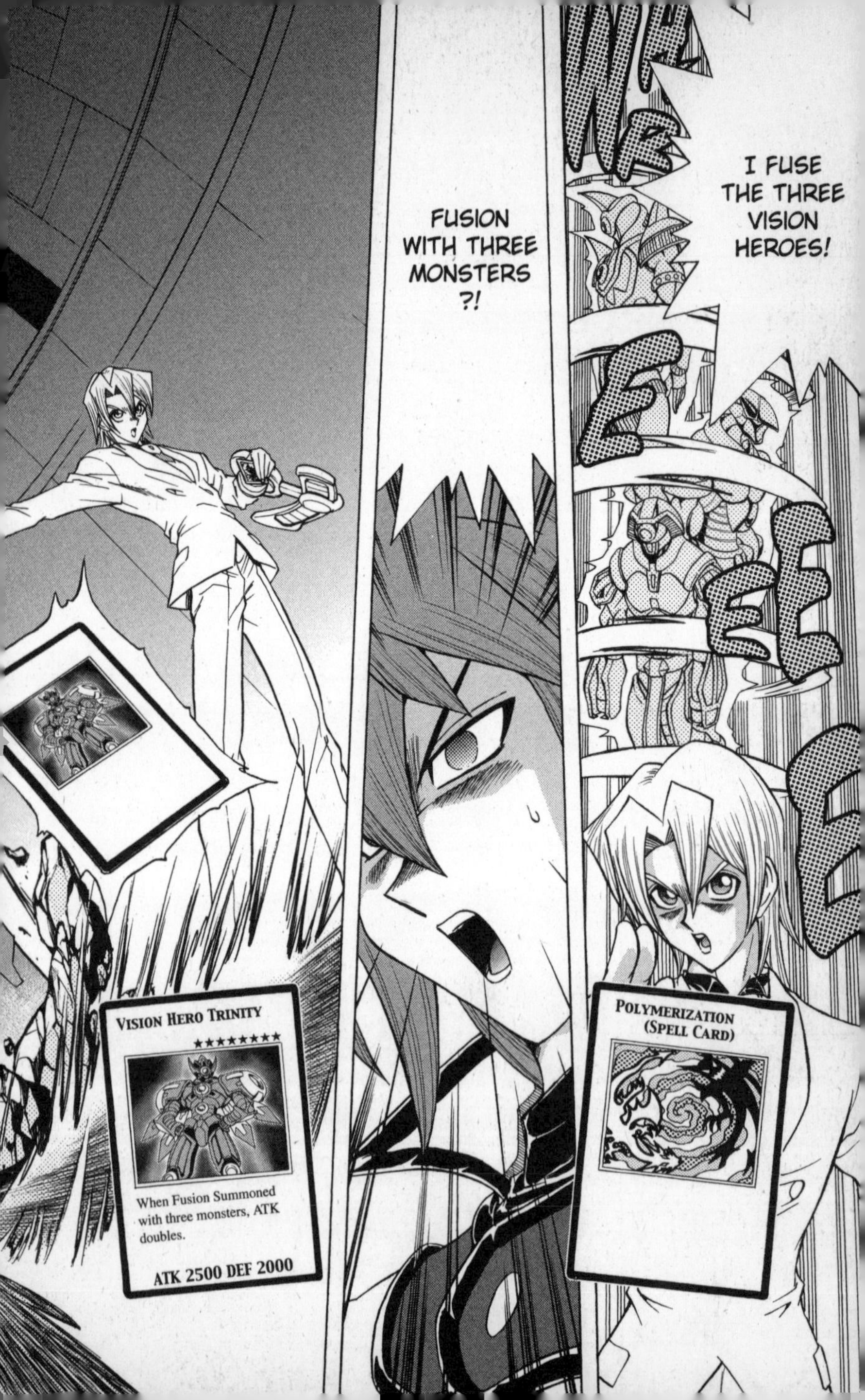
I FUSE THE THREE VISION HEROES!
POLYMERIZATION (SPELL CARD)
FUSION WITH THREE MONSTERS ?!
VISION HERO TRINITY
When Fusion Summoned with three monsters, ATK doubles.
ATK 2500 DEF 2000

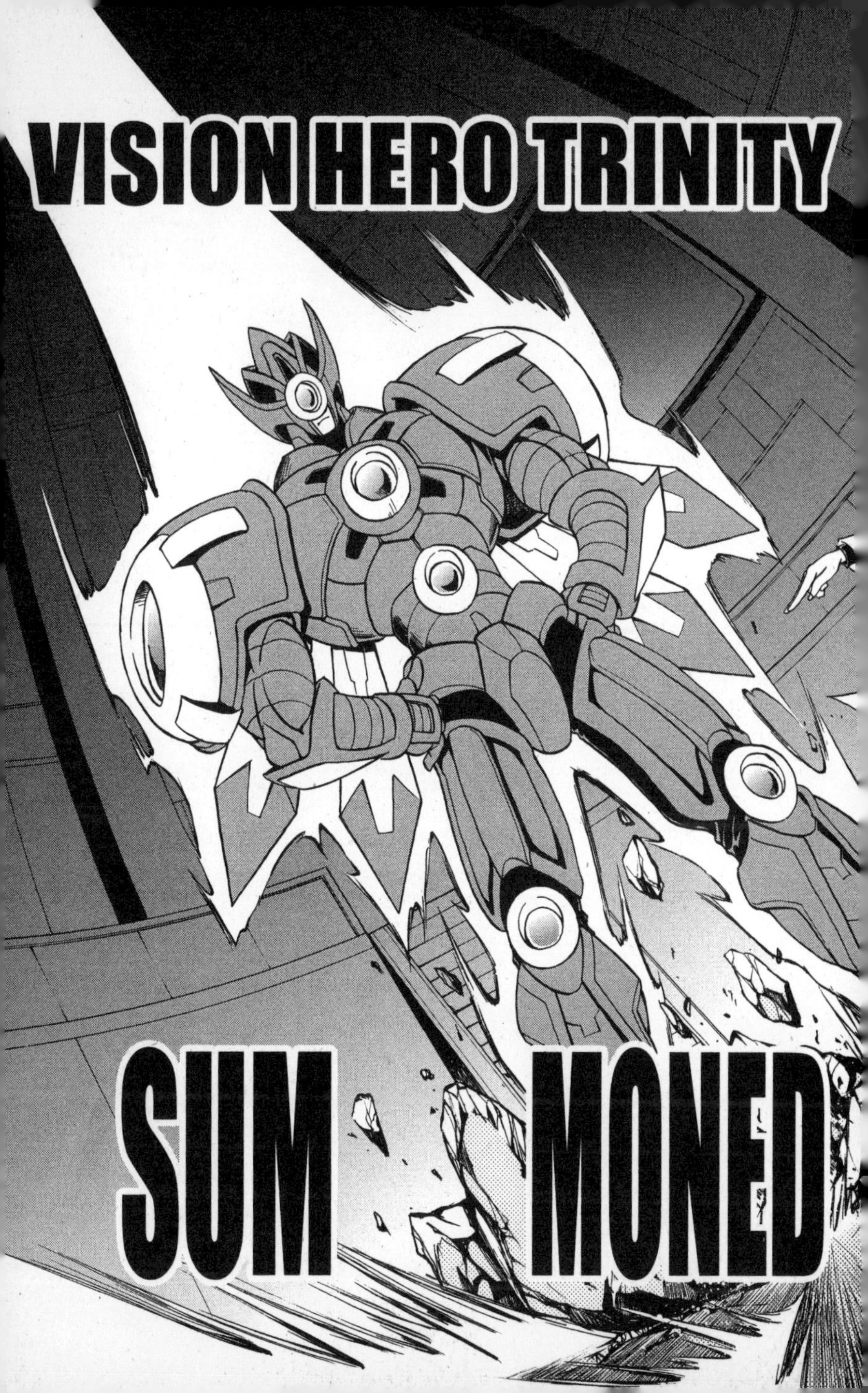
VISION HERO TRINITY
SUM MONED

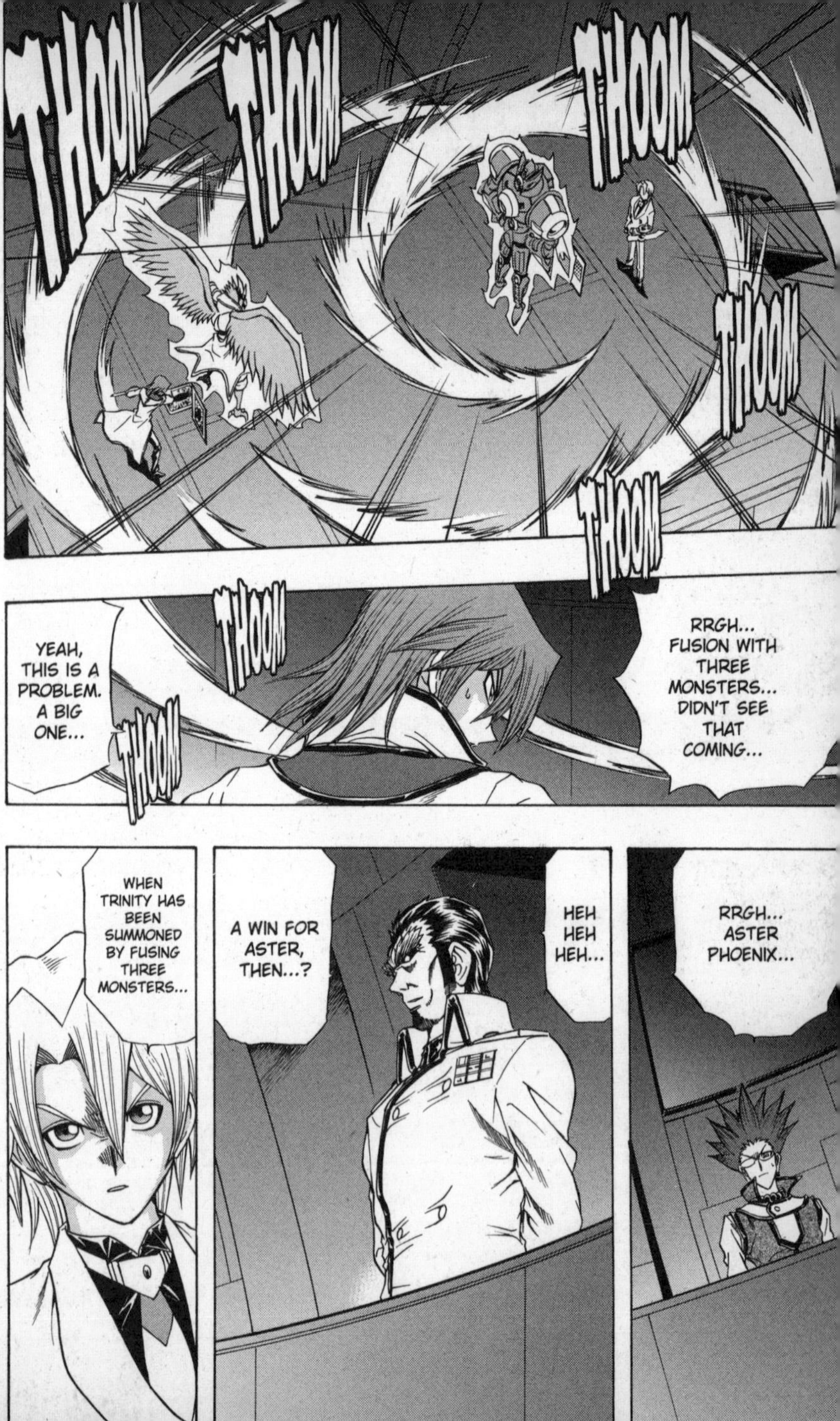
THOOM
THOOM
THOOM
THOOM
THOOM
RRGH... FUSION WITH THREE MONSTERS... DIDN'T SEE THAT COMING...
THOOM
YEAH, THIS IS A PROBLEM. A BIG ONE...
THOOM
RRGH... ASTER PHOENIX...
HEH HEH HEH...
A WIN FOR ASTER, THEN...?
WHEN TRINITY HAS BEEN SUMMONED BY FUSING THREE MONSTERS...

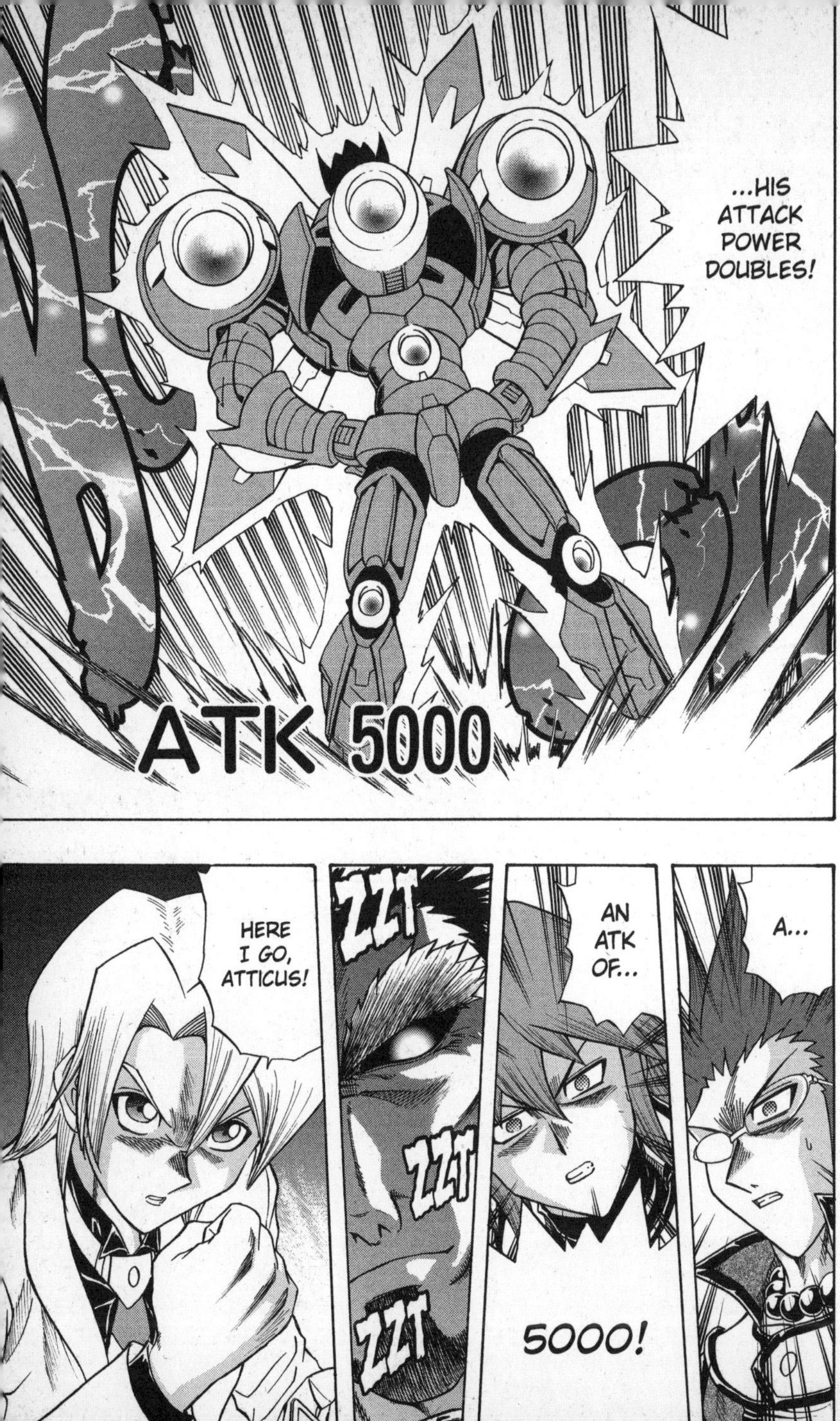
...HIS ATTACK POWER DOUBLES!
ATK 5000
A...
AN ATK OF...
5000!
ZZT
ZZT
ZZT
HERE I GO, ATTICUS!

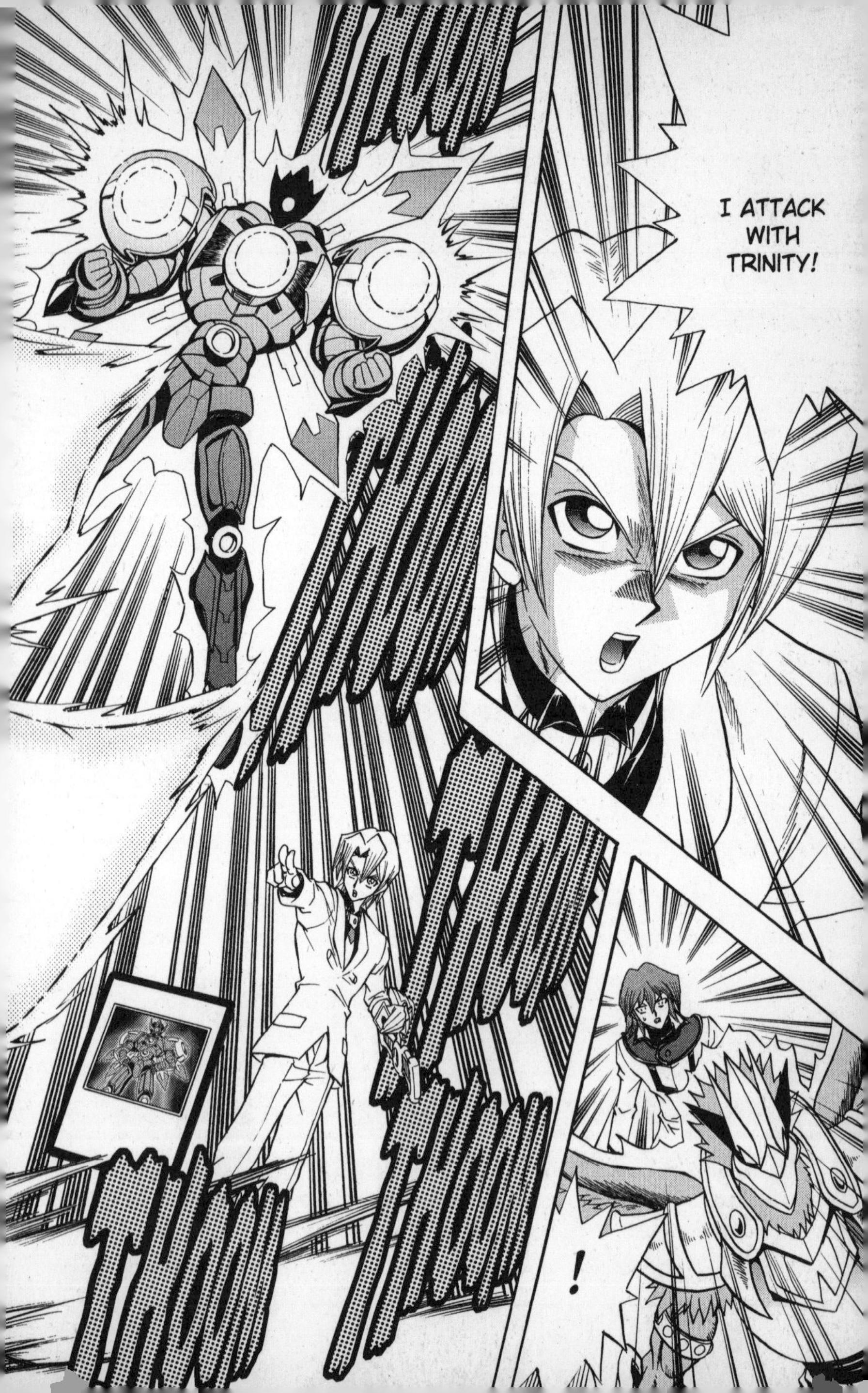
I ATTACK WITH TRINITY!
!

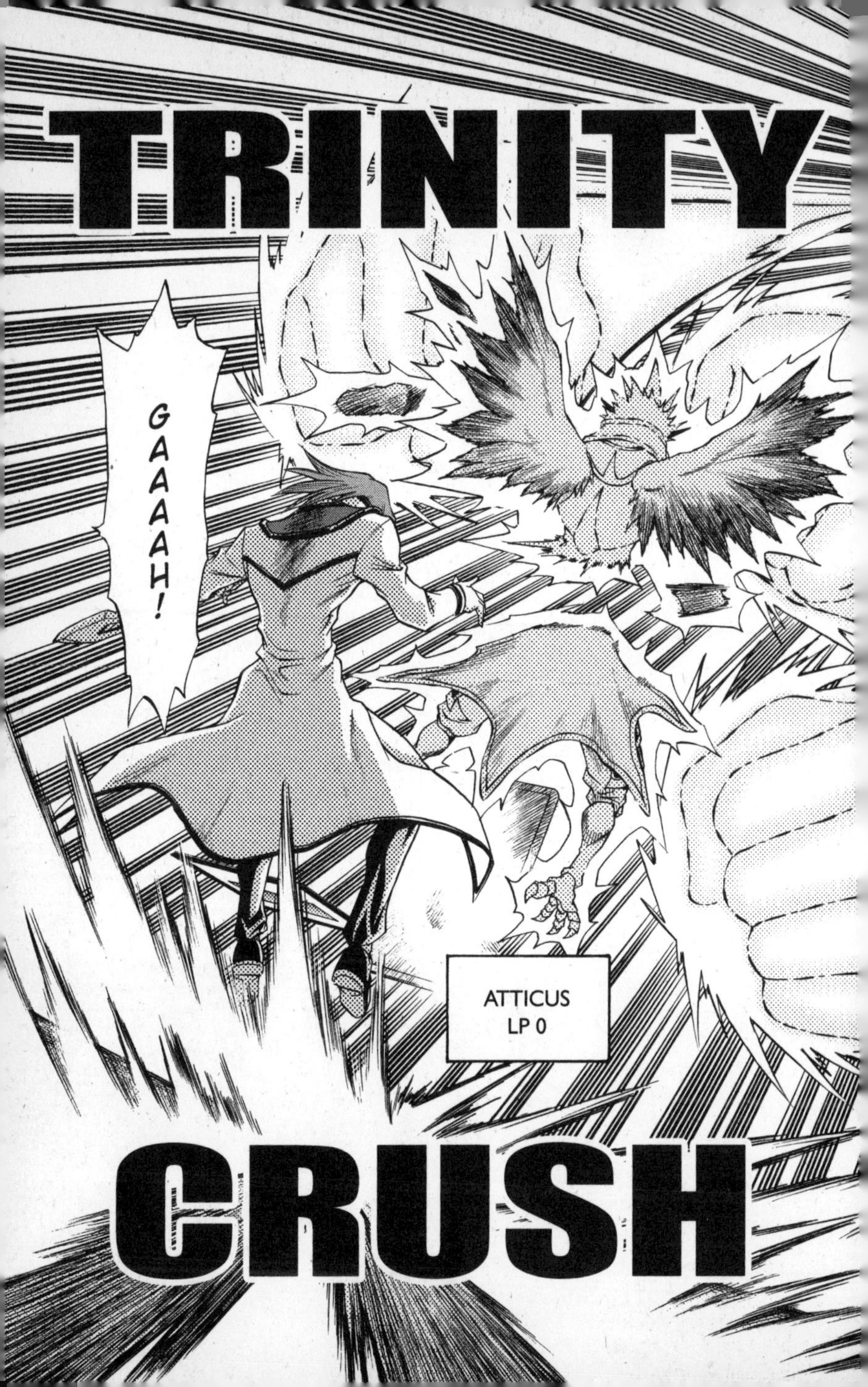
TRINITY
GAAAAAH!
ATTICUS
LP 0
CRUSH

I'LL DO ANYTHING!

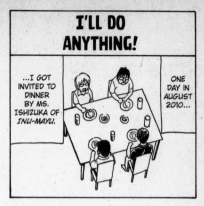

ONE DAY IN AUGUST 2010...
...I GOT INVITED TO DINNER BY MS. ISHIZUKA OF *INU-MAYU*.
I'LL HAVE AN *INU-MAYU* COMIC OUT IN SEPTEMBER!
VERY FORMAL BOW
THAT'S WONDERFUL. CONGRATULATIONS.
...AND I'M GOING TO HAVE YOU DRAW A SPECIAL GX PAGE FOR THAT COMIC, KAGEYAMA SENSEI.
RUSTLE
FUMBLE
HUH?!
PUUSH
I'VE WRITTEN THE ROUGH FOR YOU ALREADY, SEE? JUST MAKE IT LIKE THIS! THANKS!
O... OKAY...

IF THERE'S ONE WORD I JUST CAN'T SAY TO MS. ISHIZUKA, IT'S, "NO"...

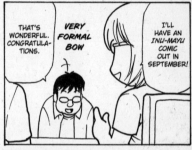

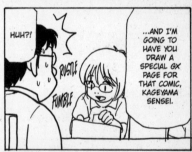

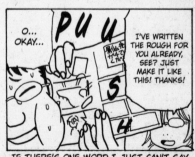

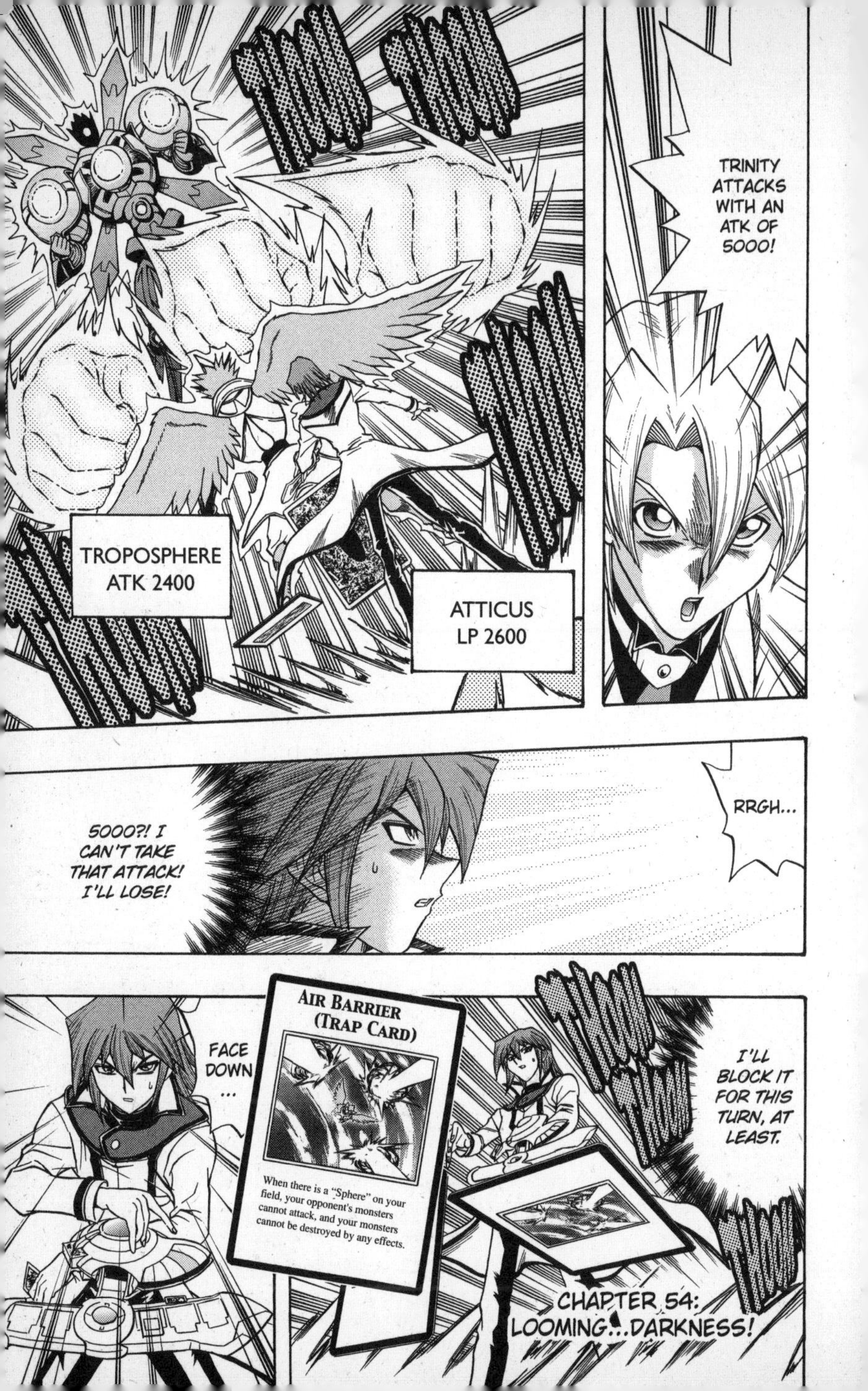
TRINITY ATTACKS WITH AN ATK OF 5000!
TROPOSPHERE ATK 2400
ATTICUS LP 2600
RRGH...
5000?! I CAN'T TAKE THAT ATTACK! I'LL LOSE!
I'LL BLOCK IT FOR THIS TURN, AT LEAST.
AIR BARRIER (TRAP CARD)
When there is a "Sphere" on your field, your opponent's monsters cannot attack, and your monsters cannot be destroyed by any effects.
CHAPTER 54: LOOMING...DARKNESS!
FACE DOWN...

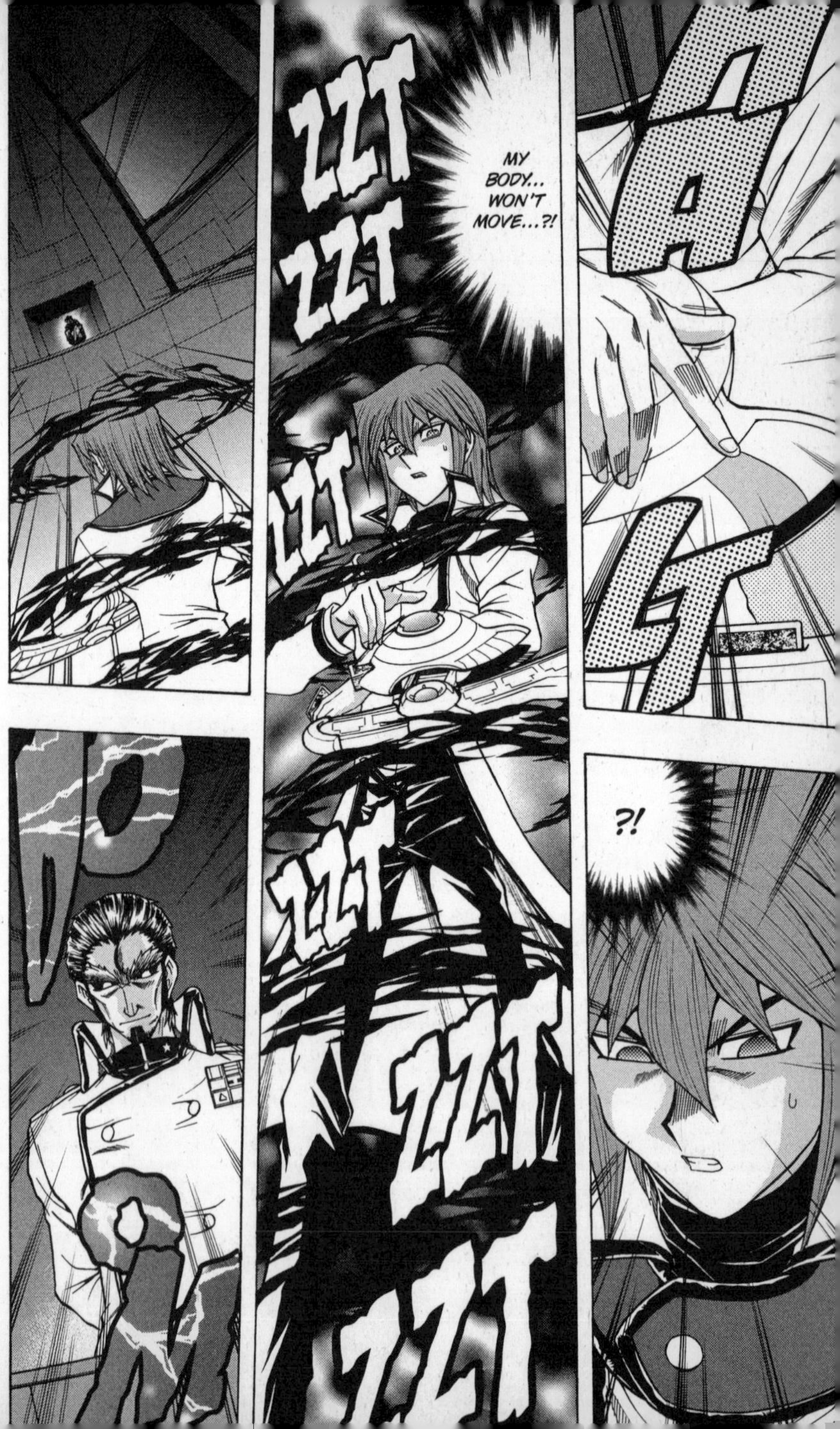
?!
ZZT
ZZT
MY BODY... WON'T MOVE...?!
ZZT
ZZT
ZZT
ZZT

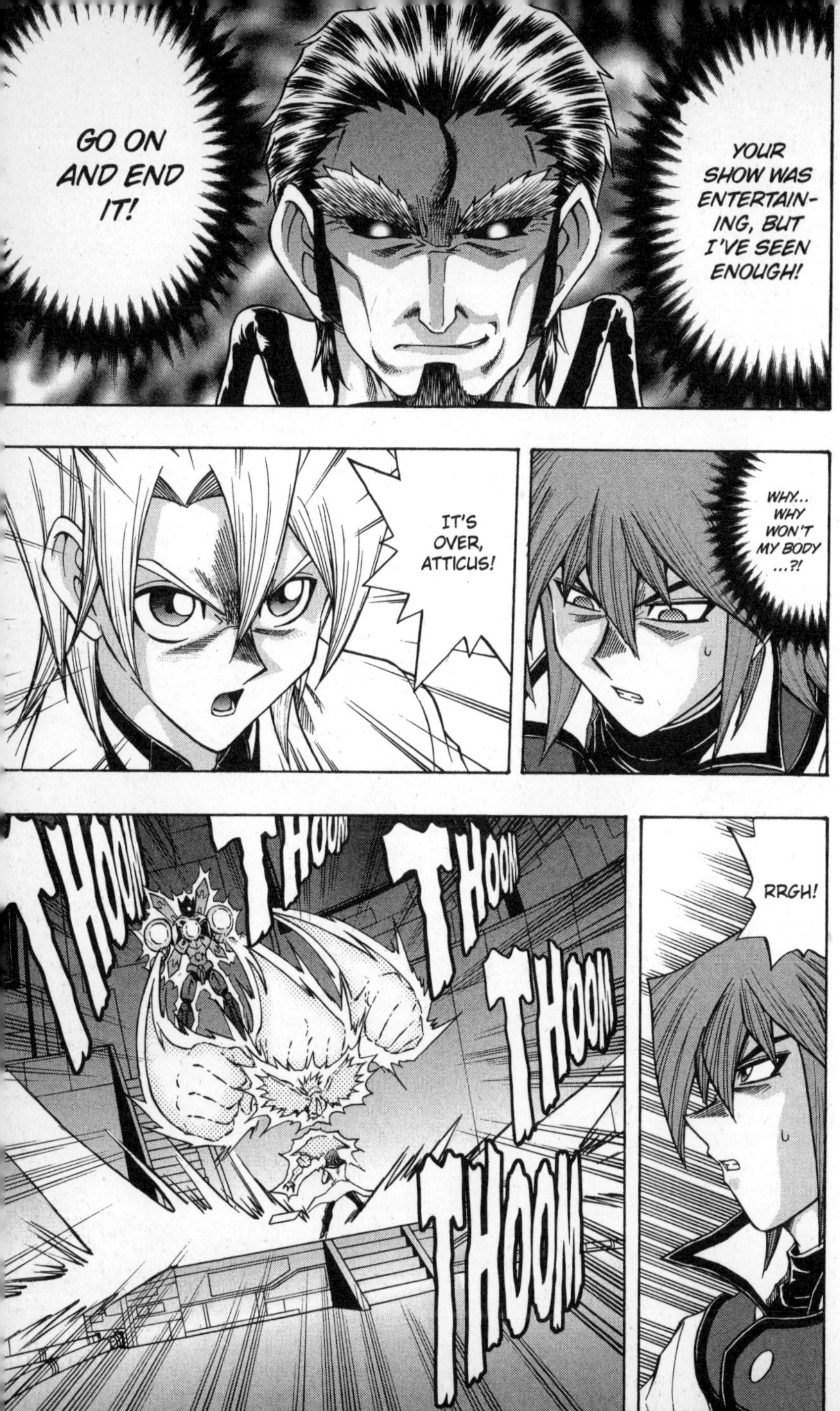
YOUR SHOW WAS ENTERTAIN-ING, BUT I'VE SEEN ENOUGH!
GO ON AND END IT!
WHY... WHY WON'T MY BODY ...?!
IT'S OVER, ATTICUS!
RRGH!
THOOM
THOOM
THOOM
THOOM
THOOM

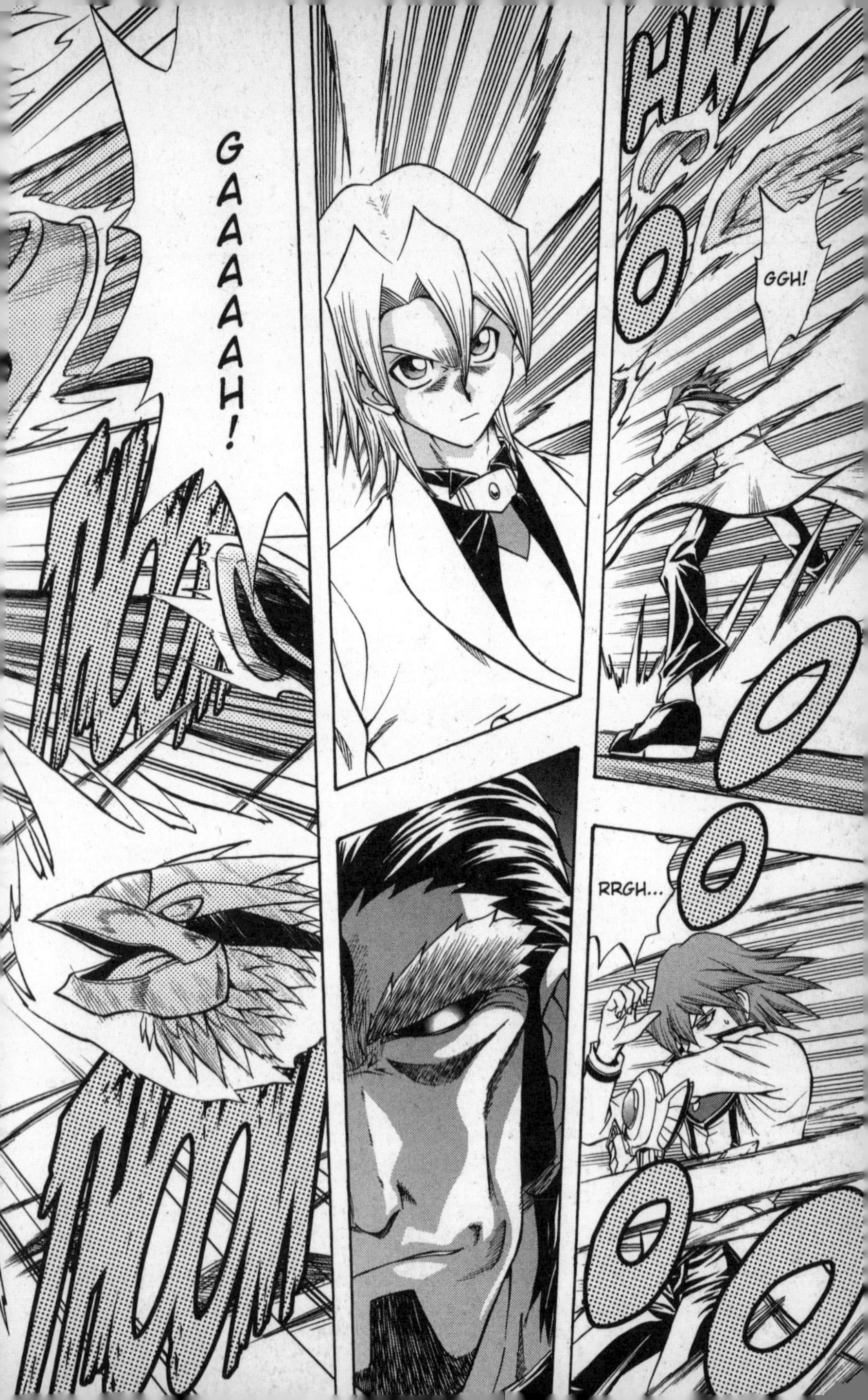
GGH!
RRGH...
GAAAAAAH!

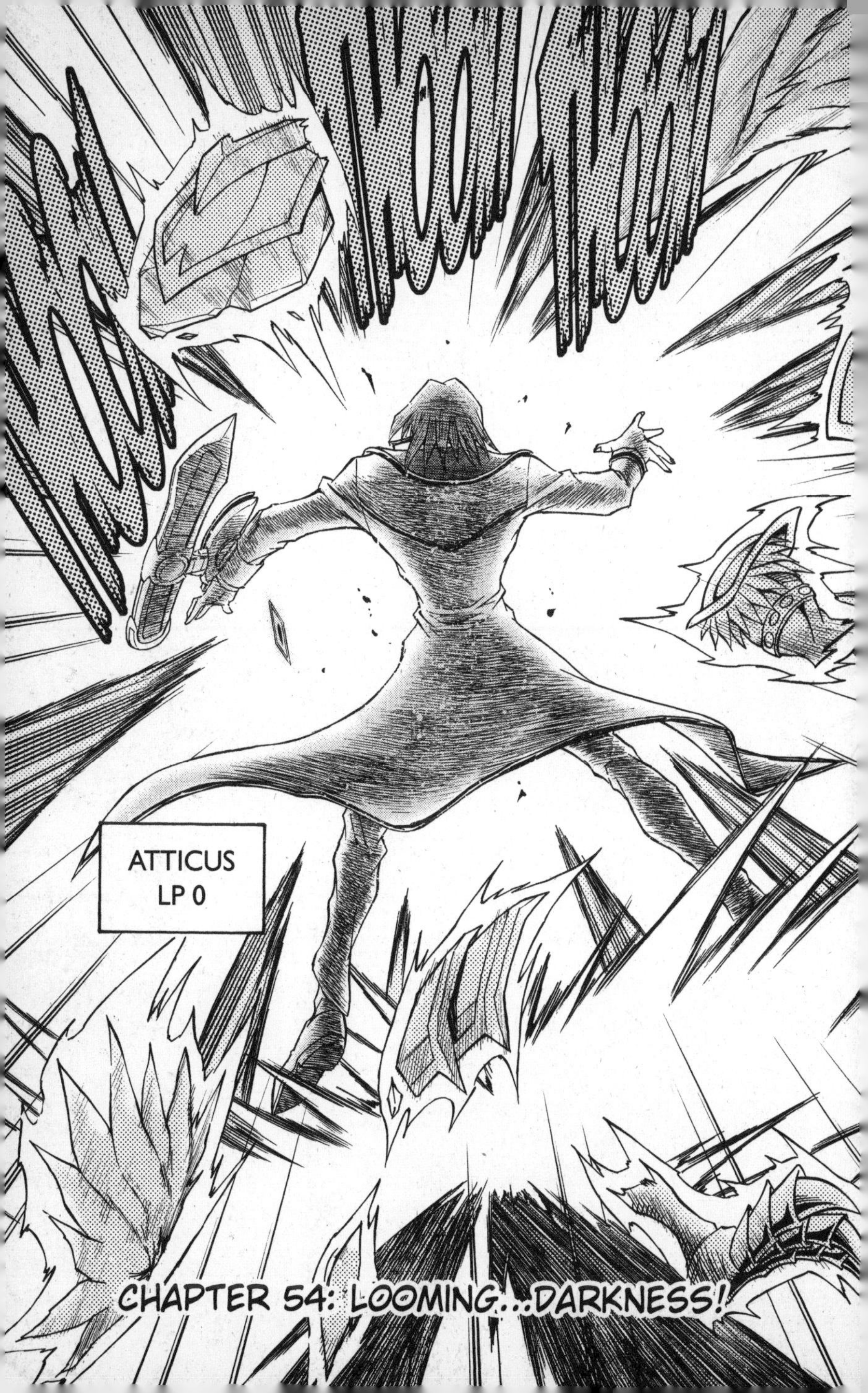
ATTICUS
LP 0
CHAPTER 54: LOOMING...DARKNESS!

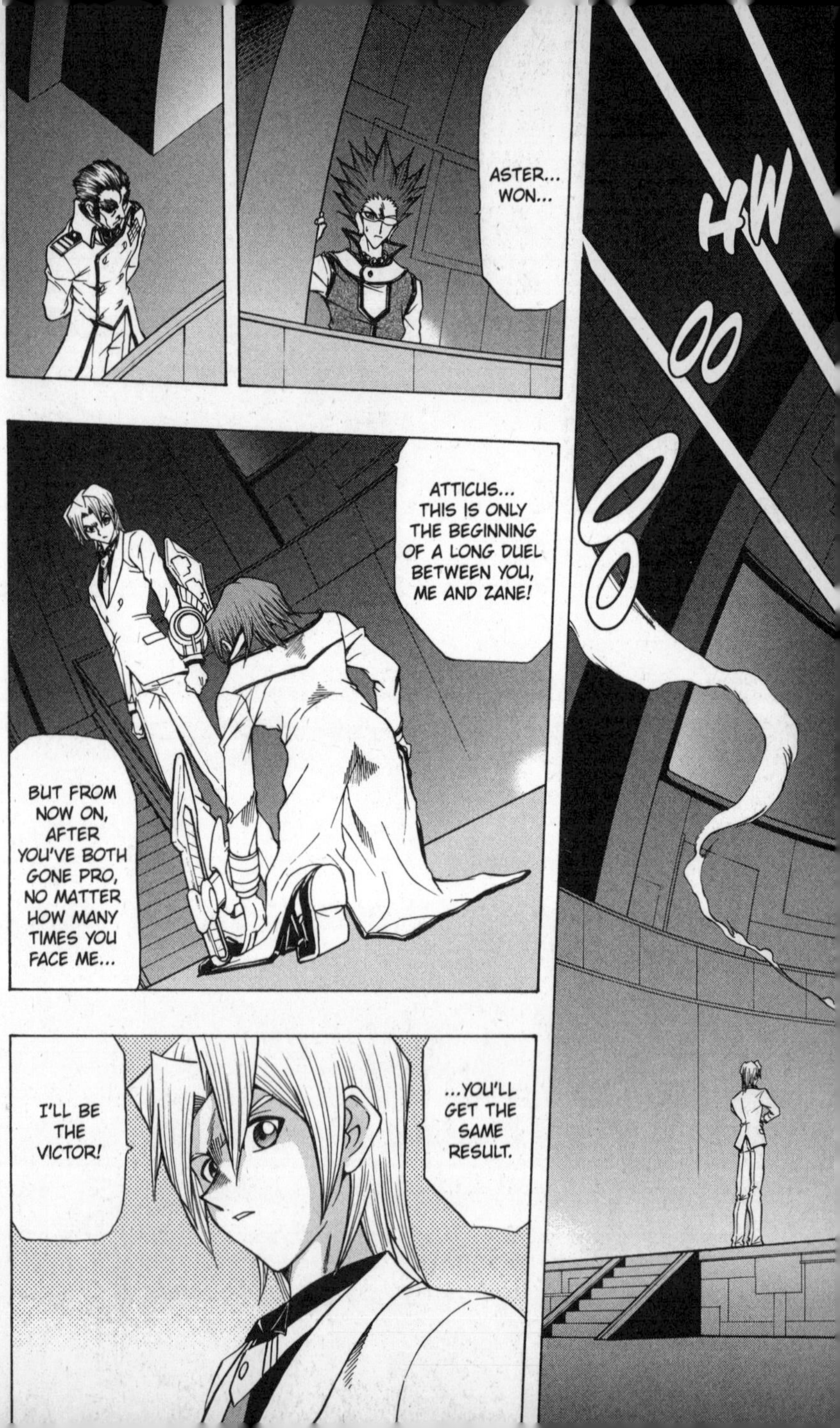
WHOOOO
ASTER... WON...
ATTICUS... THIS IS ONLY THE BEGINNING OF A LONG DUEL BETWEEN YOU, ME AND ZANE!
BUT FROM NOW ON, AFTER YOU'VE BOTH GONE PRO, NO MATTER HOW MANY TIMES YOU FACE ME...
...YOU'LL GET THE SAME RESULT.
I'LL BE THE VICTOR!

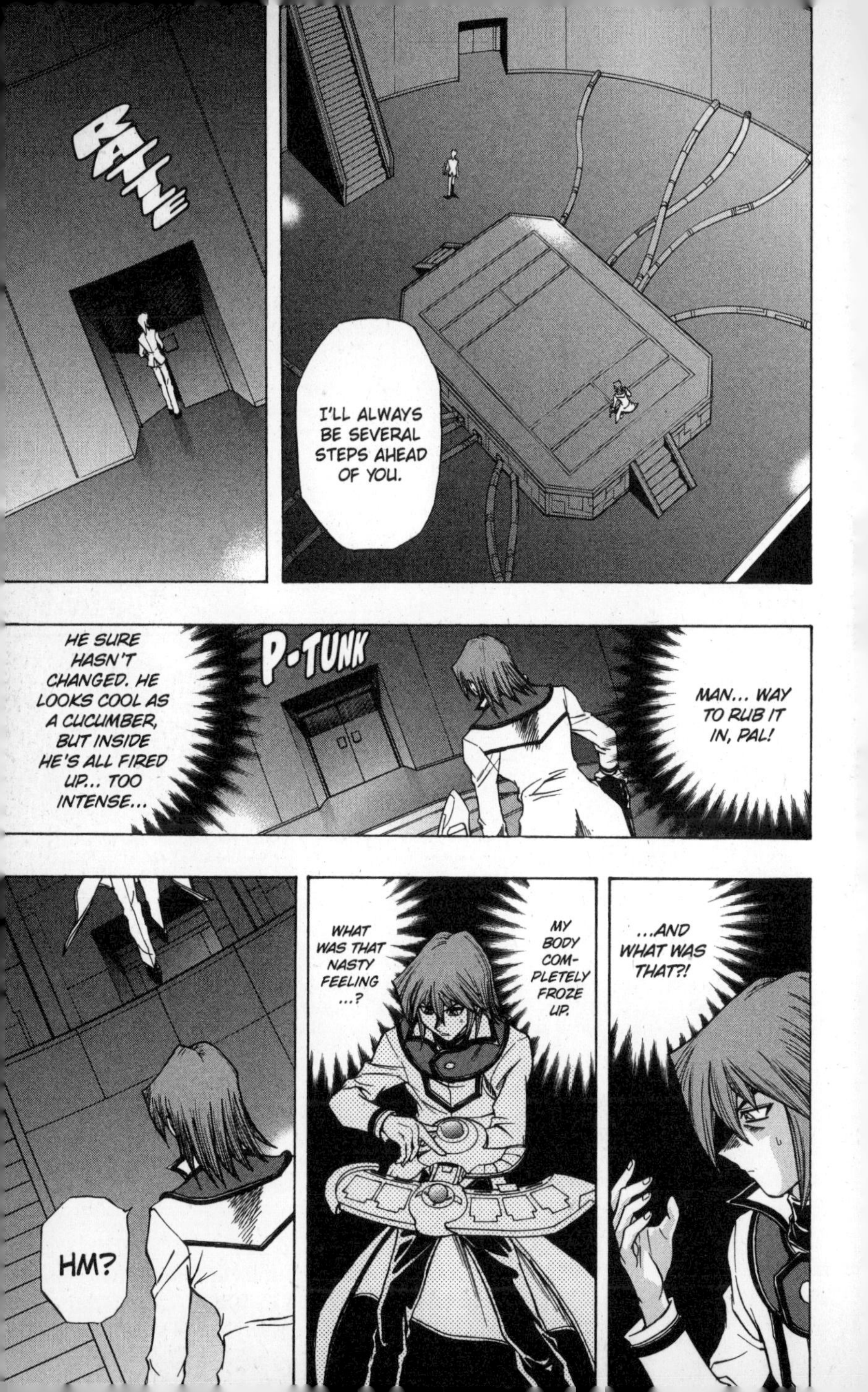
RATTLE
I'LL ALWAYS BE SEVERAL STEPS AHEAD OF YOU.
HE SURE HASN'T CHANGED. HE LOOKS COOL AS A CUCUMBER, BUT INSIDE HE'S ALL FIRED UP... TOO INTENSE...
P-TUNK
MAN... WAY TO RUB IT IN, PAL!
HM?
WHAT WAS THAT NASTY FEELING ...?
MY BODY COM-PLETELY FROZE UP.
...AND WHAT WAS THAT?!

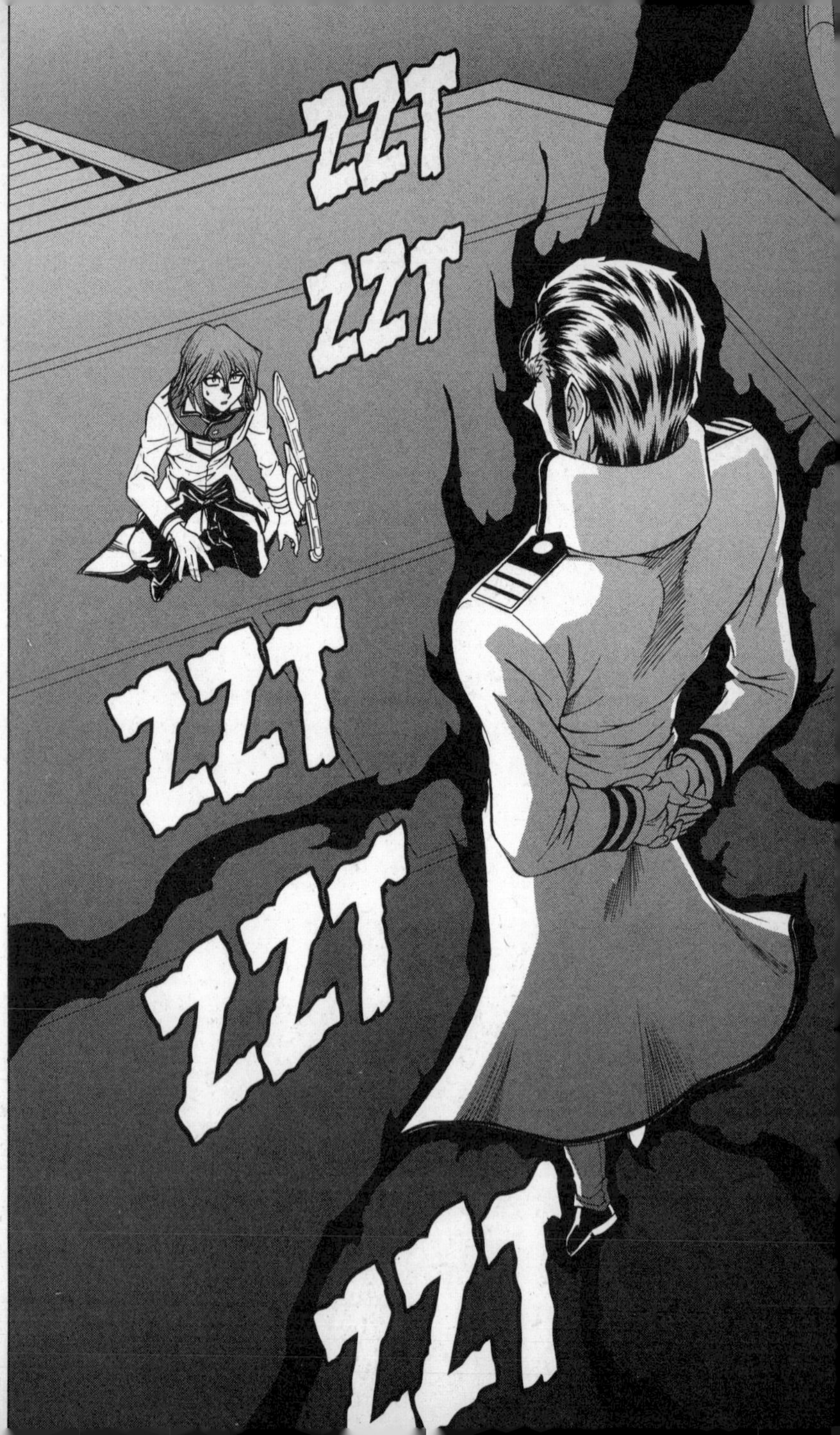
ZZT
ZZT
ZZT
ZZT
ZZT

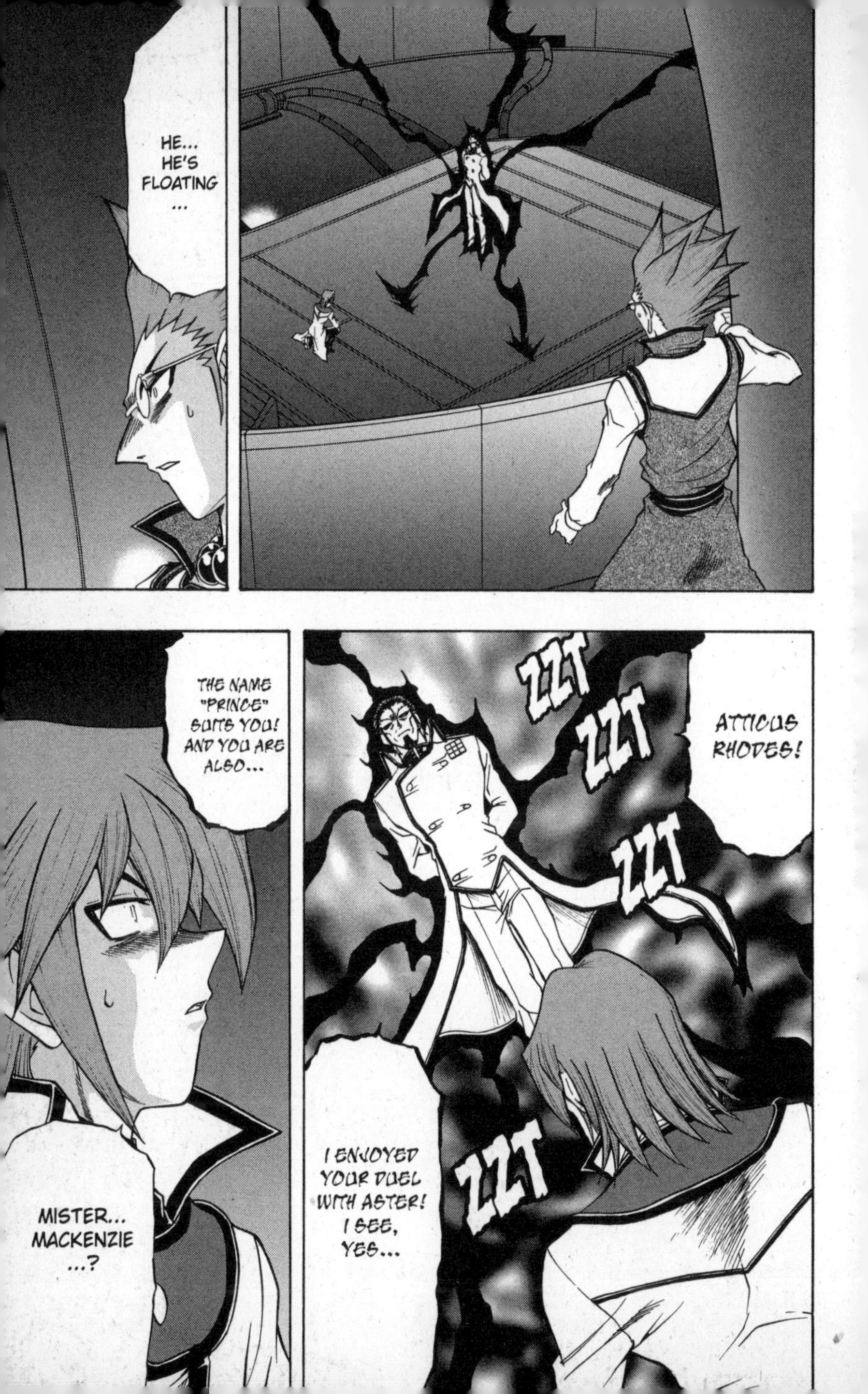
HE... HE'S FLOATING ...
ZZZT
ZZZT
ATTICUS RHODES!
ZZZT
I ENJOYED YOUR DUEL WITH ASTER! I SEE, YES...
ZZZT
THE NAME "PRINCE" SUITS YOU! AND YOU ARE ALSO...
MISTER... MACKENZIE ...?

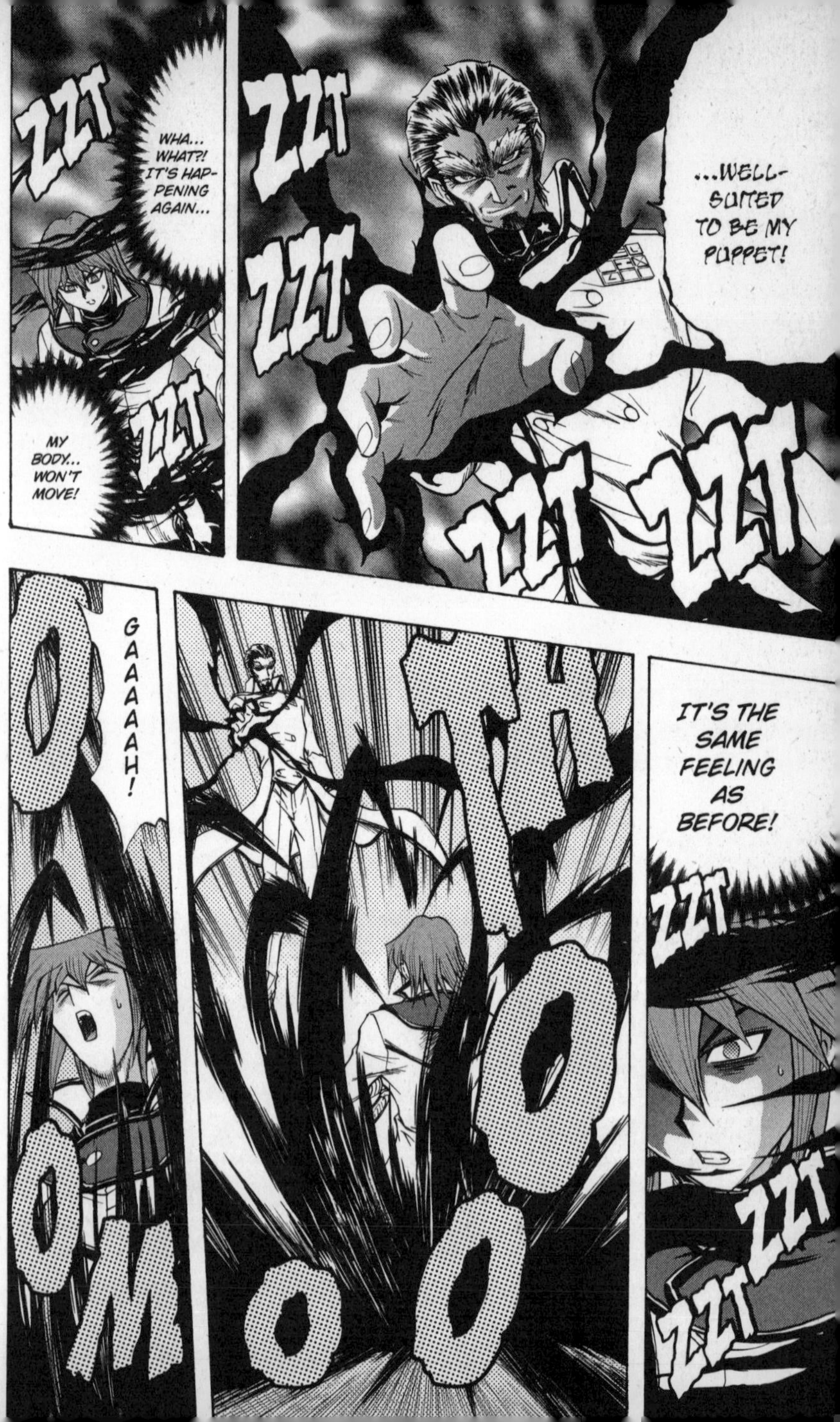
ZZT
ZZT
...WELL-SUITED TO BE MY PUPPET!
ZZT
ZZT
ZZT
WHA... WHAT?! IT'S HAPPENING AGAIN...
ZZT
MY BODY... WON'T MOVE!
IT'S THE SAME FEELING AS BEFORE!
ZZT
ZZT
ZZT
THOOOOOM
GAAAAAAH!

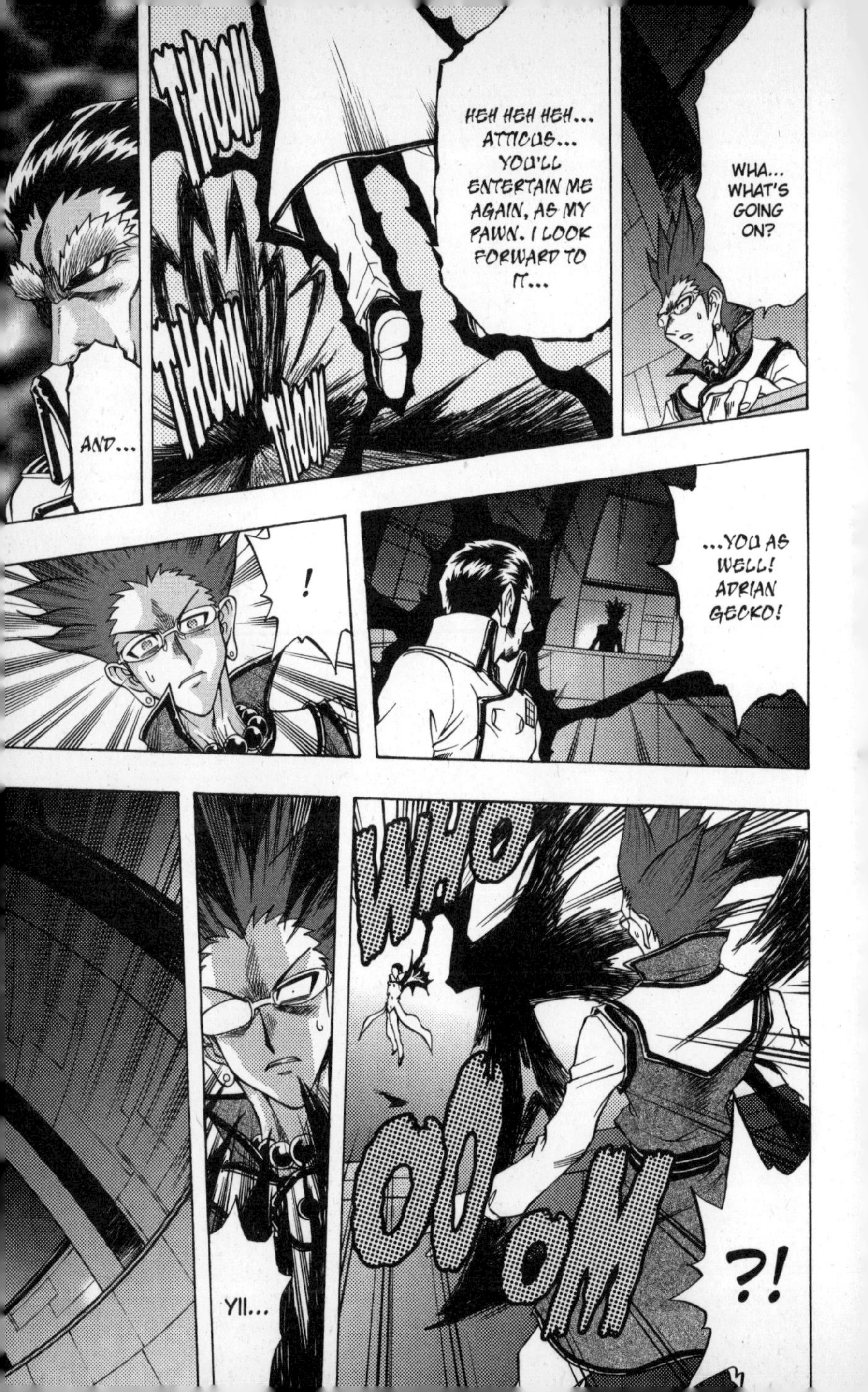
WHA... WHAT'S GOING ON?
HEH HEH HEH... ATTICUS... YOU'LL ENTERTAIN ME AGAIN, AS MY PAWN. I LOOK FORWARD TO IT...
THOOM
THOOM
THOOM
THOOM
AND...
...YOU AS WELL! ADRIAN GECKO!
!
WHOOOOM
?!
YII...

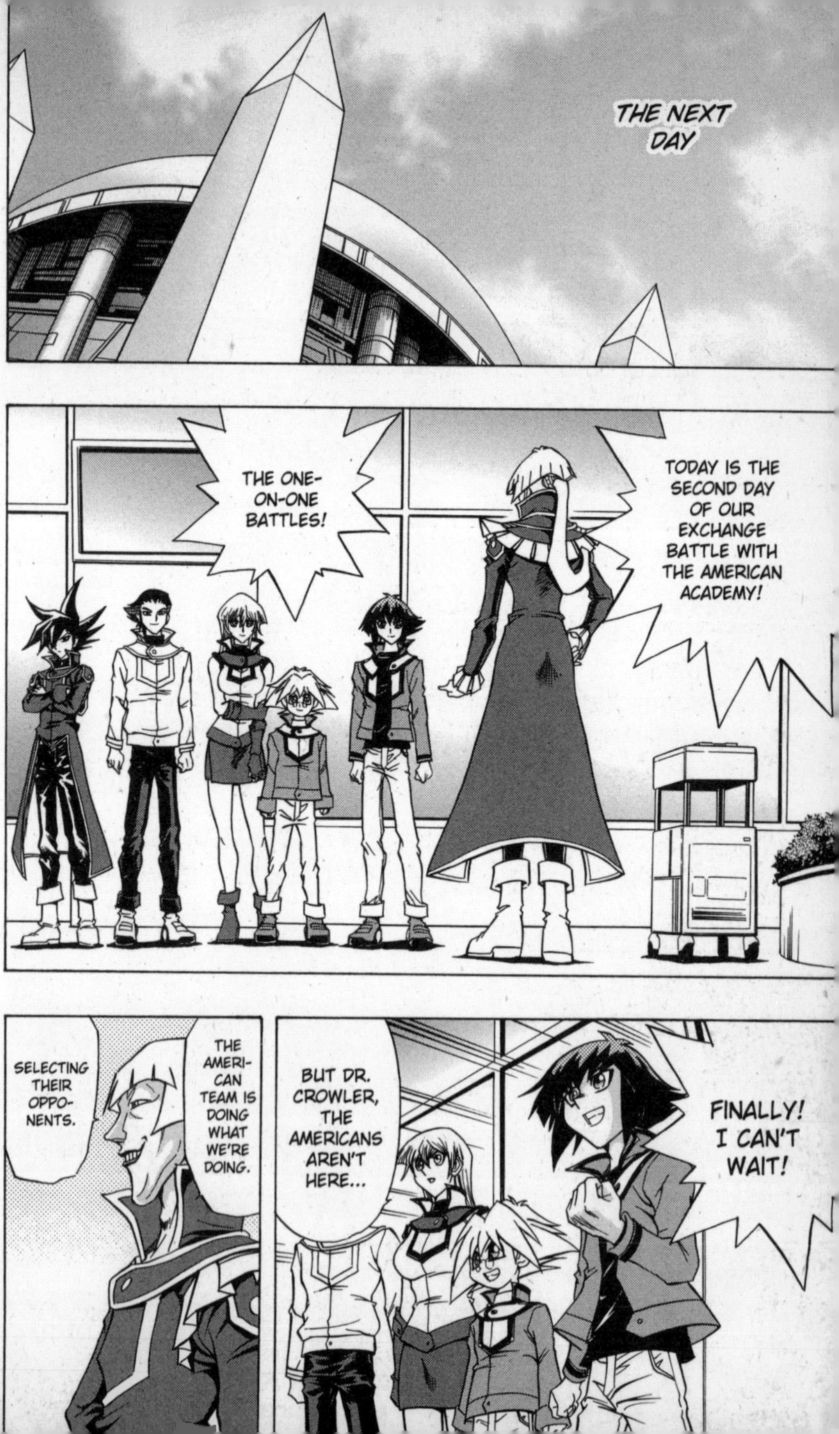
THE NEXT DAY
TODAY IS THE SECOND DAY OF OUR EXCHANGE BATTLE WITH THE AMERICAN ACADEMY!
THE ONE-ON-ONE BATTLES!
FINALLY! I CAN'T WAIT!
BUT DR. CROWLER, THE AMERICANS AREN'T HERE...
THE AMERI-CAN TEAM IS DOING WHAT WE'RE DOING.
SELECTING THEIR OPPO-NENTS.

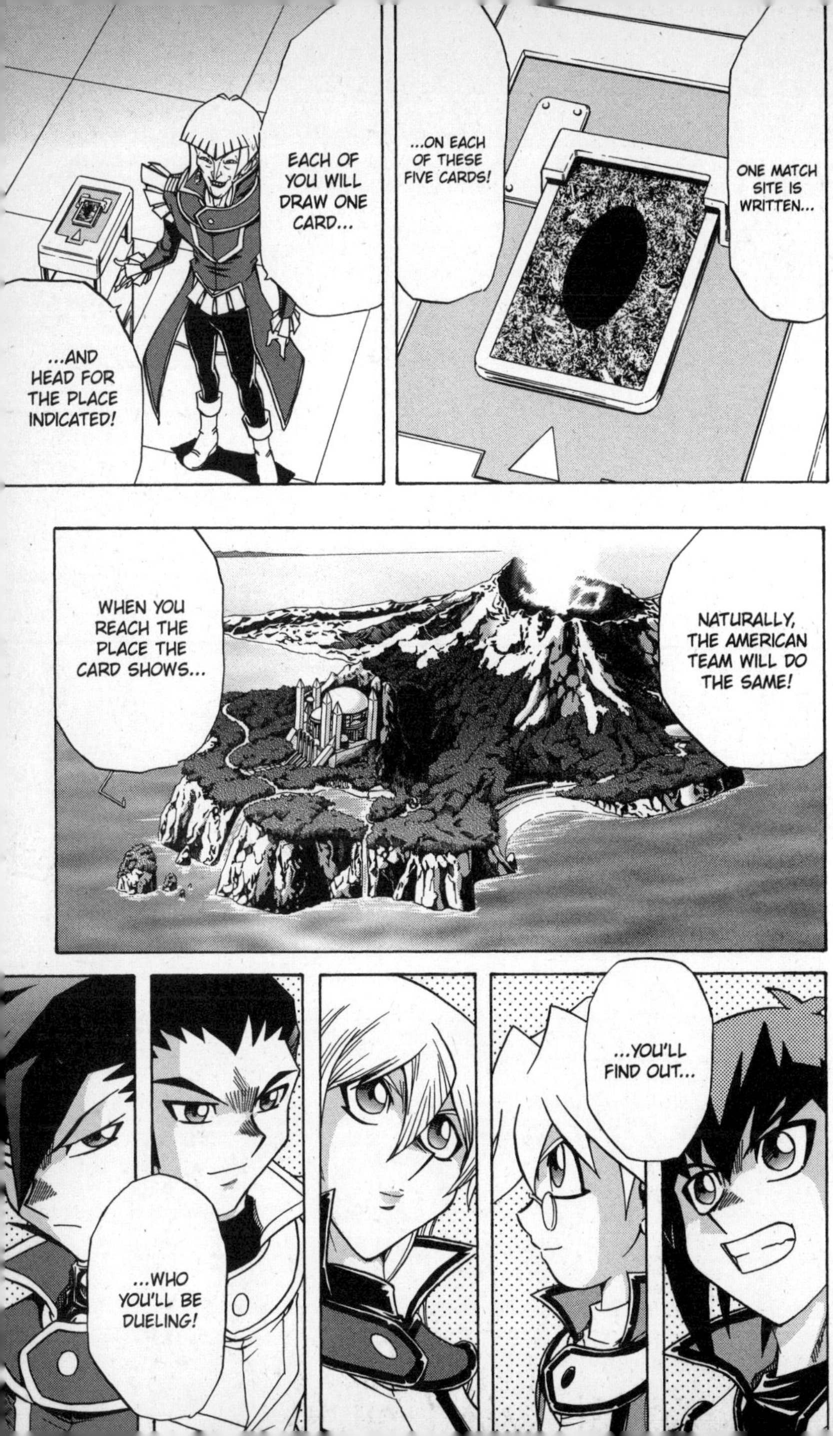
ONE MATCH SITE IS WRITTEN...
...ON EACH OF THESE FIVE CARDS!
EACH OF YOU WILL DRAW ONE CARD...
...AND HEAD FOR THE PLACE INDICATED!
NATURALLY, THE AMERICAN TEAM WILL DO THE SAME!
WHEN YOU REACH THE PLACE THE CARD SHOWS...
...YOU'LL FIND OUT...
...WHO YOU'LL BE DUELING!

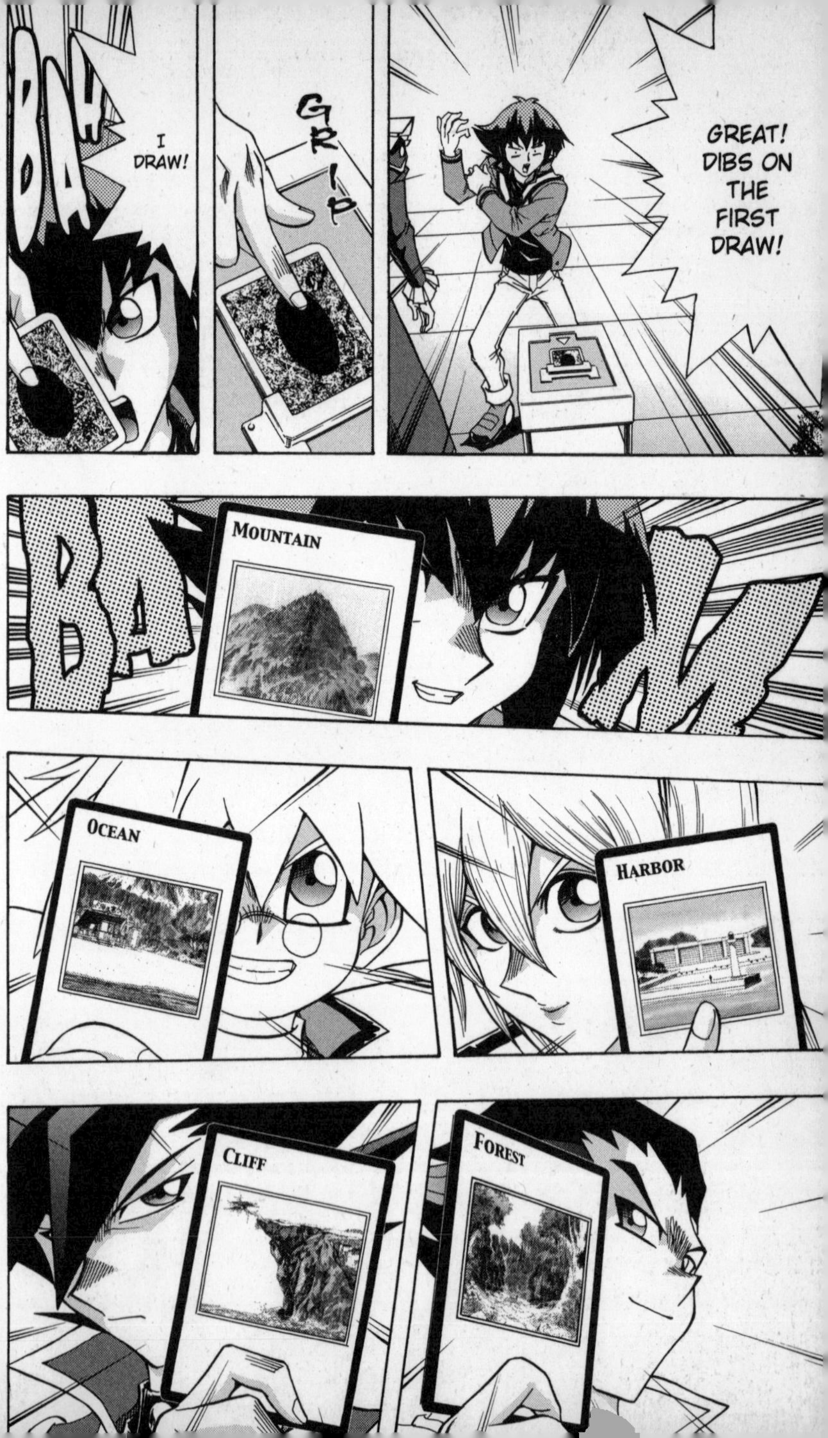
GREAT! DIBS ON THE FIRST DRAW!
GRIP
I DRAW!
BAM
MOUNTAIN
HARBOR
OCEAN
FOREST
CLIFF

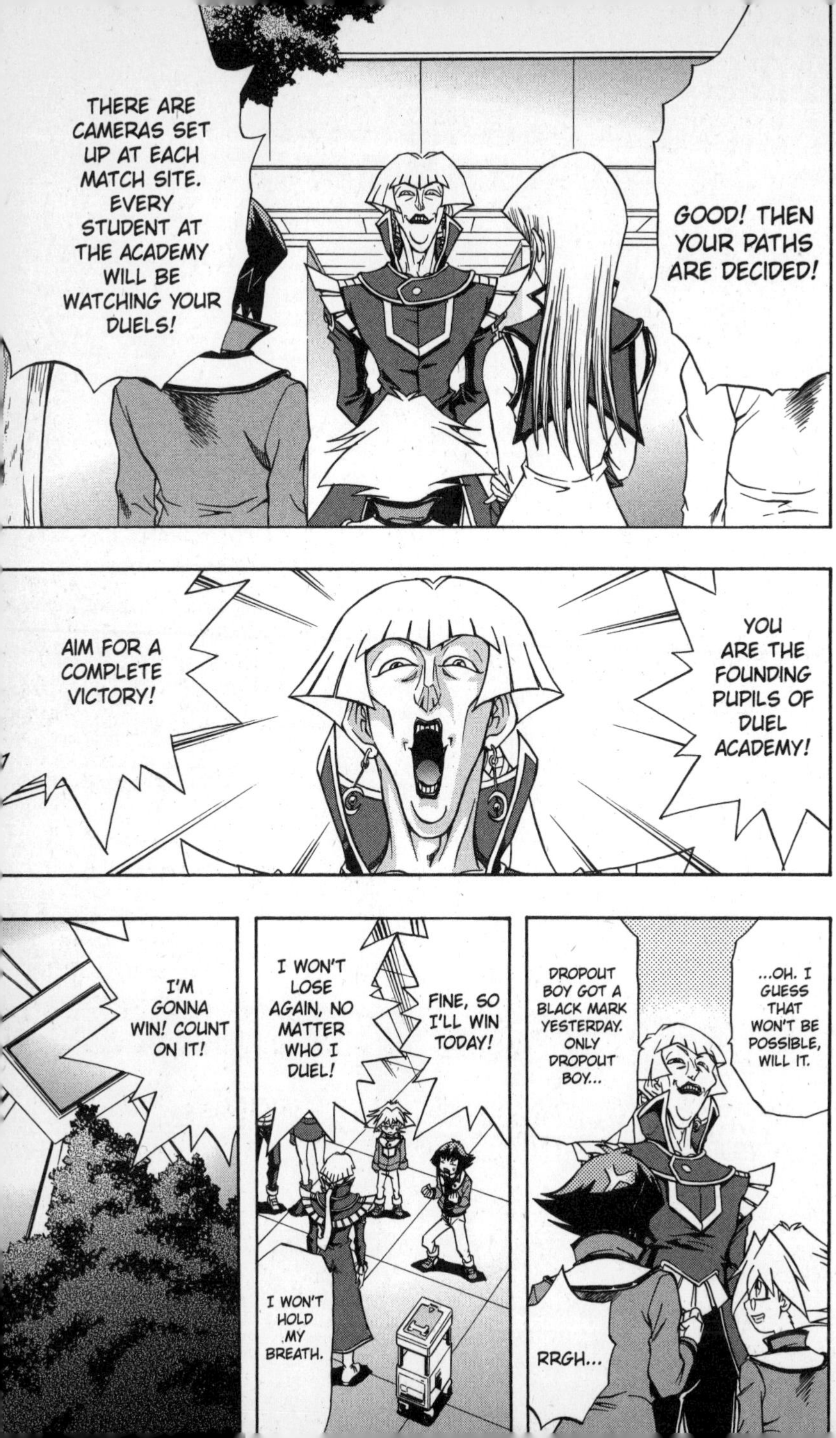
GOOD! THEN YOUR PATHS ARE DECIDED!
THERE ARE CAMERAS SET UP AT EACH MATCH SITE. EVERY STUDENT AT THE ACADEMY WILL BE WATCHING YOUR DUELS!
YOU ARE THE FOUNDING PUPILS OF DUEL ACADEMY!
AIM FOR A COMPLETE VICTORY!
...OH. I GUESS THAT WON'T BE POSSIBLE, WILL IT.
DROPOUT BOY GOT A BLACK MARK YESTERDAY. ONLY DROPOUT BOY...
RRGH...
FINE, SO I'LL WIN TODAY!
I WON'T LOSE AGAIN, NO MATTER WHO I DUEL!
I WON'T HOLD MY BREATH.
I'M GONNA WIN! COUNT ON IT!

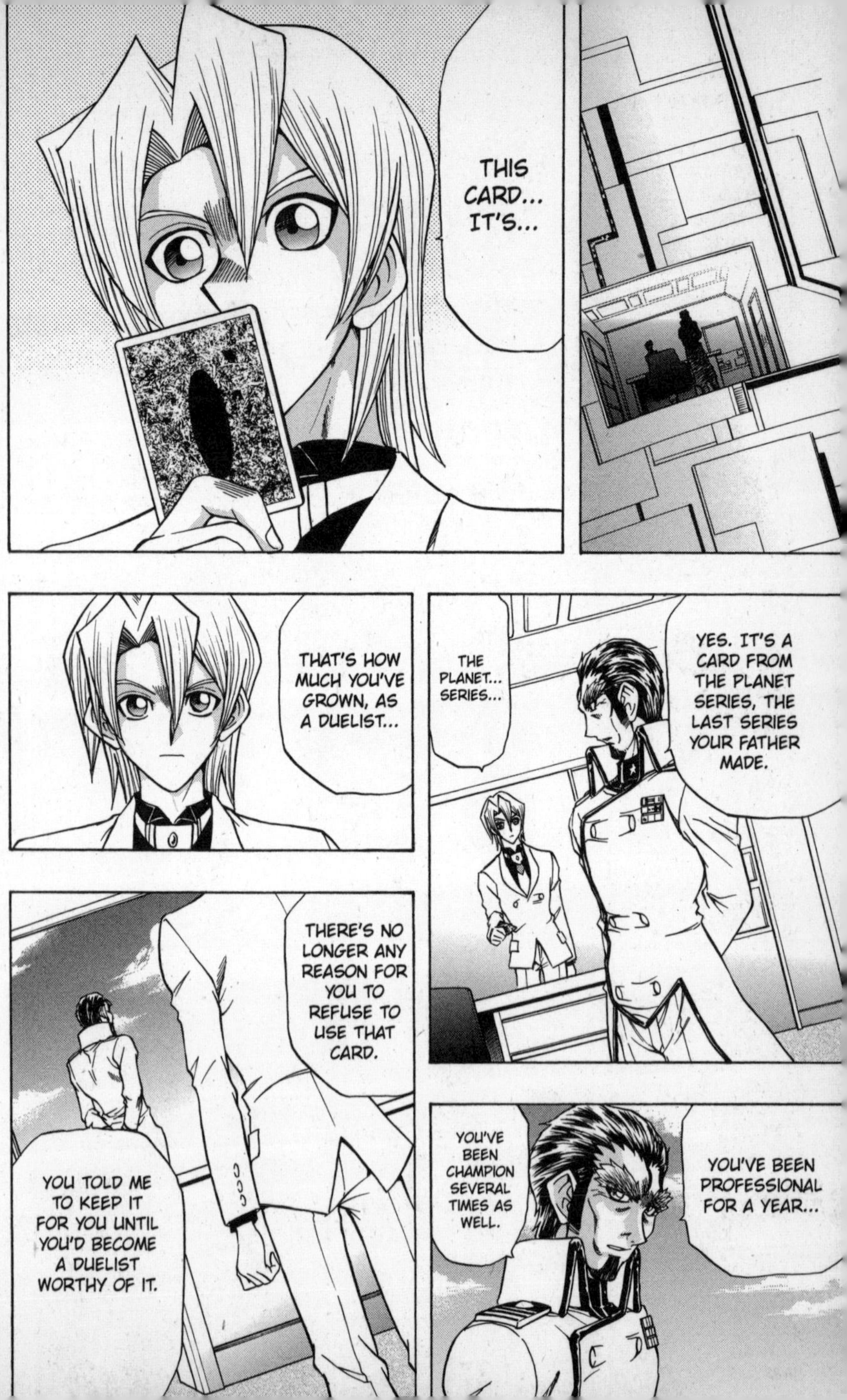
THIS CARD... IT'S...
YES. IT'S A CARD FROM THE PLANET SERIES, THE LAST SERIES YOUR FATHER MADE.
THE PLANET... SERIES...
THAT'S HOW MUCH YOU'VE GROWN, AS A DUELIST...
YOU'VE BEEN PROFESSIONAL FOR A YEAR...
YOU'VE BEEN CHAMPION SEVERAL TIMES AS WELL.
THERE'S NO LONGER ANY REASON FOR YOU TO REFUSE TO USE THAT CARD.
YOU TOLD ME TO KEEP IT FOR YOU UNTIL YOU'D BECOME A DUELIST WORTHY OF IT.

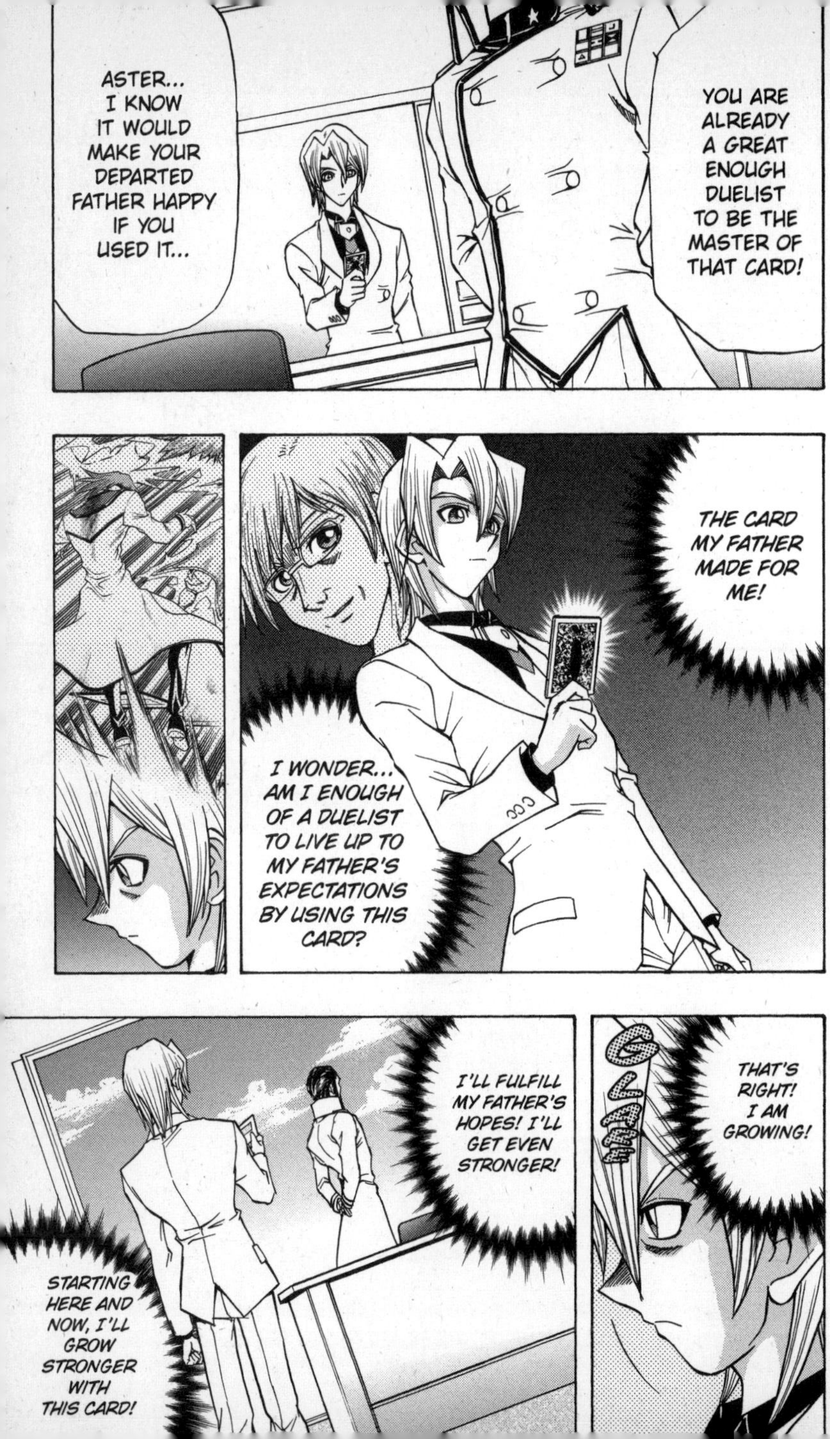
YOU ARE ALREADY A GREAT ENOUGH DUELIST TO BE THE MASTER OF THAT CARD!
ASTER... I KNOW IT WOULD MAKE YOUR DEPARTED FATHER HAPPY IF YOU USED IT...
THE CARD MY FATHER MADE FOR ME!
I WONDER... AM I ENOUGH OF A DUELIST TO LIVE UP TO MY FATHER'S EXPECTATIONS BY USING THIS CARD?
GLEAM
THAT'S RIGHT! I AM GROWING!
I'LL FULFILL MY FATHER'S HOPES! I'LL GET EVEN STRONGER!
STARTING HERE AND NOW, I'LL GROW STRONGER WITH THIS CARD!

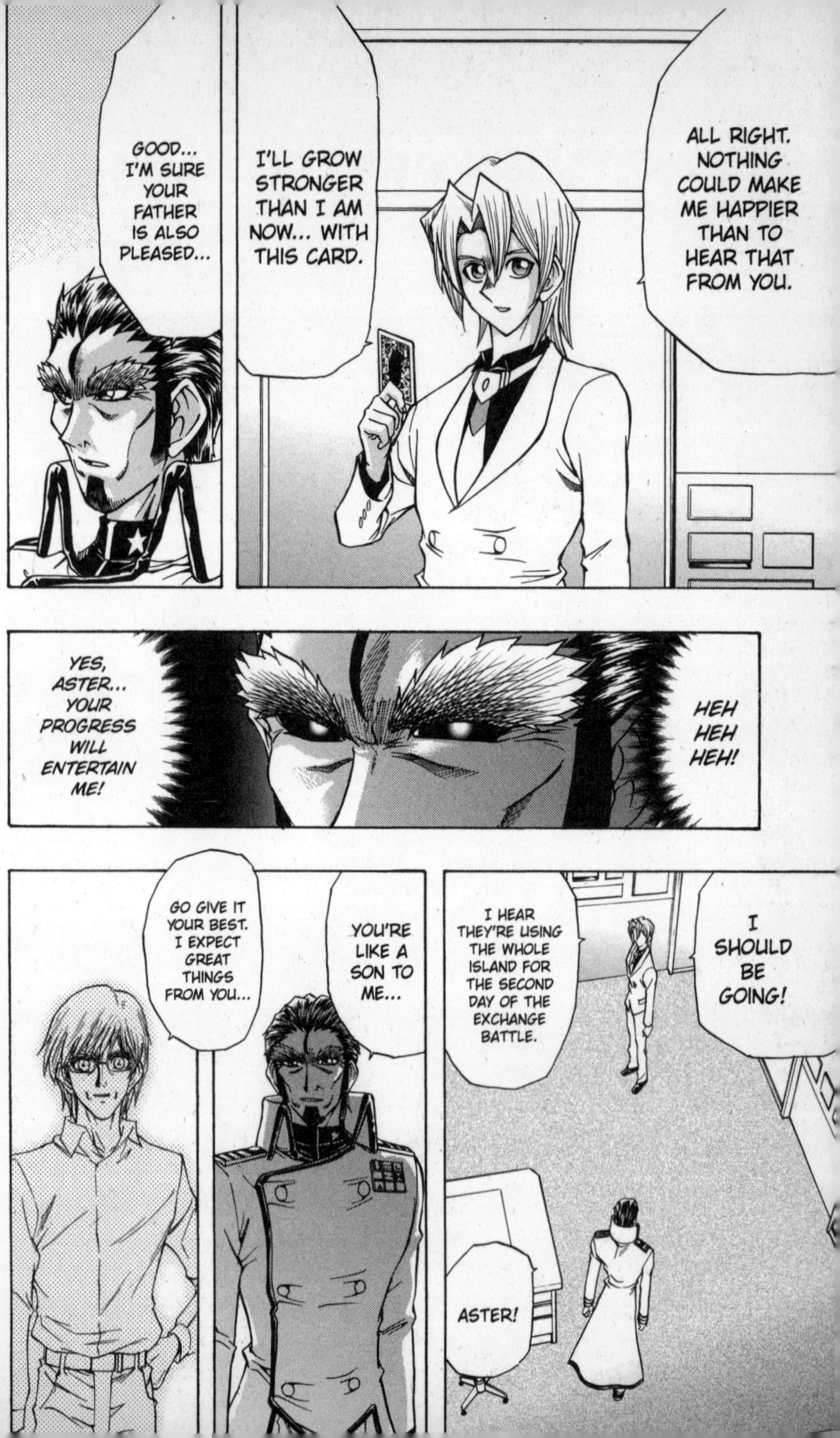
ALL RIGHT. NOTHING COULD MAKE ME HAPPIER THAN TO HEAR THAT FROM YOU.
I'LL GROW STRONGER THAN I AM NOW... WITH THIS CARD.
GOOD... I'M SURE YOUR FATHER IS ALSO PLEASED...
YES, ASTER... YOUR PROGRESS WILL ENTERTAIN ME!
HEH HEH HEH!
I SHOULD BE GOING!
I HEAR THEY'RE USING THE WHOLE ISLAND FOR THE SECOND DAY OF THE EXCHANGE BATTLE.
ASTER!
YOU'RE LIKE A SON TO ME...
GO GIVE IT YOUR BEST. I EXPECT GREAT THINGS FROM YOU...

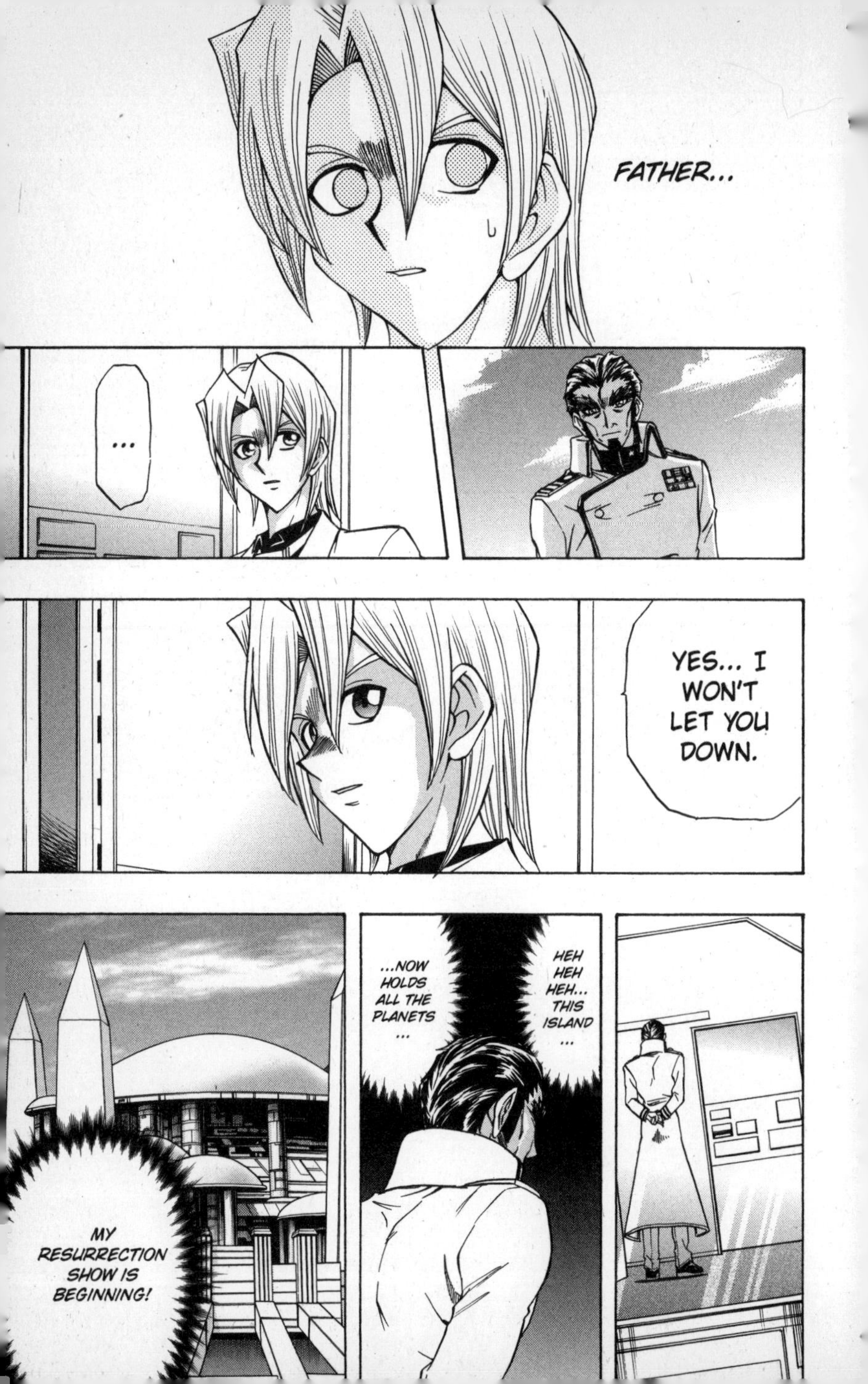
FATHER...
...
YES... I WON'T LET YOU DOWN.
HEH HEH HEH... THIS ISLAND ...
...NOW HOLDS ALL THE PLANETS ...
MY RESURRECTION SHOW IS BEGINNING!

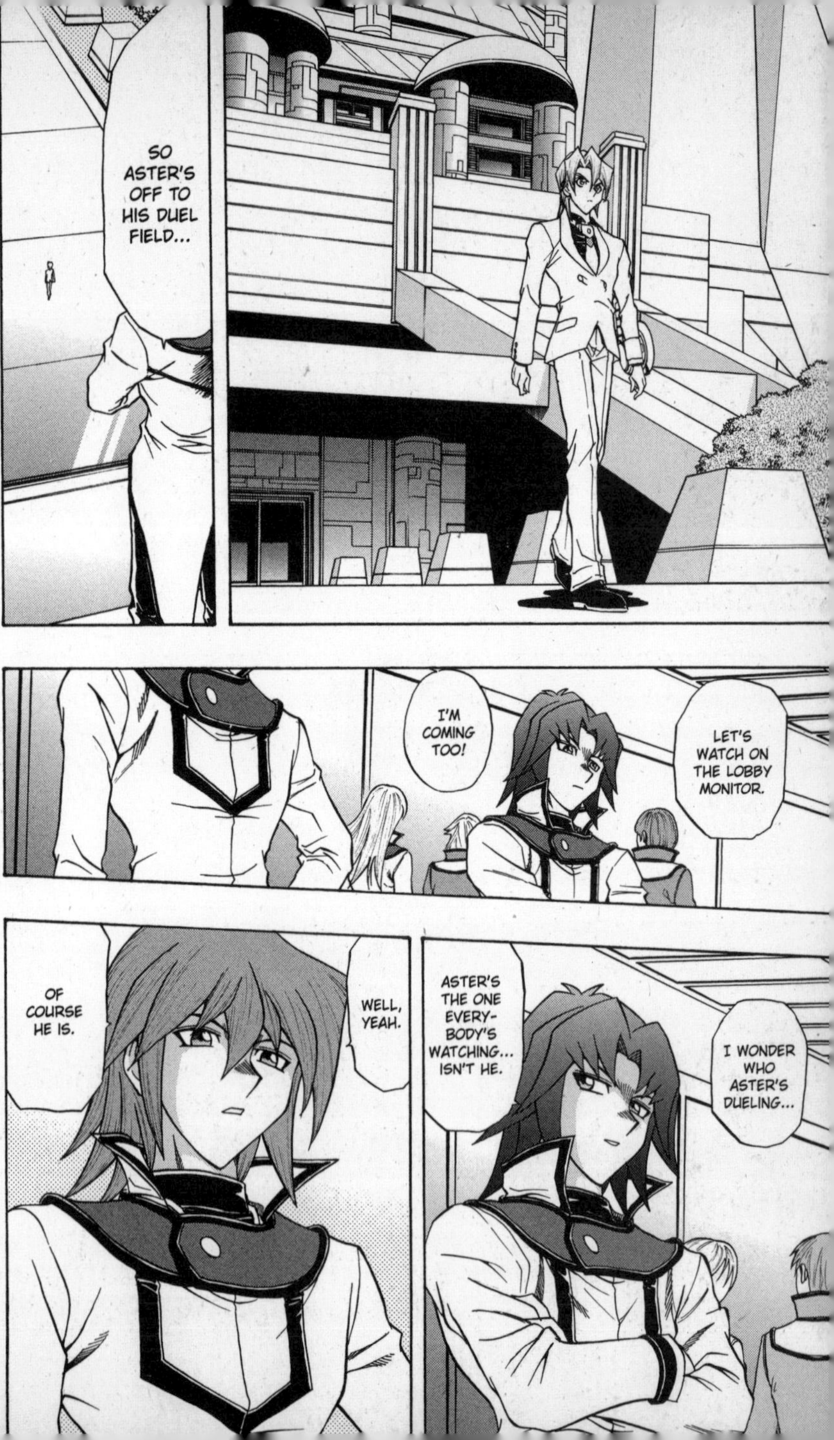
SO ASTER'S OFF TO HIS DUEL FIELD...
LET'S WATCH ON THE LOBBY MONITOR.
I'M COMING TOO!
I WONDER WHO ASTER'S DUELING...
ASTER'S THE ONE EVERY-BODY'S WATCHING... ISN'T HE.
WELL, YEAH.
OF COURSE HE IS.

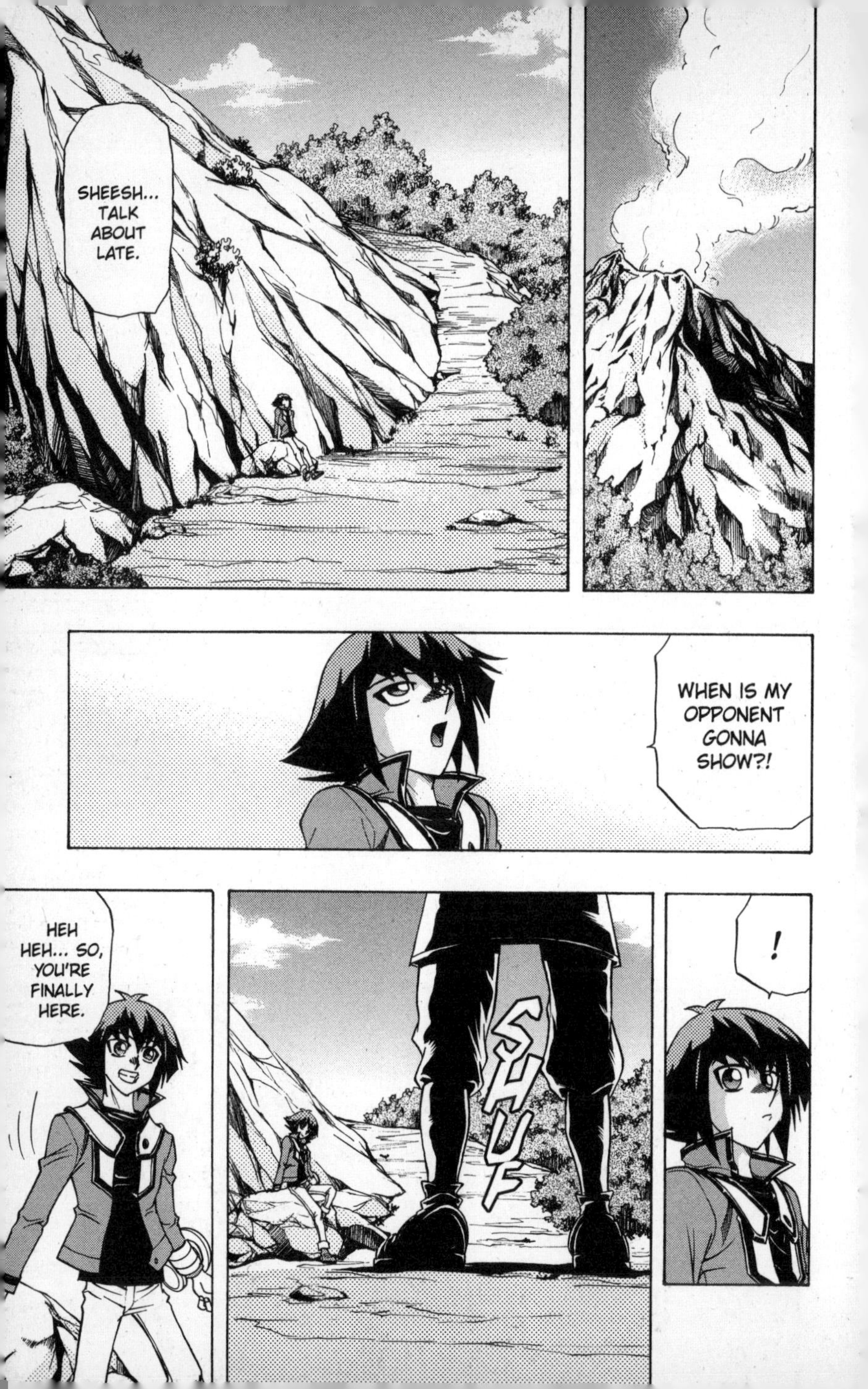
SHEESH... TALK ABOUT LATE.
WHEN IS MY OPPONENT GONNA SHOW?!
!
SHUF
HEH HEH... SO, YOU'RE FINALLY HERE.

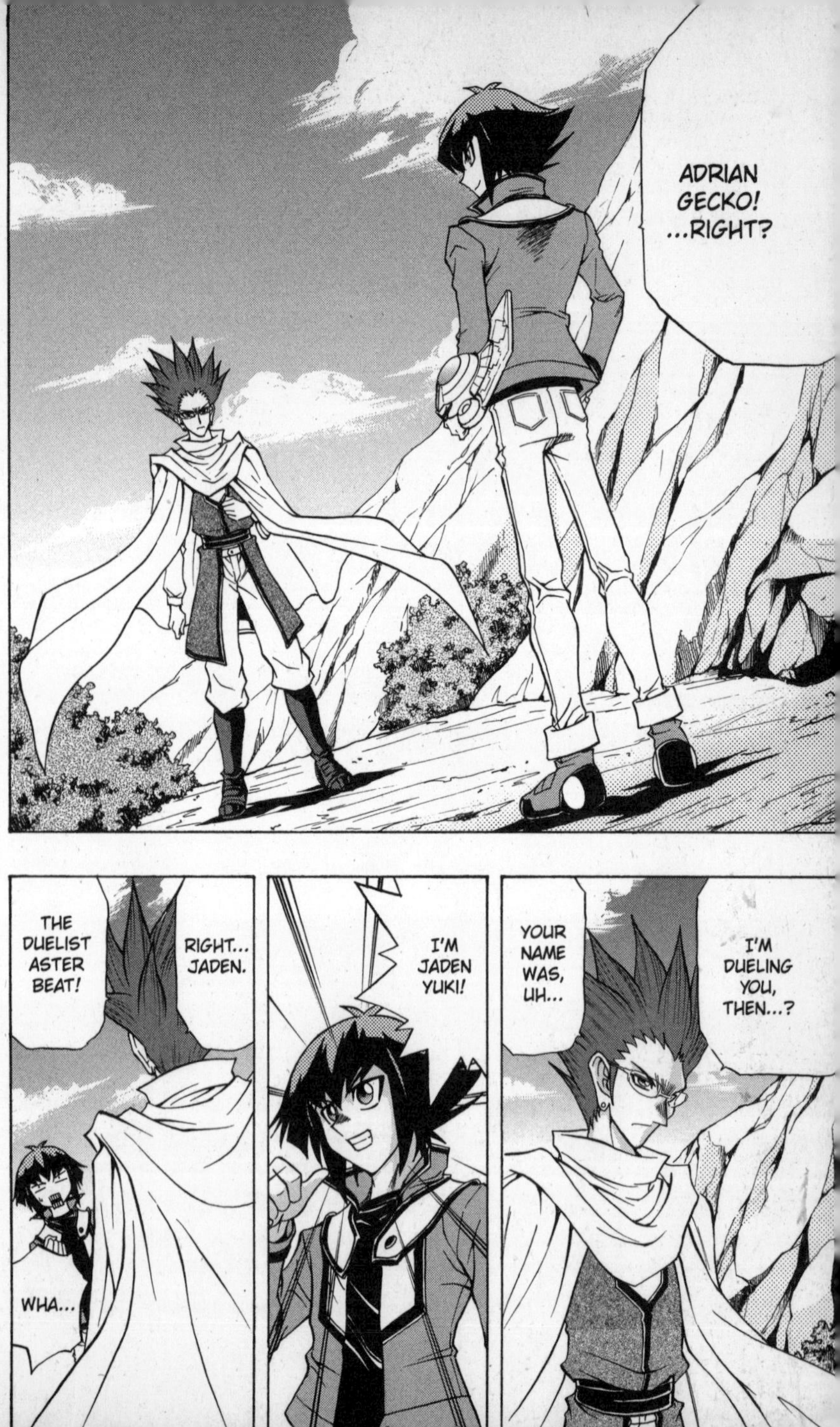
ADRIAN GECKO! ...RIGHT?
I'M DUELING YOU, THEN...?
YOUR NAME WAS, UH...
I'M JADEN YUKI!
RIGHT... JADEN.
THE DUELIST ASTER BEAT!
WHA...

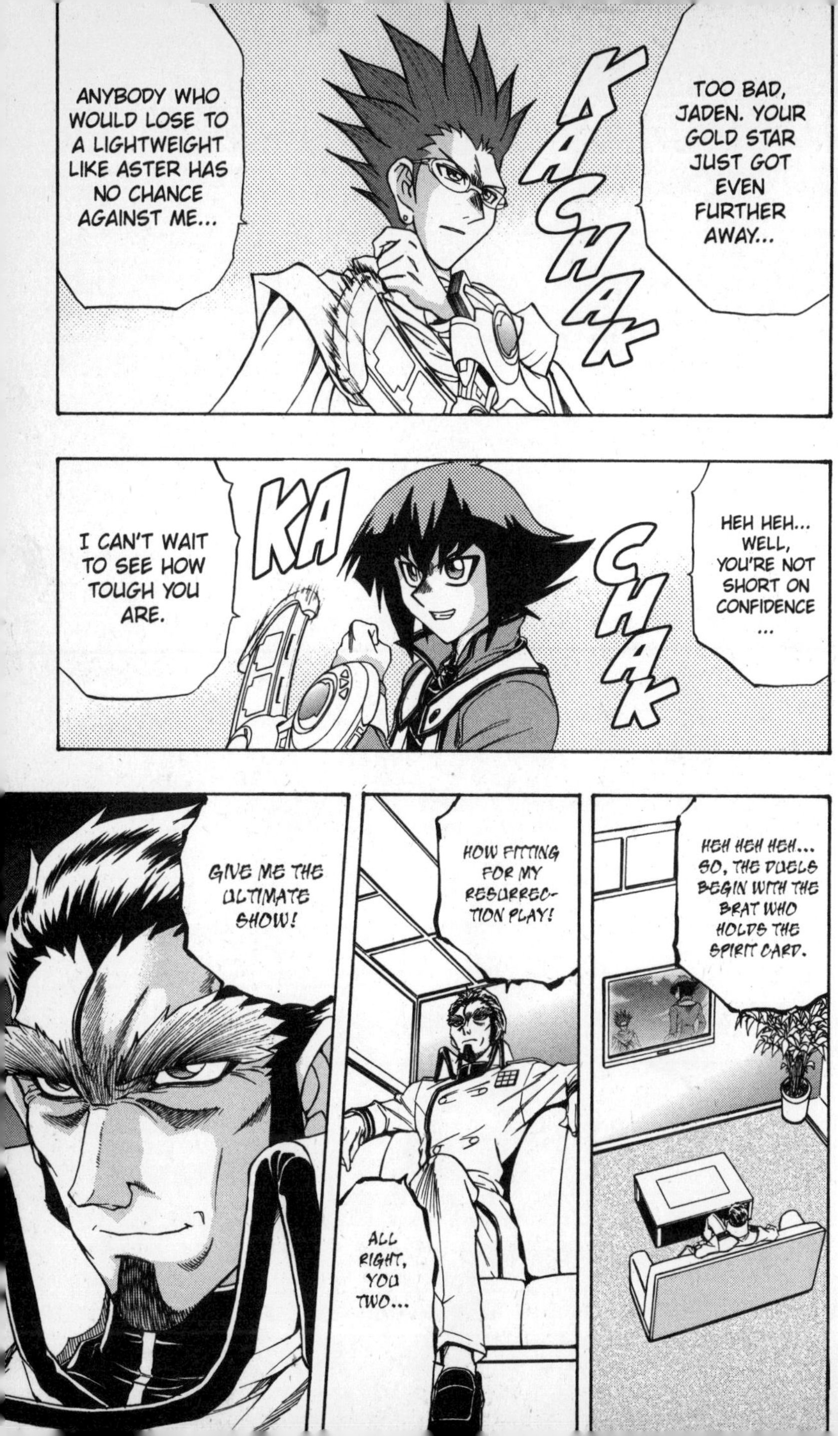
TOO BAD, JADEN. YOUR GOLD STAR JUST GOT EVEN FURTHER AWAY...
KACHAK
ANYBODY WHO WOULD LOSE TO A LIGHTWEIGHT LIKE ASTER HAS NO CHANCE AGAINST ME...
HEH HEH... WELL, YOU'RE NOT SHORT ON CONFIDENCE ...
KA
CHAK
I CAN'T WAIT TO SEE HOW TOUGH YOU ARE.
HEH HEH HEH... SO, THE DUELS BEGIN WITH THE BRAT WHO HOLDS THE SPIRIT CARD.
HOW FITTING FOR MY RESURREC-TION PLAY!
ALL RIGHT, YOU TWO...
GIVE ME THE ULTIMATE SHOW!

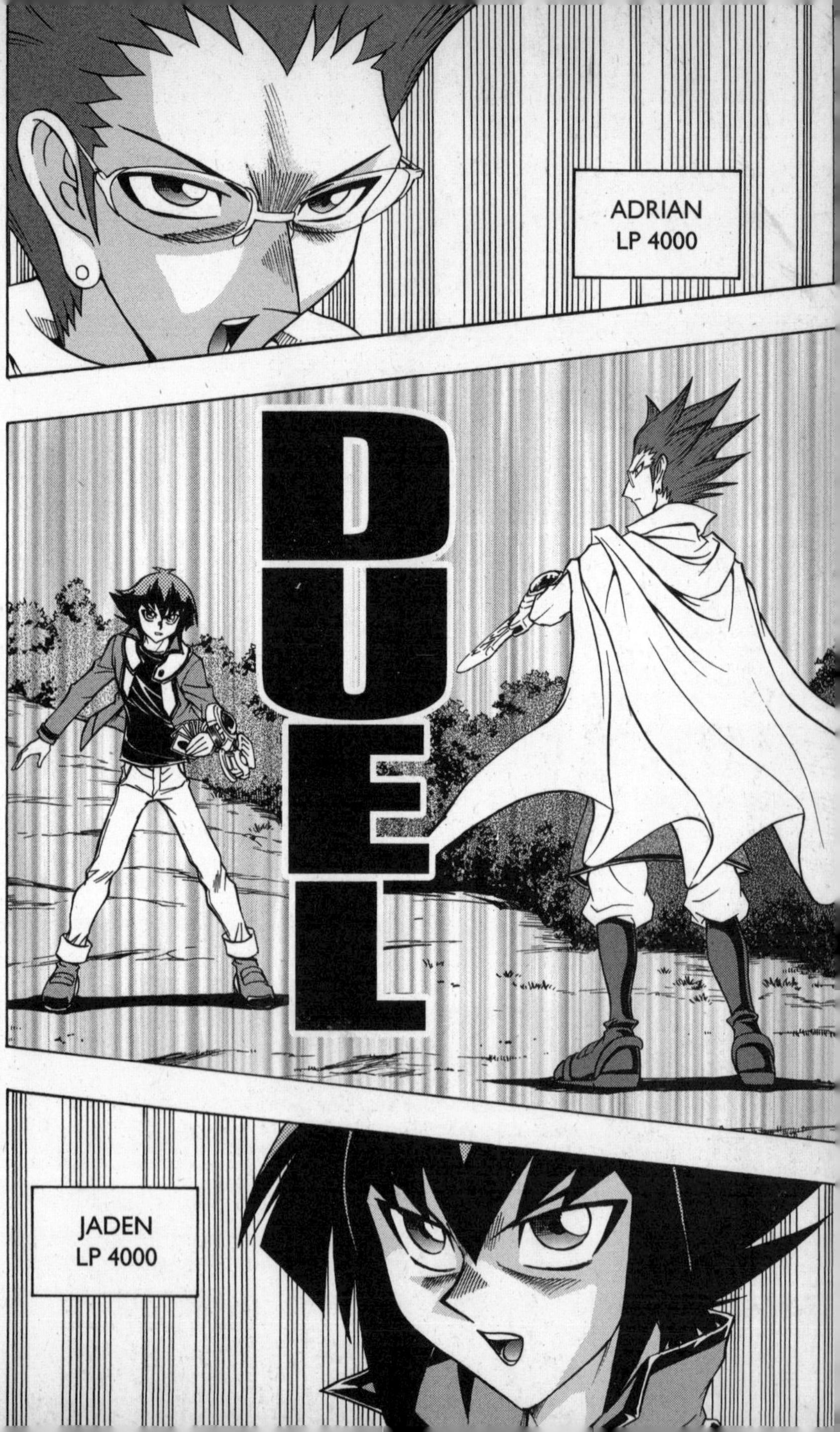
ADRIAN
LP 4000
DUEL
JADEN
LP 4000

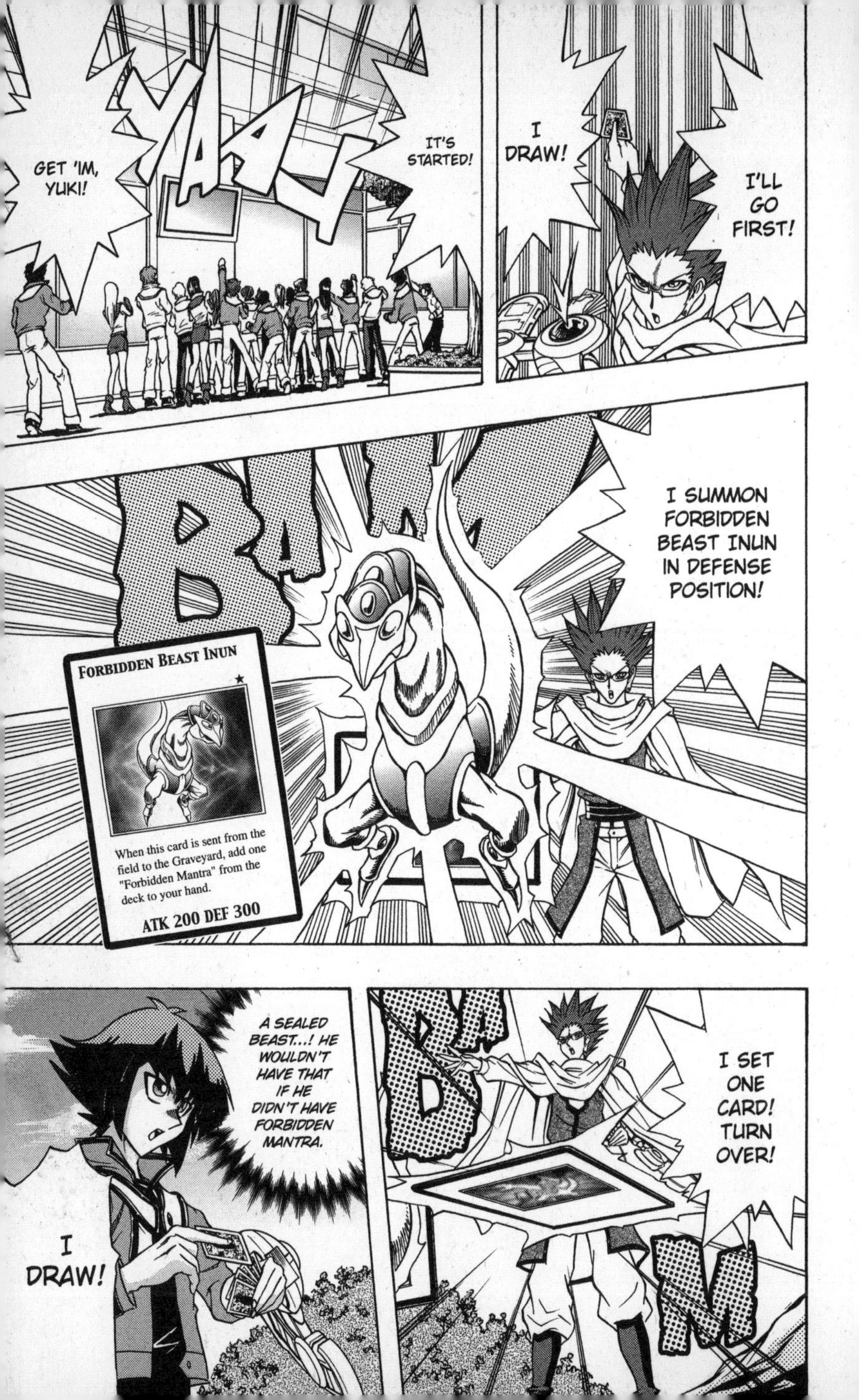
I DRAW!
I'LL GO FIRST!
IT'S STARTED!
YAAY
GET 'IM, YUKI!
I SUMMON FORBIDDEN BEAST INUN IN DEFENSE POSITION!
BAM
FORBIDDEN BEAST INUN
When this card is sent from the field to the Graveyard, add one "Forbidden Mantra" from the deck to your hand.
ATK 200 DEF 300
I SET ONE CARD! TURN OVER!
BAM
A SEALED BEAST...! HE WOULDN'T HAVE THAT IF HE DIDN'T HAVE FORBIDDEN MANTRA.
I DRAW!

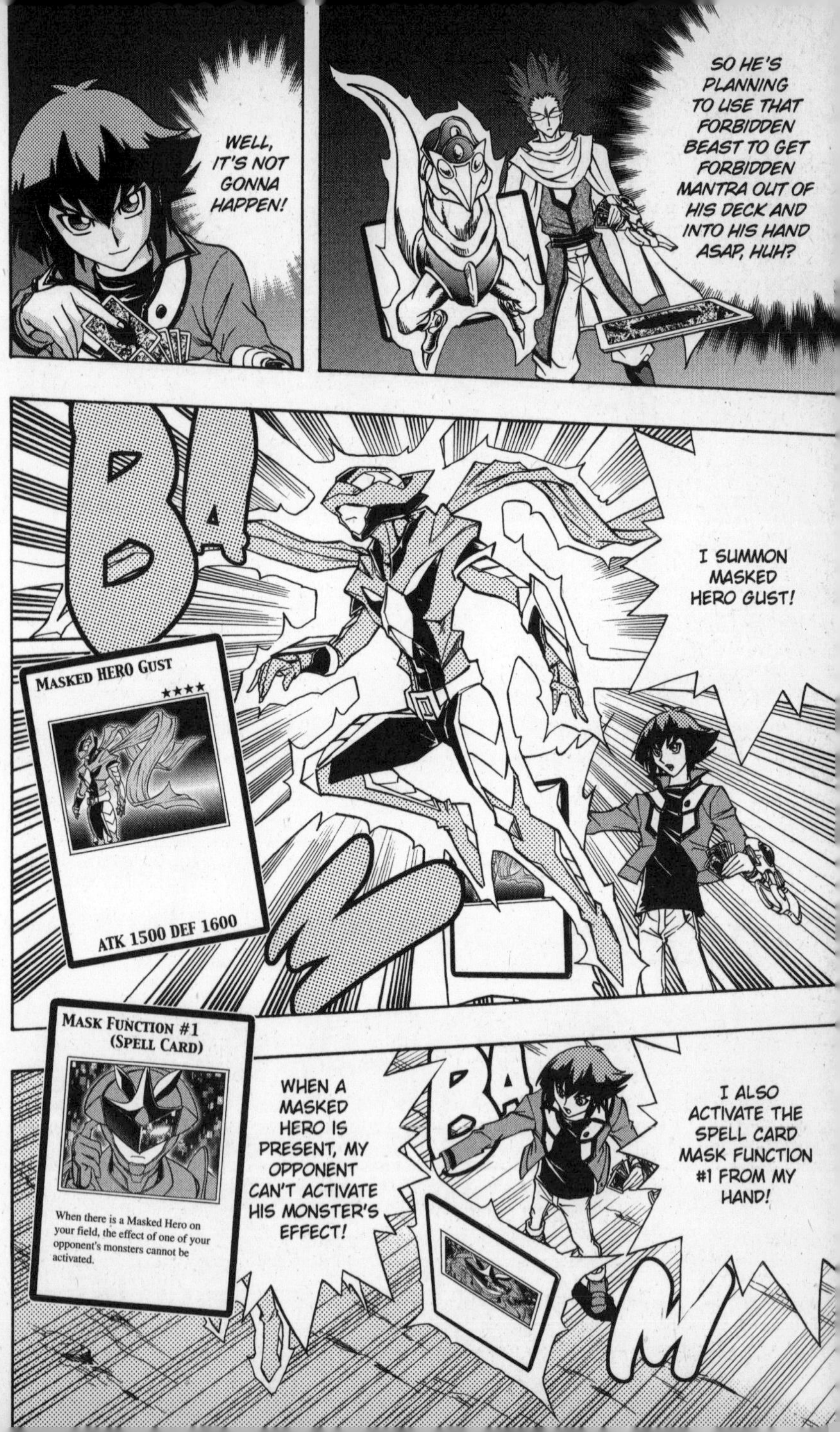
SO HE'S PLANNING TO USE THAT FORBIDDEN BEAST TO GET FORBIDDEN MANTRA OUT OF HIS DECK AND INTO HIS HAND ASAP, HUH?
WELL, IT'S NOT GONNA HAPPEN!
I SUMMON MASKED HERO GUST!
MASKED HERO GUST
★★★★
ATK 1500 DEF 1600
I ALSO ACTIVATE THE SPELL CARD MASK FUNCTION #1 FROM MY HAND!
WHEN A MASKED HERO IS PRESENT, MY OPPONENT CAN'T ACTIVATE HIS MONSTER'S EFFECT!
MASK FUNCTION #1 (SPELL CARD)
When there is a Masked Hero on your field, the effect of one of your opponent's monsters cannot be activated.

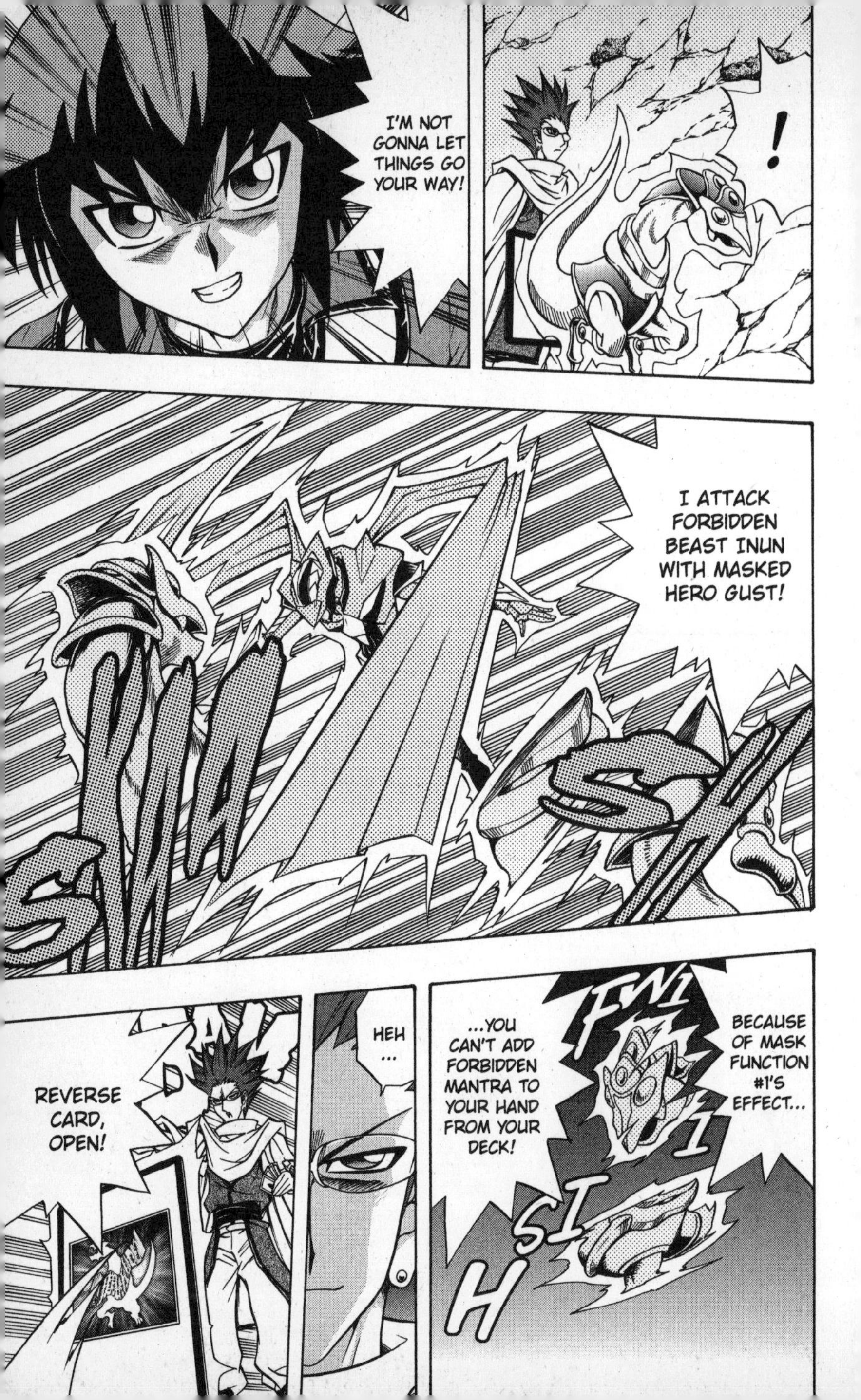
!
I'M NOT GONNA LET THINGS GO YOUR WAY!
I ATTACK FORBIDDEN BEAST INUN WITH MASKED HERO GUST!
BECAUSE OF MASK FUNCTION #1'S EFFECT...
...YOU CAN'T ADD FORBIDDEN MANTRA TO YOUR HAND FROM YOUR DECK!
HEH ...
REVERSE CARD, OPEN!

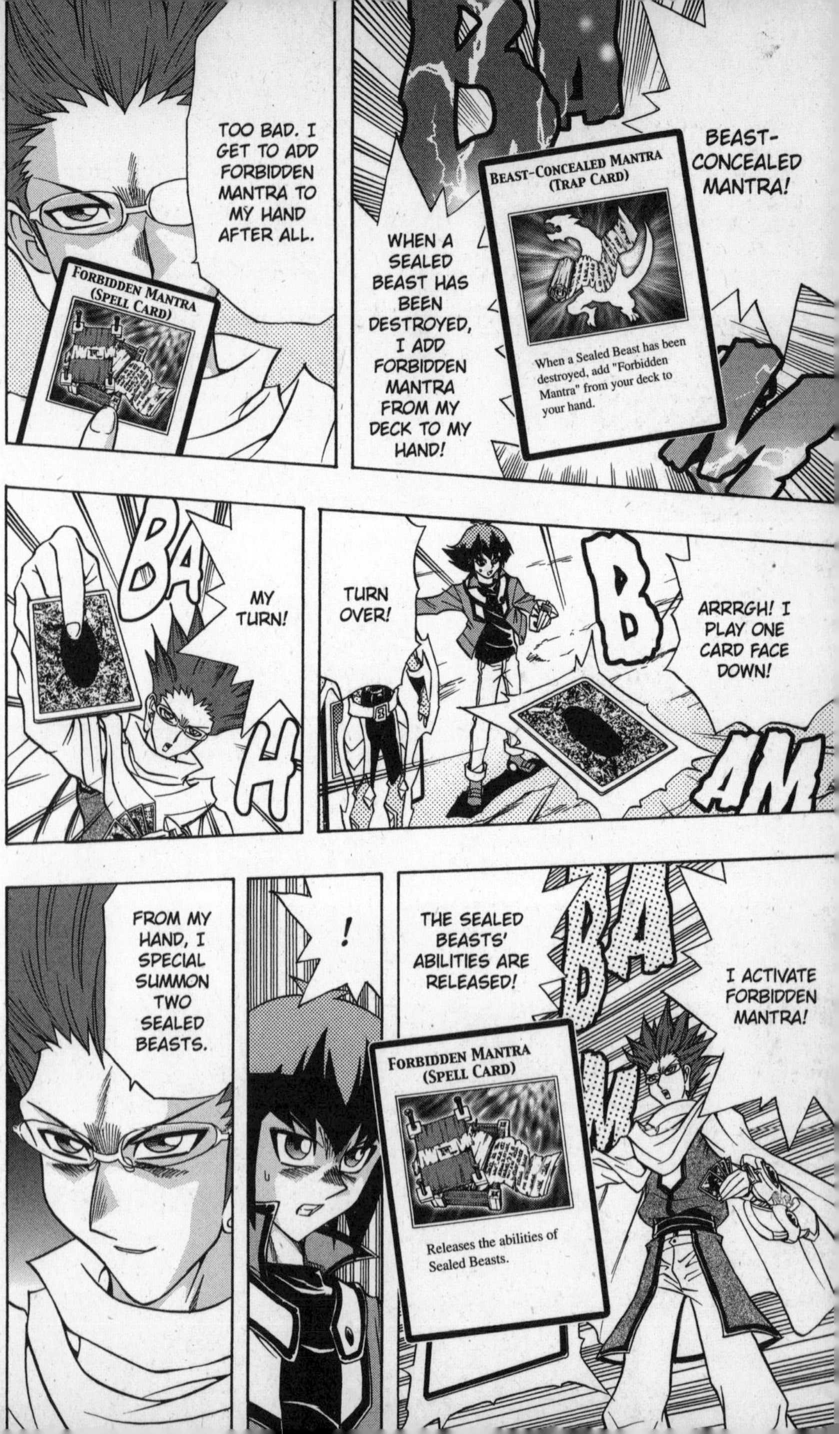
BA
BEAST-CONCEALED MANTRA!
BEAST-CONCEALED MANTRA (TRAP CARD)
When a Sealed Beast has been destroyed, add "Forbidden Mantra" from your deck to your hand.
WHEN A SEALED BEAST HAS BEEN DESTROYED, I ADD FORBIDDEN MANTRA FROM MY DECK TO MY HAND!
TOO BAD. I GET TO ADD FORBIDDEN MANTRA TO MY HAND AFTER ALL.
FORBIDDEN MANTRA (SPELL CARD)
ARRRGH! I PLAY ONE CARD FACE DOWN!
B
AM
TURN OVER!
MY TURN!
BA
H
I ACTIVATE FORBIDDEN MANTRA!
BA
THE SEALED BEASTS' ABILITIES ARE RELEASED!
FORBIDDEN MANTRA (SPELL CARD)
Releases the abilities of Sealed Beasts.
!
FROM MY HAND, I SPECIAL SUMMON TWO SEALED BEASTS.

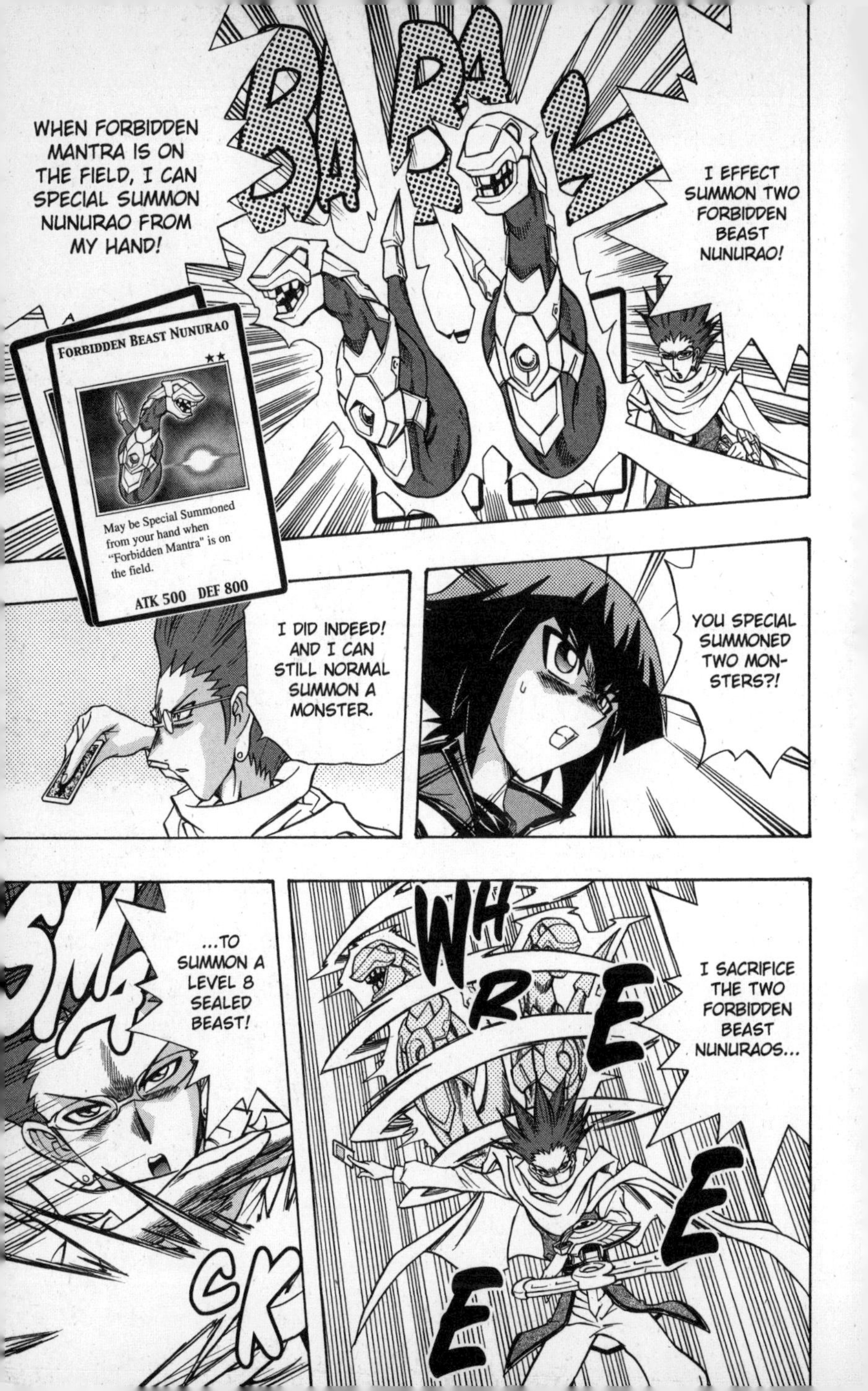
I EFFECT SUMMON TWO FORBIDDEN BEAST NUNURAO!
WHEN FORBIDDEN MANTRA IS ON THE FIELD, I CAN SPECIAL SUMMON NUNURAO FROM MY HAND!
FORBIDDEN BEAST NUNURAO
May be Special Summoned from your hand when "Forbidden Mantra" is on the field.
ATK 500 DEF 800
YOU SPECIAL SUMMONED TWO MONSTERS?!
I DID INDEED! AND I CAN STILL NORMAL SUMMON A MONSTER.
I SACRIFICE THE TWO FORBIDDEN BEAST NUNURAOS...
...TO SUMMON A LEVEL 8 SEALED BEAST!

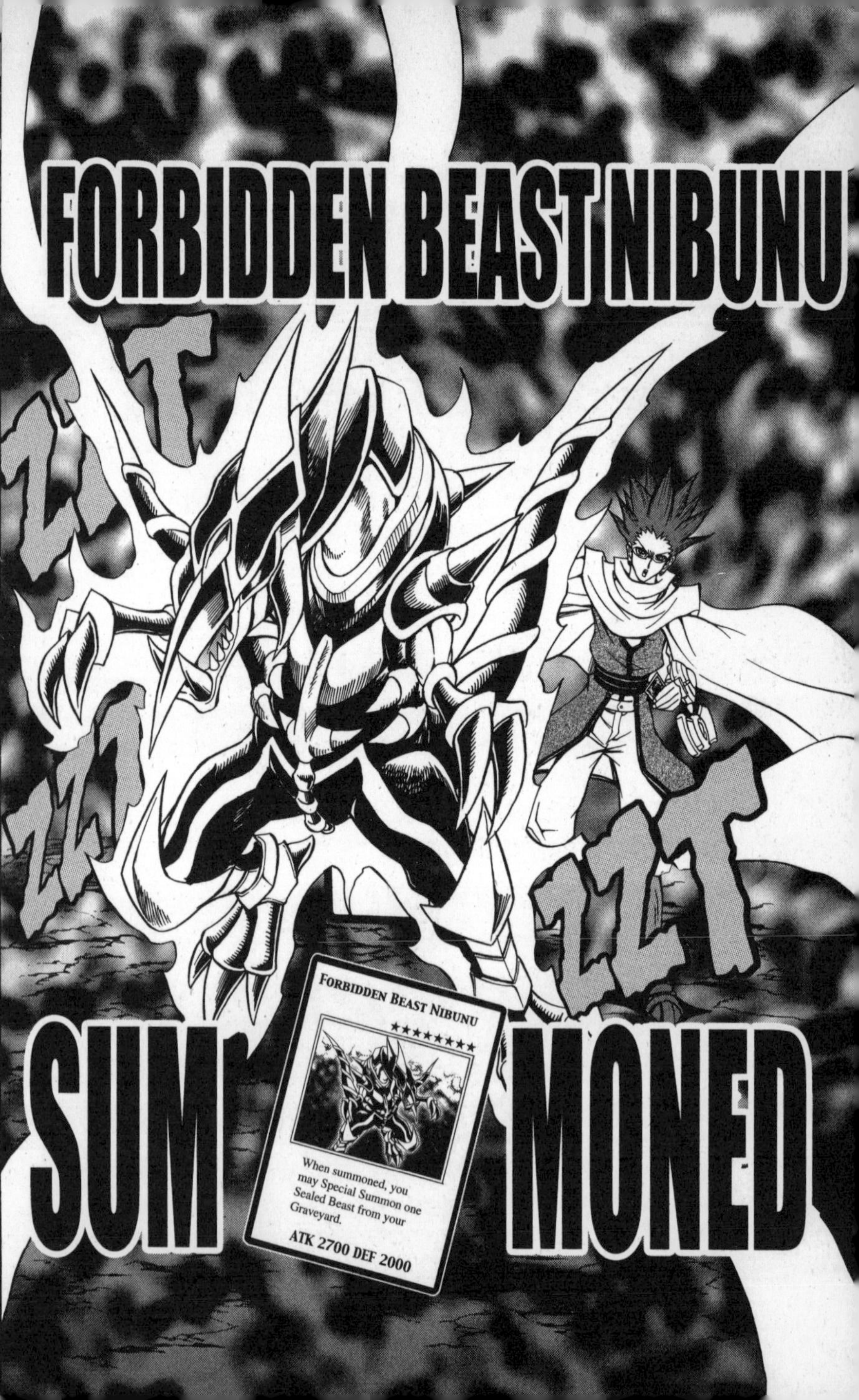
FORBIDDEN BEAST NIBUNU
ZZT
ZZT
ZZT
SUMMONED
FORBIDDEN BEAST NIBUNU
When summoned, you may Special Summon one Sealed Beast from your Graveyard.
ATK 2700 DEF 2000

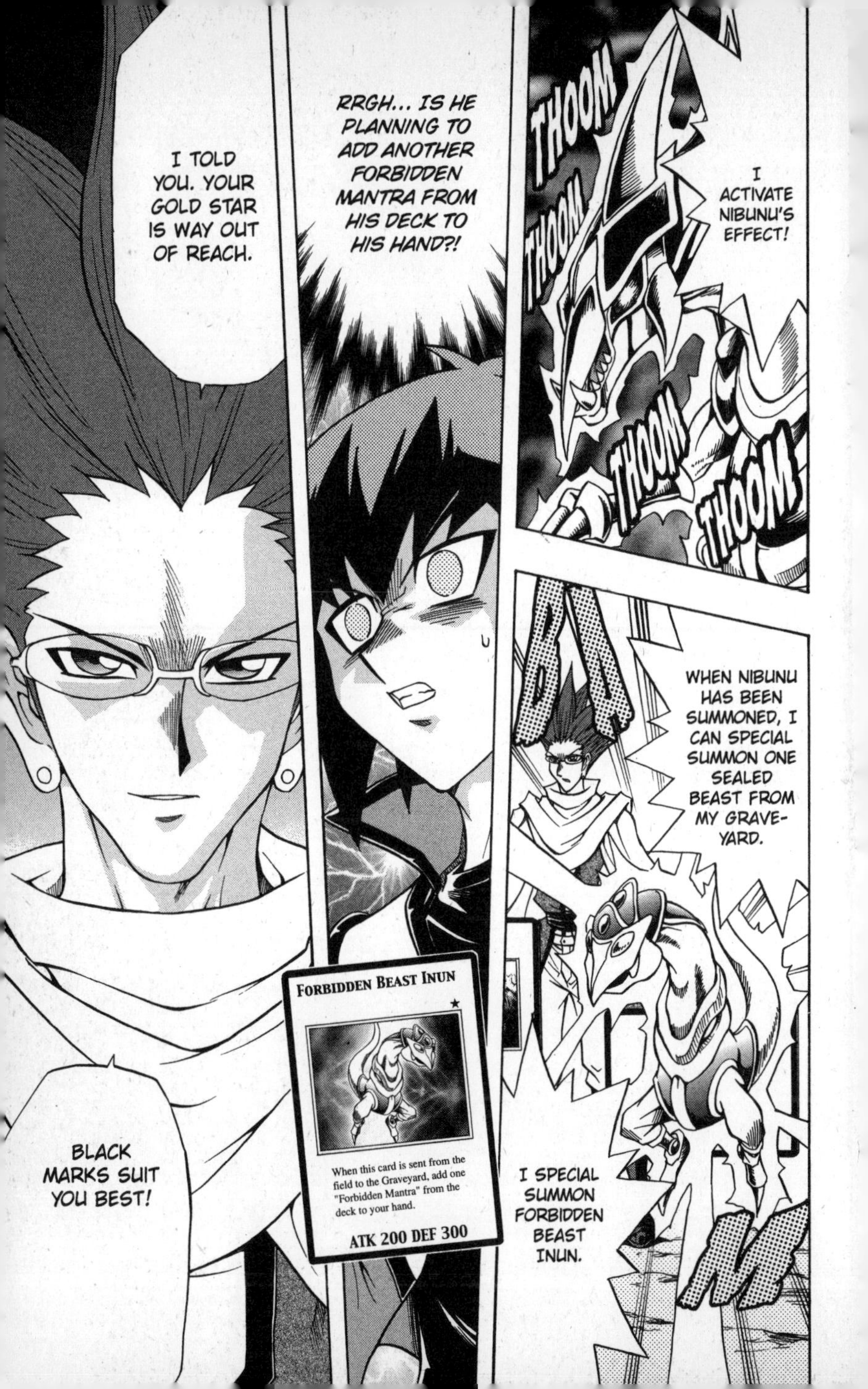
I ACTIVATE NIBUNU'S EFFECT!
THOOM
THOOM
THOOM
THOOM
BA
WHEN NIBUNU HAS BEEN SUMMONED, I CAN SPECIAL SUMMON ONE SEALED BEAST FROM MY GRAVEYARD.
I SPECIAL SUMMON FORBIDDEN BEAST INUN.
RRGH... IS HE PLANNING TO ADD ANOTHER FORBIDDEN MANTRA FROM HIS DECK TO HIS HAND?!
FORBIDDEN BEAST INUN
When this card is sent from the field to the Graveyard, add one "Forbidden Mantra" from the deck to your hand.
ATK 200 DEF 300
I TOLD YOU. YOUR GOLD STAR IS WAY OUT OF REACH.
BLACK MARKS SUIT YOU BEST!

TALK SHOW!

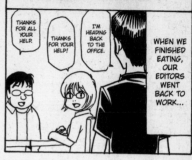

WHEN WE FINISHED EATING, OUR EDITORS WENT BACK TO WORK...
I'M HEADING BACK TO THE OFFICE.
THANKS FOR YOUR HELP!
THANKS FOR ALL YOUR HELP.
...BUT WE WEREN'T THROUGH YET.
YOU'VE STILL GOT TIME, RIGHT?
OH... SURE...
ISHIZUKA-SAN HADN'T CHATTED ENOUGH YET...
...SO SHE ASKED ME OUT FOR A CUP OF COFFEE AT A NEARBY COFFEE SHOP.
WE TALKED FOR THREE HOURS ON ONE CUP OF COFFEE EACH!
ENDLESS STREAM OF ALL SORTS OF TOPICS
OF THAT TIME, TWO HOURS AND FORTY MINUTES WAS A YUKO ISHIZUKA 2 "TALK SHOW".

I DID HAVE A LOT OF FUN.

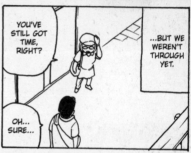

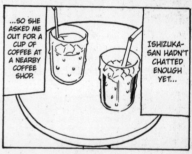

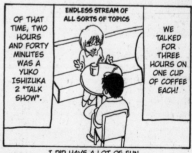

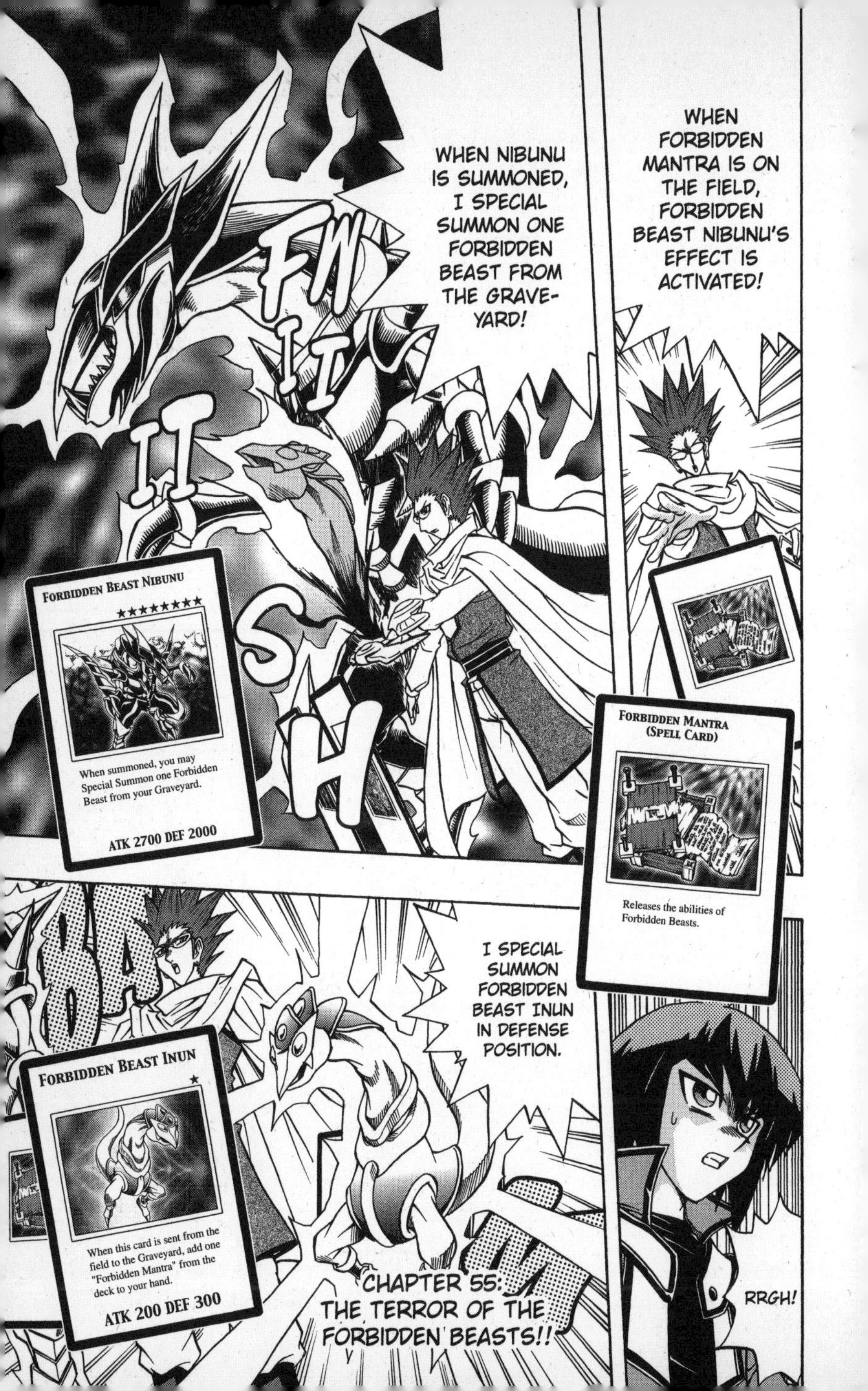
WHEN FORBIDDEN MANTRA IS ON THE FIELD, FORBIDDEN BEAST NIBUNU'S EFFECT IS ACTIVATED!
FORBIDDEN MANTRA (SPELL CARD)
Releases the abilities of Forbidden Beasts.
WHEN NIBUNU IS SUMMONED, I SPECIAL SUMMON ONE FORBIDDEN BEAST FROM THE GRAVEYARD!
FWIIII
FORBIDDEN BEAST NIBUNU
When summoned, you may Special Summon one Forbidden Beast from your Graveyard.
ATK 2700 DEF 2000
RRGH!
I SPECIAL SUMMON FORBIDDEN BEAST INUN IN DEFENSE POSITION.
FORBIDDEN BEAST INUN
When this card is sent from the field to the Graveyard, add one "Forbidden Mantra" from the deck to your hand.
ATK 200 DEF 300
CHAPTER 55: THE TERROR OF THE FORBIDDEN BEASTS!!

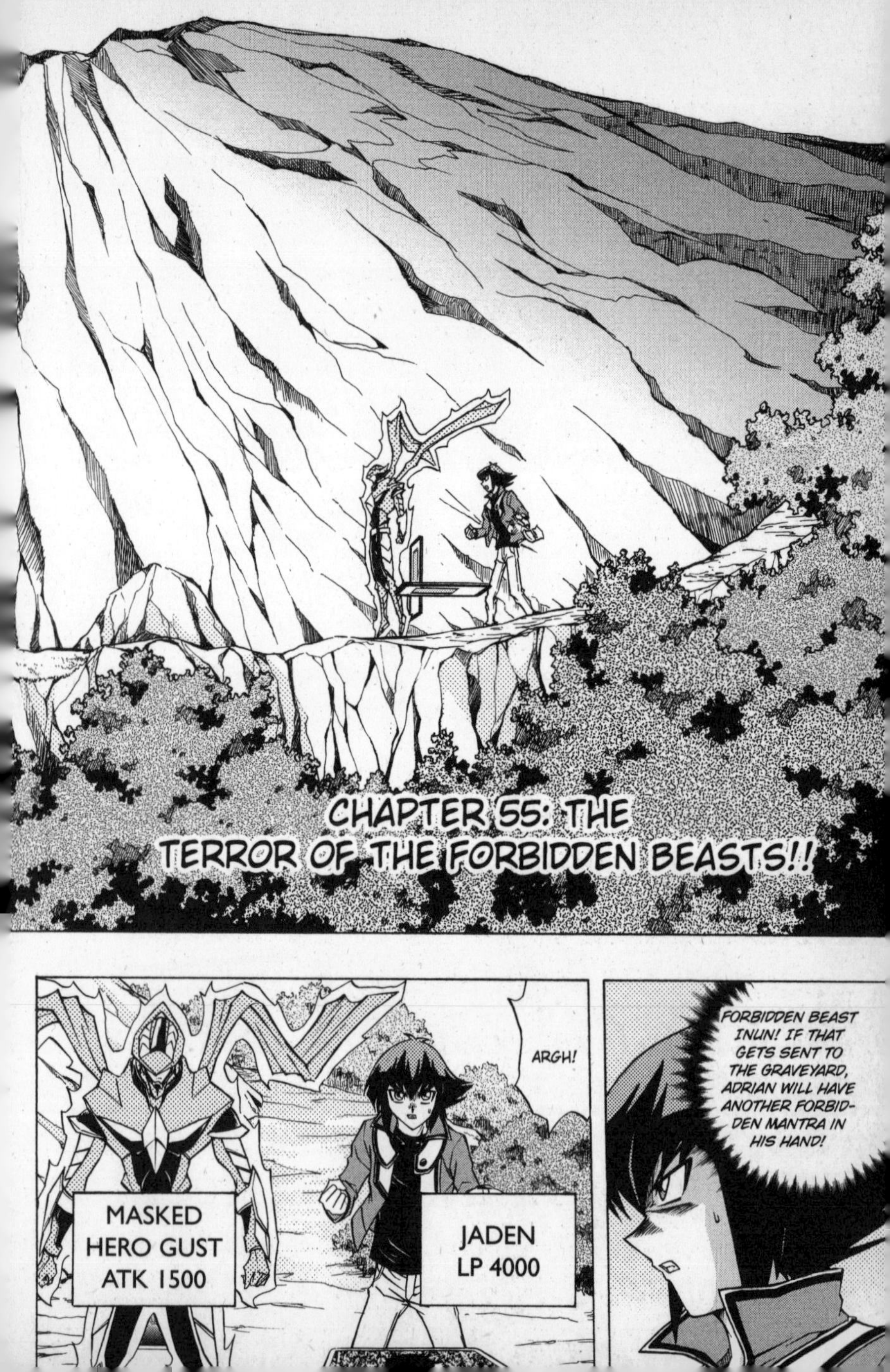
CHAPTER 55: THE
TERROR OF THE FORBIDDEN BEASTS!!
FORBIDDEN BEAST INUN! IF THAT GETS SENT TO THE GRAVEYARD, ADRIAN WILL HAVE ANOTHER FORBID-DEN MANTRA IN HIS HAND!
ARGH!
JADEN LP 4000
MASKED HERO GUST ATK 1500

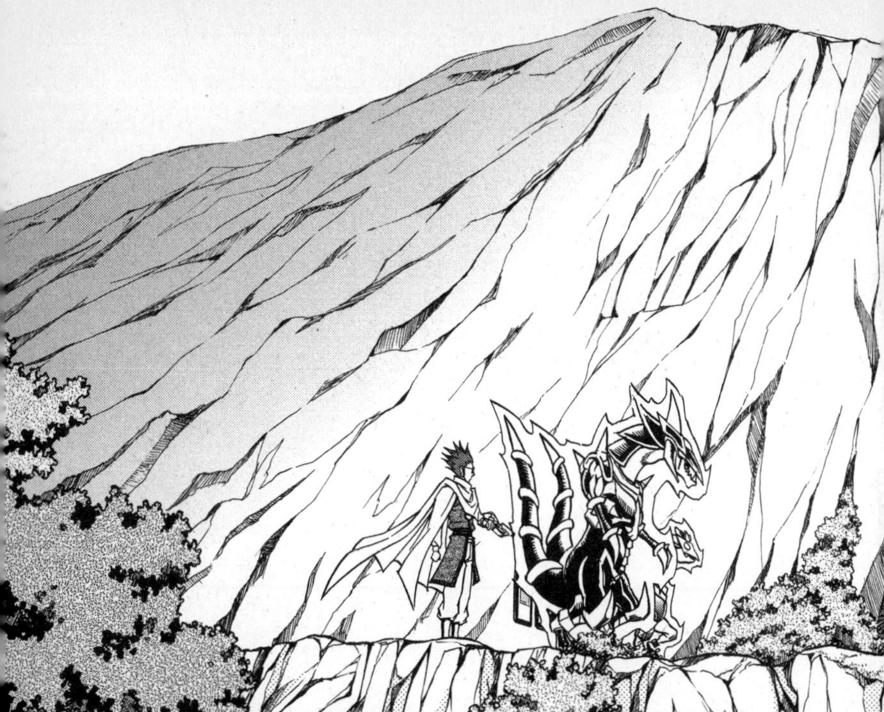

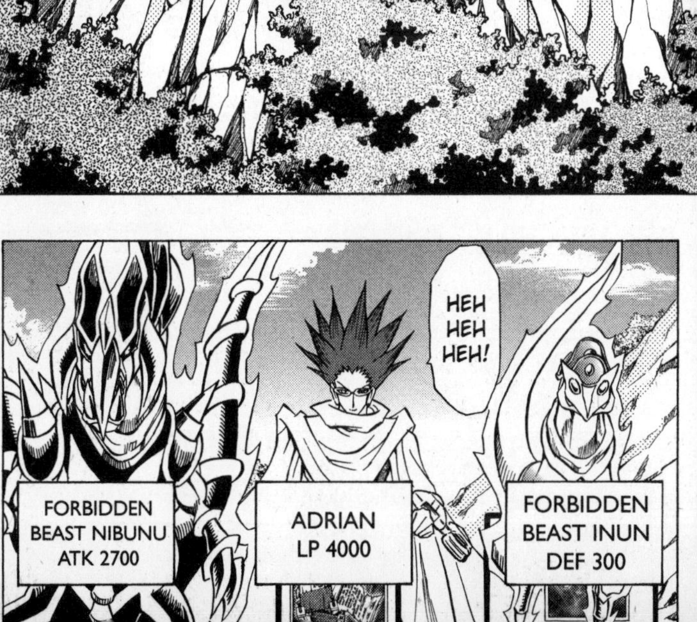
HEH HEH HEH!
FORBIDDEN BEAST INUN DEF 300
ADRIAN LP 4000
FORBIDDEN BEAST NIBUNU ATK 2700

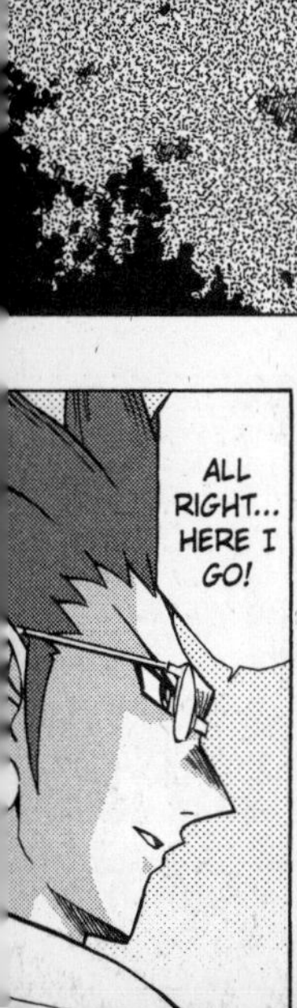
ALL RIGHT... HERE I GO!

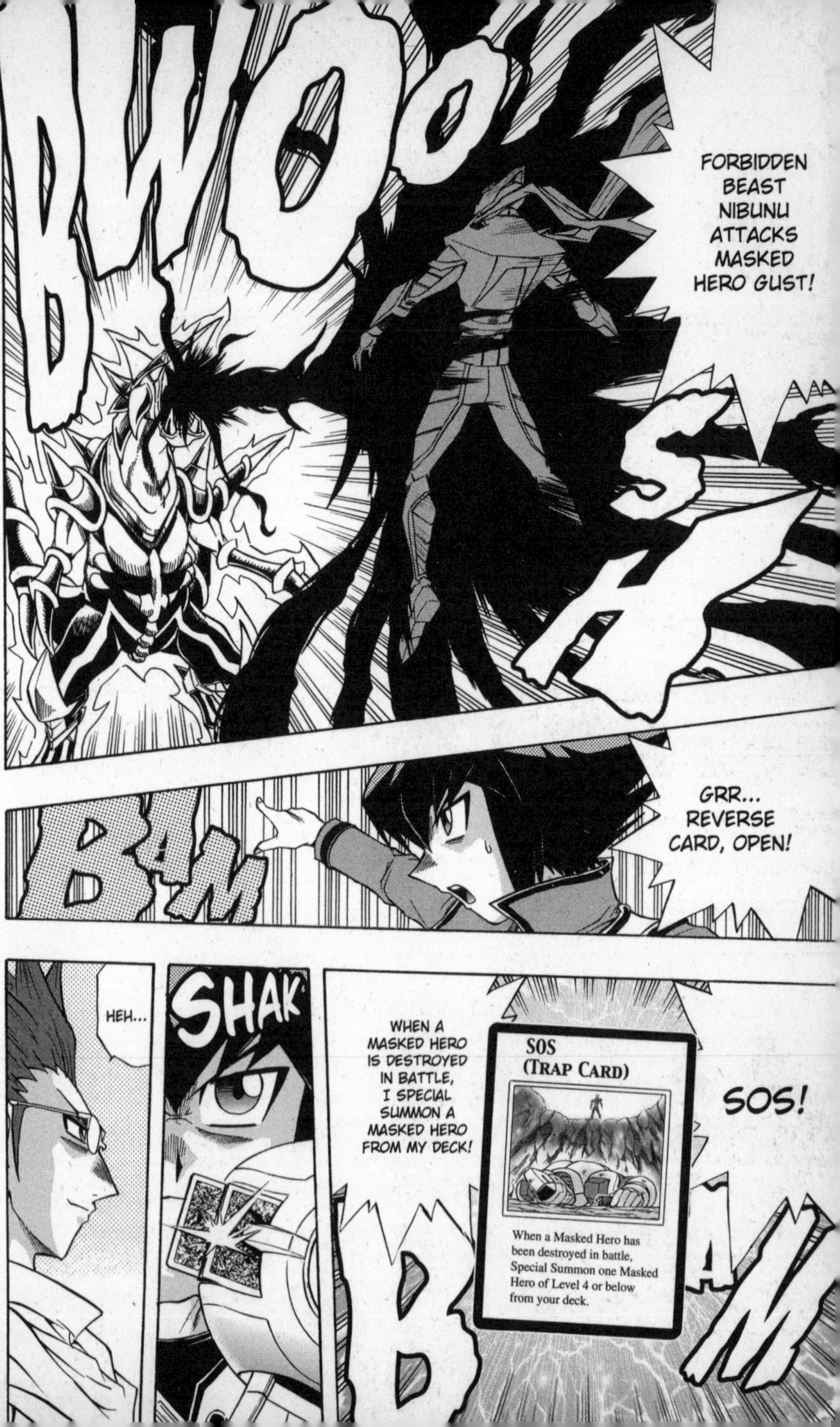
FORBIDDEN BEAST NIBUNU ATTACKS MASKED HERO GUST!
GRR... REVERSE CARD, OPEN!
BAM
SOS!
SOS
(TRAP CARD)
When a Masked Hero has been destroyed in battle, Special Summon one Masked Hero of Level 4 or below from your deck.
WHEN A MASKED HERO IS DESTROYED IN BATTLE, I SPECIAL SUMMON A MASKED HERO FROM MY DECK!
BAM
SHAK
HEH...

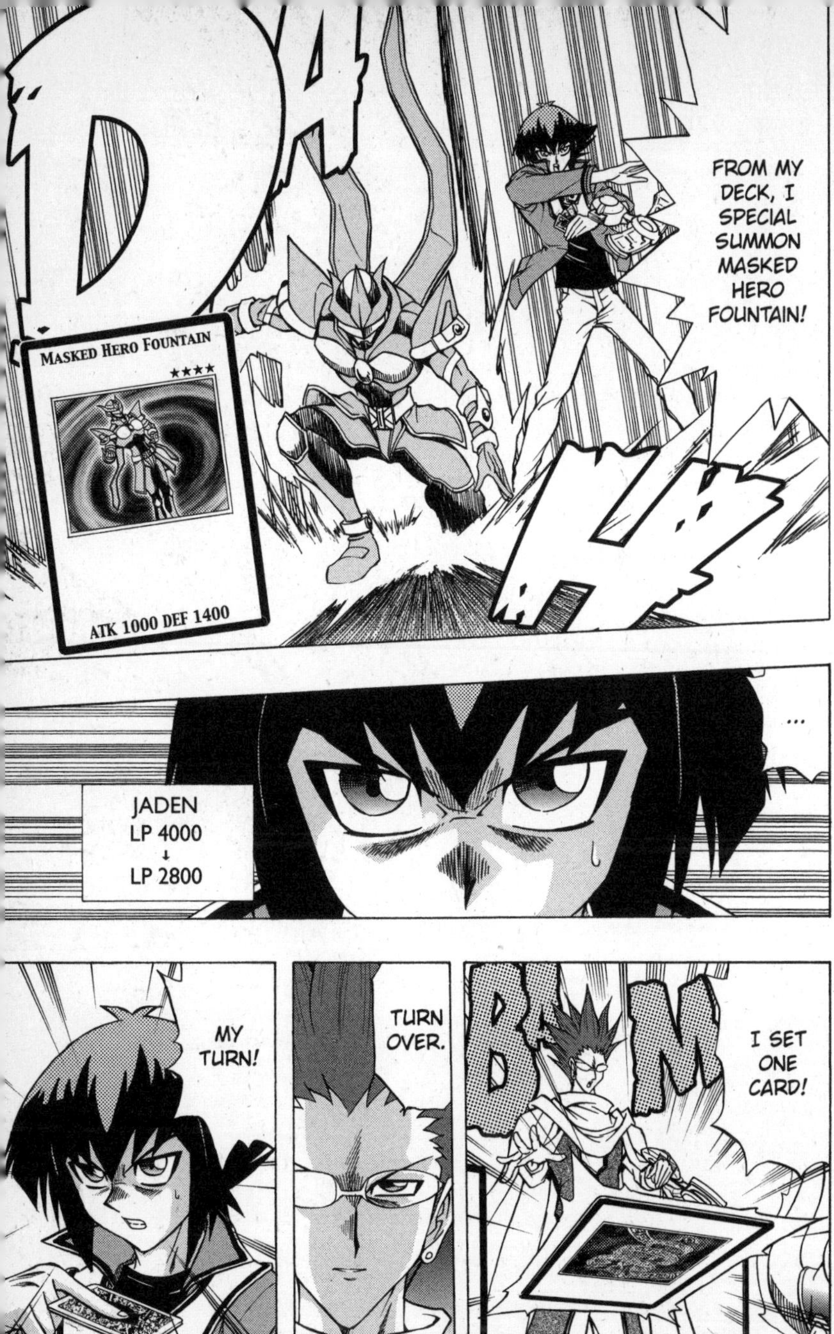
FROM MY DECK, I SPECIAL SUMMON MASKED HERO FOUNTAIN!
Masked Hero Fountain
ATK 1000 DEF 1400
...
JADEN
LP 4000
↓
LP 2800
I SET ONE CARD!
TURN OVER.
MY TURN!

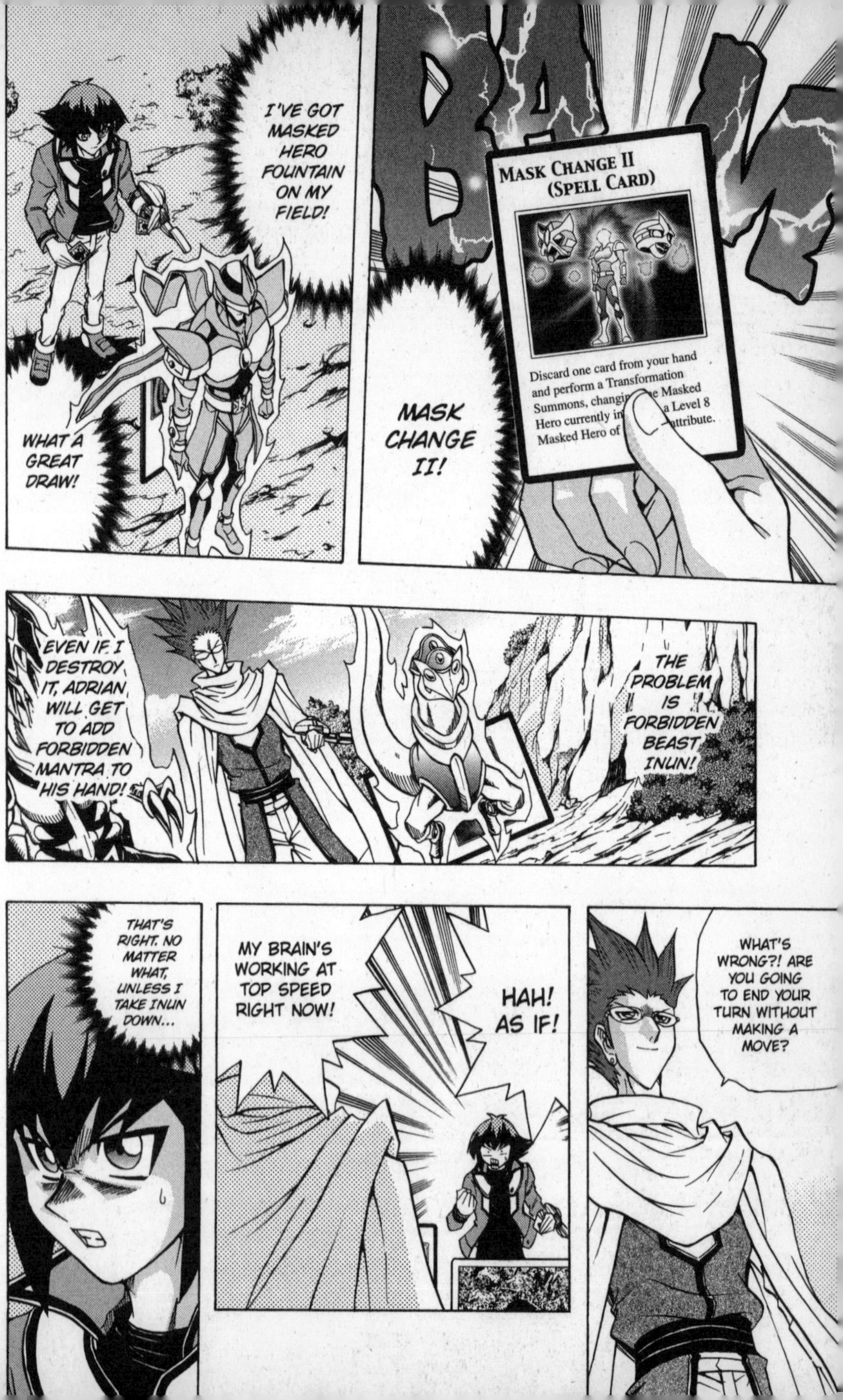
MASK CHANGE II
(SPELL CARD)
Discard one card from your hand and perform a Transformation Summons, changin e Masked Hero currently in a Level 8 Masked Hero of attribute.
MASK CHANGE II!
I'VE GOT MASKED HERO FOUNTAIN ON MY FIELD!
WHAT A GREAT DRAW!
THE PROBLEM IS FORBIDDEN BEAST INUN!
EVEN IF I DESTROY IT, ADRIAN WILL GET TO ADD FORBIDDEN MANTRA TO HIS HAND!
WHAT'S WRONG?! ARE YOU GOING TO END YOUR TURN WITHOUT MAKING A MOVE?
HAH! AS IF!
MY BRAIN'S WORKING AT TOP SPEED RIGHT NOW!
THAT'S RIGHT. NO MATTER WHAT, UNLESS I TAKE INUN DOWN...

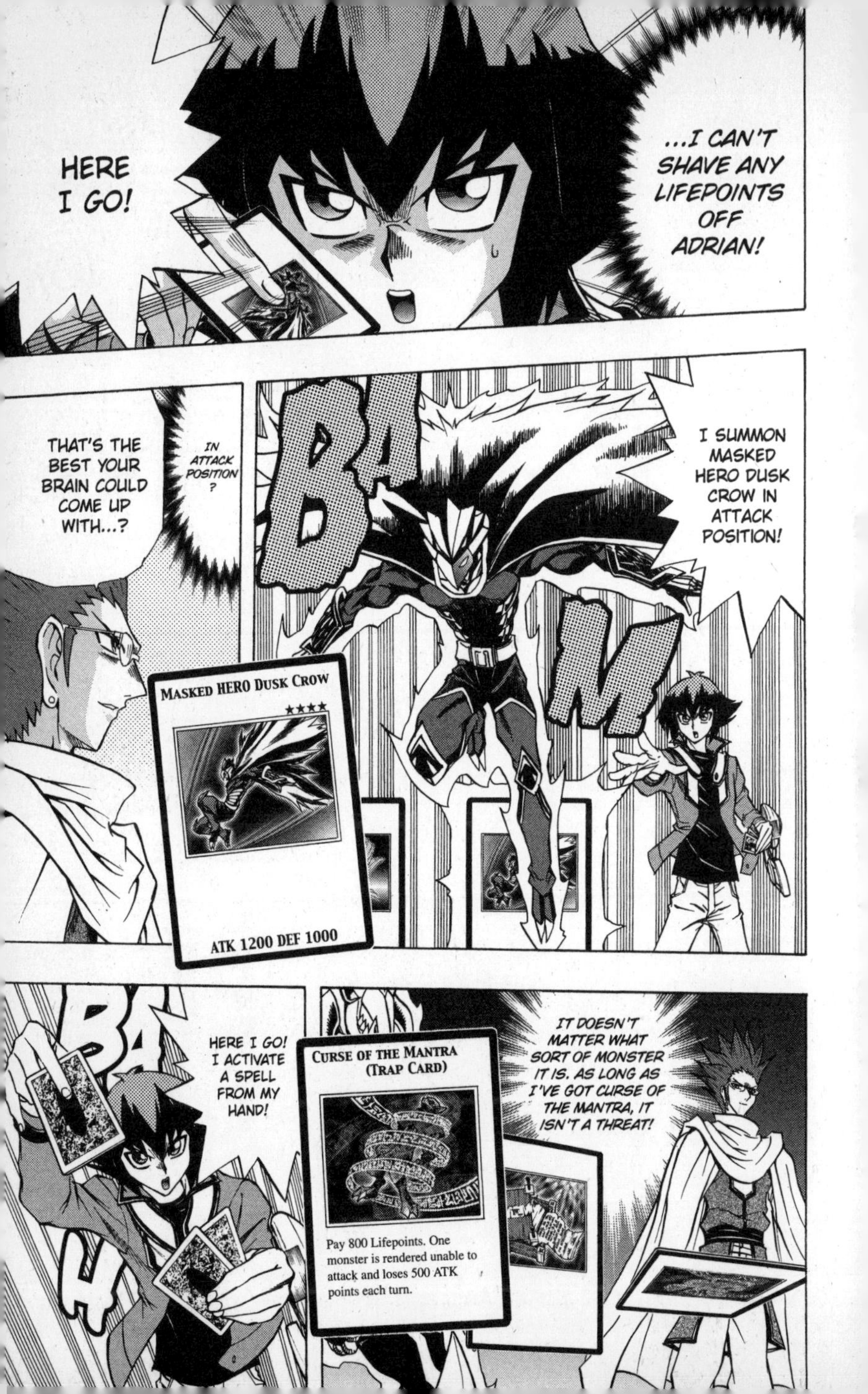
...I CAN'T SHAVE ANY LIFEPOINTS OFF ADRIAN!
HERE I GO!
I SUMMON MASKED HERO DUSK CROW IN ATTACK POSITION!
BAM
MASKED HERO DUSK CROW
ATK 1200 DEF 1000
IN ATTACK POSITION?
THAT'S THE BEST YOUR BRAIN COULD COME UP WITH...?
IT DOESN'T MATTER WHAT SORT OF MONSTER IT IS. AS LONG AS I'VE GOT CURSE OF THE MANTRA, IT ISN'T A THREAT!
CURSE OF THE MANTRA (TRAP CARD)
Pay 800 Lifepoints. One monster is rendered unable to attack and loses 500 ATK points each turn.
HERE I GO! I ACTIVATE A SPELL FROM MY HAND!

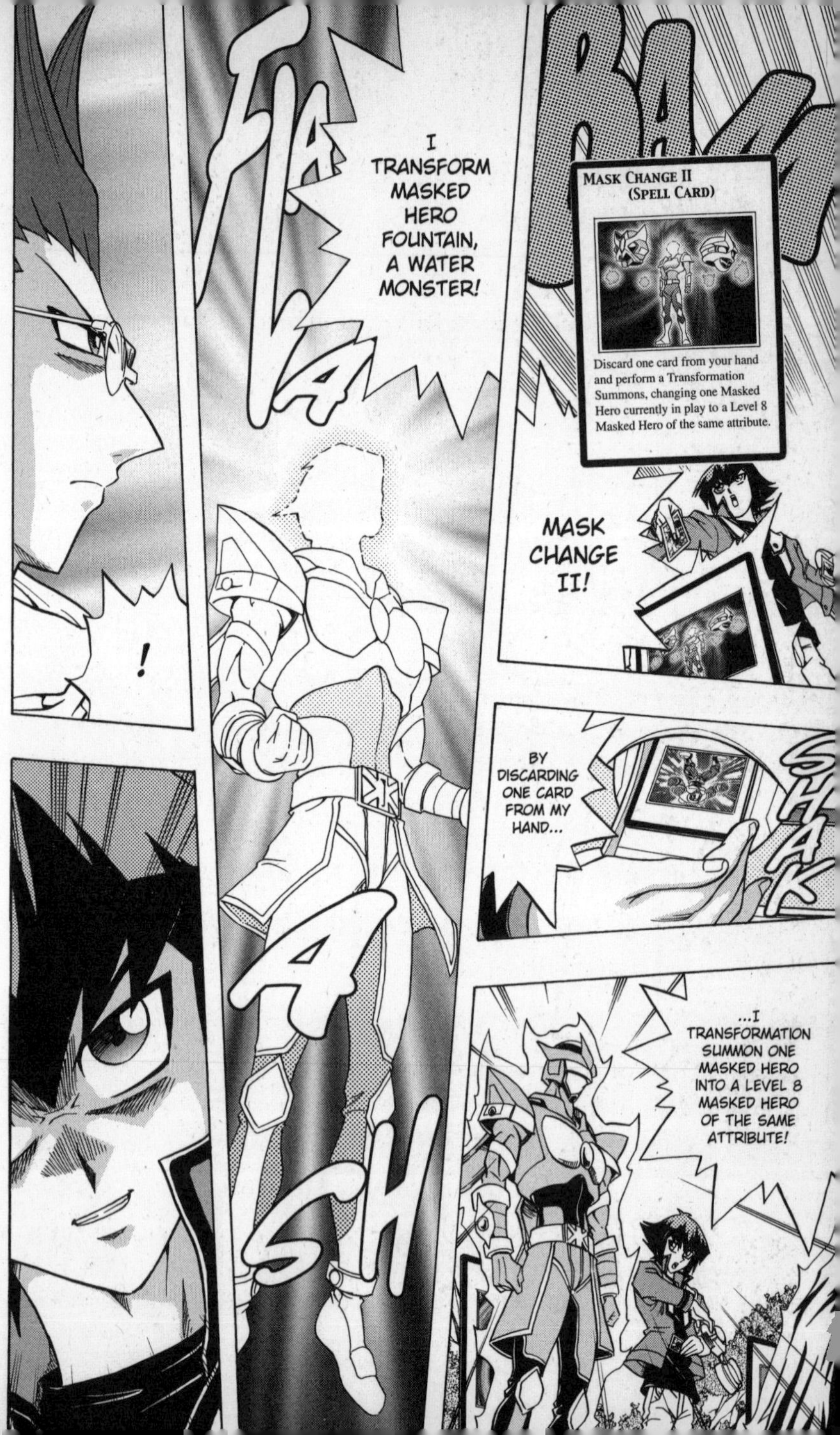
BAA
MASK CHANGE II
(SPELL CARD)
Discard one card from your hand and perform a Transformation Summons, changing one Masked Hero currently in play to a Level 8 Masked Hero of the same attribute.
MASK CHANGE II!
BY DISCARDING ONE CARD FROM MY HAND...
SHAK
...I TRANSFORMATION SUMMON ONE MASKED HERO INTO A LEVEL 8 MASKED HERO OF THE SAME ATTRIBUTE!
FLA
A
I TRANSFORM MASKED HERO FOUNTAIN, A WATER MONSTER!
A
SH
!

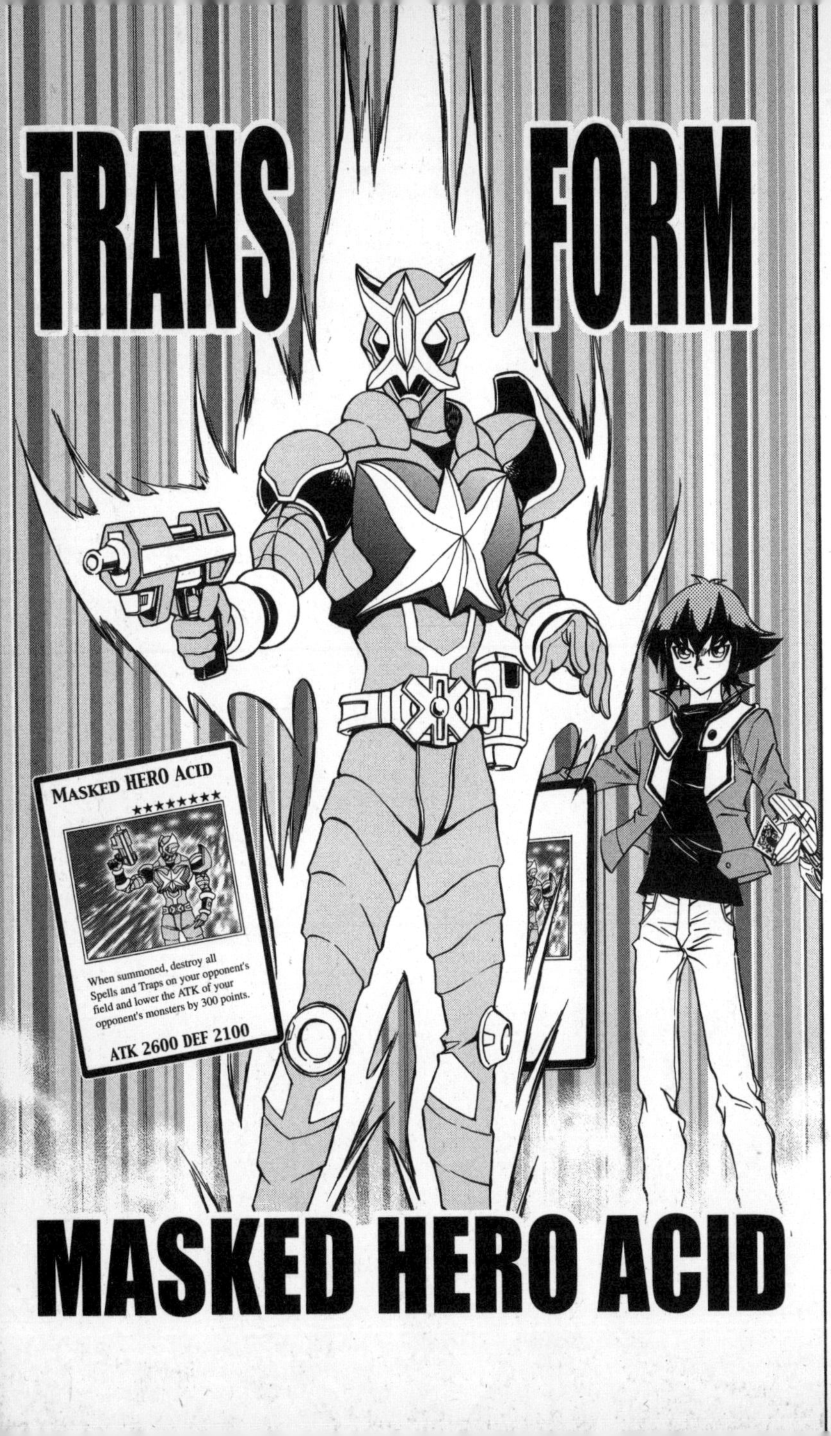

TRANS FORM
MASKED HERO ACID
MASKED HERO ACID
★★★★★★★★
When summoned, destroy all Spells and Traps on your opponent's field and lower the ATK of your opponent's monsters by 300 points.
ATK 2600 DEF 2100
MASKED HERO ACID

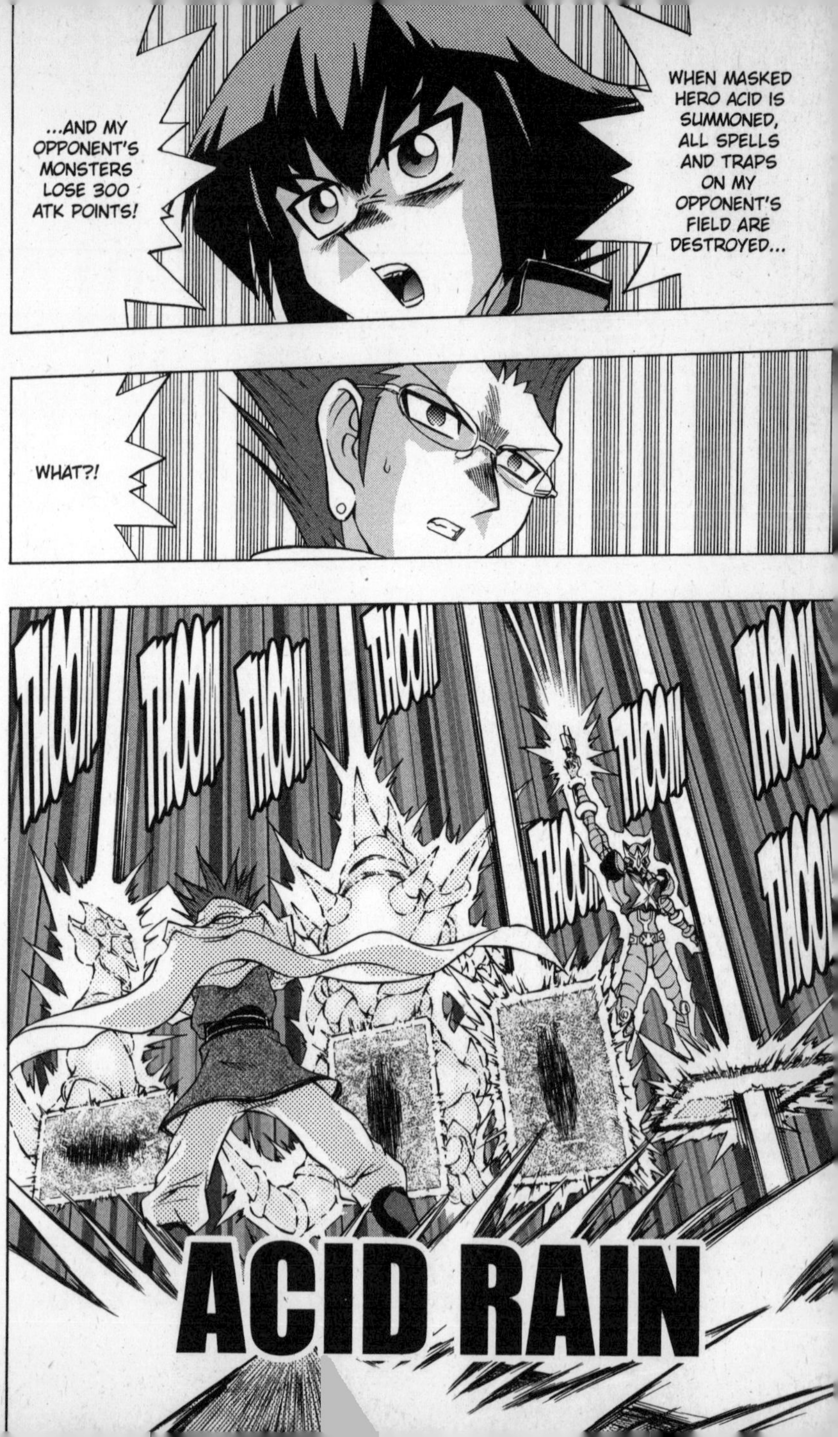
WHEN MASKED HERO ACID IS SUMMONED, ALL SPELLS AND TRAPS ON MY OPPONENT'S FIELD ARE DESTROYED...
...AND MY OPPONENT'S MONSTERS LOSE 300 ATK POINTS!
WHAT?!
THOOM
THOOM
THOOM
THOOM
THOOM
THOOM
THOOM
ACID RAIN

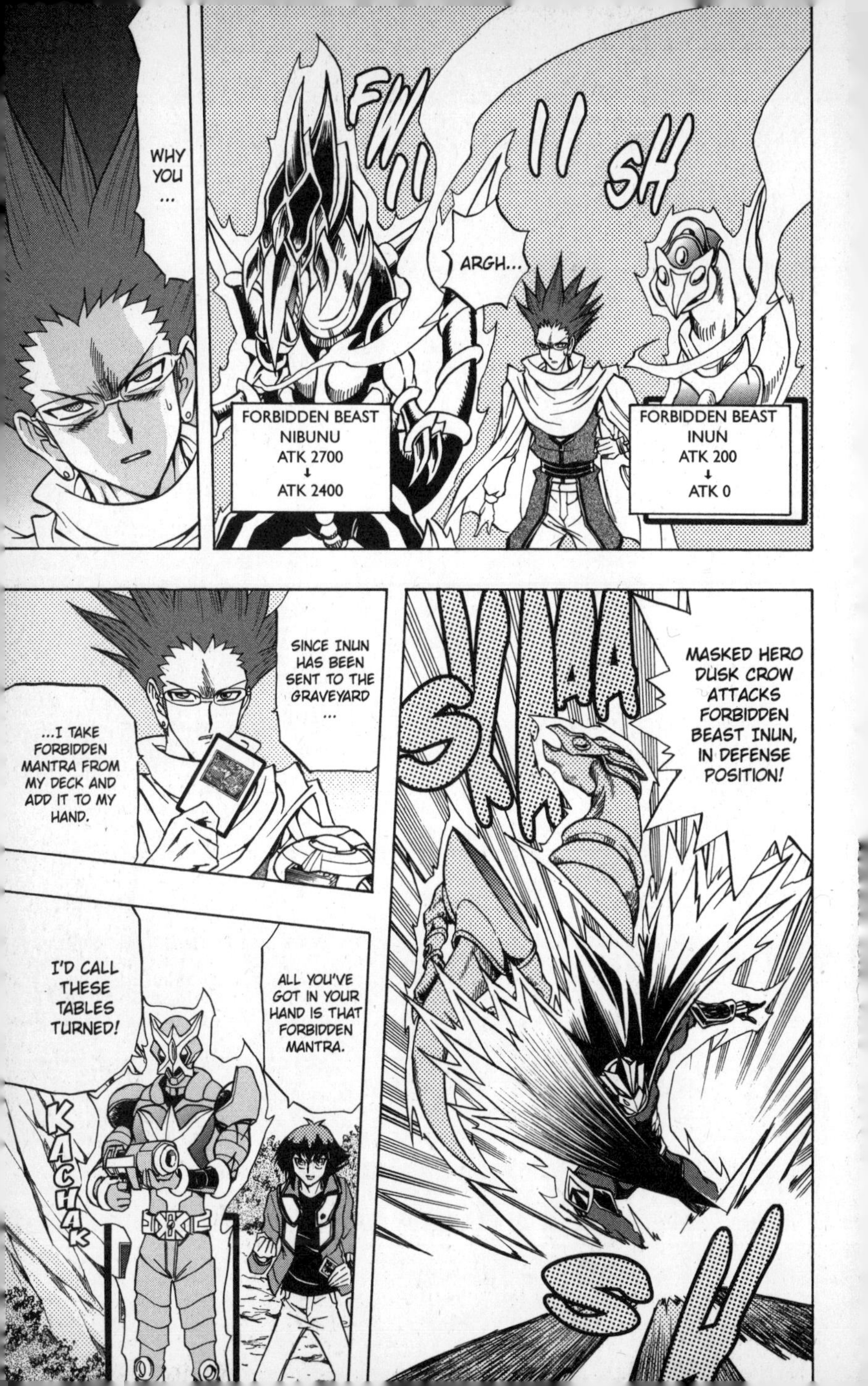
FWIIISH
ARGH...
FORBIDDEN BEAST
INUN
ATK 200
↓
ATK 0
FORBIDDEN BEAST
NIBUNU
ATK 2700
↓
ATK 2400
WHY YOU ...
MASKED HERO DUSK CROW ATTACKS FORBIDDEN BEAST INUN, IN DEFENSE POSITION!
SHAA
SH
SINCE INUN HAS BEEN SENT TO THE GRAVEYARD ...
...I TAKE FORBIDDEN MANTRA FROM MY DECK AND ADD IT TO MY HAND.
ALL YOU'VE GOT IN YOUR HAND IS THAT FORBIDDEN MANTRA.
I'D CALL THESE TABLES TURNED!
KACHAK

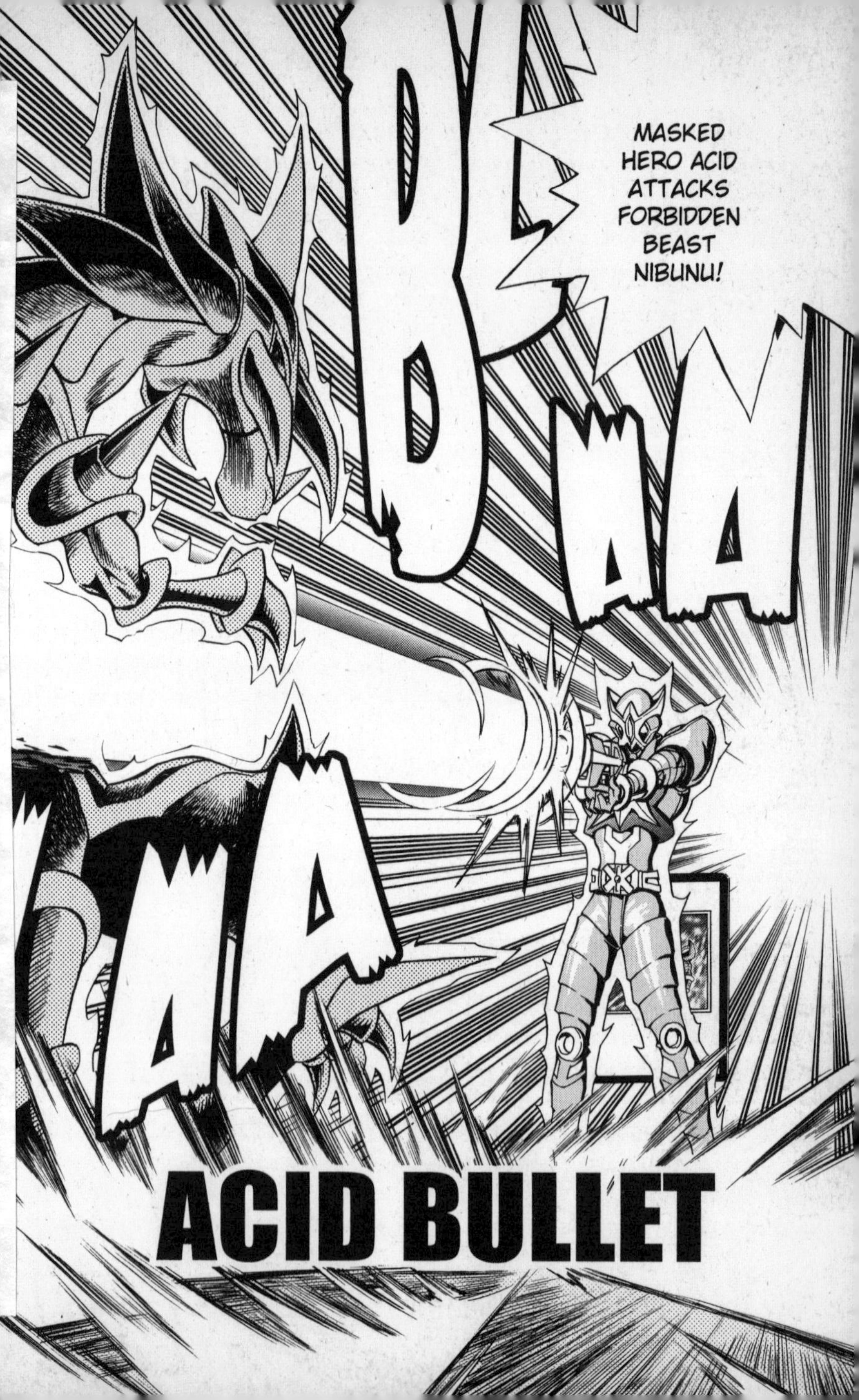
MASKED HERO ACID ATTACKS FORBIDDEN BEAST NIBUNU!
BDAAAA
ACID BULLET

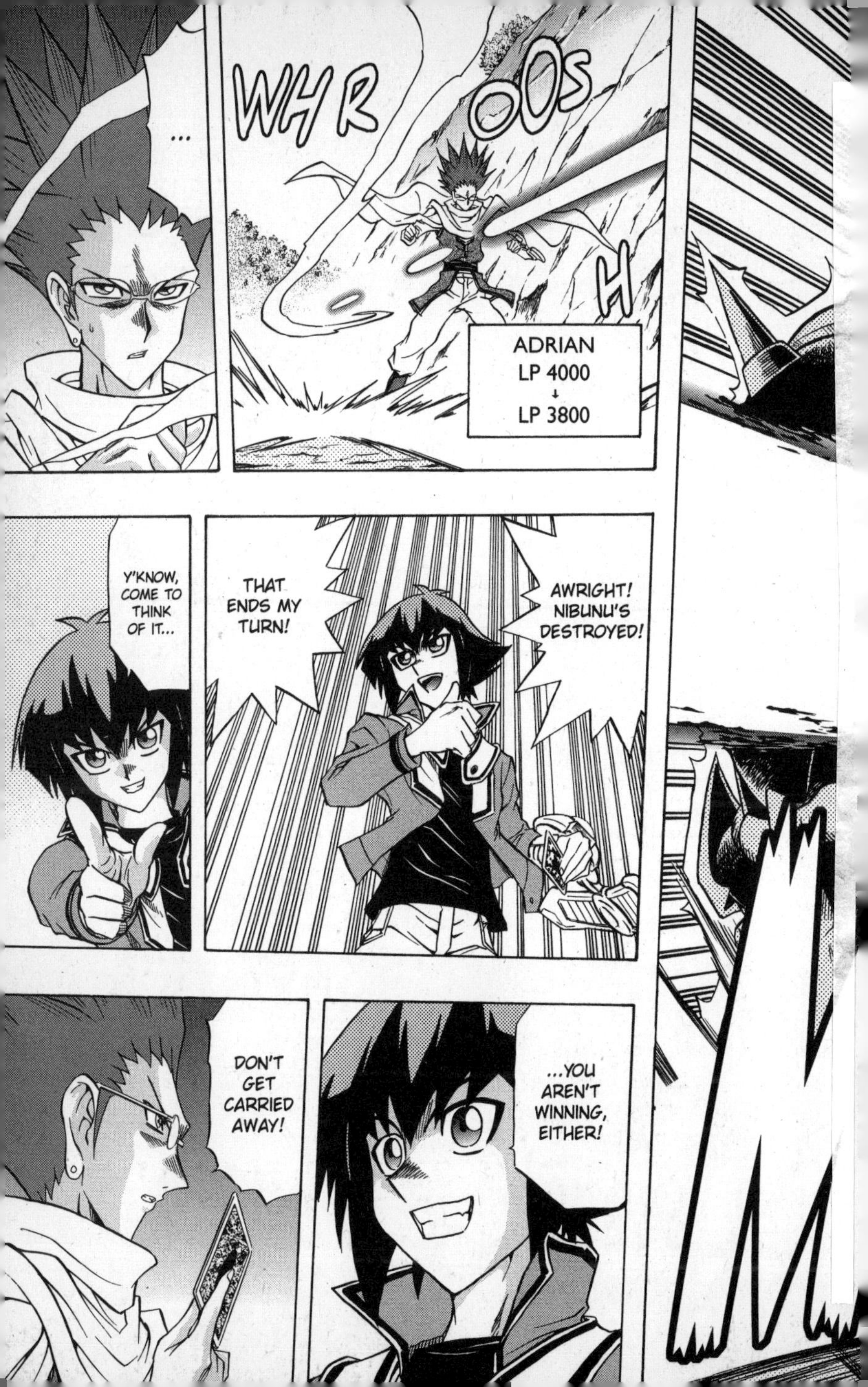
WHROOSH
ADRIAN
LP 4000
↓
LP 3800
...
AWRIGHT! NIBUNU'S DESTROYED!
THAT ENDS MY TURN!
Y'KNOW, COME TO THINK OF IT...
...YOU AREN'T WINNING, EITHER!
DON'T GET CARRIED AWAY!

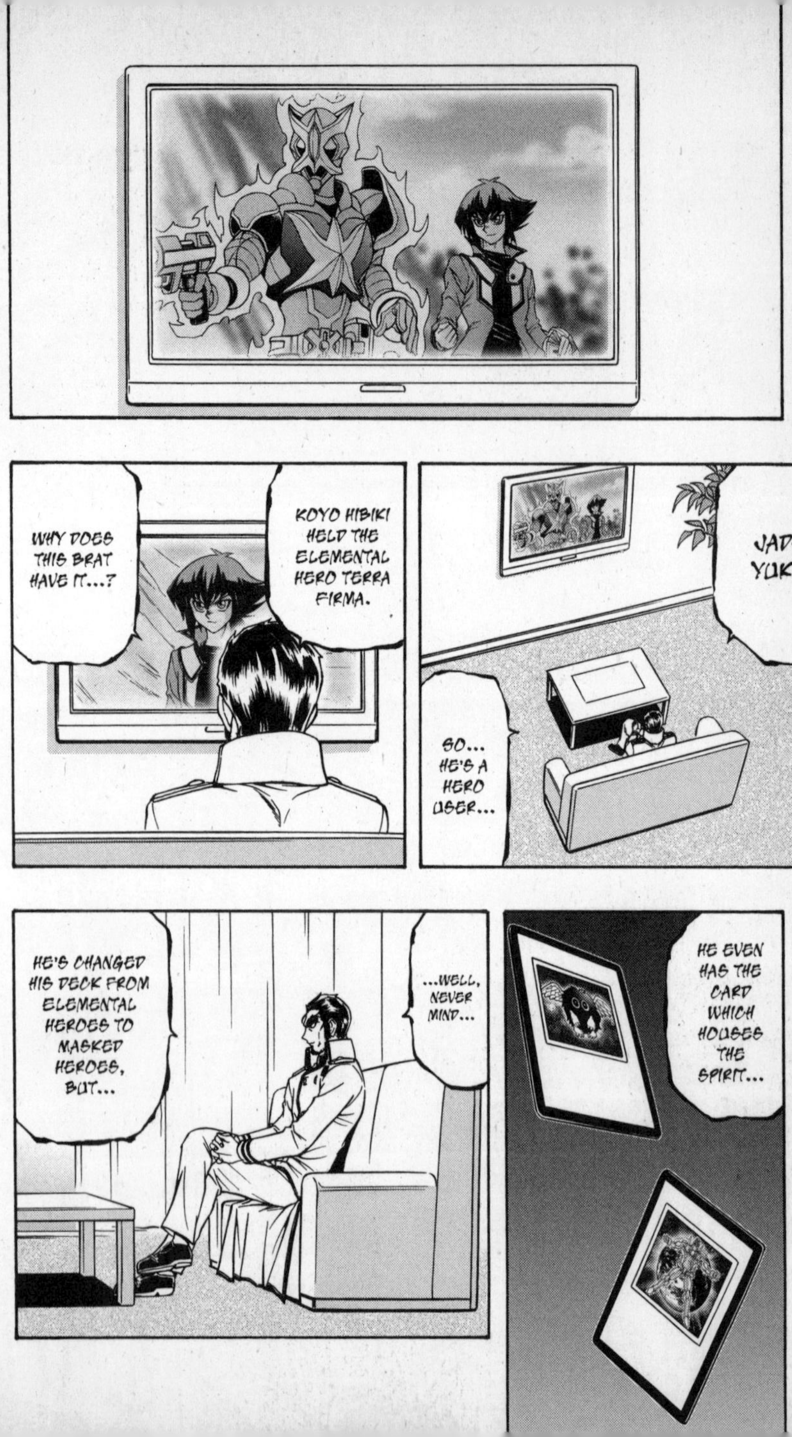
JADEN YUKI...
SO... HE'S A HERO USER...
KOYO HIBIKI HELD THE ELEMENTAL HERO TERRA FIRMA.
WHY DOES THIS BRAT HAVE IT...?
HE EVEN HAS THE CARD WHICH HOUSES THE SPIRIT...
HE'S CHANGED HIS DECK FROM ELEMENTAL HEROES TO MASKED HEROES, BUT...
...WELL, NEVER MIND...

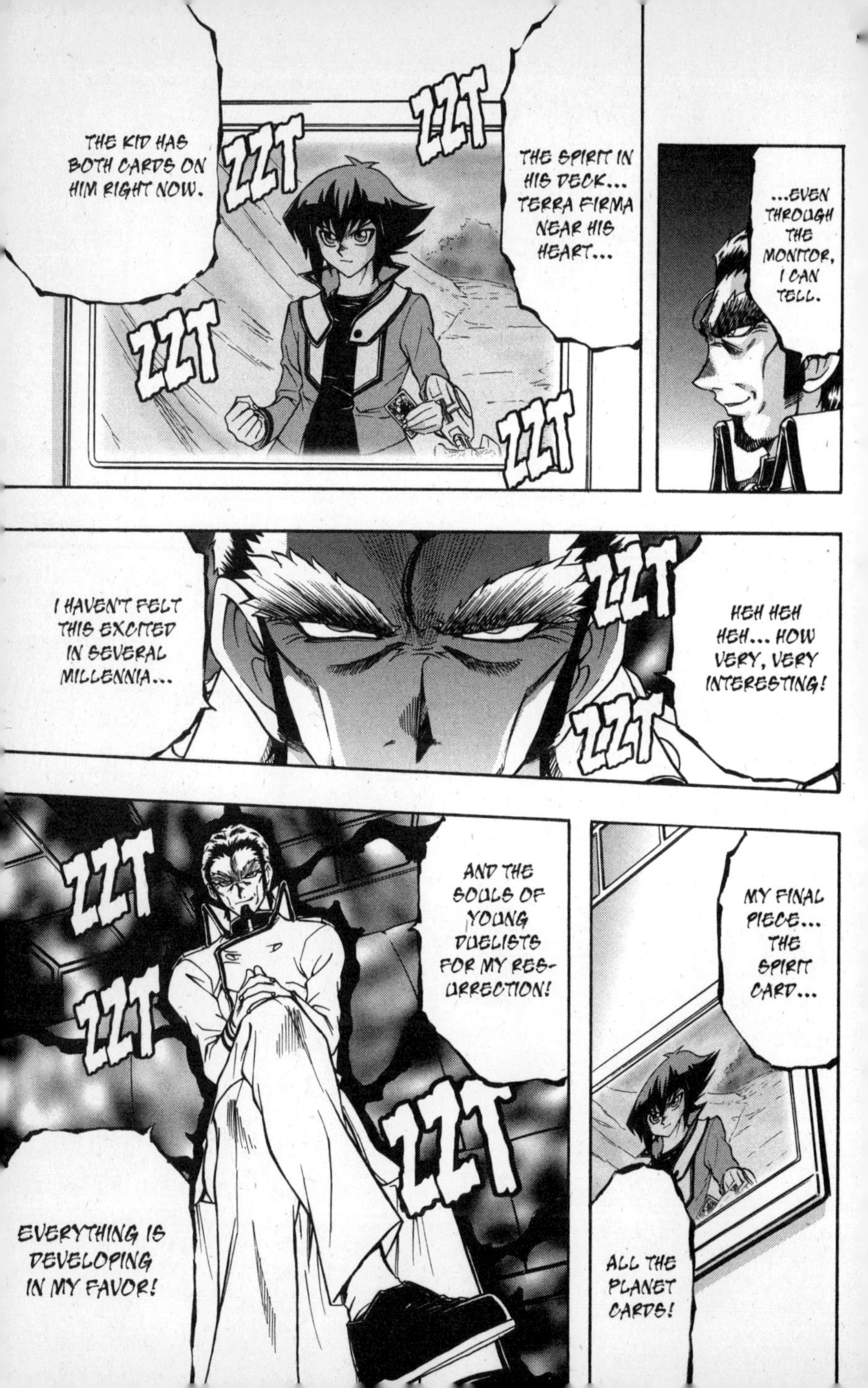
...EVEN THROUGH THE MONITOR, I CAN TELL.
THE SPIRIT IN HIS DECK... TERRA FIRMA NEAR HIS HEART...
THE KID HAS BOTH CARDS ON HIM RIGHT NOW.
ZZT
ZZT
ZZT
ZZT
HEH HEH HEH... HOW VERY, VERY INTERESTING!
I HAVEN'T FELT THIS EXCITED IN SEVERAL MILLENNIA...
ZZT
ZZT
MY FINAL PIECE... THE SPIRIT CARD...
ALL THE PLANET CARDS!
AND THE SOULS OF YOUNG DUELISTS FOR MY RES-URRECTION!
EVERYTHING IS DEVELOPING IN MY FAVOR!
ZZT
ZZT
ZZT

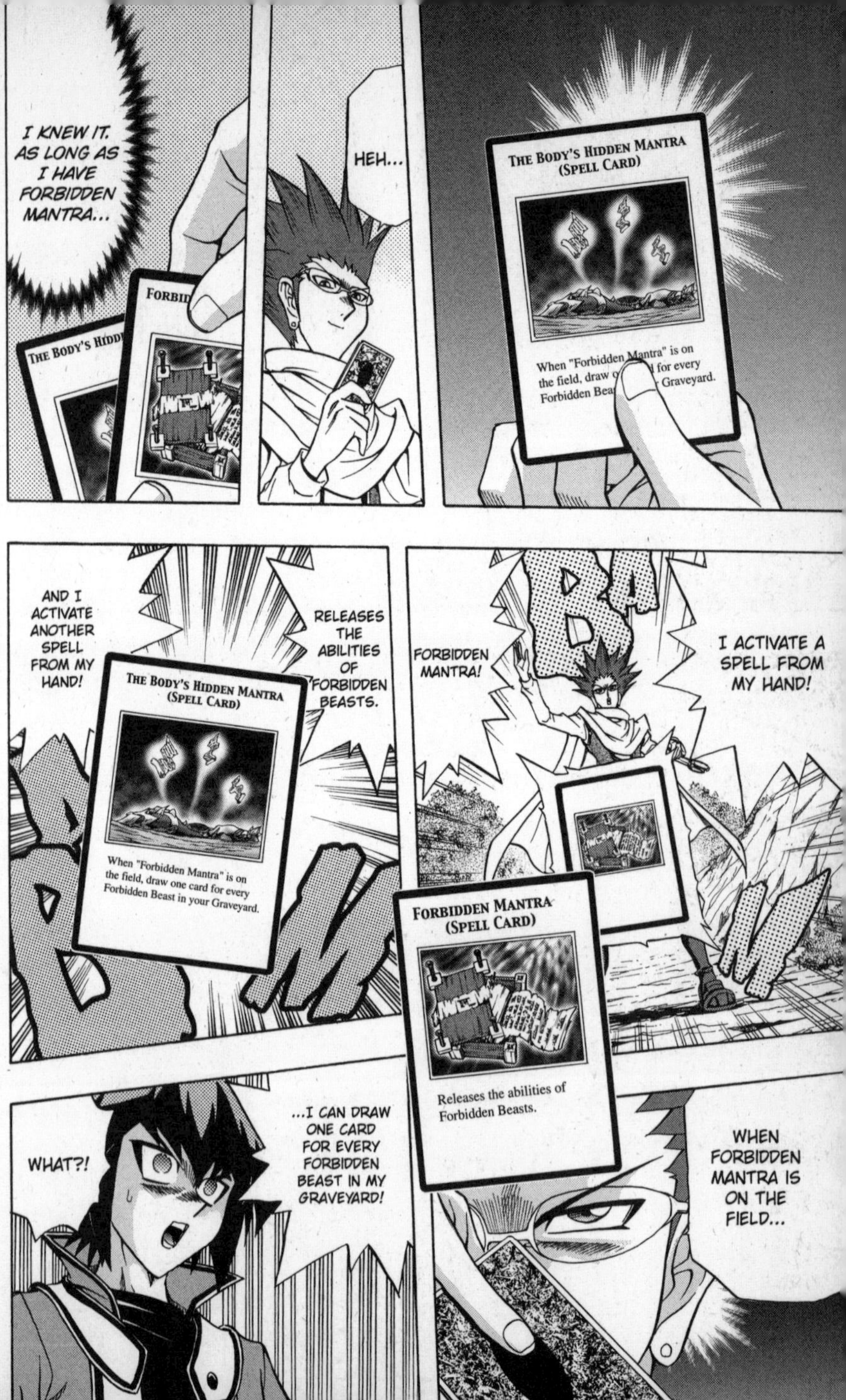

THE BODY'S HIDDEN MANTRA (SPELL CARD)
HEH...
I KNEW IT. AS LONG AS I HAVE FORBIDDEN MANTRA...
I ACTIVATE A SPELL FROM MY HAND!
FORBIDDEN MANTRA!
BAM
FORBIDDEN MANTRA (SPELL CARD)
Releases the abilities of Forbidden Beasts.
RELEASES THE ABILITIES OF FORBIDDEN BEASTS.
AND I ACTIVATE ANOTHER SPELL FROM MY HAND!
THE BODY'S HIDDEN MANTRA (SPELL CARD)
When "Forbidden Mantra" is on the field, draw one card for every Forbidden Beast in your Graveyard.
WHEN FORBIDDEN MANTRA IS ON THE FIELD...
...I CAN DRAW ONE CARD FOR EVERY FORBIDDEN BEAST IN MY GRAVEYARD!
WHAT?!

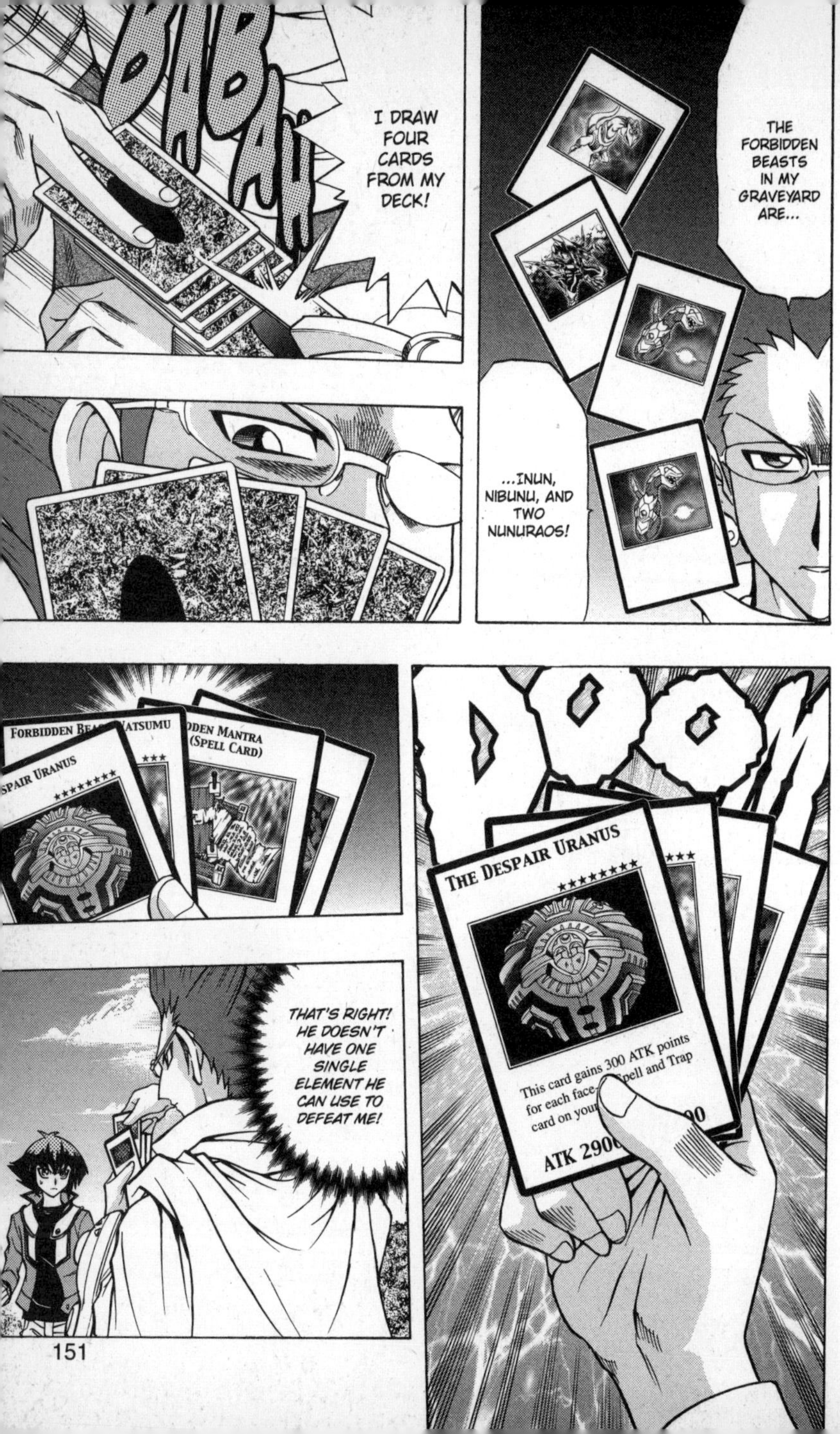
THE FORBIDDEN BEASTS IN MY GRAVEYARD ARE...
...INUN, NIBUNU, AND TWO NUNURAOS!
BABAH
I DRAW FOUR CARDS FROM MY DECK!
DOOM
THE DESPAIR URANUS
This card gains 300 ATK points
for each face-
pell and Trap
card on you
ATK 290
FORBIDDEN BEA
ATSUMU
DDEN MANTRA
(SPELL CARD)
SPAIR URANUS
THAT'S RIGHT! HE DOESN'T HAVE ONE SINGLE ELEMENT HE CAN USE TO DEFEAT ME!

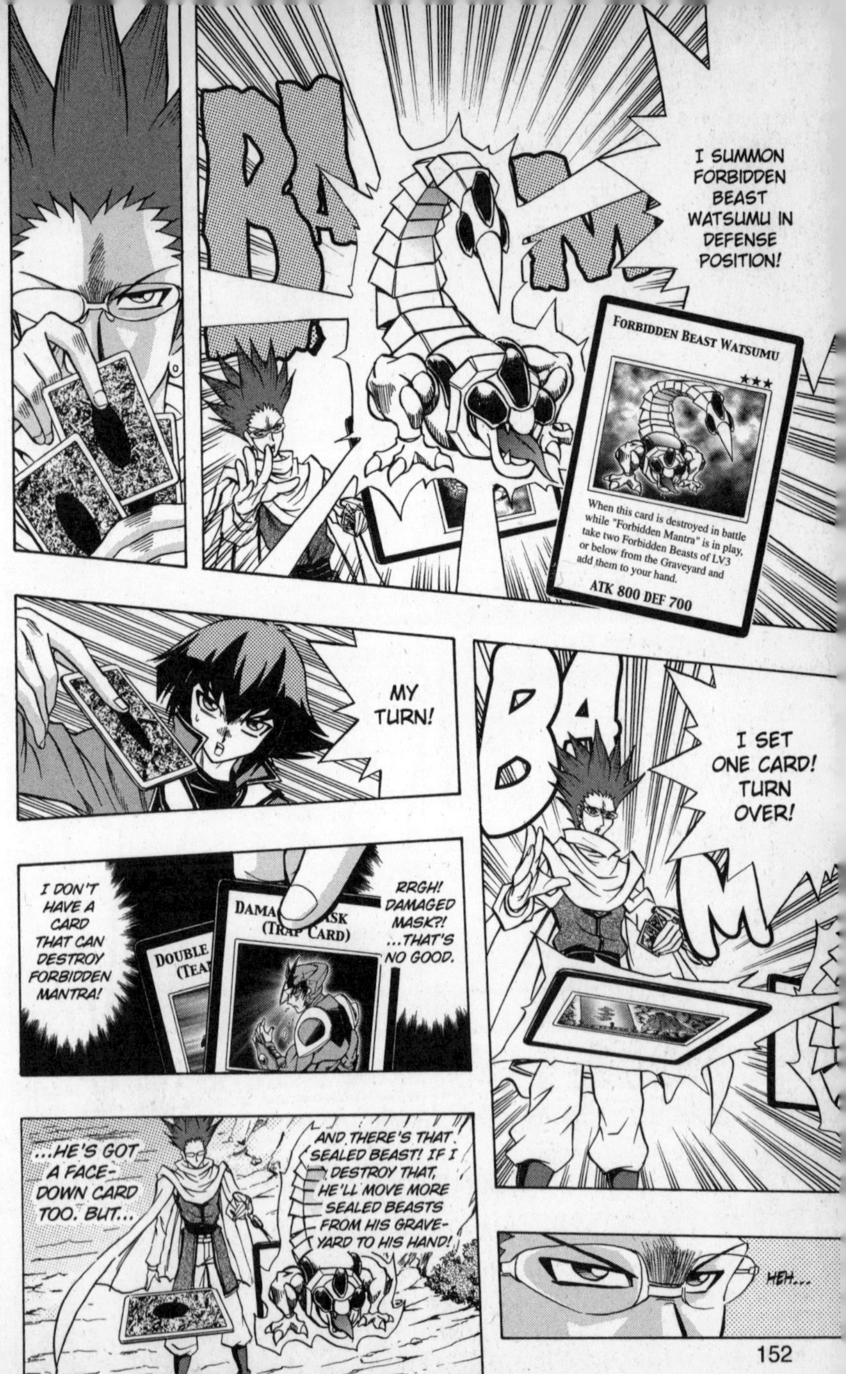
I SUMMON FORBIDDEN BEAST WATSUMU IN DEFENSE POSITION!
FORBIDDEN BEAST WATSUMU
When this card is destroyed in battle while "Forbidden Mantra" is in play, take two Forbidden Beasts of LV3 or below from the Graveyard and add them to your hand.
ATK 800 DEF 700
I SET ONE CARD! TURN OVER!
MY TURN!
RRGH! DAMAGED MASK?! ...THAT'S NO GOOD.
I DON'T HAVE A CARD THAT CAN DESTROY FORBIDDEN MANTRA!
HEH...
AND THERE'S THAT SEALED BEAST! IF I DESTROY THAT, HE'LL MOVE MORE SEALED BEASTS FROM HIS GRAVEYARD TO HIS HAND!
...HE'S GOT A FACE-DOWN CARD TOO. BUT...

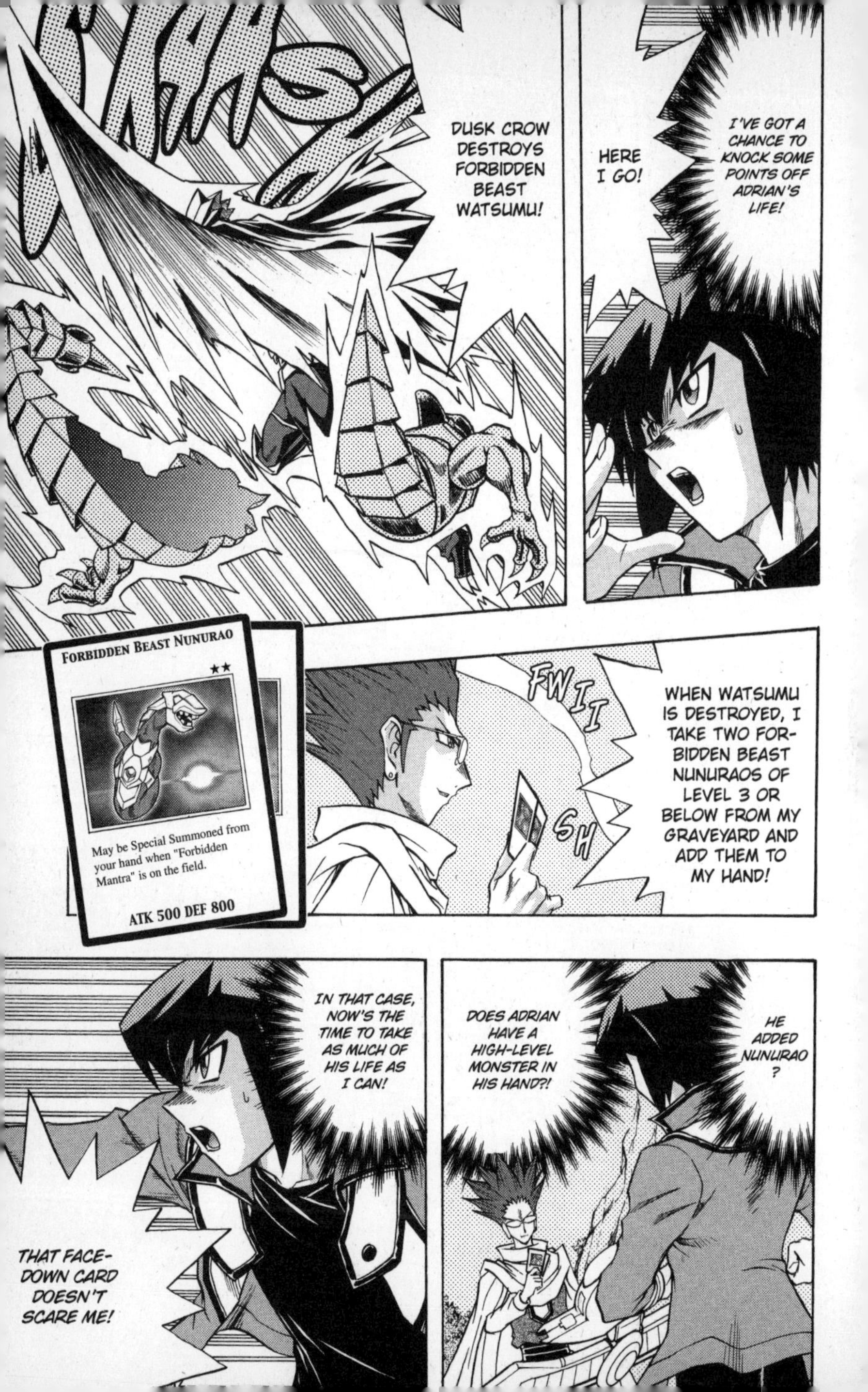

I'VE GOT A CHANCE TO KNOCK SOME POINTS OFF ADRIAN'S LIFE!
HERE I GO!
DUSK CROW DESTROYS FORBIDDEN BEAST WATSUMU!
WHEN WATSUMU IS DESTROYED, I TAKE TWO FOR-BIDDEN BEAST NUNURAOS OF LEVEL 3 OR BELOW FROM MY GRAVEYARD AND ADD THEM TO MY HAND!
FWIII
SH
FORBIDDEN BEAST NUNURAO
★★
May be Special Summoned from your hand when "Forbidden Mantra" is on the field.
ATK 500 DEF 800
HE ADDED NUNURAO?
DOES ADRIAN HAVE A HIGH-LEVEL MONSTER IN HIS HAND?!
IN THAT CASE, NOW'S THE TIME TO TAKE AS MUCH OF HIS LIFE AS I CAN!
THAT FACE-DOWN CARD DOESN'T SCARE ME!

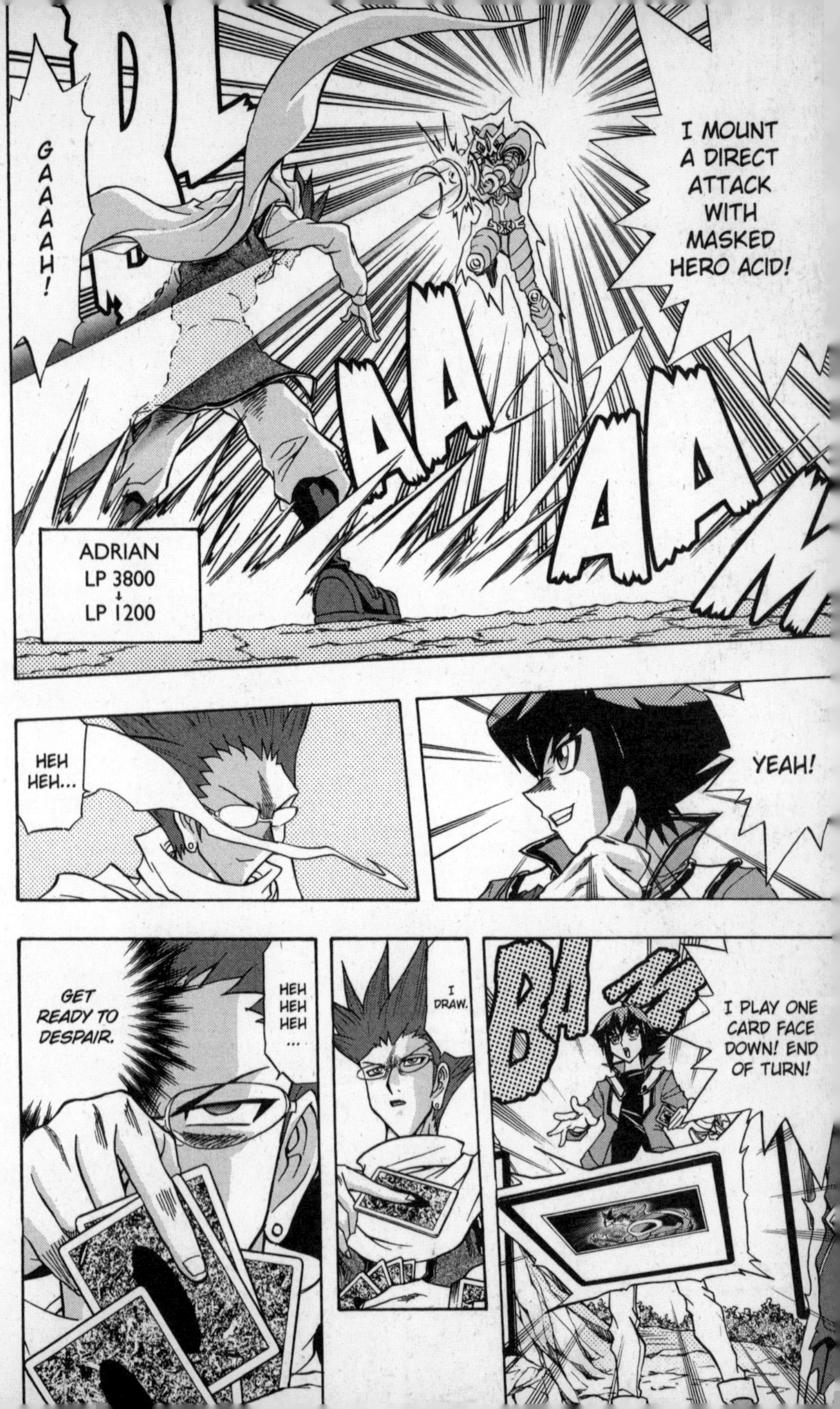
I MOUNT A DIRECT ATTACK WITH MASKED HERO ACID!
GAAAAAH!
ADRIAN
LP 3800
↓
LP 1200
YEAH!
HEH HEH...
I PLAY ONE CARD FACE DOWN! END OF TURN!
I DRAW.
HEH HEH HEH ...
GET READY TO DESPAIR.

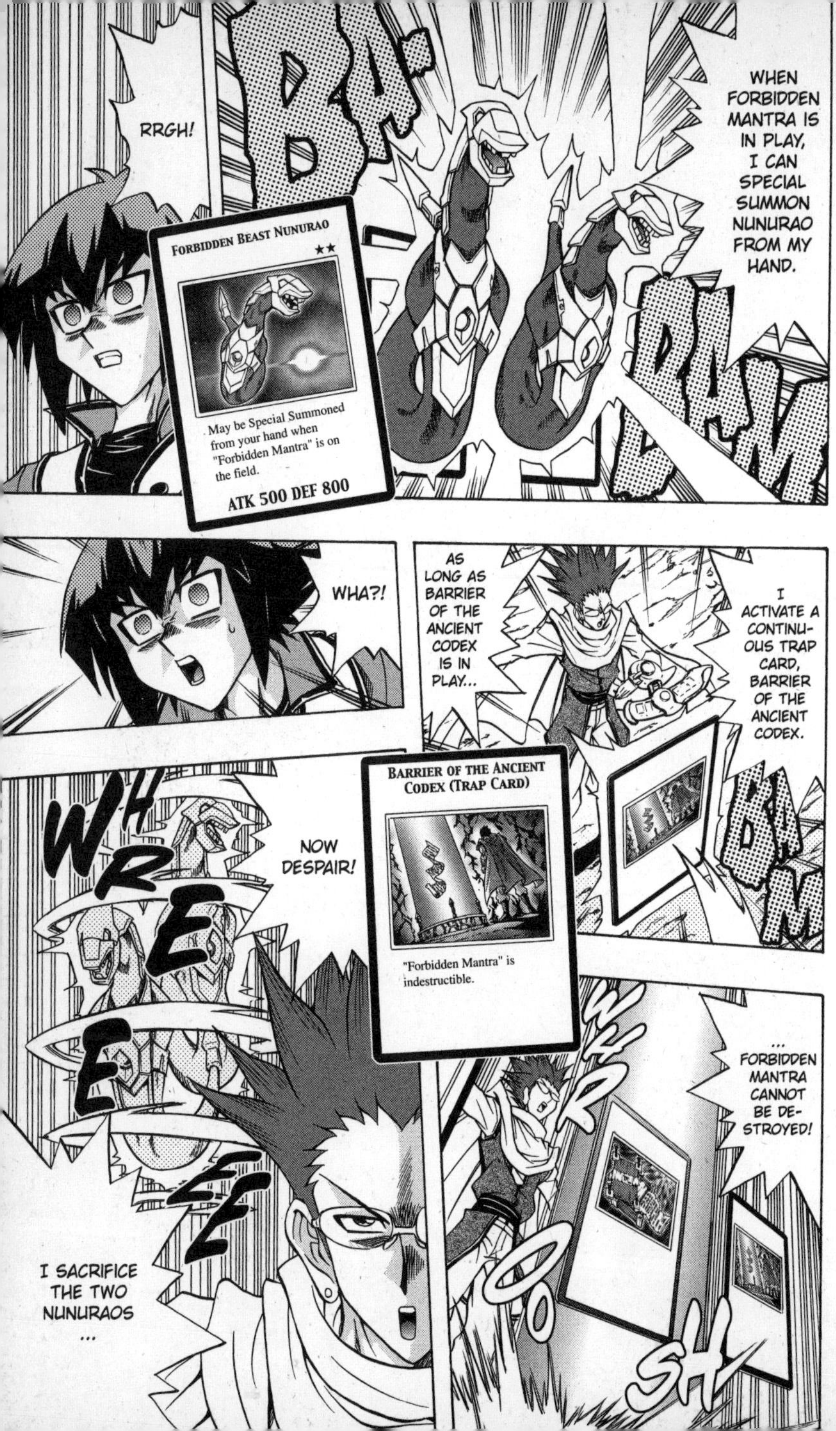
WHEN FORBIDDEN MANTRA IS IN PLAY, I CAN SPECIAL SUMMON NUNURAO FROM MY HAND.
BAM
FORBIDDEN BEAST NUNURAO
★★
May be Special Summoned from your hand when "Forbidden Mantra" is on the field.
ATK 500 DEF 800
RRGH!
I ACTIVATE A CONTINUOUS TRAP CARD, BARRIER OF THE ANCIENT CODEX.
AS LONG AS BARRIER OF THE ANCIENT CODEX IS IN PLAY...
WHA?!
BAM
BARRIER OF THE ANCIENT CODEX (TRAP CARD)
"Forbidden Mantra" is indestructible.
...FORBIDDEN MANTRA CANNOT BE DE-STROYED!
NOW DESPAIR!
WHREEEE
I SACRIFICE THE TWO NUNURAOS ...

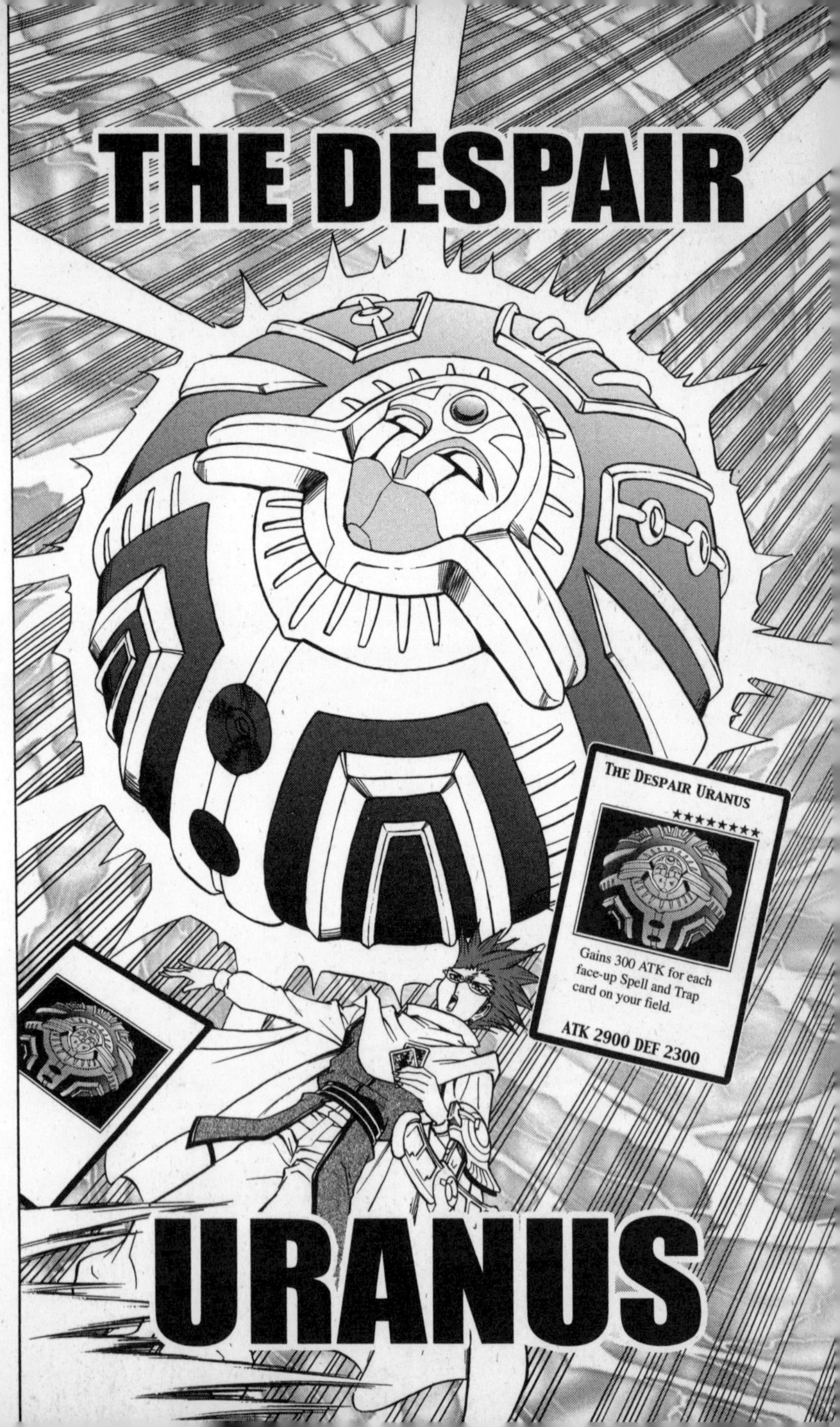
THE DESPAIR
THE DESPAIR URANUS
★★★★★★★★★
Gains 300 ATK for each face-up Spell and Trap card on your field.
ATK 2900 DEF 2300
URANUS

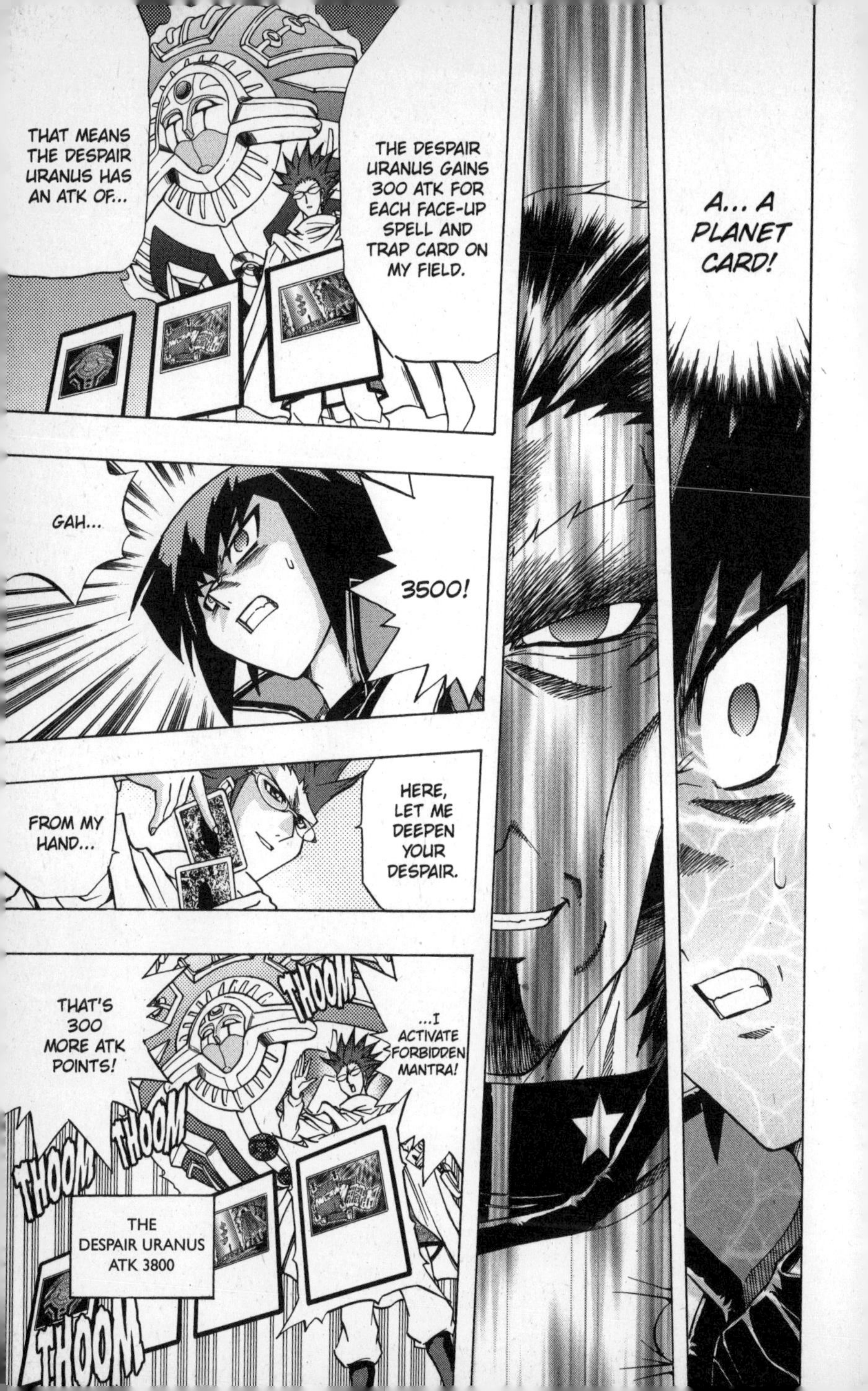
A... A PLANET CARD!
THE DESPAIR URANUS GAINS 300 ATK FOR EACH FACE-UP SPELL AND TRAP CARD ON MY FIELD.
THAT MEANS THE DESPAIR URANUS HAS AN ATK OF...
3500!
GAH...
HERE, LET ME DEEPEN YOUR DESPAIR.
FROM MY HAND...
THOOM
...I ACTIVATE FORBIDDEN MANTRA!
THAT'S 300 MORE ATK POINTS!
THOOM
THOOM
THOOM
THE DESPAIR URANUS ATK 3800
THOOM

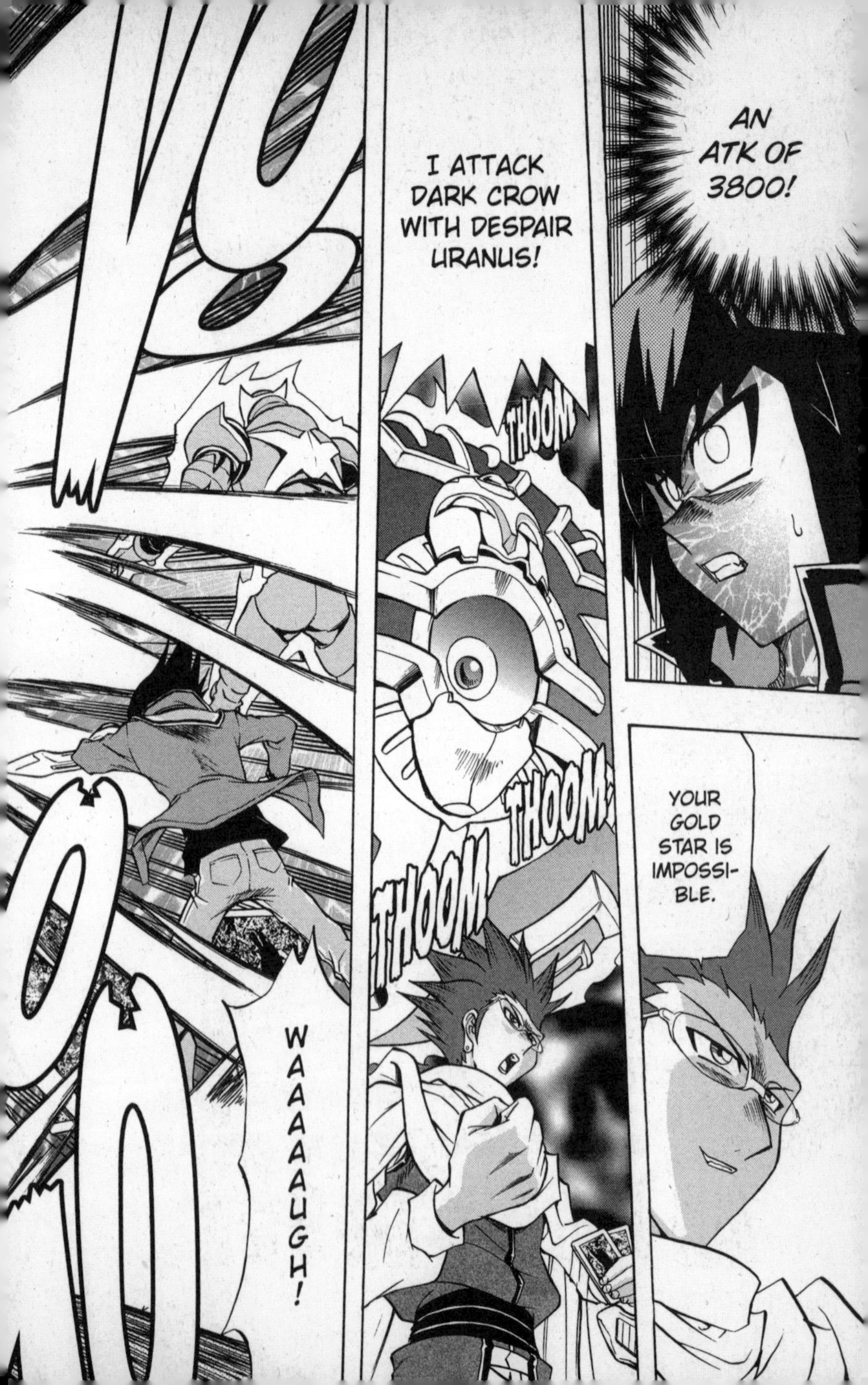
AN ATK OF 3800!
YOUR GOLD STAR IS IMPOSSI-BLE.
I ATTACK DARK CROW WITH DESPAIR URANUS!
THOOM
THOOM
THOOM
THOOM
WAAAAAAUGH!

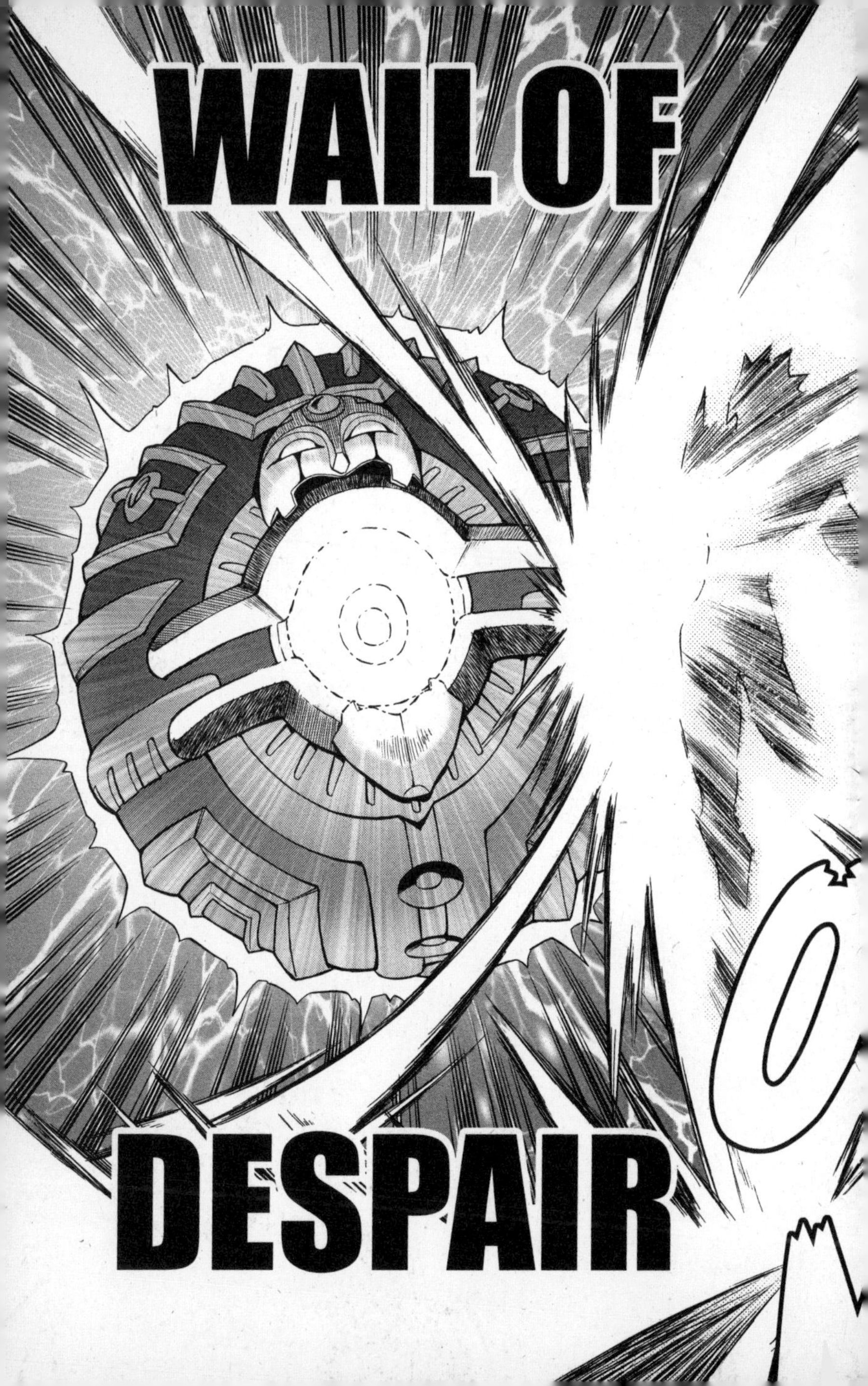
WAIL OF DESPAIR

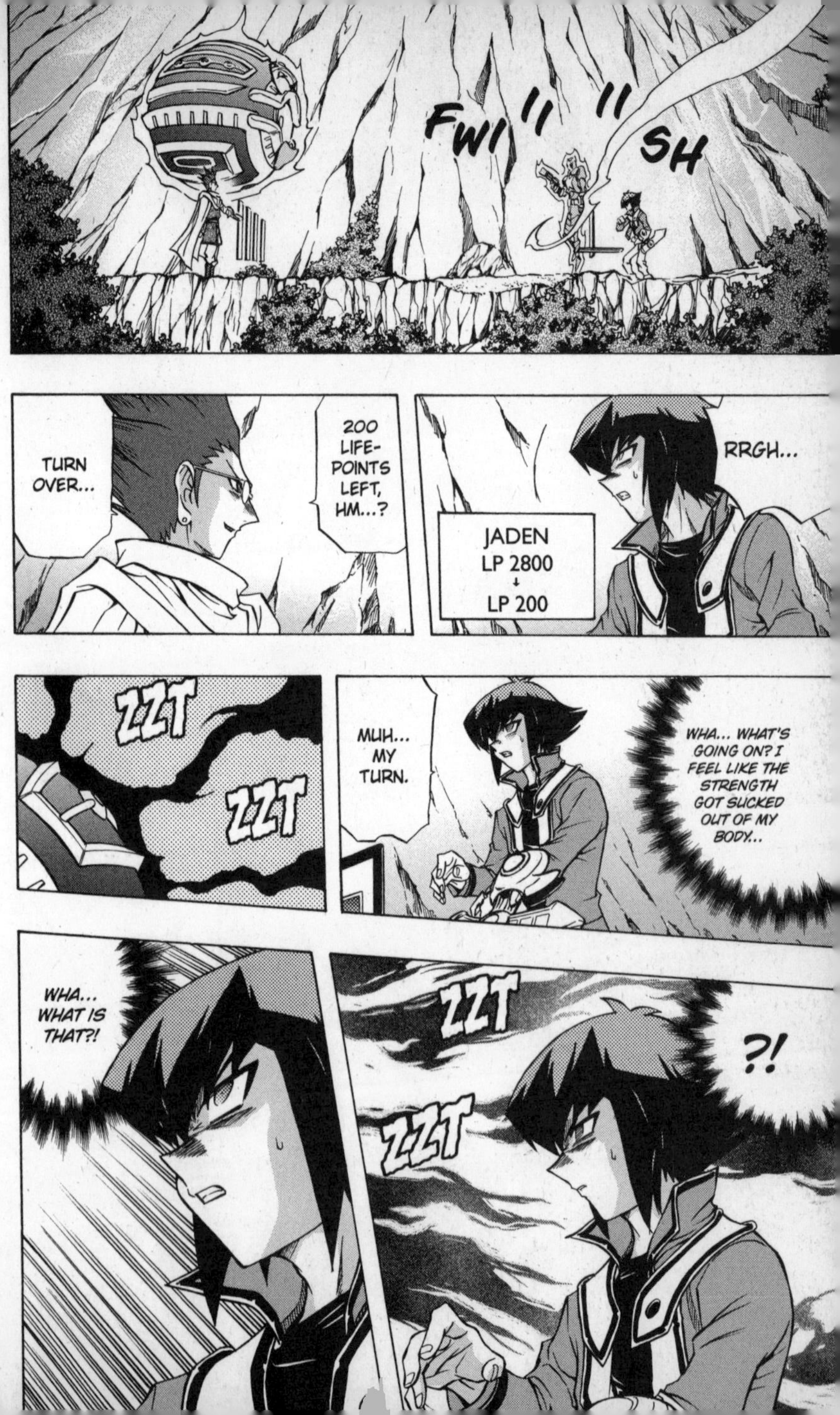
FWISH
RRGH...
JADEN LP 2800 ↓ LP 200
200 LIFE-POINTS LEFT, HM...?
TURN OVER...
WHA... WHAT'S GOING ON? I FEEL LIKE THE STRENGTH GOT SUCKED OUT OF MY BODY...
MUH... MY TURN.
ZZT
ZZT
?!
ZZT
ZZT
WHA... WHAT IS THAT?!

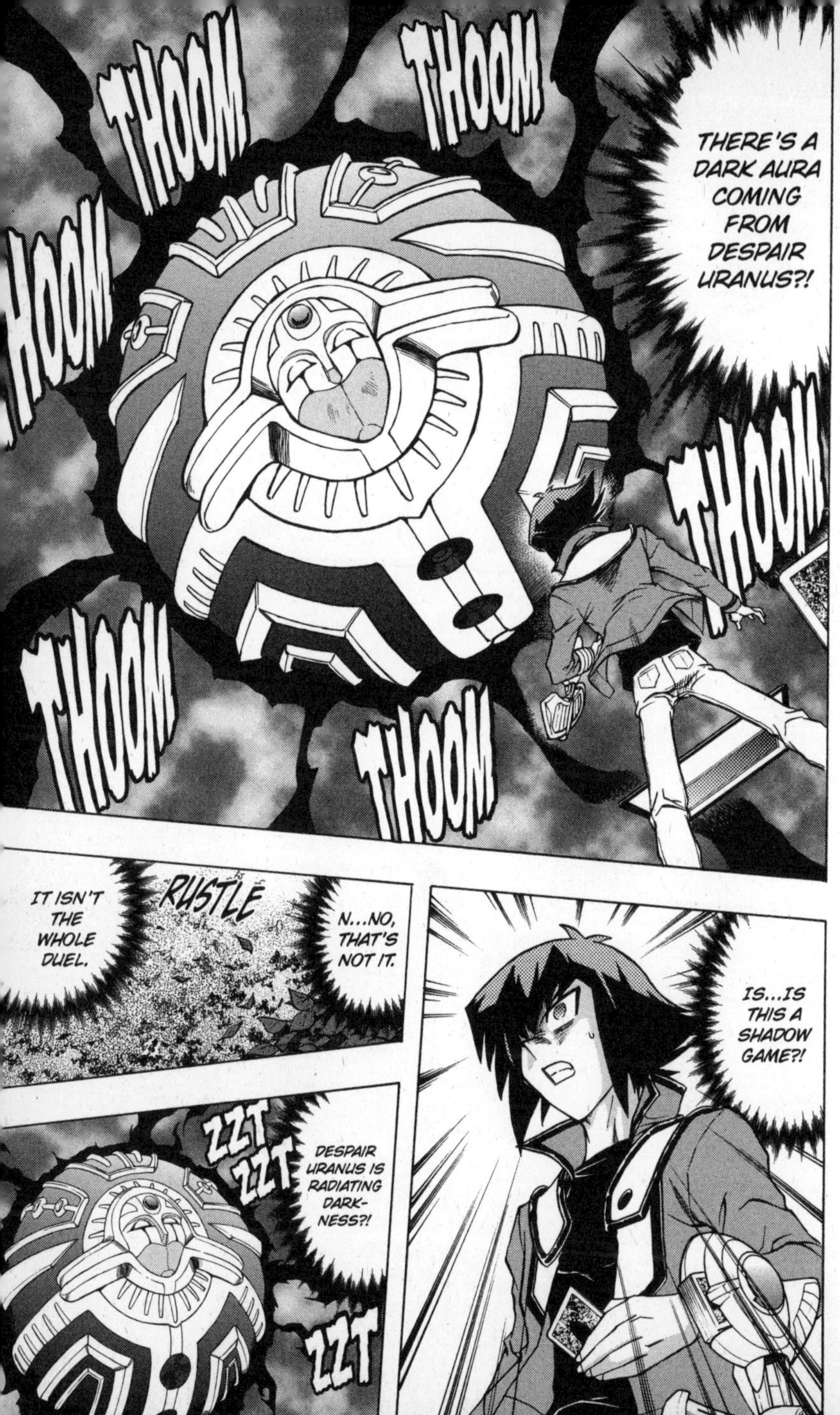
THOOM
THERE'S A DARK AURA COMING FROM DESPAIR URANUS?!
THOOM
HOOM
THOOM
THOOM
THOOM
IS...IS THIS A SHADOW GAME?!
N...NO, THAT'S NOT IT.
RUSTLE
IT ISN'T THE WHOLE DUEL.
ZZT
ZZT
DESPAIR URANUS IS RADIATING DARK-NESS?!
ZZT

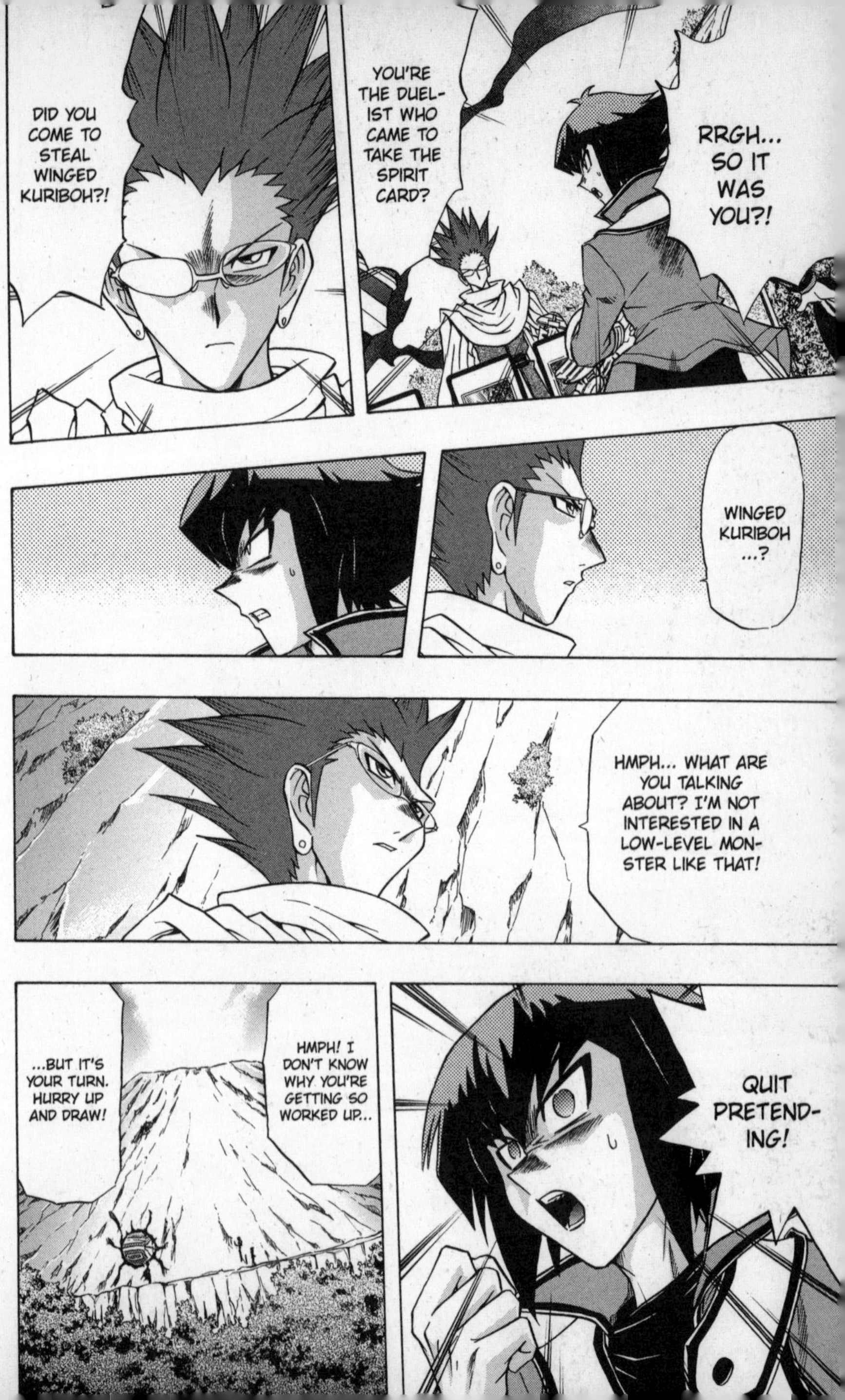
RRGH... SO IT WAS YOU?!
YOU'RE THE DUEL-IST WHO CAME TO TAKE THE SPIRIT CARD?
DID YOU COME TO STEAL WINGED KURIBOH?!
WINGED KURIBOH ...?
HMPH... WHAT ARE YOU TALKING ABOUT? I'M NOT INTERESTED IN A LOW-LEVEL MON-STER LIKE THAT!
QUIT PRETEND-ING!
HMPH! I DON'T KNOW WHY YOU'RE GETTING SO WORKED UP...
...BUT IT'S YOUR TURN. HURRY UP AND DRAW!

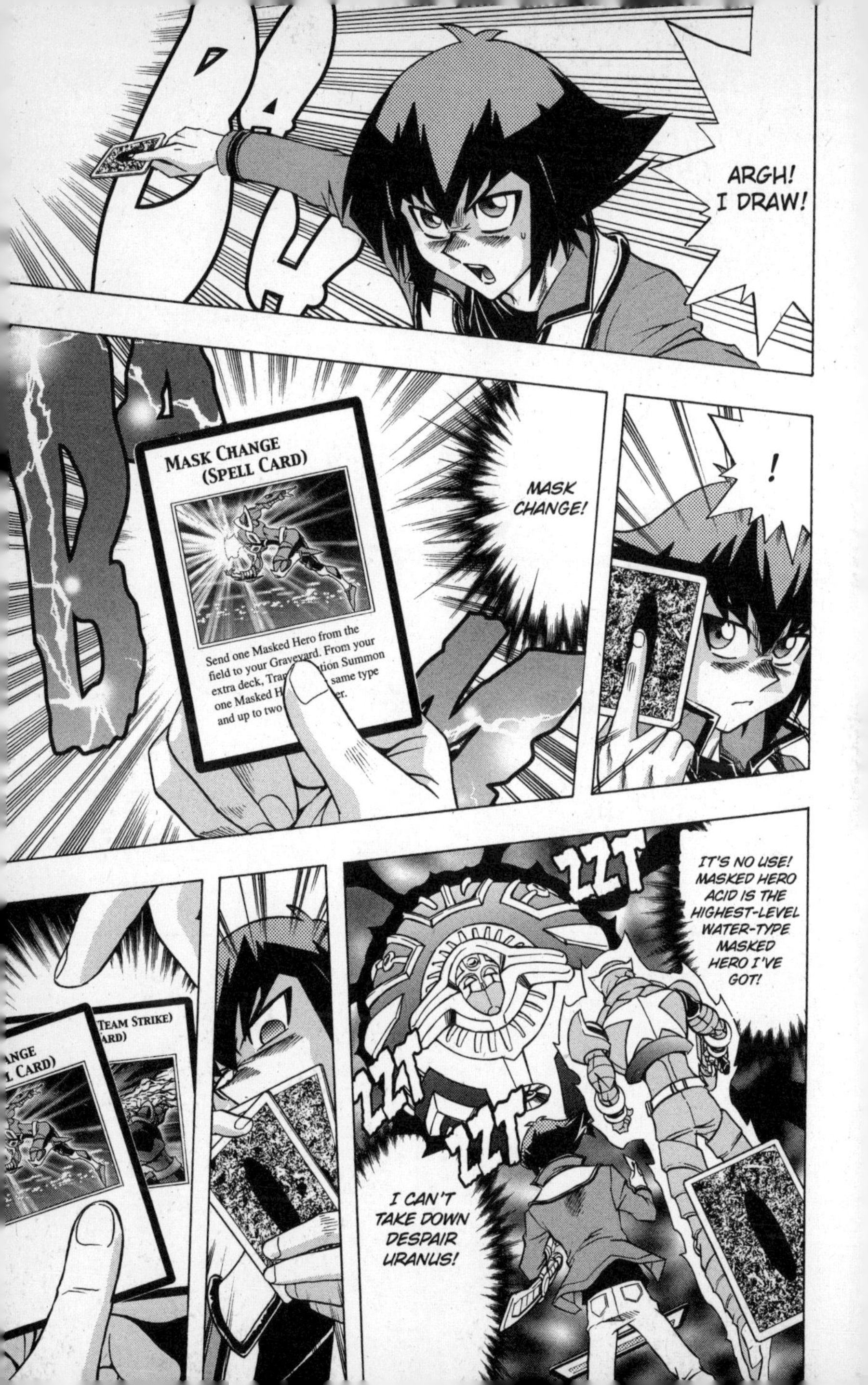
ARGH! I DRAW!
!
MASK CHANGE!
MASK CHANGE (SPELL CARD)
Send one Masked Hero from the field to your Graveyard. From your extra deck, Tran
ation Summon
same type
one Masked H
and up to two
er.
IT'S NO USE! MASKED HERO ACID IS THE HIGHEST-LEVEL WATER-TYPE MASKED HERO I'VE GOT!
ZZT
ZZT
ZZT
I CAN'T TAKE DOWN DESPAIR URANUS!
(TEAM STRIKE)
ARD)
ANGE
L CARD)

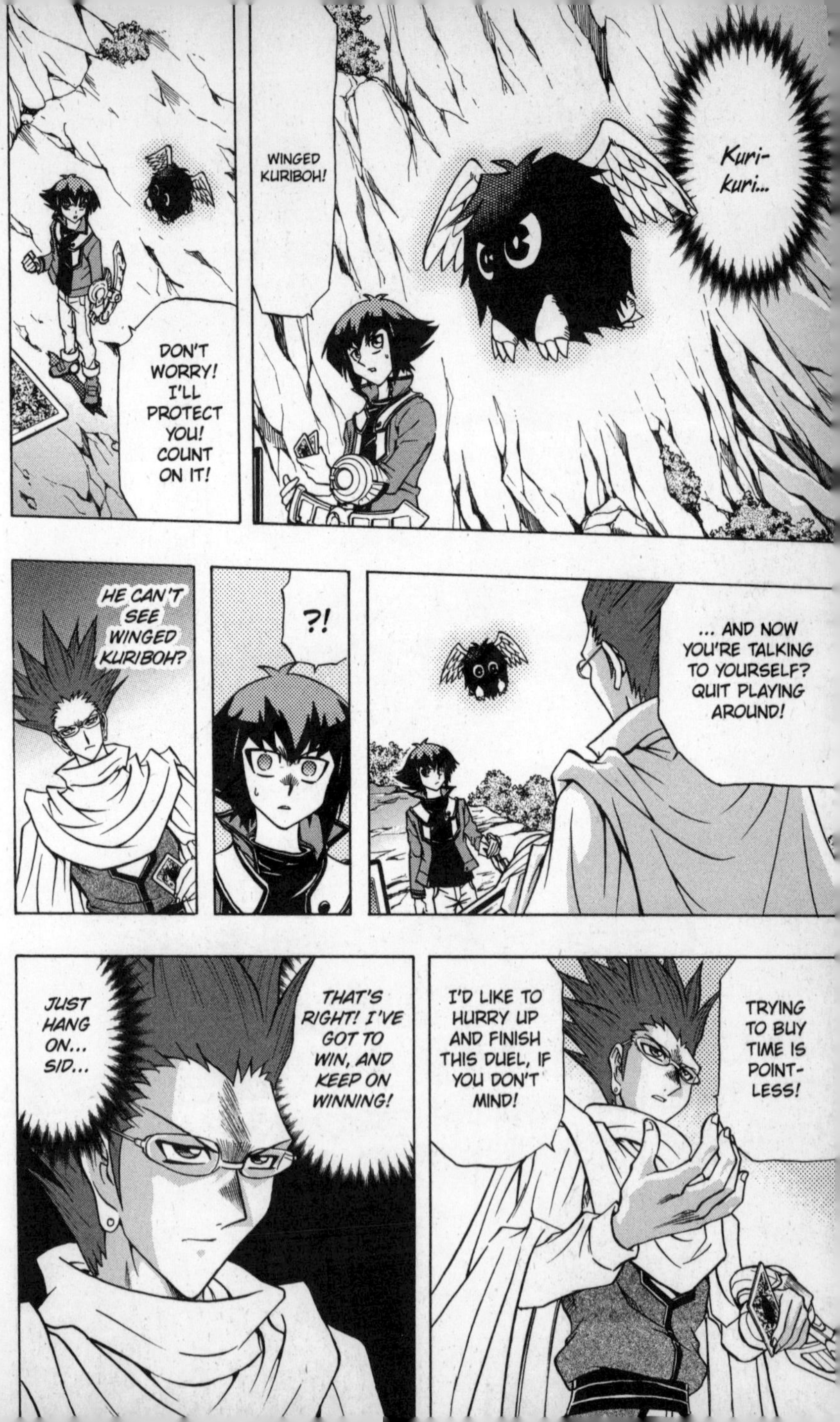
Kuri-kuri...
WINGED KURIBOH!
DON'T WORRY! I'LL PROTECT YOU! COUNT ON IT!
... AND NOW YOU'RE TALKING TO YOURSELF? QUIT PLAYING AROUND!
?!
HE CAN'T SEE WINGED KURIBOH?
TRYING TO BUY TIME IS POINT-LESS!
I'D LIKE TO HURRY UP AND FINISH THIS DUEL, IF YOU DON'T MIND!
THAT'S RIGHT! I'VE GOT TO WIN, AND KEEP ON WINNING!
JUST HANG ON... SID...

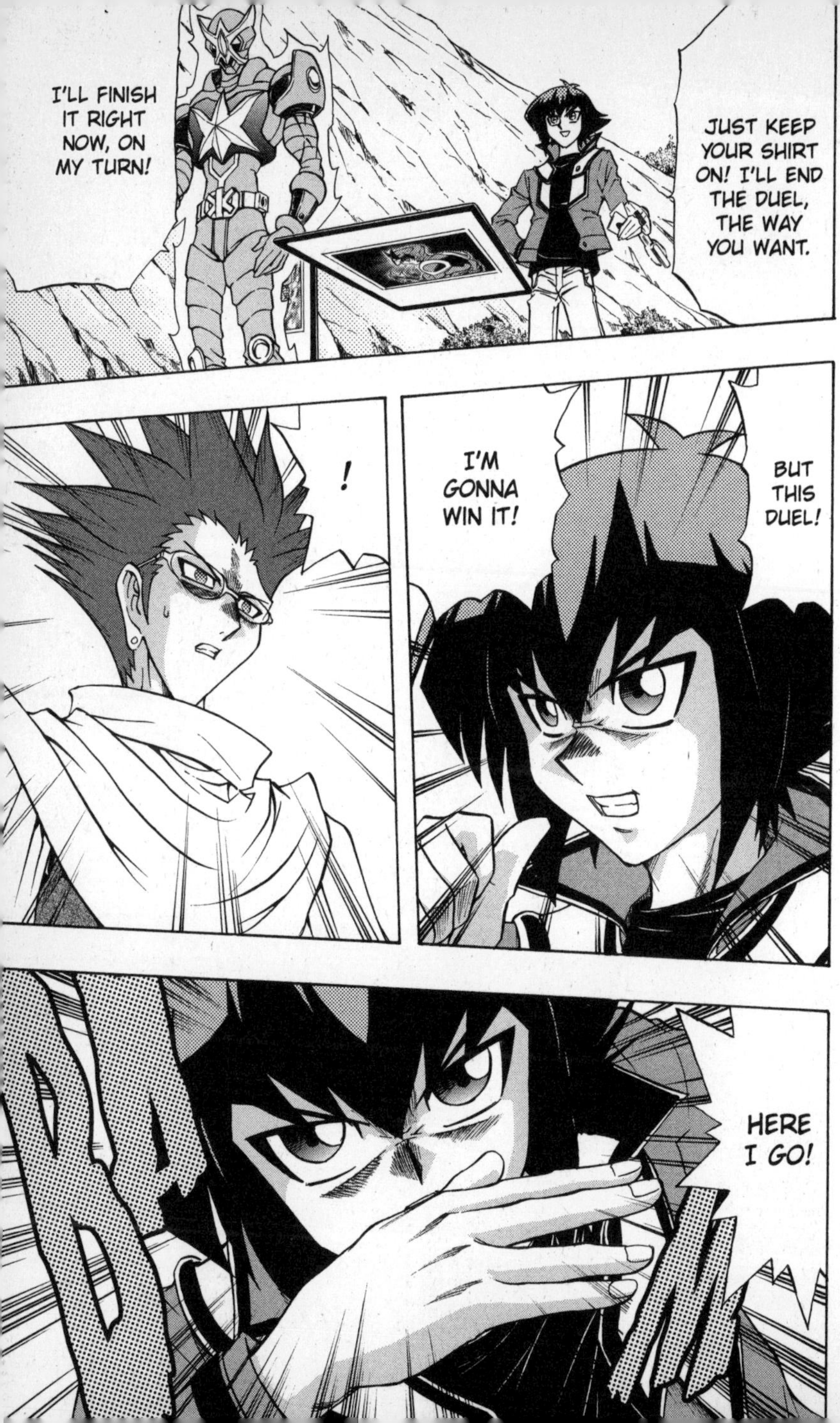
JUST KEEP YOUR SHIRT ON! I'LL END THE DUEL, THE WAY YOU WANT.
I'LL FINISH IT RIGHT NOW, ON MY TURN!
BUT THIS DUEL!
I'M GONNA WIN IT!
!
HERE I GO!

ANNOUNCEMENT

STUDIO DICE NOW HAS A HOMEPAGE!

WHETHER YOU KNEW ABOUT IT ALREADY OR JUST FOUND OUT, PLEASE CHECK IT OUT!

IT HAS MR. TAKAHASHI'S JOURNAL(?), "BUTTON," A LAID BACK ANIME PRODUCED BY DICE, AND A *YU-GI-OH!* GALLERY. WE'VE UPLOADED LOTS OF AMAZING ILLUSTRATIONS DRAWN BY MR. TAKAHASHI!

HTTP://STUDIO-DICE.COM
*JAPANESE ONLY

STUDIO DICE	SEARCH

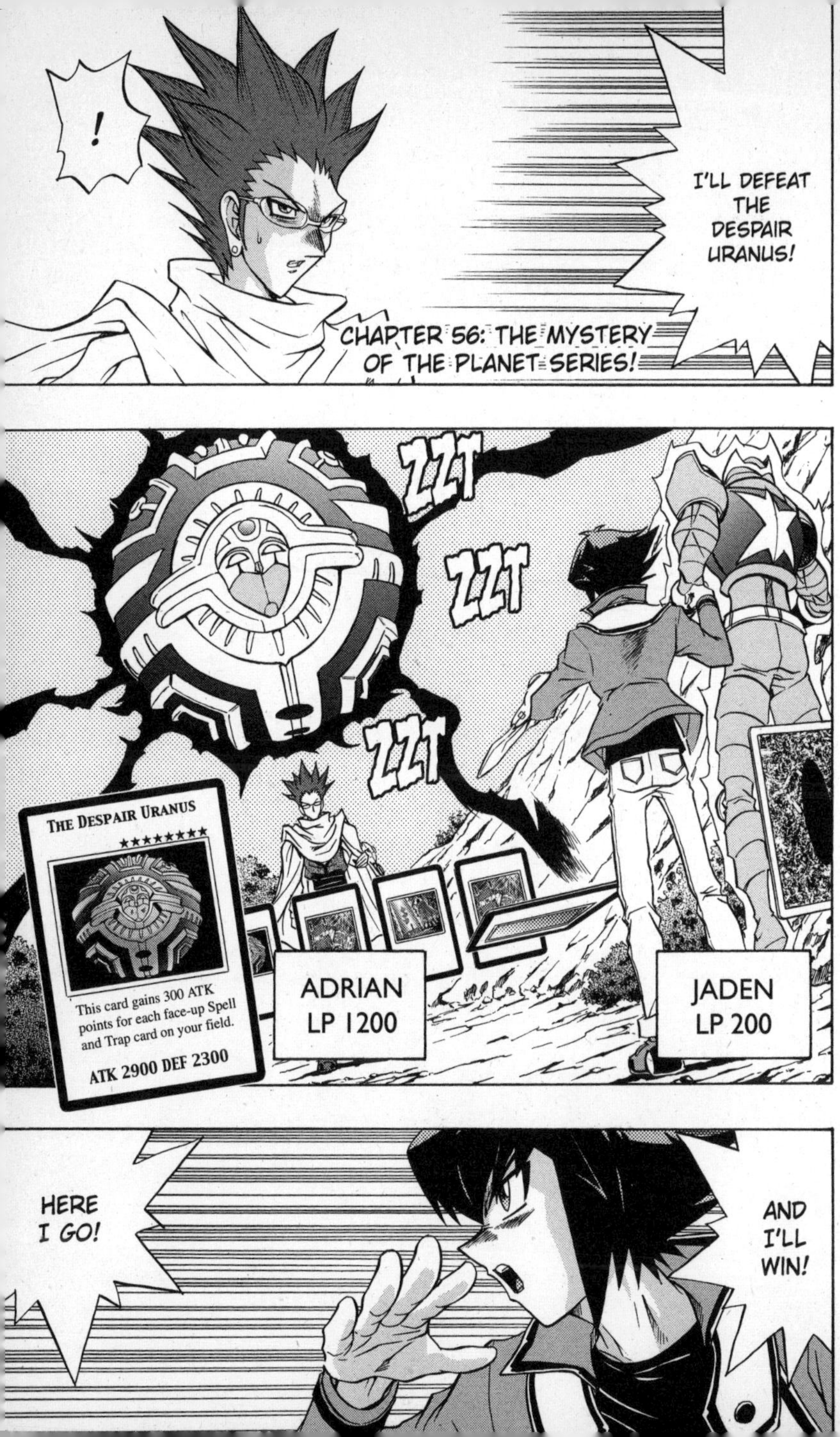
I'LL DEFEAT THE DESPAIR URANUS!
!
CHAPTER 56: THE MYSTERY OF THE PLANET SERIES!
ZZT
ZZT
ZZT
JADEN
LP 200
ADRIAN
LP 1200
THE DESPAIR URANUS
This card gains 300 ATK points for each face-up Spell and Trap card on your field.
ATK 2900 DEF 2300
HERE I GO!
AND I'LL WIN!

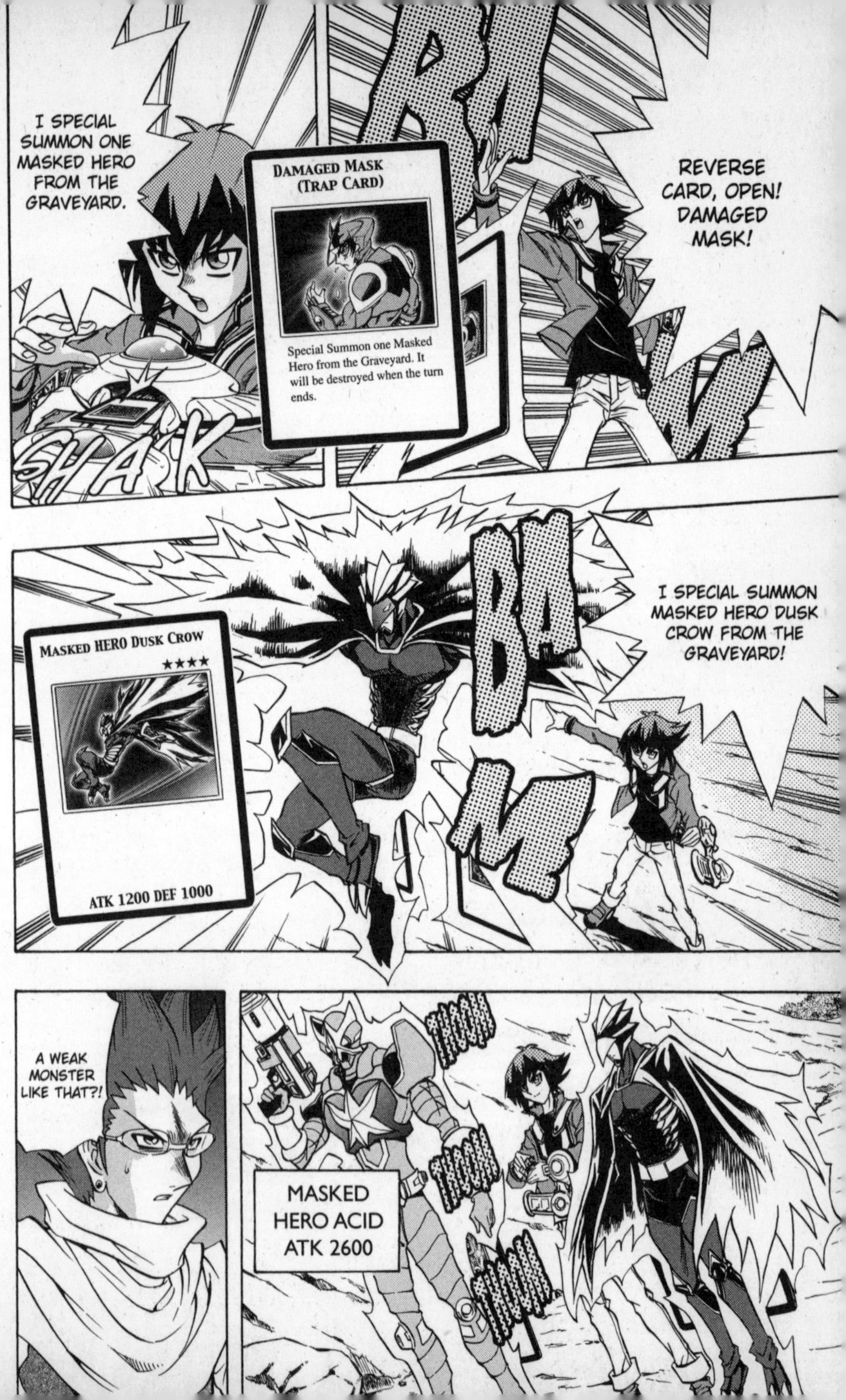
REVERSE CARD, OPEN! DAMAGED MASK!
DAMAGED MASK (TRAP CARD)
Special Summon one Masked Hero from the Graveyard. It will be destroyed when the turn ends.
I SPECIAL SUMMON ONE MASKED HERO FROM THE GRAVEYARD.
SHAK
I SPECIAL SUMMON MASKED HERO DUSK CROW FROM THE GRAVEYARD!
BAM
MASKED HERO DUSK CROW
★★★★
ATK 1200 DEF 1000
THOOM
THOOM
THOOM
MASKED HERO ACID ATK 2600
A WEAK MONSTER LIKE THAT?!

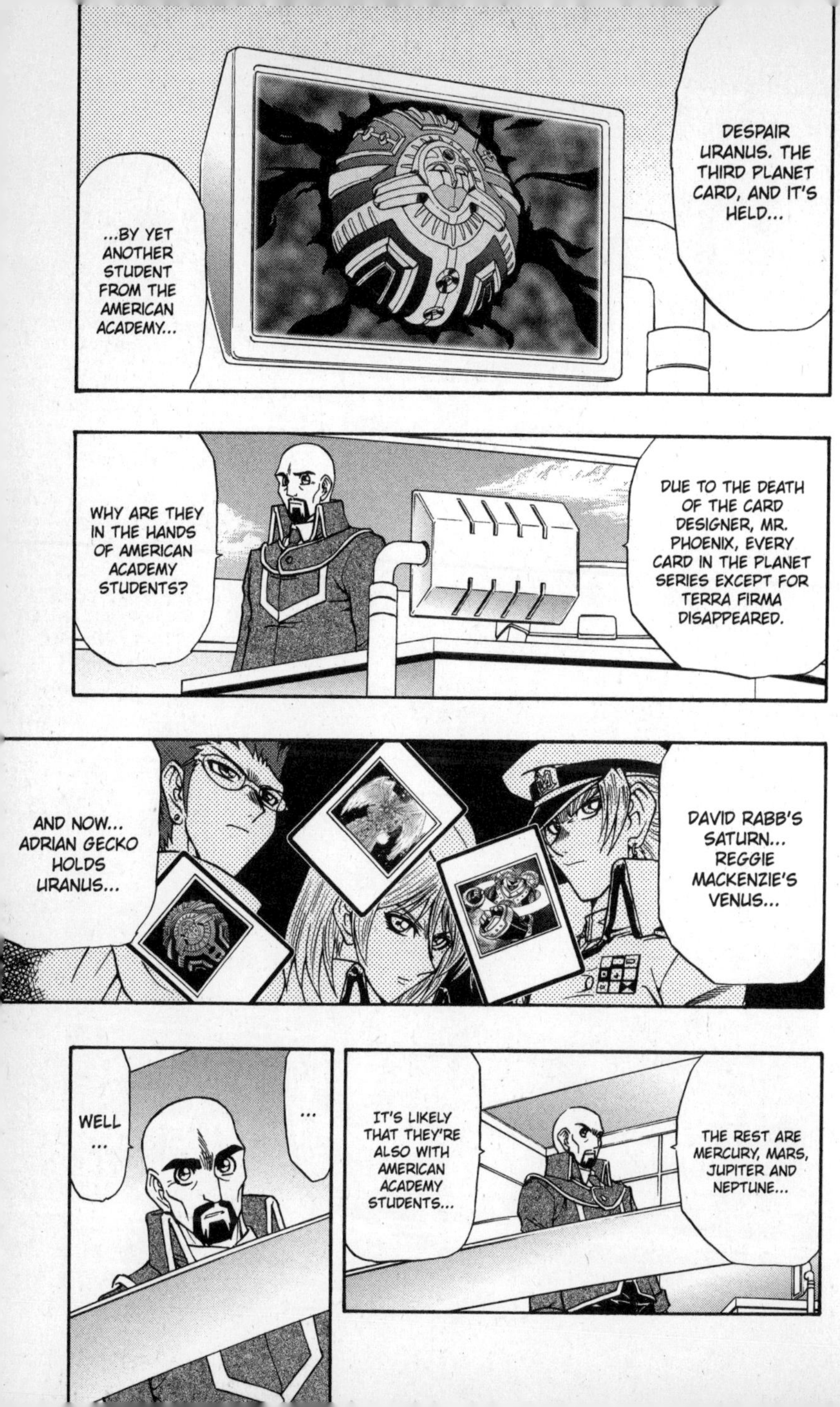
DESPAIR URANUS. THE THIRD PLANET CARD, AND IT'S HELD...
...BY YET ANOTHER STUDENT FROM THE AMERICAN ACADEMY...
DUE TO THE DEATH OF THE CARD DESIGNER, MR. PHOENIX, EVERY CARD IN THE PLANET SERIES EXCEPT FOR TERRA FIRMA DISAPPEARED.
WHY ARE THEY IN THE HANDS OF AMERICAN ACADEMY STUDENTS?
DAVID RABB'S SATURN... REGGIE MACKENZIE'S VENUS...
AND NOW... ADRIAN GECKO HOLDS URANUS...
THE REST ARE MERCURY, MARS, JUPITER AND NEPTUNE...
IT'S LIKELY THAT THEY'RE ALSO WITH AMERICAN ACADEMY STUDENTS...
...
WELL ...

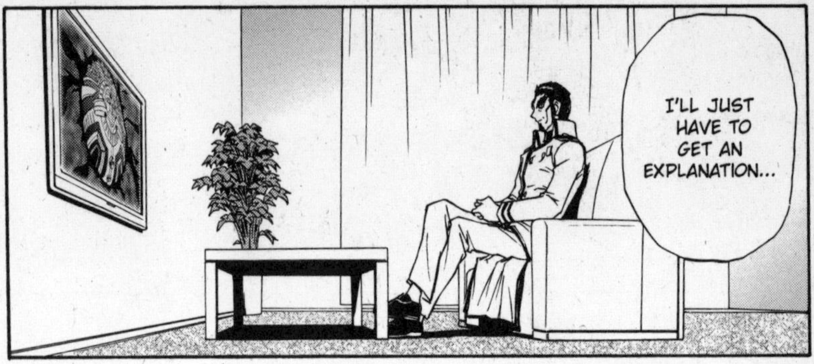
I'LL JUST HAVE TO GET AN EXPLANATION...

CHAPTER 56:
THE MYSTERY OF THE PLANET SERIES!!

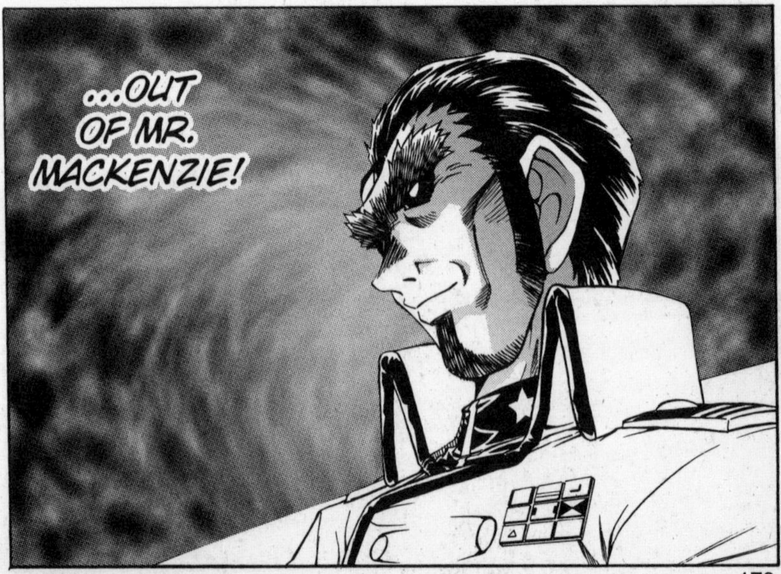
...OUT OF MR. MACKENZIE!

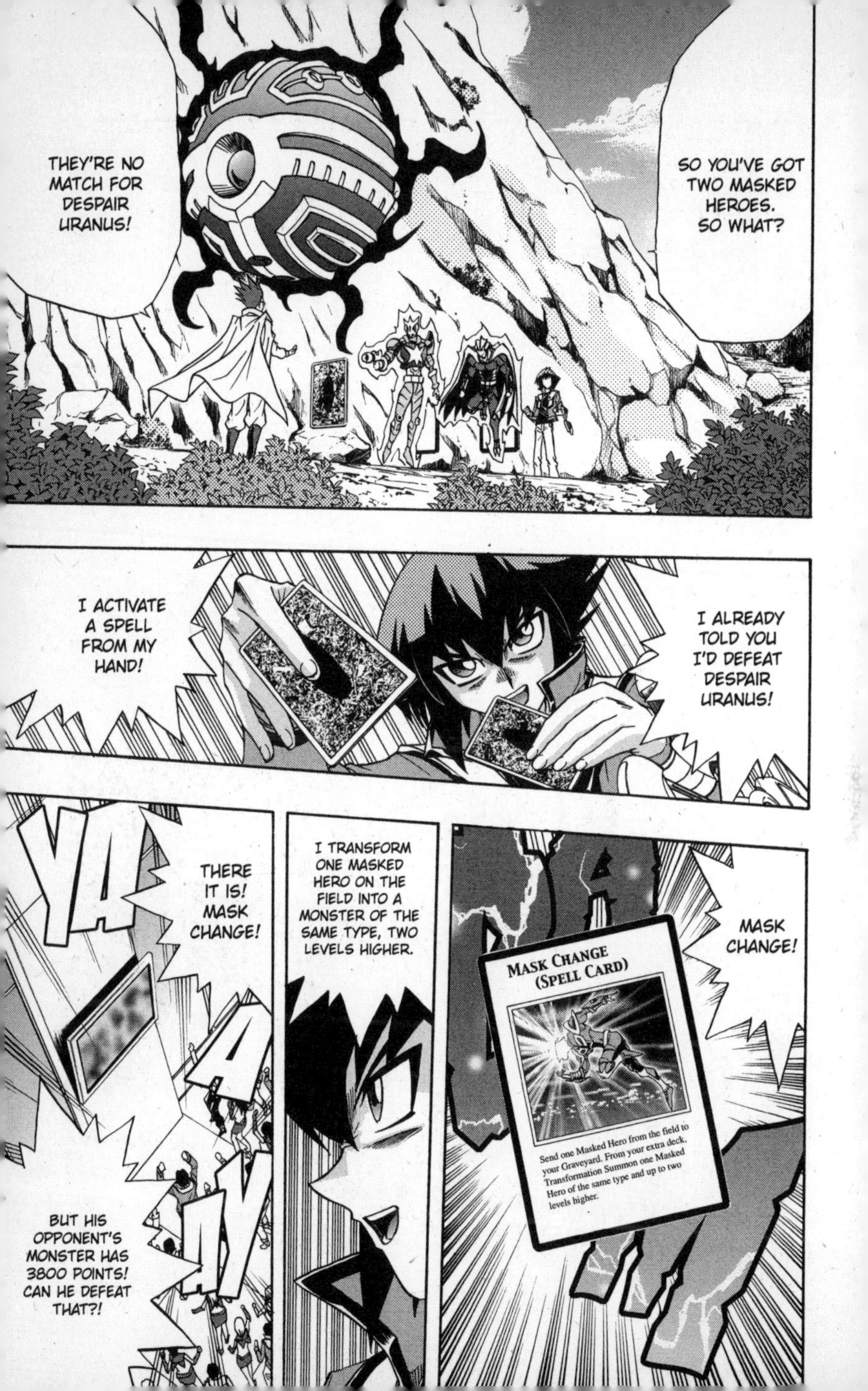
SO YOU'VE GOT TWO MASKED HEROES. SO WHAT?
THEY'RE NO MATCH FOR DESPAIR URANUS!
I ALREADY TOLD YOU I'D DEFEAT DESPAIR URANUS!
I ACTIVATE A SPELL FROM MY HAND!
MASK CHANGE!
MASK CHANGE (SPELL CARD)
Send one Masked Hero from the field to your Graveyard. From your extra deck, Transformation Summon one Masked Hero of the same type and up to two levels higher.
I TRANSFORM ONE MASKED HERO ON THE FIELD INTO A MONSTER OF THE SAME TYPE, TWO LEVELS HIGHER.
THERE IT IS! MASK CHANGE!
YA
A
BUT HIS OPPONENT'S MONSTER HAS 3800 POINTS! CAN HE DEFEAT THAT?!

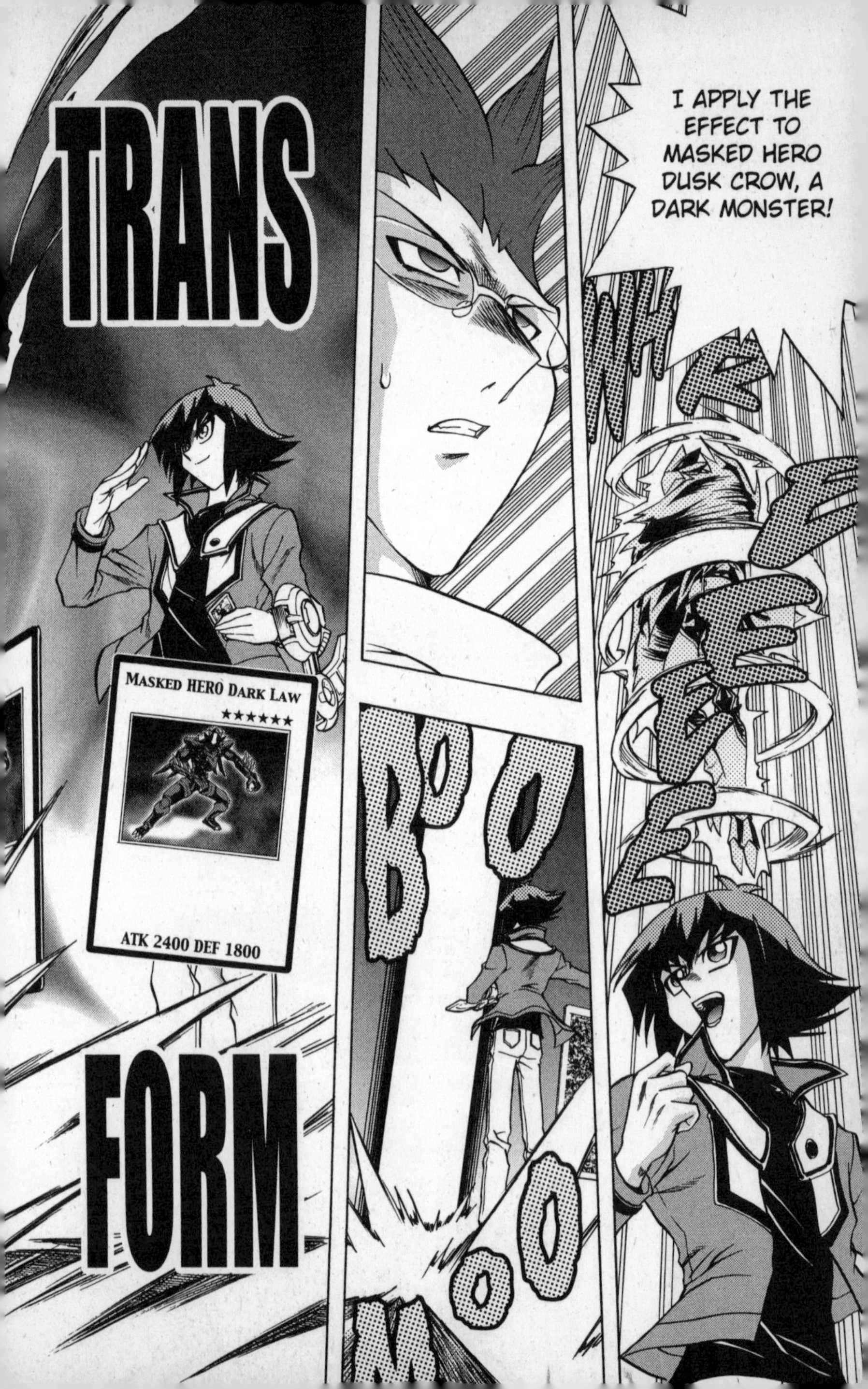
I APPLY THE EFFECT TO MASKED HERO DUSK CROW, A DARK MONSTER!
TRANS
FORM
MASKED HERO DARK LAW
ATK 2400 DEF 1800

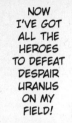

NOW I'VE GOT ALL THE HEROES TO DEFEAT DESPAIR URANUS ON MY FIELD!

?!!

MASKED HERO

DARK LAW

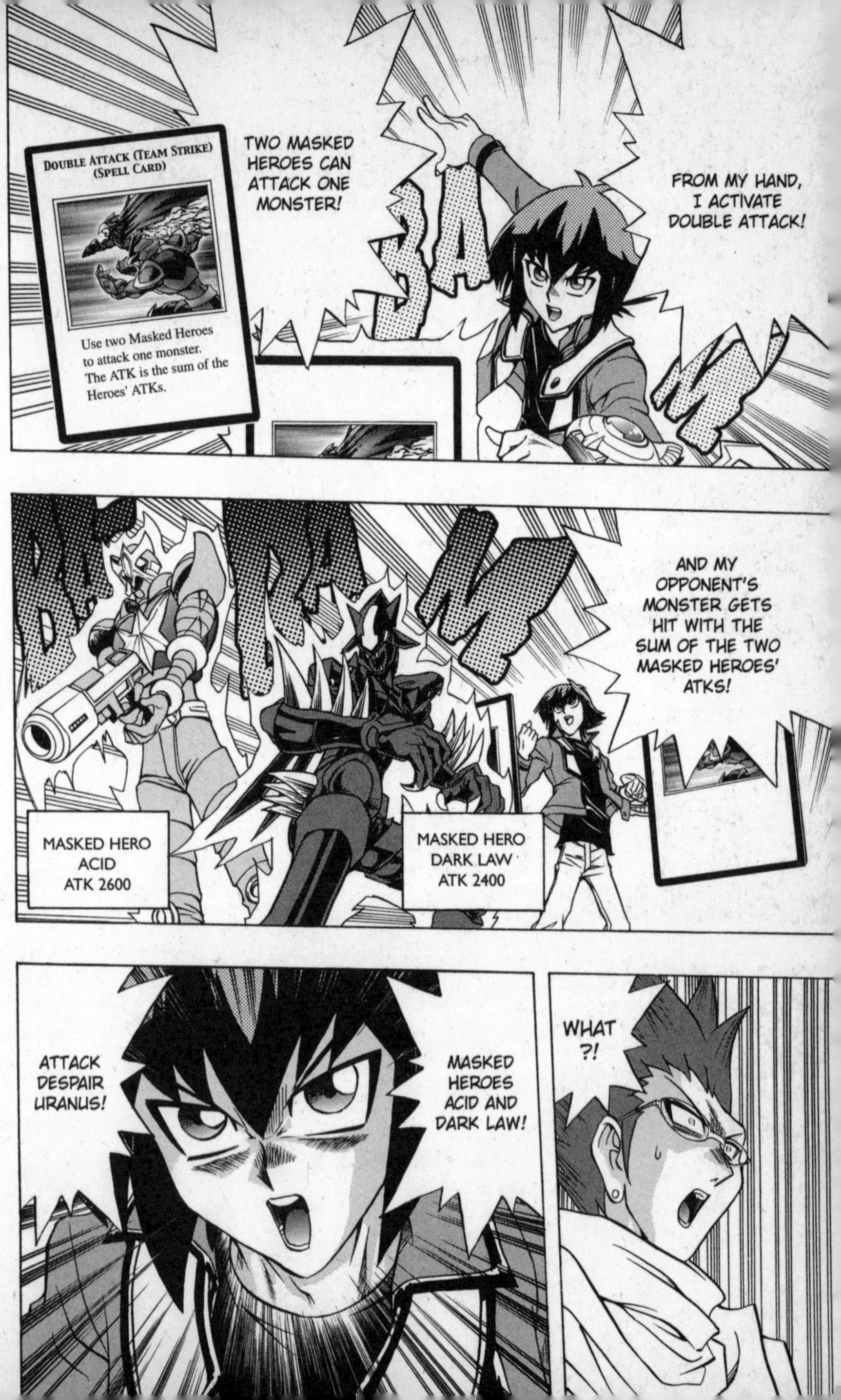
FROM MY HAND, I ACTIVATE DOUBLE ATTACK!
BAM
TWO MASKED HEROES CAN ATTACK ONE MONSTER!
DOUBLE ATTACK (TEAM STRIKE) (SPELL CARD)
Use two Masked Heroes to attack one monster. The ATK is the sum of the Heroes' ATKs.
AND MY OPPONENT'S MONSTER GETS HIT WITH THE SUM OF THE TWO MASKED HEROES' ATKS!
BAM
MASKED HERO DARK LAW ATK 2400
MASKED HERO ACID ATK 2600
WHAT ?!
MASKED HEROES ACID AND DARK LAW!
ATTACK DESPAIR URANUS!

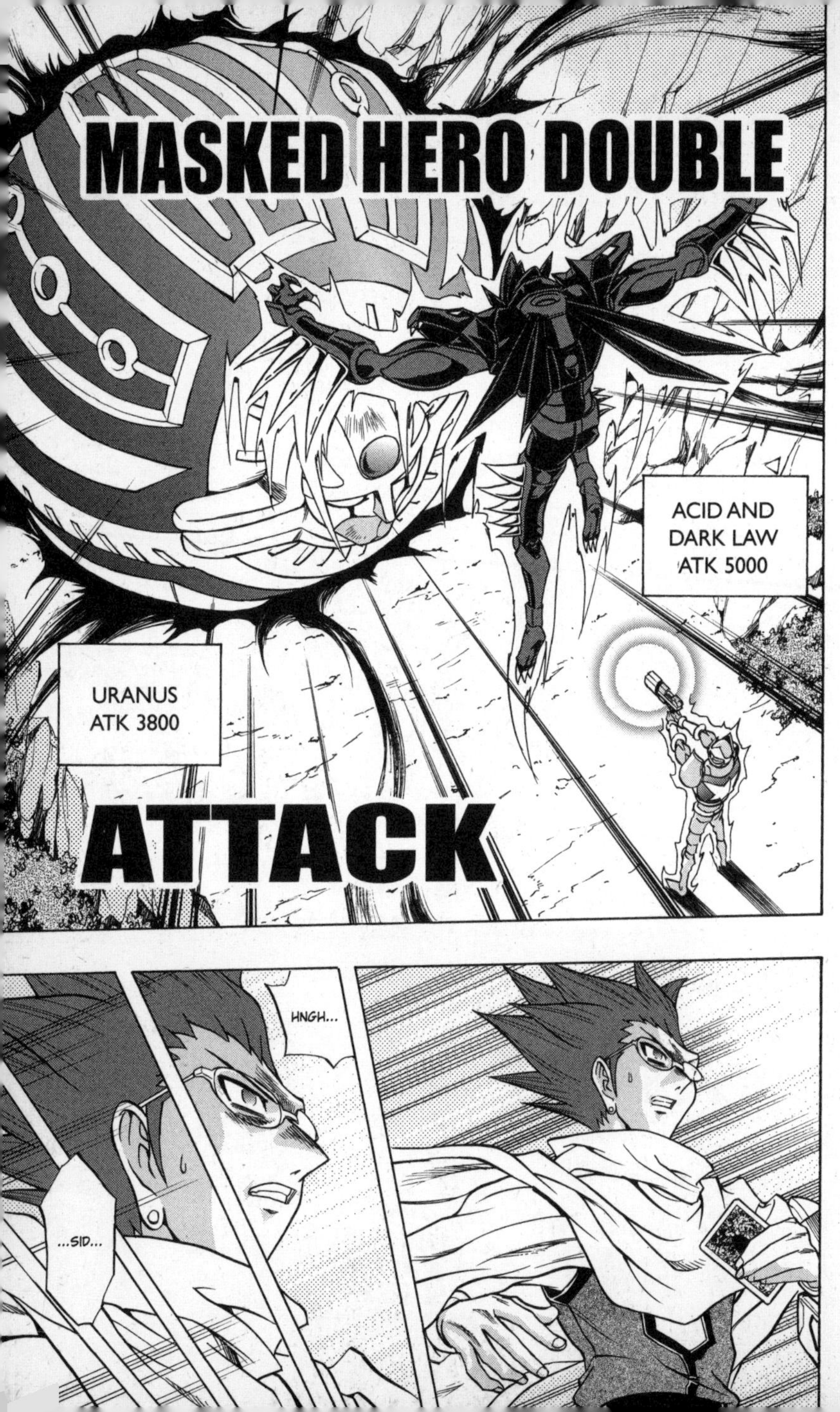
MASKED HERO DOUBLE
ACID AND DARK LAW ATK 5000
URANUS ATK 3800
ATTACK
HNGH...
...SID...

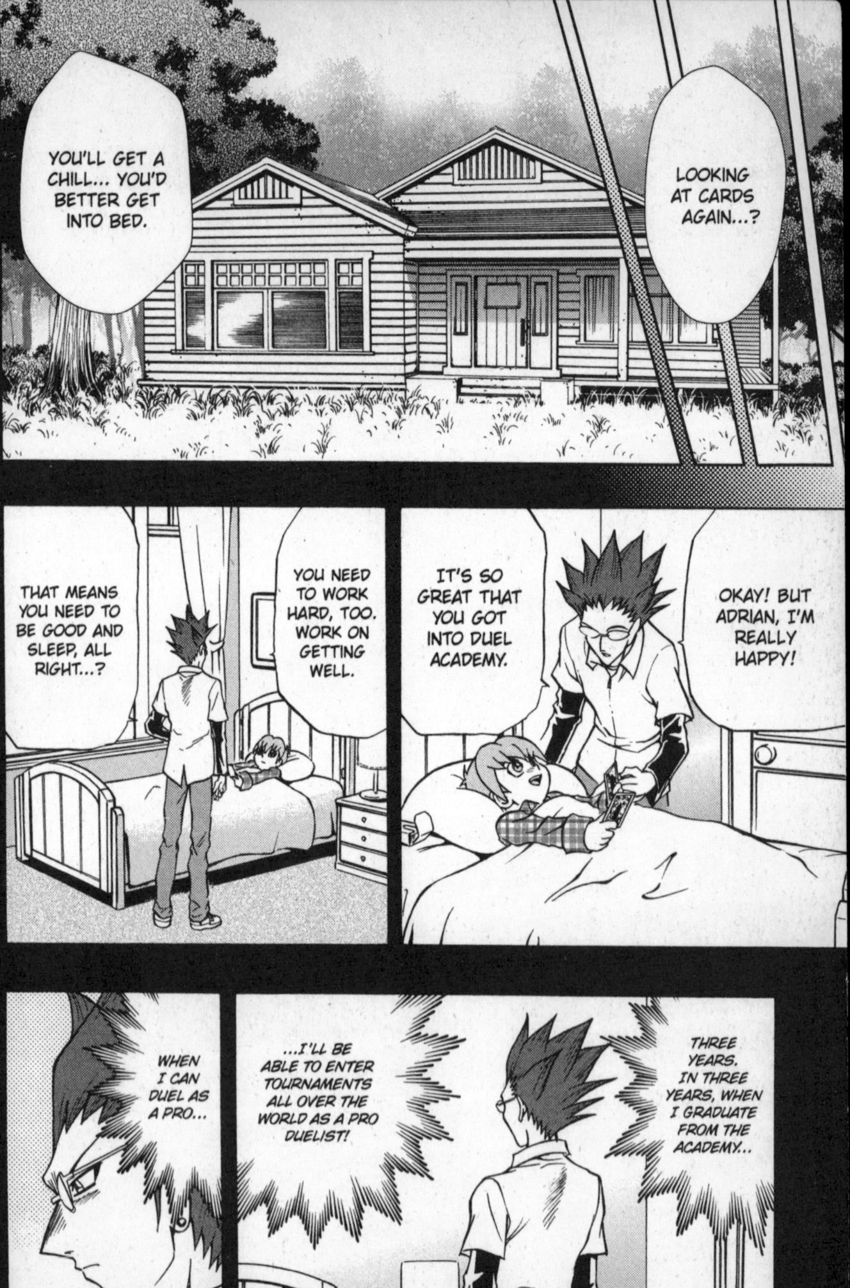
LOOKING AT CARDS AGAIN...?
YOU'LL GET A CHILL... YOU'D BETTER GET INTO BED.
OKAY! BUT ADRIAN, I'M REALLY HAPPY!
IT'S SO GREAT THAT YOU GOT INTO DUEL ACADEMY.
YOU NEED TO WORK HARD, TOO. WORK ON GETTING WELL.
THAT MEANS YOU NEED TO BE GOOD AND SLEEP, ALL RIGHT...?
THREE YEARS. IN THREE YEARS, WHEN I GRADUATE FROM THE ACADEMY...
...I'LL BE ABLE TO ENTER TOURNAMENTS ALL OVER THE WORLD AS A PRO DUELIST!
WHEN I CAN DUEL AS A PRO...

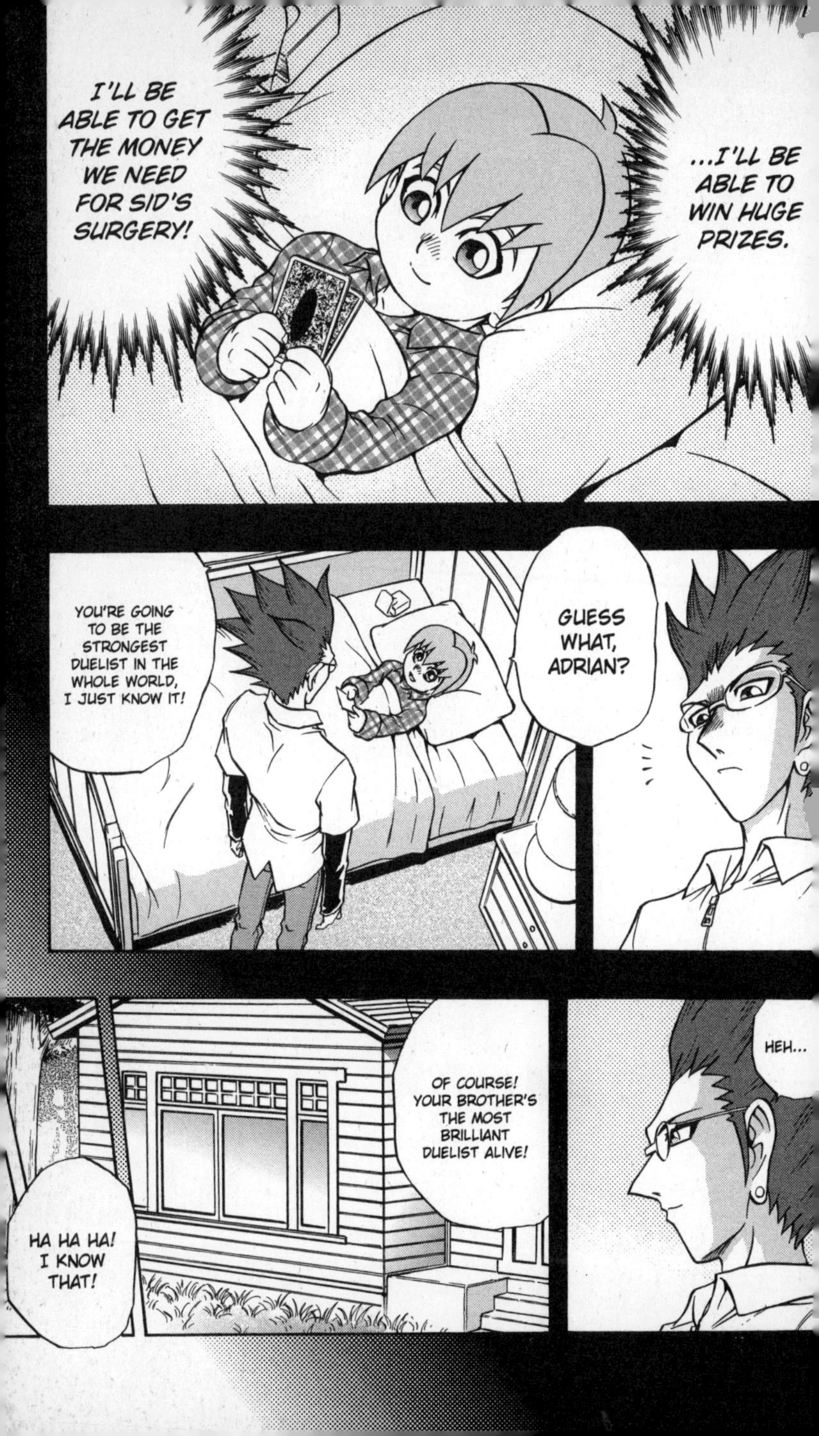
...I'LL BE ABLE TO WIN HUGE PRIZES.
I'LL BE ABLE TO GET THE MONEY WE NEED FOR SID'S SURGERY!
GUESS WHAT, ADRIAN?
YOU'RE GOING TO BE THE STRONGEST DUELIST IN THE WHOLE WORLD, I JUST KNOW IT!
HEH...
OF COURSE! YOUR BROTHER'S THE MOST BRILLIANT DUELIST ALIVE!
HA HA HA! I KNOW THAT!

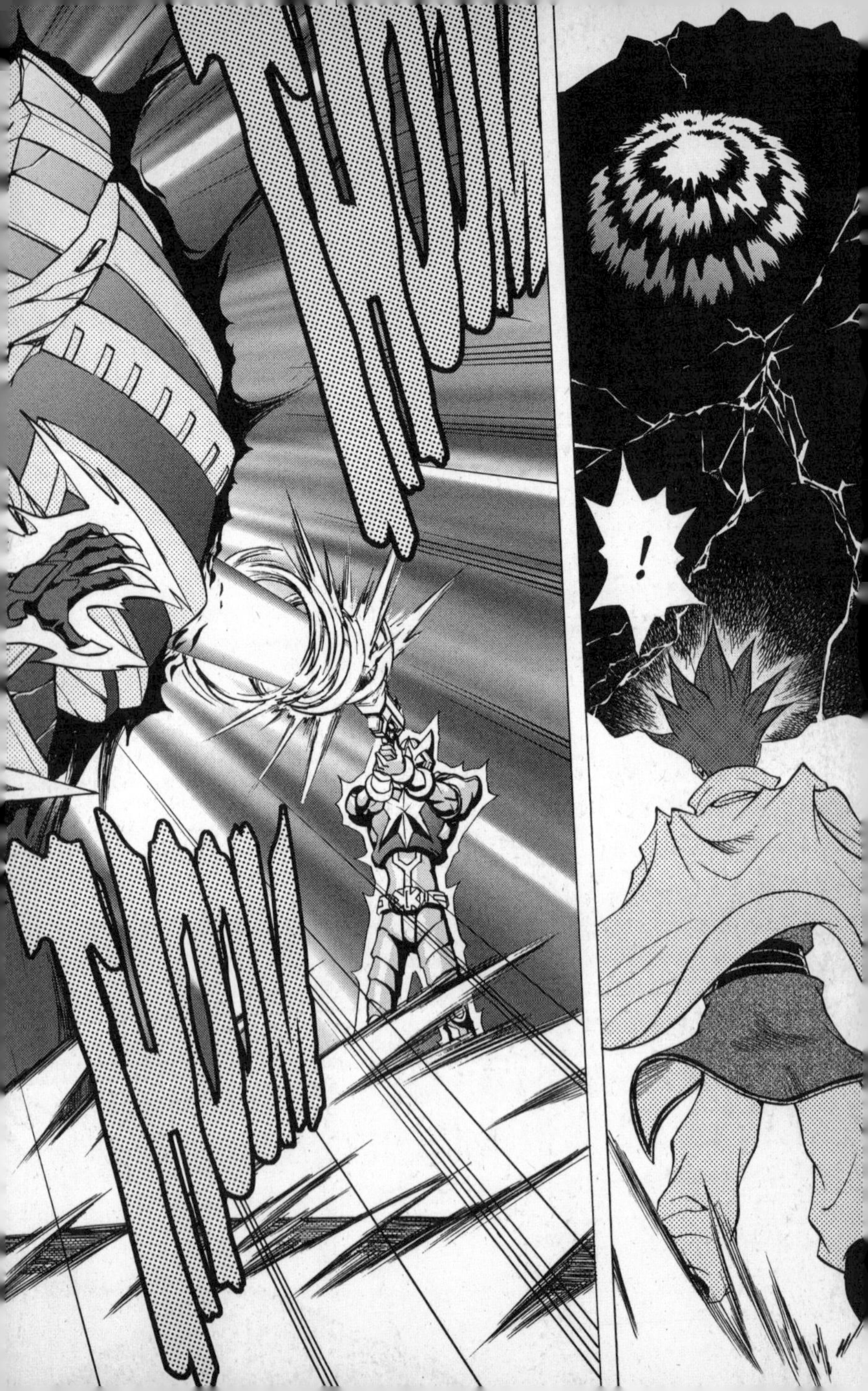
!
THOOM
THOOM

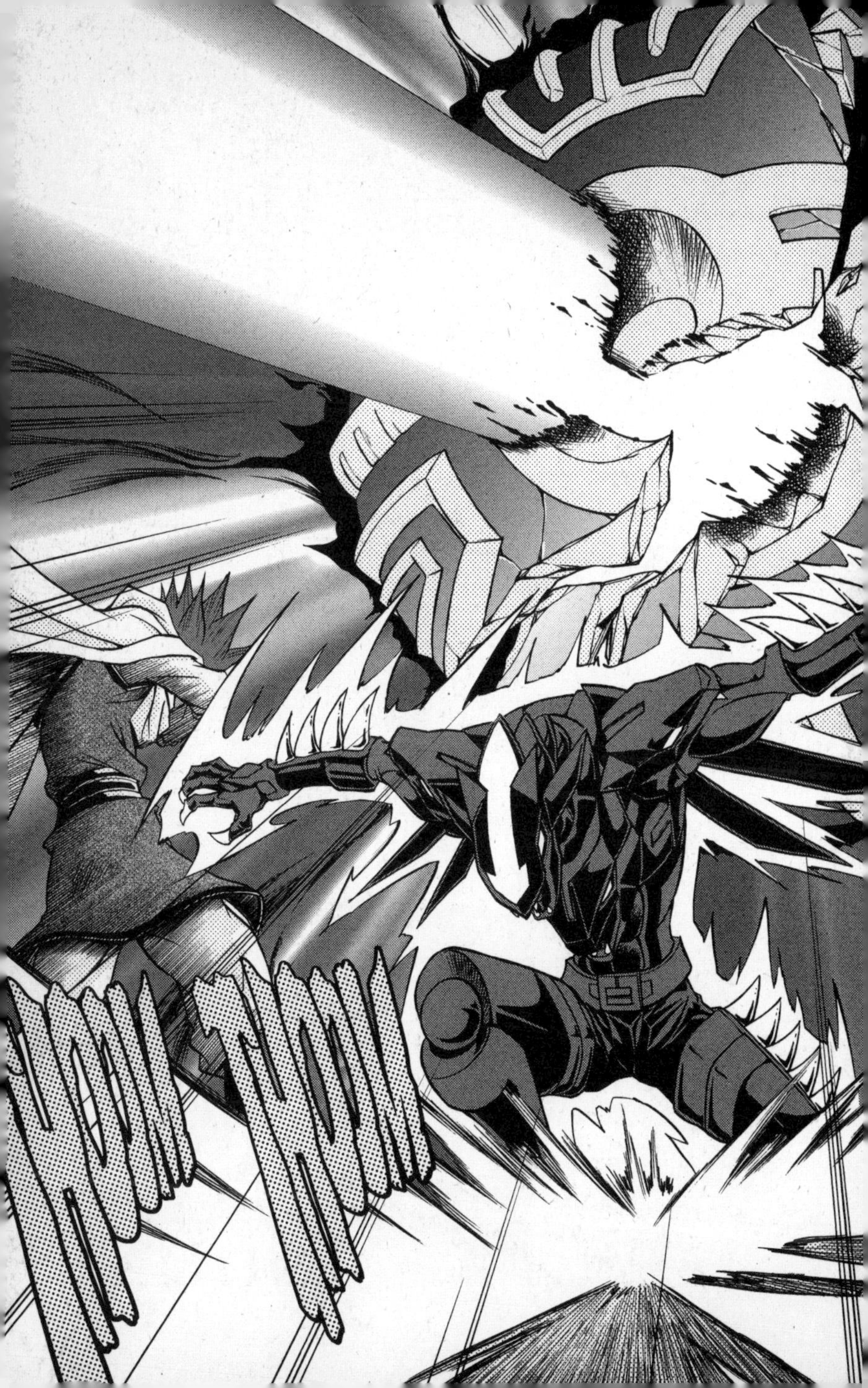

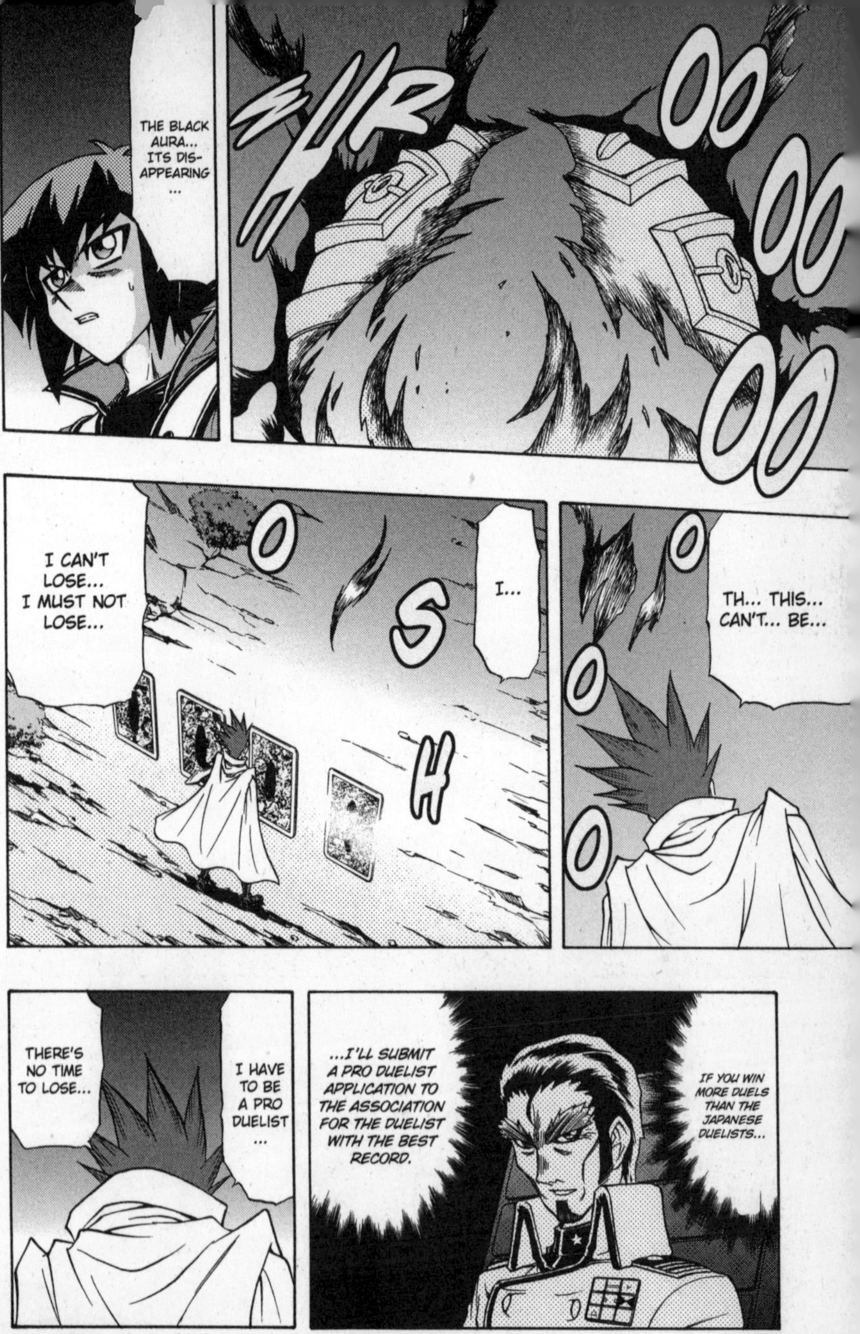
THE BLACK AURA... ITS DIS- APPEARING ...
TH... THIS... CAN'T... BE...
I...
I CAN'T LOSE... I MUST NOT LOSE...
IF YOU WIN MORE DUELS THAN THE JAPANESE DUELISTS...
...I'LL SUBMIT A PRO DUELIST APPLICATION TO THE ASSOCIATION FOR THE DUELIST WITH THE BEST RECORD.
I HAVE TO BE A PRO DUELIST ...
THERE'S NO TIME TO LOSE...

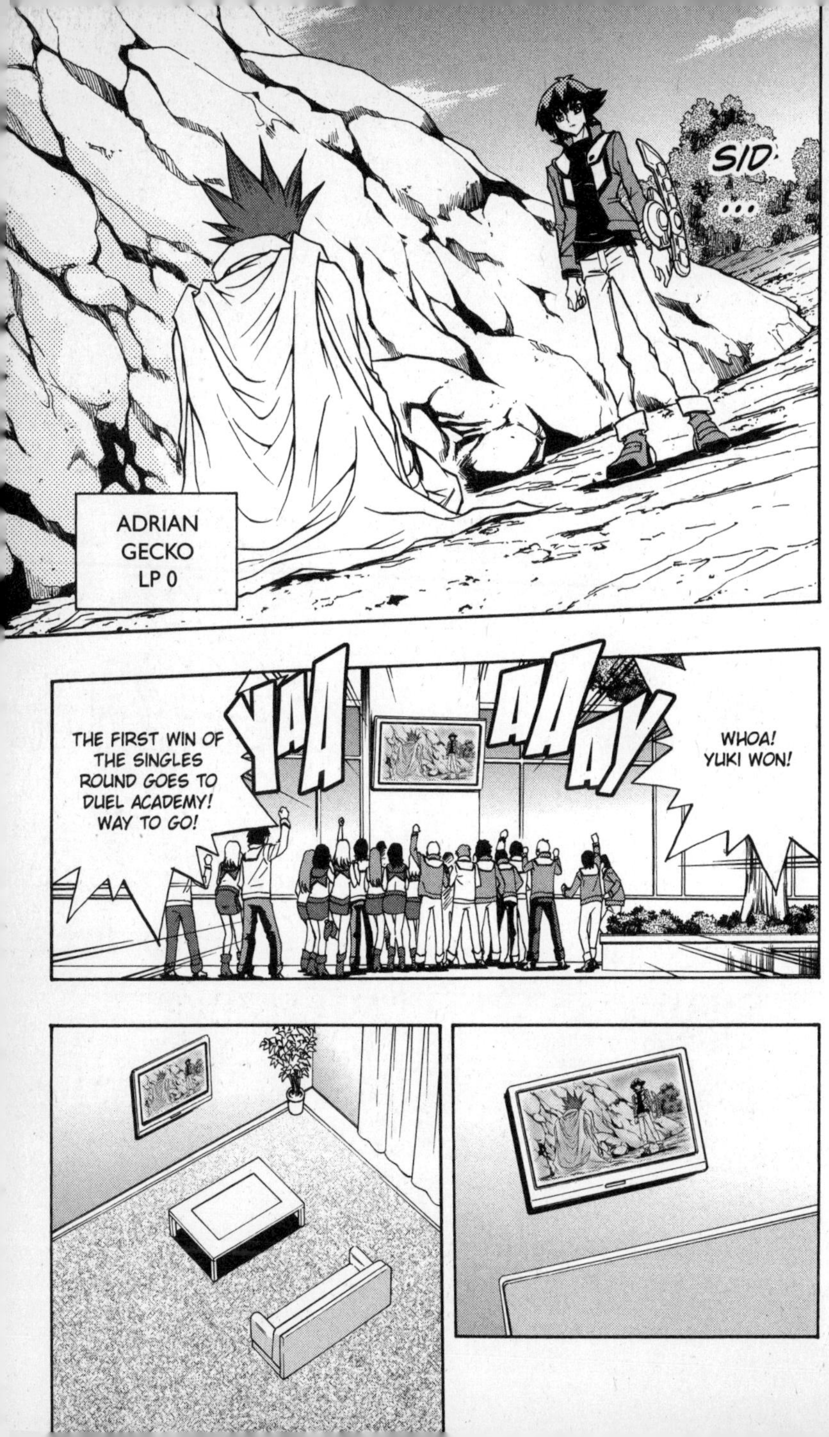
SID...
ADRIAN GECKO LP 0
WHOA! YUKI WON!
YAA AAAY
THE FIRST WIN OF THE SINGLES ROUND GOES TO DUEL ACADEMY! WAY TO GO!

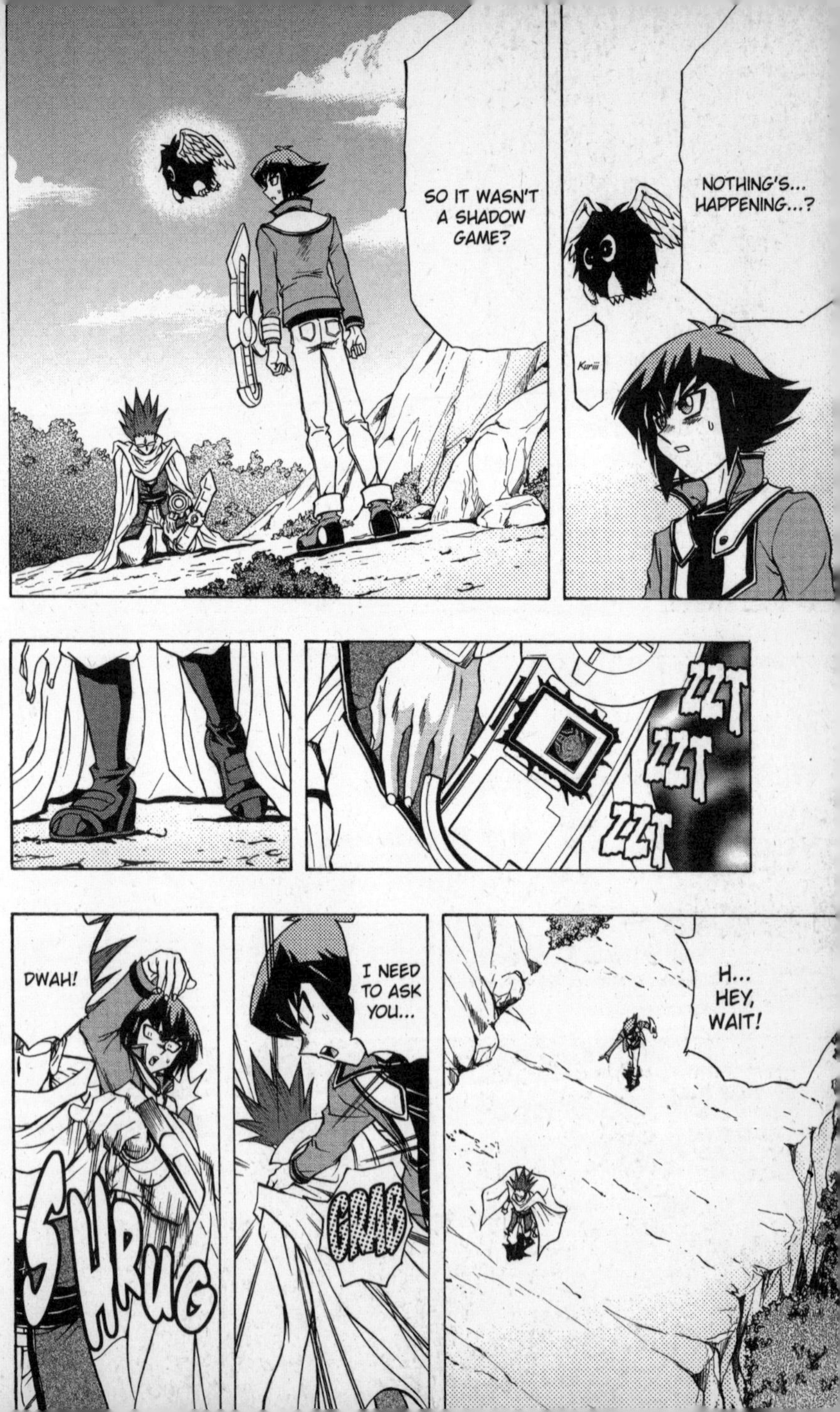
NOTHING'S... HAPPENING...?
Kuriii
SO IT WASN'T A SHADOW GAME?
ZZT
ZZT
ZZT
H... HEY, WAIT!
I NEED TO ASK YOU...
GRAB
DWAH!
SHRUG

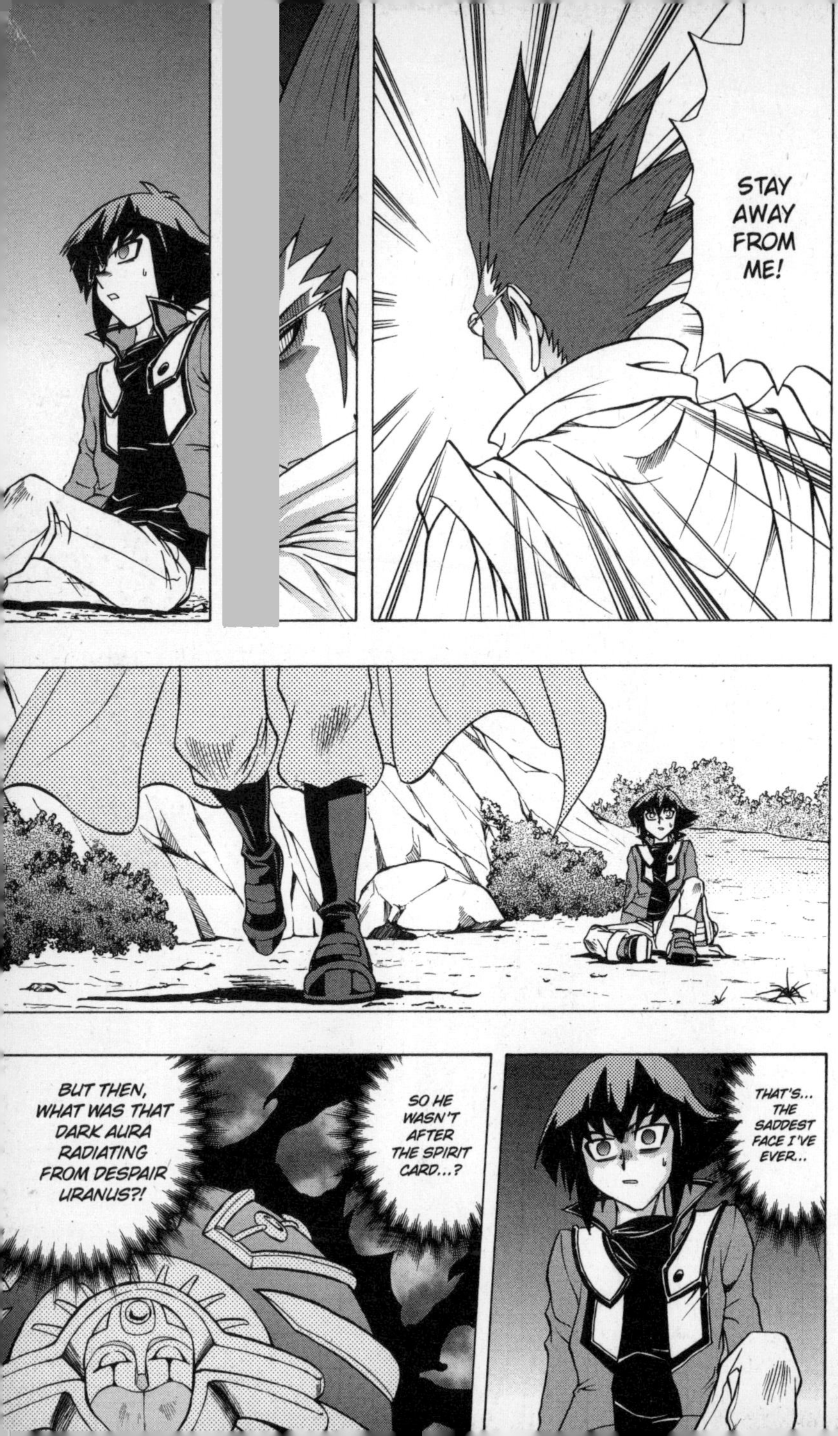
STAY AWAY FROM ME!
THAT'S... THE SADDEST FACE I'VE EVER...
SO HE WASN'T AFTER THE SPIRIT CARD...?
BUT THEN, WHAT WAS THAT DARK AURA RADIATING FROM DESPAIR URANUS?!

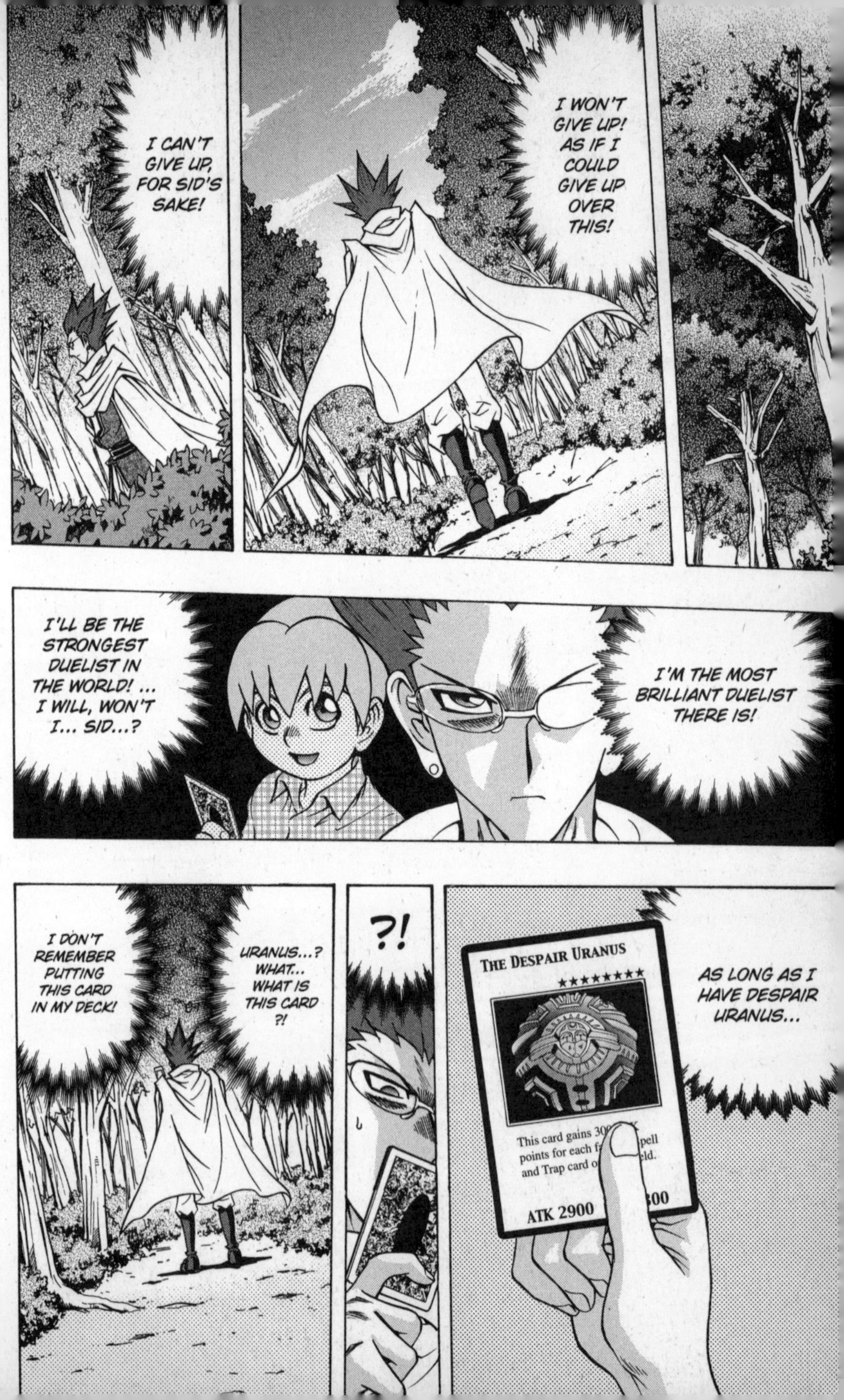
I WON'T GIVE UP! AS IF I COULD GIVE UP OVER THIS!
I CAN'T GIVE UP, FOR SID'S SAKE!
I'M THE MOST BRILLIANT DUELIST THERE IS!
I'LL BE THE STRONGEST DUELIST IN THE WORLD! ... I WILL, WON'T I... SID...?
AS LONG AS I HAVE DESPAIR URANUS...
THE DESPAIR URANUS
ATK 2900
?!
URANUS...? WHAT... WHAT IS THIS CARD ?!
I DON'T REMEMBER PUTTING THIS CARD IN MY DECK!

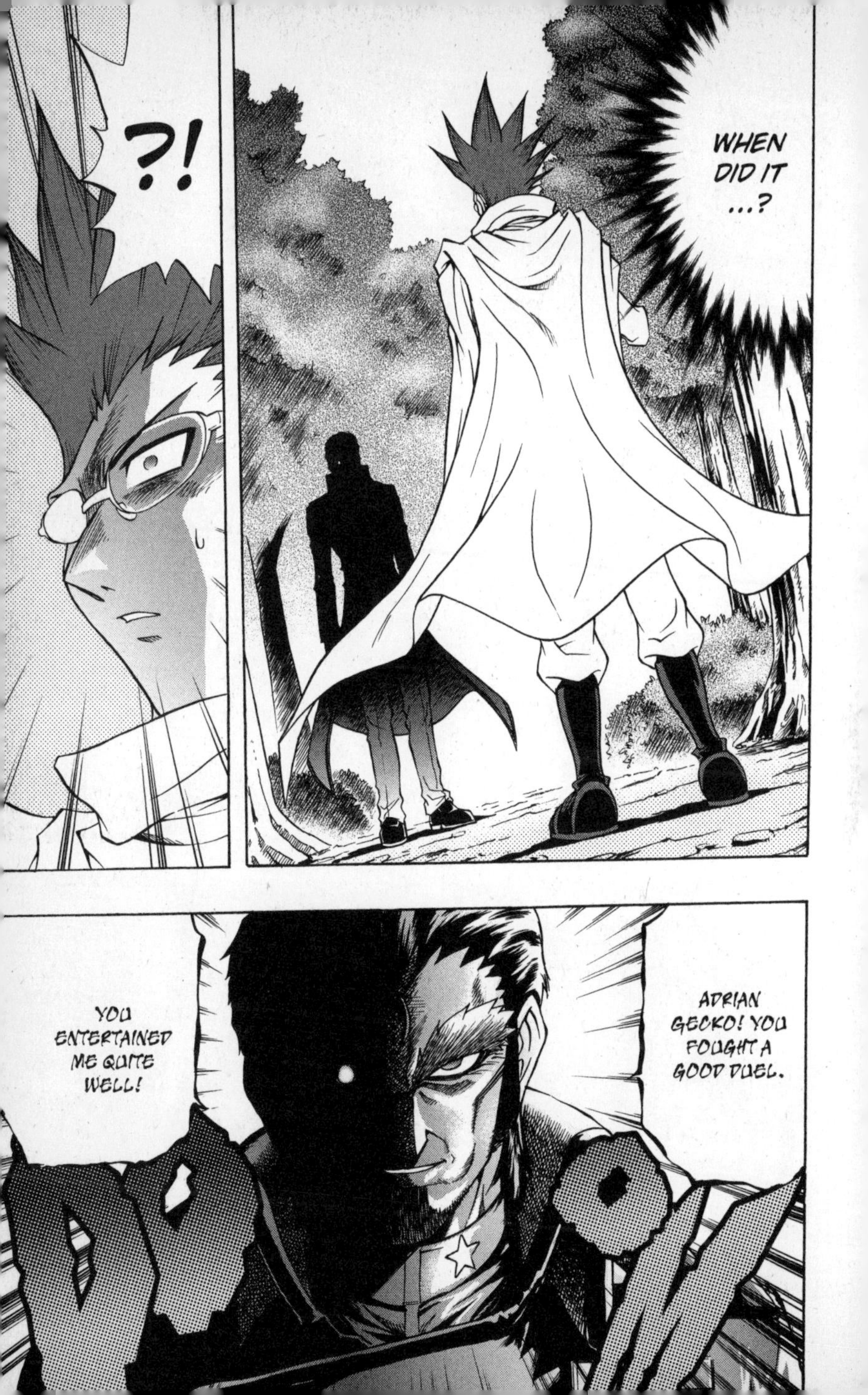
WHEN DID IT ...?
?!
ADRIAN GECKO! YOU FOUGHT A GOOD DUEL.
YOU ENTERTAINED ME QUITE WELL!

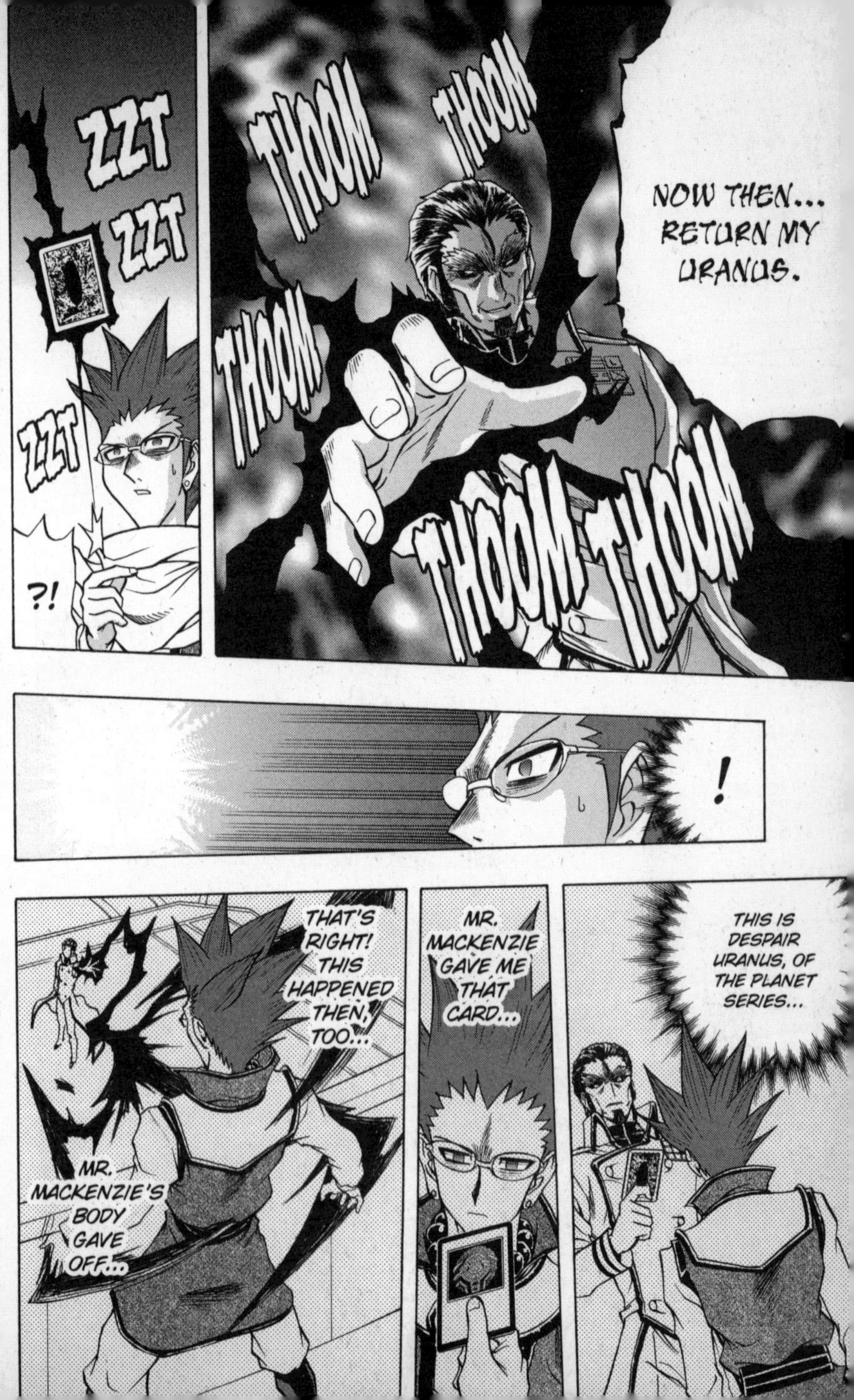
THOOM
THOOM
NOW THEN... RETURN MY URANUS.
THOOM
THOOM THOOM
ZZT
ZZT
ZZT
?!
!
THIS IS DESPAIR URANUS, OF THE PLANET SERIES...
MR. MACKENZIE GAVE ME THAT CARD...
THAT'S RIGHT! THIS HAPPENED THEN, TOO...
MR. MACKENZIE'S BODY GAVE OFF...

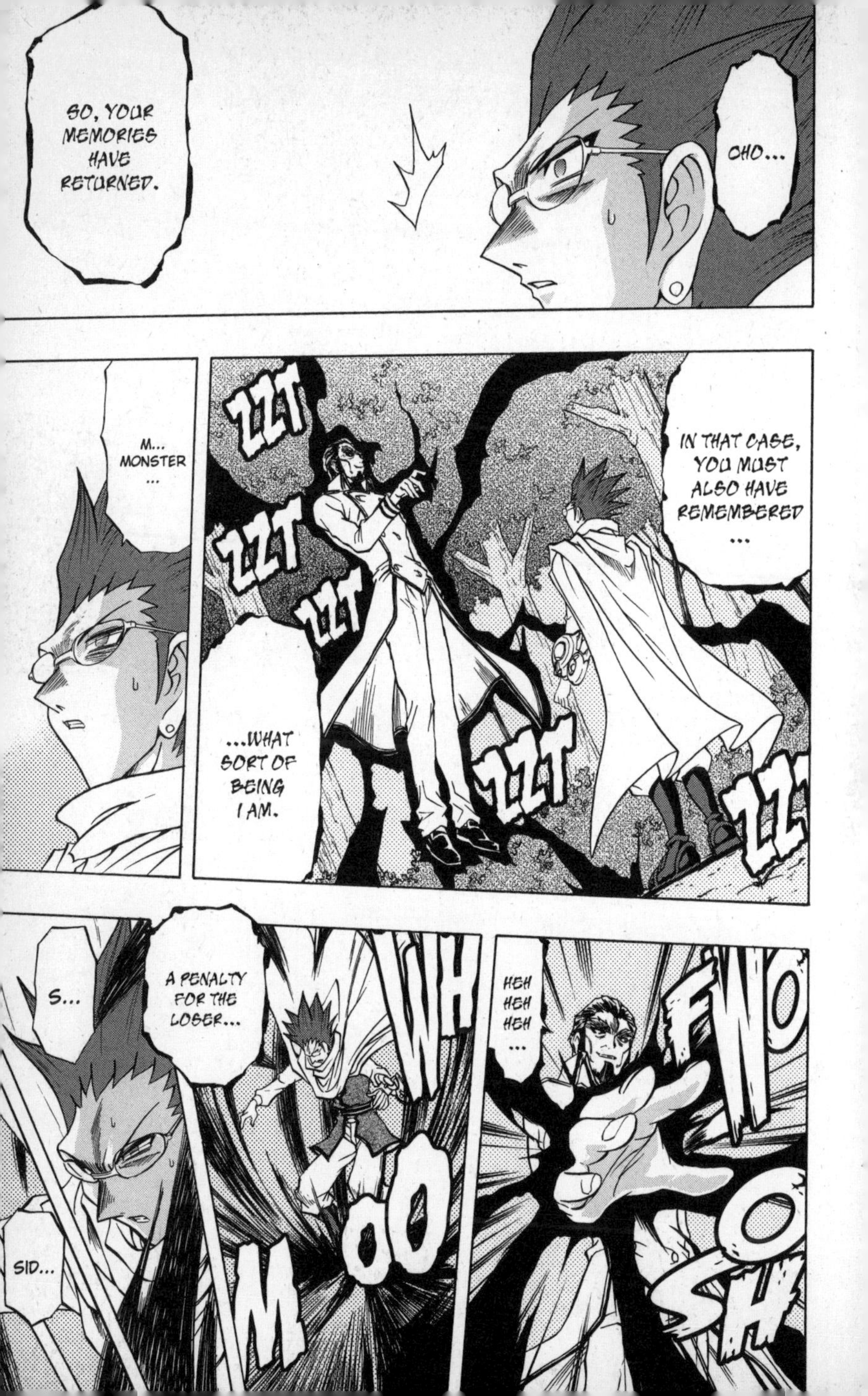
CHO...
SO, YOUR MEMORIES HAVE RETURNED.
IN THAT CASE, YOU MUST ALSO HAVE REMEMBERED ...
...WHAT SORT OF BEING I AM.
ZZT
ZZT
ZZT
ZZT
M... MONSTER ...
HEH HEH HEH ...
FWOOSH
A PENALTY FOR THE LOSER...
WHOOM
S...
SID...

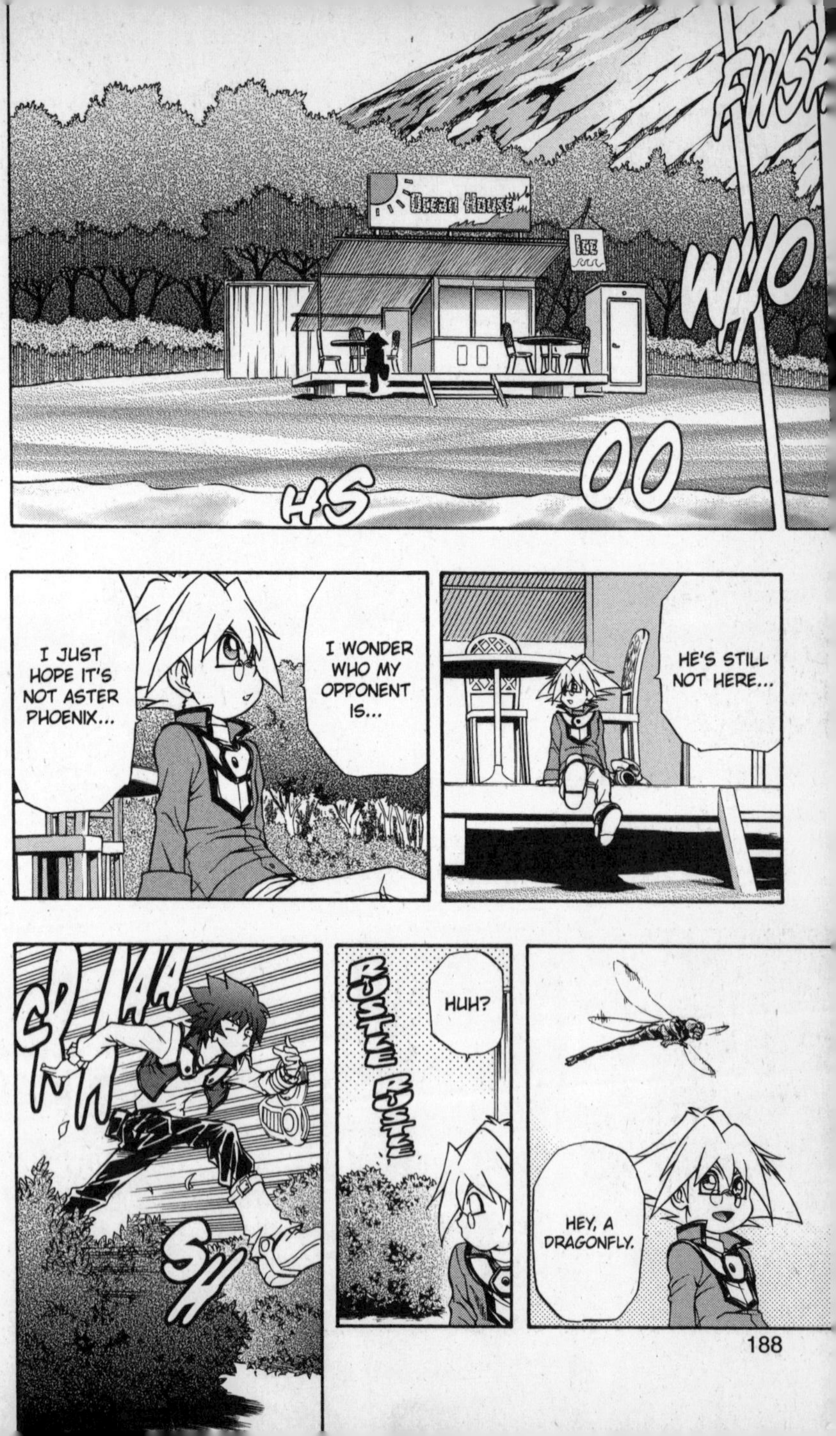
FWSH
WHO
OO
HS
HE'S STILL NOT HERE...
I WONDER WHO MY OPPONENT IS...
I JUST HOPE IT'S NOT ASTER PHOENIX...
HEY, A DRAGONFLY.
HUH?
RUSTLE RUSTLE
SH

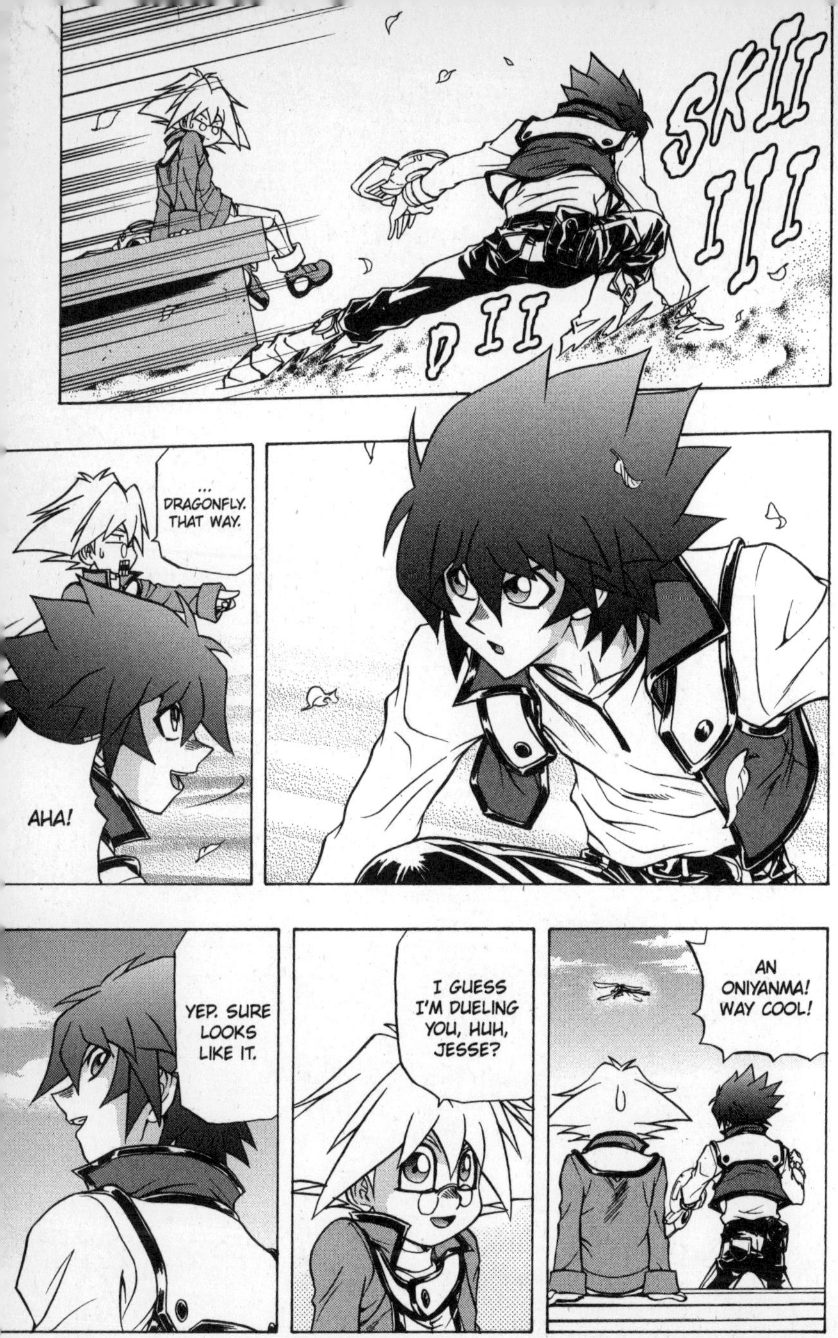

SKIIIII
DII
... DRAGONFLY. THAT WAY.
AHA!
AN ONIYANMA! WAY COOL!
I GUESS I'M DUELING YOU, HUH, JESSE?
YEP. SURE LOOKS LIKE IT.

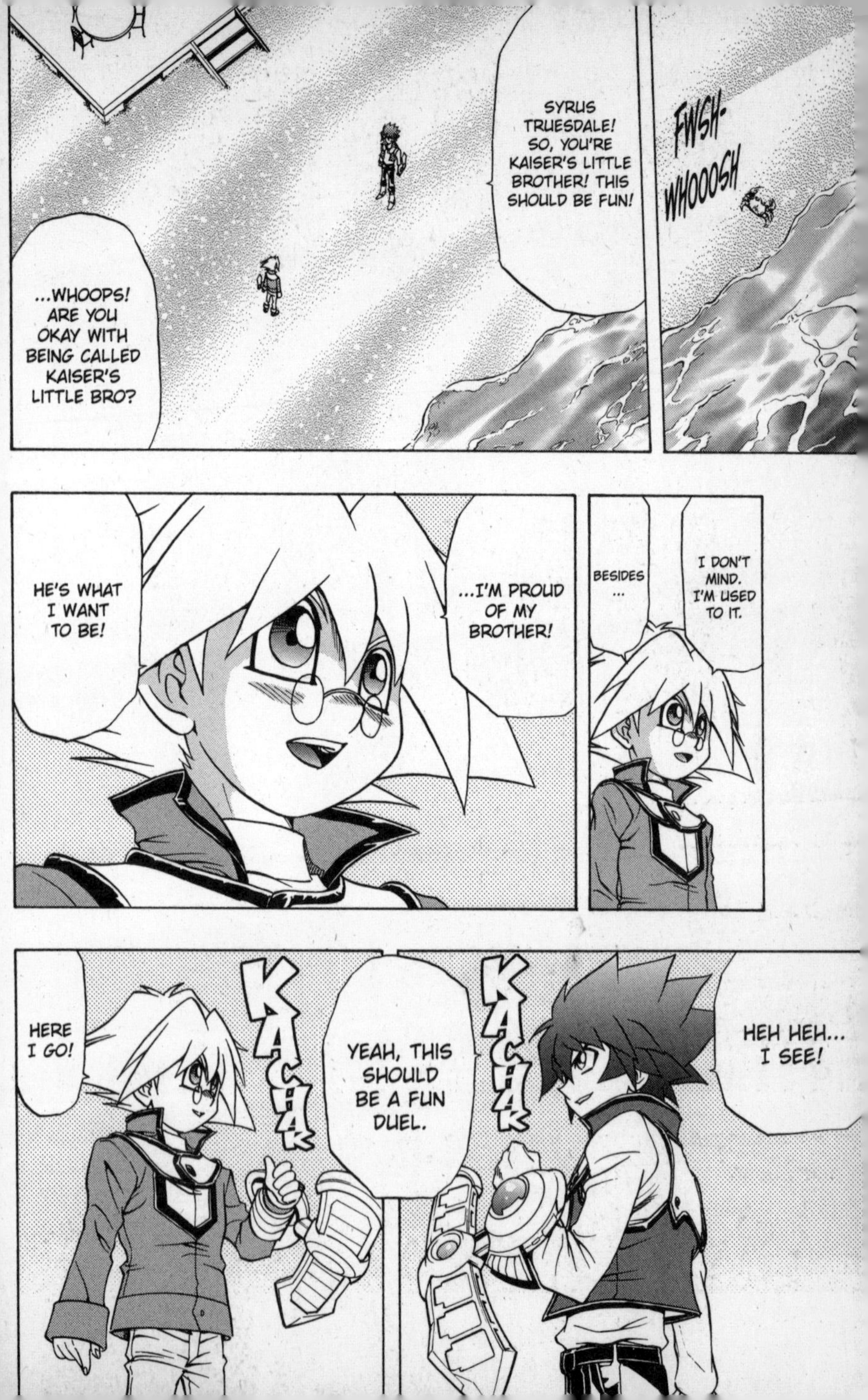
FWSH-WHOOOSH
SYRUS TRUESDALE! SO, YOU'RE KAISER'S LITTLE BROTHER! THIS SHOULD BE FUN!
...WHOOPS! ARE YOU OKAY WITH BEING CALLED KAISER'S LITTLE BRO?
I DON'T MIND. I'M USED TO IT.
BESIDES ...
...I'M PROUD OF MY BROTHER!
HE'S WHAT I WANT TO BE!
HEH HEH... I SEE!
KACHAK
YEAH, THIS SHOULD BE A FUN DUEL.
KACHAK
HERE I GO!

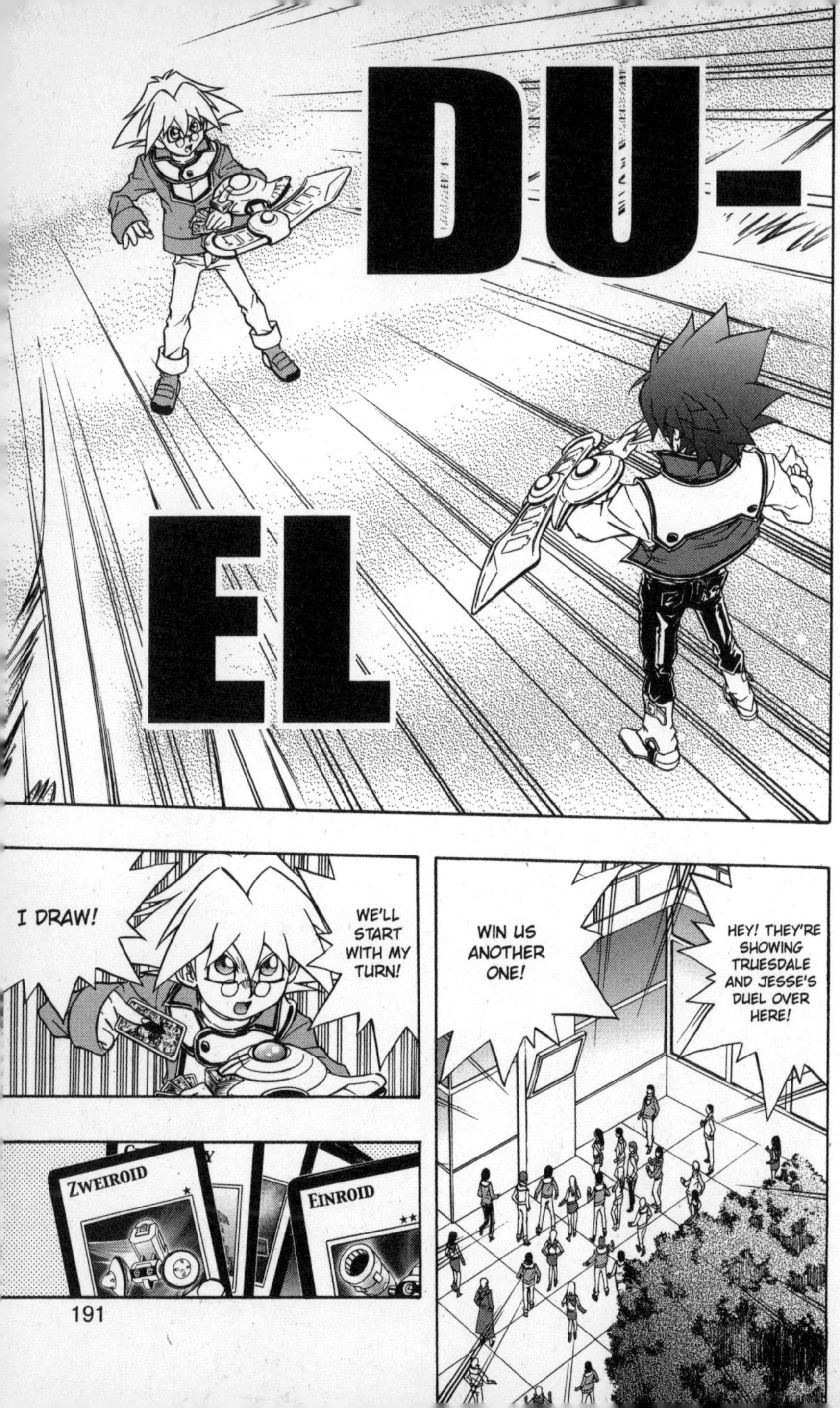
DU-
EL
HEY! THEY'RE SHOWING TRUESDALE AND JESSE'S DUEL OVER HERE!
WIN US ANOTHER ONE!
WE'LL START WITH MY TURN!
I DRAW!
EINROID
ZWEIROID

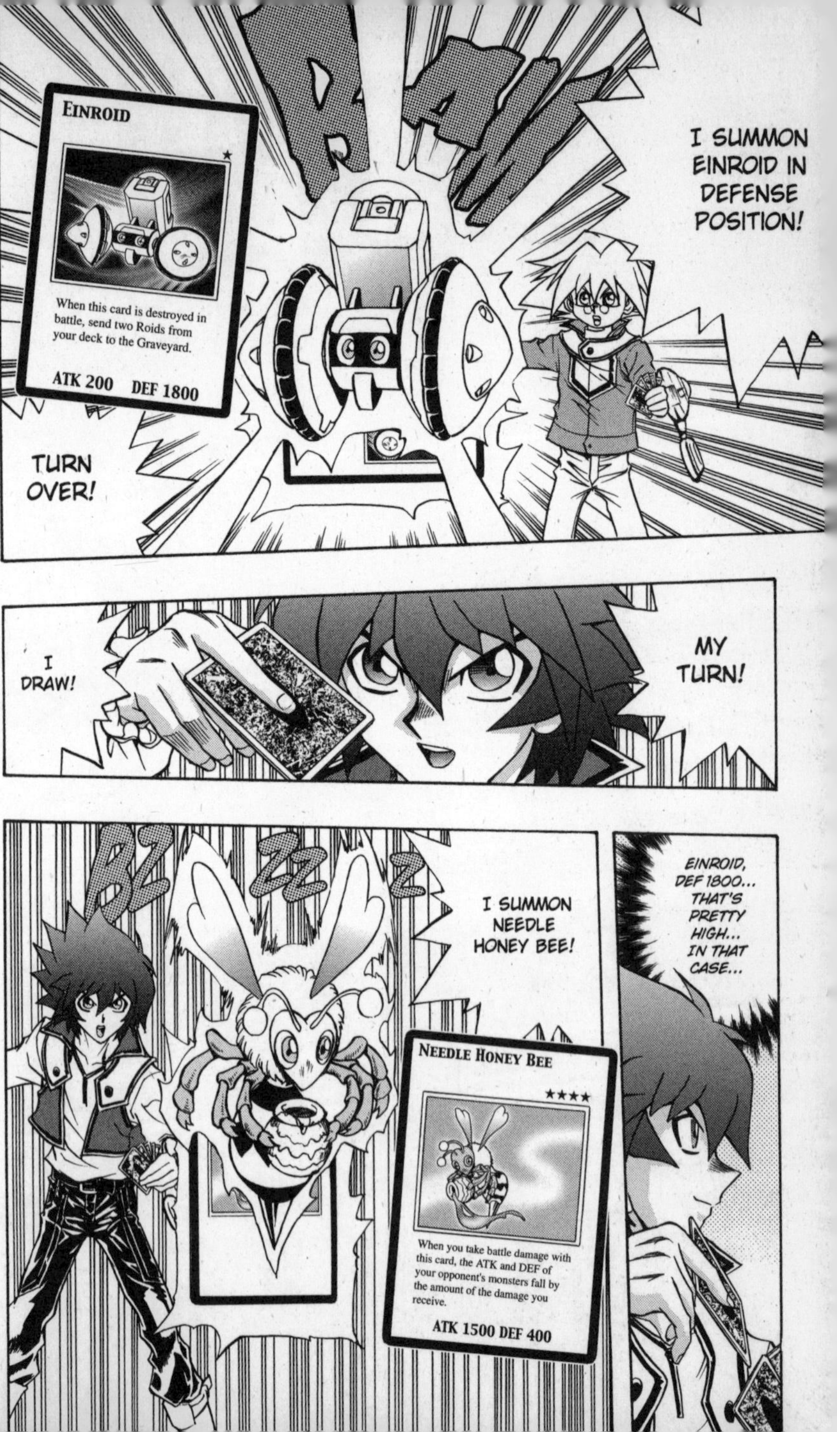
I SUMMON EINROID IN DEFENSE POSITION!
EINROID
When this card is destroyed in battle, send two Roids from your deck to the Graveyard.
ATK 200 DEF 1800
TURN OVER!
MY TURN!
I DRAW!
EINROID, DEF 1800... THAT'S PRETTY HIGH... IN THAT CASE...
I SUMMON NEEDLE HONEY BEE!
NEEDLE HONEY BEE
When you take battle damage with this card, the ATK and DEF of your opponent's monsters fall by the amount of the damage you receive.
ATK 1500 DEF 400

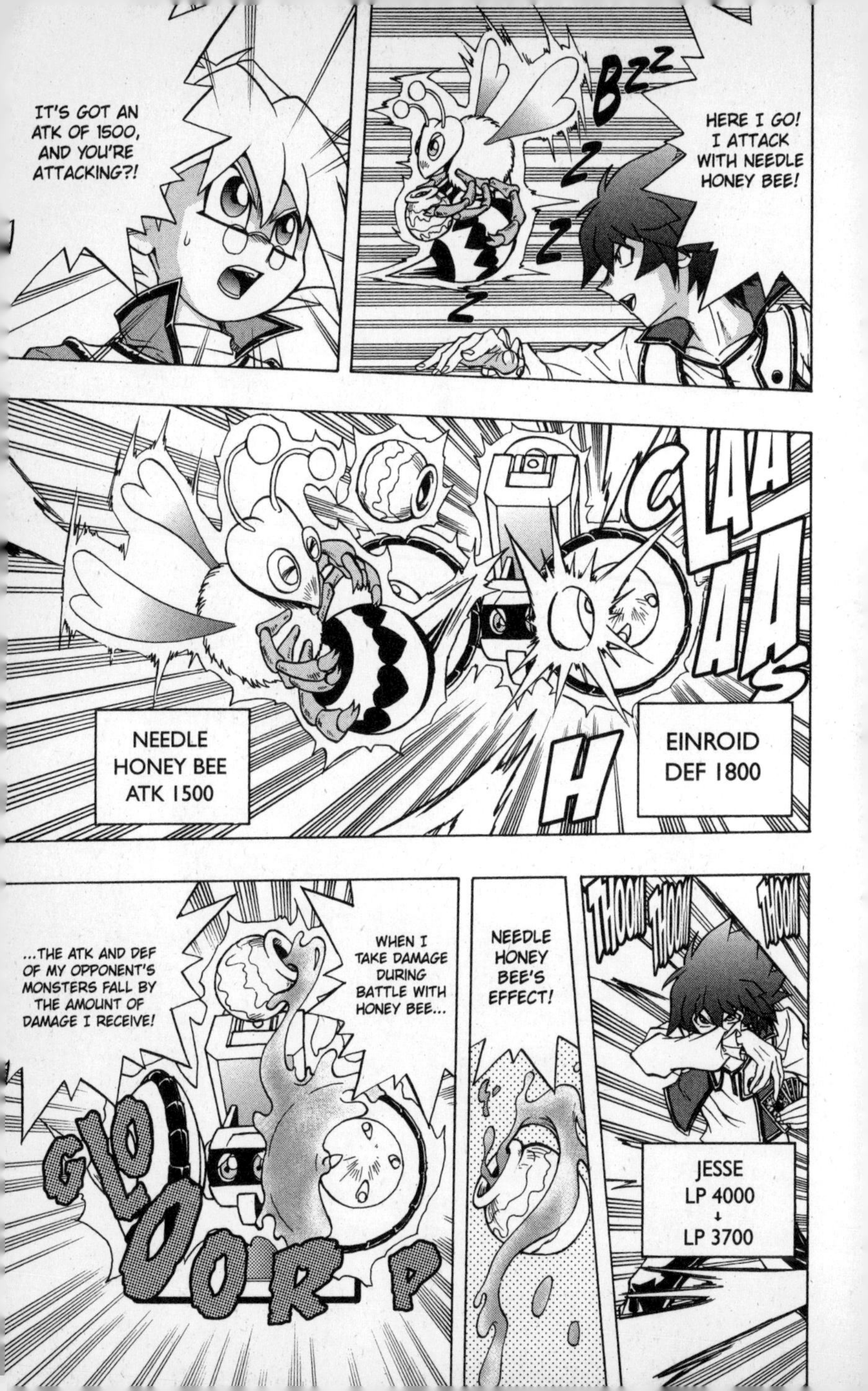
BZZZ
HERE I GO! I ATTACK WITH NEEDLE HONEY BEE!
IT'S GOT AN ATK OF 1500, AND YOU'RE ATTACKING?!
CLAAAASH
EINROID DEF 1800
NEEDLE HONEY BEE ATK 1500
THOOM THOOM THOOM
JESSE LP 4000 ↓ LP 3700
NEEDLE HONEY BEE'S EFFECT!
WHEN I TAKE DAMAGE DURING BATTLE WITH HONEY BEE...
...THE ATK AND DEF OF MY OPPONENT'S MONSTERS FALL BY THE AMOUNT OF DAMAGE I RECEIVE!
GLOOORP

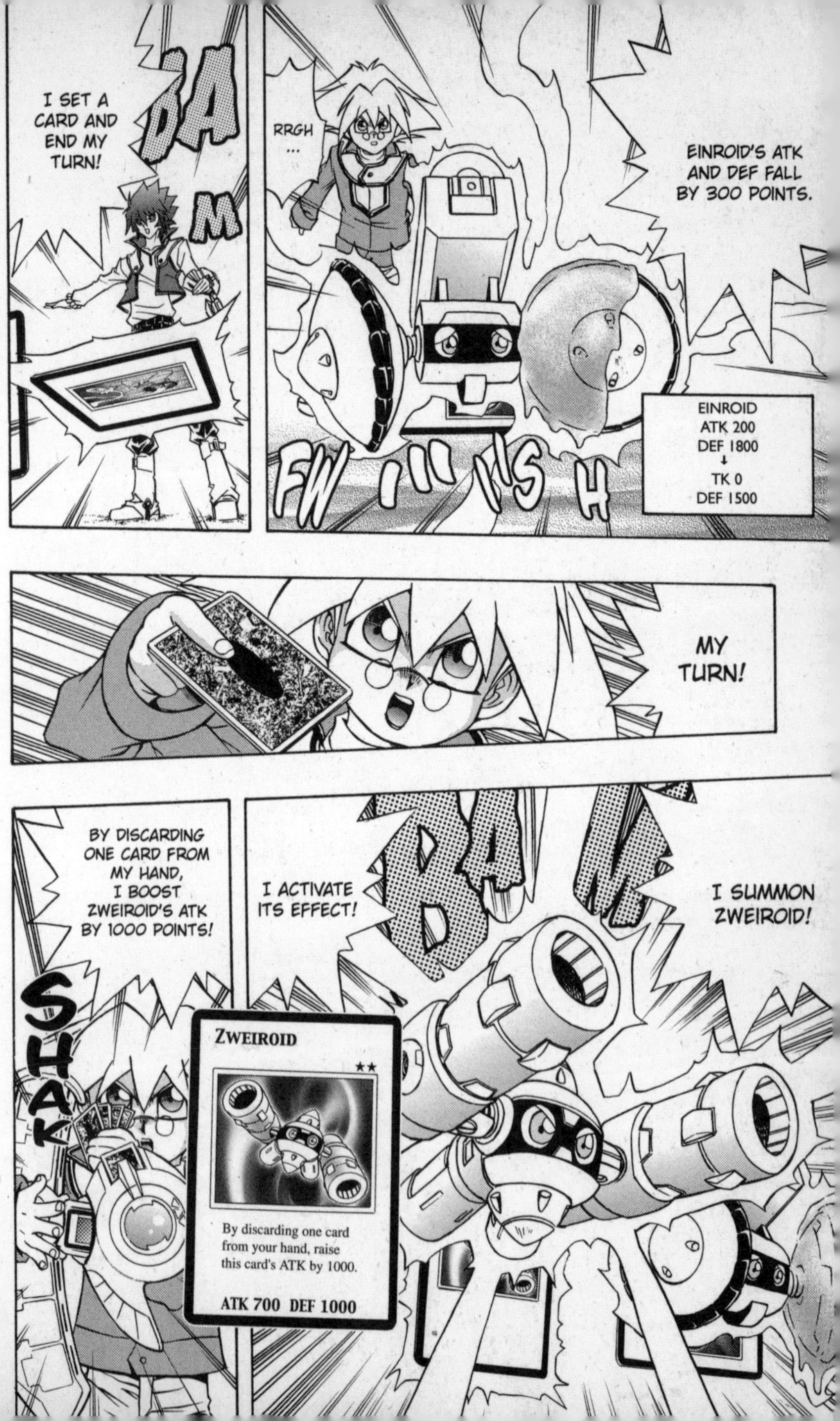
EINROID'S ATK AND DEF FALL BY 300 POINTS.
RRGH ...
EINROID
ATK 200
DEF 1800
↓
TK 0
DEF 1500
FWISH
BAM
I SET A CARD AND END MY TURN!
MY TURN!
I SUMMON ZWEIROID!
BAM
I ACTIVATE ITS EFFECT!
BY DISCARDING ONE CARD FROM MY HAND, I BOOST ZWEIROID'S ATK BY 1000 POINTS!
SHAK
ZWEIROID
By discarding one card from your hand, raise this card's ATK by 1000.
ATK 700 DEF 1000

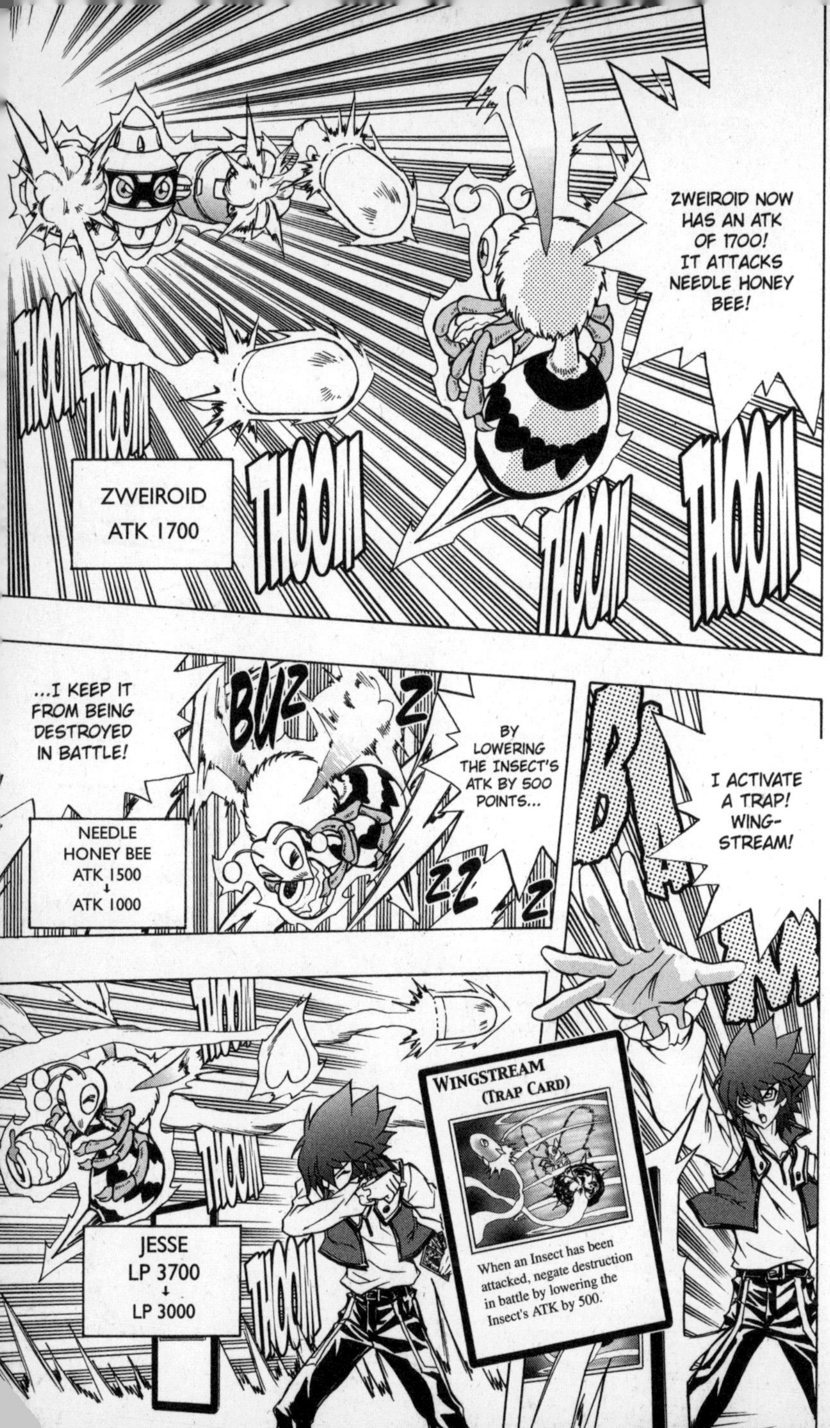
ZWEIROID NOW HAS AN ATK OF 1700! IT ATTACKS NEEDLE HONEY BEE!
THOOM
THOOM
THOOM
THOOM
THOOM
ZWEIROID ATK 1700
BAM
I ACTIVATE A TRAP! WING-STREAM!
BY LOWERING THE INSECT'S ATK BY 500 POINTS...
BUZZZZ
...I KEEP IT FROM BEING DESTROYED IN BATTLE!
NEEDLE HONEY BEE ATK 1500 ↓ ATK 1000
WINGSTREAM (TRAP CARD)
When an Insect has been attacked, negate destruction in battle by lowering the Insect's ATK by 500.
THOOM
THOOM
THOOM
JESSE LP 3700 ↓ LP 3000

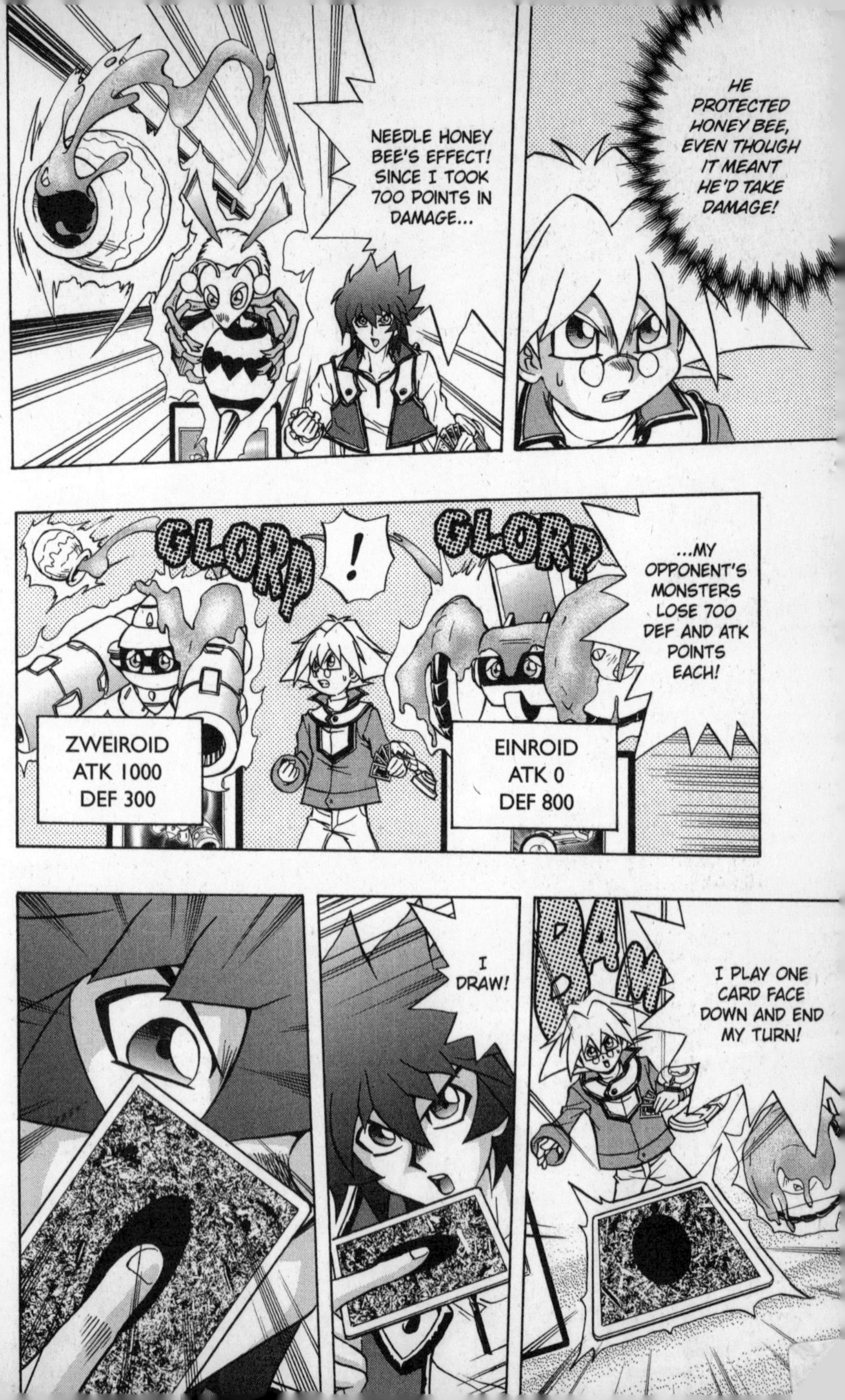
HE PROTECTED HONEY BEE, EVEN THOUGH IT MEANT HE'D TAKE DAMAGE!
NEEDLE HONEY BEE'S EFFECT! SINCE I TOOK 700 POINTS IN DAMAGE...
GLORP
!
GLORP
...MY OPPONENT'S MONSTERS LOSE 700 DEF AND ATK POINTS EACH!
EINROID ATK 0 DEF 800
ZWEIROID ATK 1000 DEF 300
BAM
I PLAY ONE CARD FACE DOWN AND END MY TURN!
I DRAW!

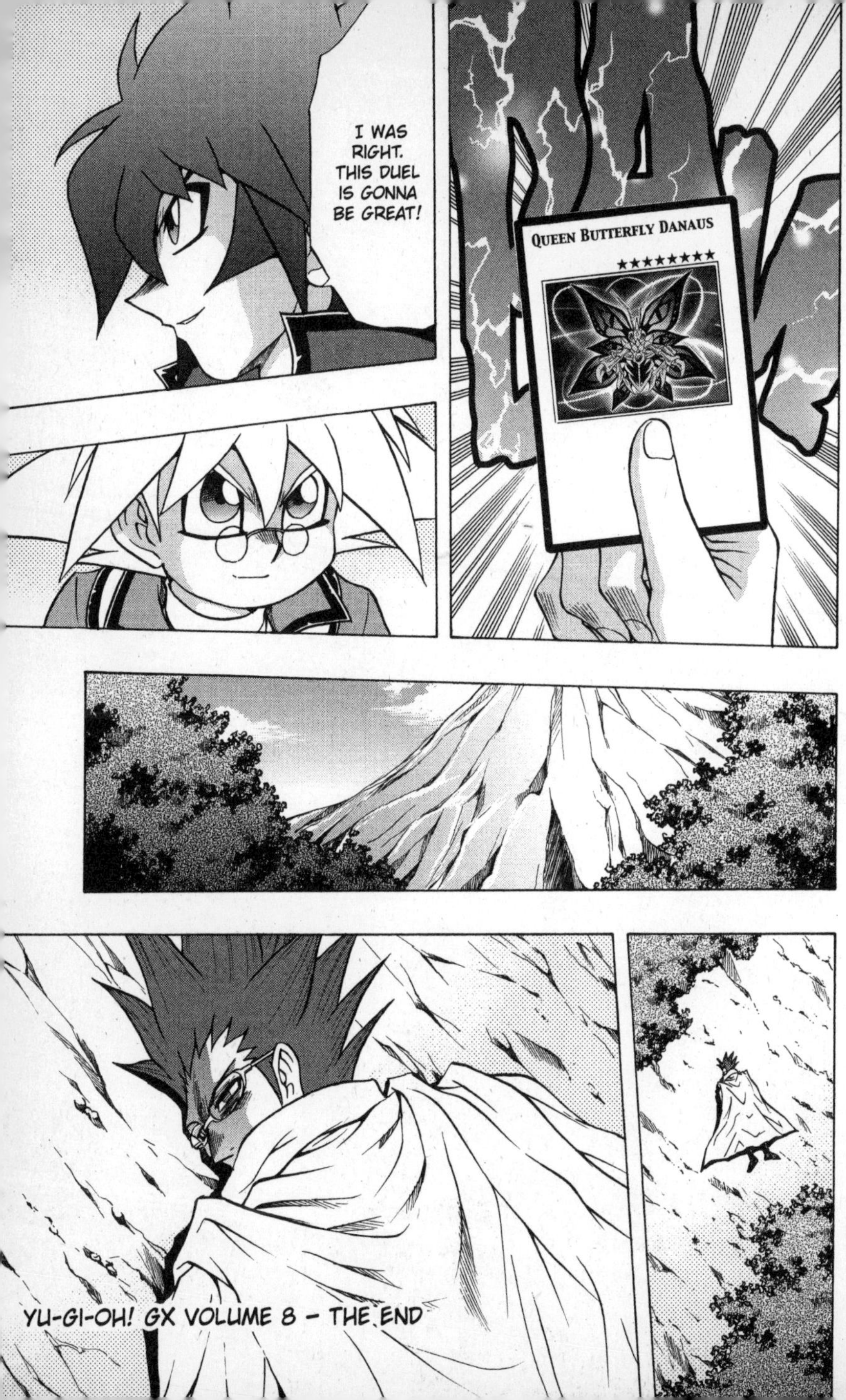
QUEEN BUTTERFLY DANAUS
I WAS RIGHT. THIS DUEL IS GONNA BE GREAT!
YU-GI-OH! GX VOLUME 8 - THE END

STAFF
YUJI KOIKE
MAKOTO SHIMIZU
TAKASHI UCHIDA
AKIRA ITO
TOSHIO NAGAOKA

DUEL COMPOSITION COOPERATION
MASAHIRO UCHIDA

COLORING
NABETARO

EDITING
DAISUKE TERASHI

MASTER OF THE CARDS

Jaden Yuki and the rest of the next generation of Duelists have introduced their own cards into the *Yu-Gi-Oh!* TCG, which also make their first appearance here in the seventh volume of the *Yu-Gi-Oh!: GX* manga! As with all original *Yu-Gi-Oh!* cards, names can differ slightly between the Japanese and English versions, so we're showing you both for reference. Plus, we show you the card even if the card itself doesn't show up in the manga but the monster or trap does! And some cards you may have already seen in the original *Yu-Gi-Oh!*, but we still note them the first time they appear in this volume anyway!

First Appearance in This Volume	Japanese Card Name	English Card Name <<!>> = Not yet available in the TCG.
p.10	Vision Hero Increase V•HERO インクリース	Vision HERO Increase <<!>>
p.11	Vision Hero Minimum Ray V•HERO ミニマム・レイ	Vision HERO Minimum Ray <<!>>
p.12	Mask Change マスク・チェンジ	Mask Change
p.13	Damaged Mask 破損した仮面	Damaged Mask <<!>>
p.13	Fiend's Pitfall 魔人の落とし穴	Fiendish Trap Hole <<!>>
p.15	Masked Hero Goka M•HERO 剛火	Masked HERO Goka
p.17	Holy Barrier - Mirror Force 聖なるバリアーミラーフォース―	Mirror Force
p.17	Form Change フォーム・チェンジ	Form Change <<!>>
p.18	Masked Hero Vapor M•HERO ヴェイパー	Masked HERO Vapor
p.20	Vision Hero Multiply Guy V•HERO マルティプリ・ガイ	Vision HERO Multiply Guy <<!>>
p.23	Vision Fusion 幻影融合	Vision Fusion <<!>>
p.23	Vision Hero Poisoner V•HERO ポイズナー	Vision HERO Poisoner <<!>>

p.24	Masked Hero Dusk Crow **M•HERO** ダスク·クロウ	Masked HERO Dusk Crow <<!>>
p.27	Hero Soul ヒーロー·ソウル	Hero Soul <<!>>
p.29	Negate Attack 攻撃の無力化	Negate Attack
p.29	Vision Hero Witch Raid **V•HERO** ウィッチ·レイド	Vision HERO Witch Raider <<!>>
p.30	Vision Release 幻影解放	Vision Release <<!>>
p.33	Vision Hero Adoration **V•HERO** アドレイション	Vision HERO Adoration
p.61	Vision Hero Faris **V•HERO** ファリス	Vision HERO Farris <<!>>
p.62	The Atmosphere The アトモスフィア	The Atmosphere
p.63	Excavation Work 発掘作業	Excavation Work <<!>>
p.63	Breeze Sphere ブリーズ・スフィア	Breeze Sphere <<!>>
p.64	Virtual Sphere バーチャル·スフィア	Virtual Sphere <<!>>
p.74	Synthesize Sphere シンセサイズ·スフィア	Synthetic Sphere <<!>>
p.75	Atmospheric Transference 大気伝達	Atmospheric Transference <<!>>
p.75	Air Sphere エアースフィア	Air Sphere <<!>>
p.84	Illusion 幻惑	Illusion <<!>>
p.85	Appearing Vision 出幻	Apparition <<!>>

p.85	Vision Hero Vaion **V•HERO** ヴァイオン	Vision HERO Vyon <<!>>
p.88	Vision Hero Gravito **V•HERO** グラビート	Vision HERO Gravito <<!>>
p.88	Fusion 融合	Polymerization
p.90	Trafasphere トラファスフィア	Troposphere
p.93	Hallucination 幻覚	Hallucination <<!>>
p.96	Vision Hero Trinity **V•HERO** トリニティー	Vision Hero Trinity
p.103	Air Barrier 大気障壁	Air Barrier <<!>>
p.127	Sealed Beast Inun 封印獣イヌン	Forbidden Beast Inun <<!>>
p.128	Masked Hero Gusto **M•HERO** ガスト	Masked HERO Gust <<!>>
p.128	Mask Function 1 マスク·ファンクシャン1	Mask Function #1 <<!>>
p.130	Beast Concealed Mantra 獣に隠された真言	Beast-Concealed Mantra <<!>>
p.130	Sealed Mantra 封印の真言	Forbidden Mantra <<!>>
p.131	Sealed Beast Nunurao 封印獣ヌヌラオ	Forbidden Beast Nunurao <<!>>
p.132	Sealed Beast Nibunu 封印獣ニブヌ	Forbidden Beast Nibunu <<!>>
p.138	Urgent Line アージャント·ライン	SOS <<!>>
p.139	Masked Hero Fountain **M•HERO** ファウンティン	Masked HERO Fountain <<!>>

p.140	Mask Change Second マスク·チェンジ·セカンド	Mask Change II <<!>>
p.141	Curse of Mantra 真言の呪縛	Curse of the Mantra <<!>>
p.143	Masked Hero Acid **M•HERO** アシッド	Masked HERO Acid <<!>>
p.150	Mantra Within the Corpse 屍の中の真言	The Body's Hidden Mantra <<!>>
p.151	The Despair Uranus	The Despair Uranus <<!>>
p.152	Sealed Beast Watsumu 封印獣ワツム	Forbidden Beast Watsumu <<!>>
p.155	Barrier of the Ancient Document 古文書の結界	Barrier of the Ancient Codex <<!>>
p.172	Masked Hero Dusk Crow **M•HERO** ダスク·クロウ	Masked HERO Dusk Crow <<!>>
p.174	Double Attack (Team Strike) ダブルアタック(合体攻撃)	Double Attack (Team Strike) <<!>>
p.187	Zwei Roid ツバァイ·ロイド	Zweiroid <<!>>
p.187	Ein Roid アイン·ロイド	Einroid <<!>>
p.192	Needle Honey Bee ニードル·ハニー·ビィ	Needle Honey Bee <<!>>
p.195	Wing Stream ウイング·ストリーム	Wingstream <<!>>
p.197	Queen Butterfly Danaus クイーン·バタフライ ダナウス	Queen Butterfly Danaus <<!>>

IN THE NEXT VOLUME...

The possessed Principal Mackenzie makes his final bid to crush the students of Duel Academy and seize Chazz and Jaden's Spirit Cards! Jaden will need all his dueling skill as he battles his way through to the final Duel, fighting for his friends, his mentor Koyo Hibiki, and the fate of Duel Academy itself!

COMING AUGUST 2012!

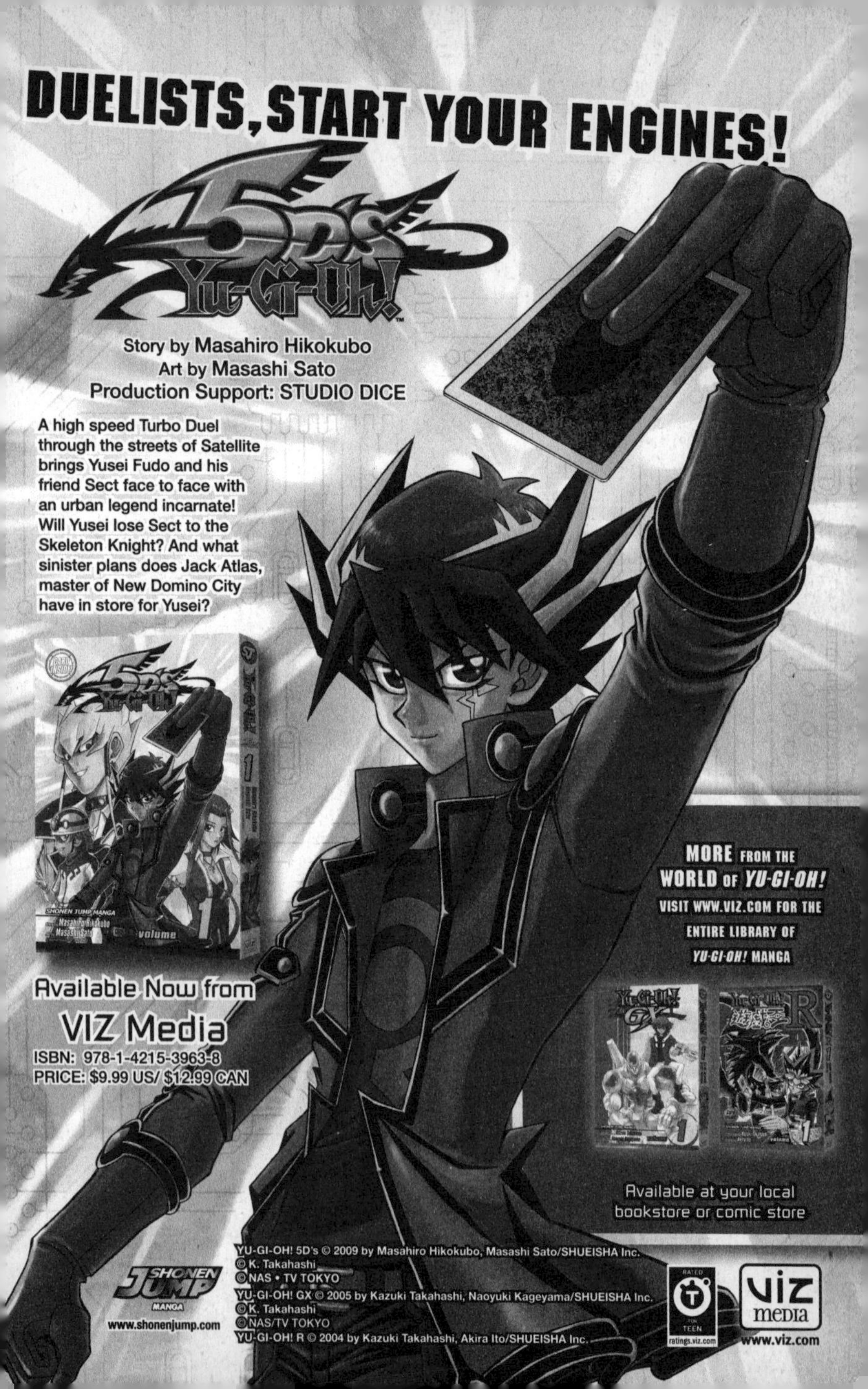

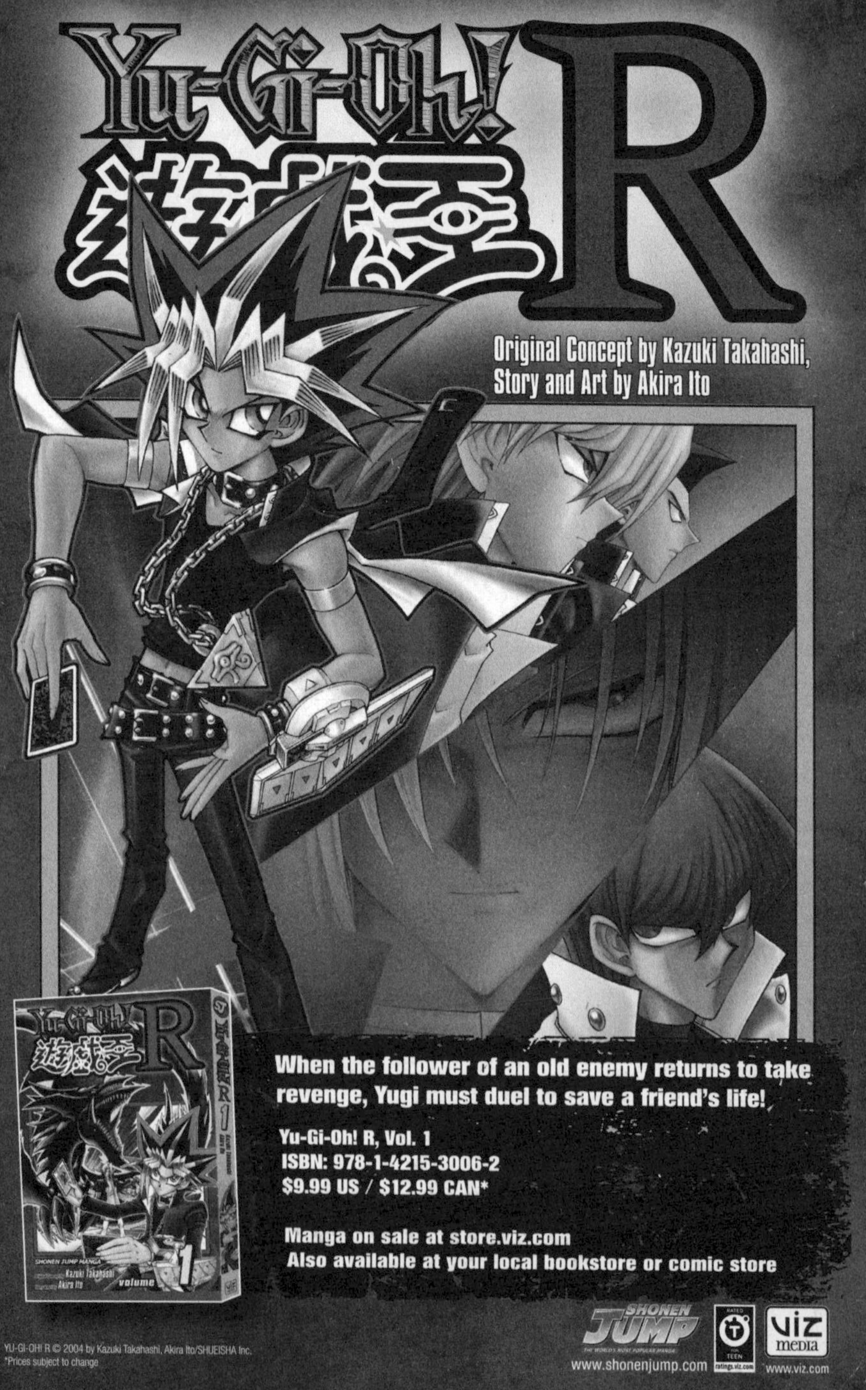
Yu-Gi-Oh! R
Original Concept by Kazuki Takahashi,
Story and Art by Akira Ito
When the follower of an old enemy returns to take revenge, Yugi must duel to save a friend's life!
Yu-Gi-Oh! R, Vol. 1
ISBN: 978-1-4215-3006-2
$9.99 US / $12.99 CAN*
Manga on sale at store.viz.com
Also available at your local bookstore or comic store
SHONEN JUMP MANGA
Kazuki Takahashi
Akira Ito
volume 1
SHONEN JUMP
www.shonenjump.com
RATED T FOR TEEN
ratings.viz.com
VIZ media
www.viz.com
YU-GI-OH! R © 2004 by Kazuki Takahashi, Akira Ito/SHUEISHA Inc.
*Prices subject to change

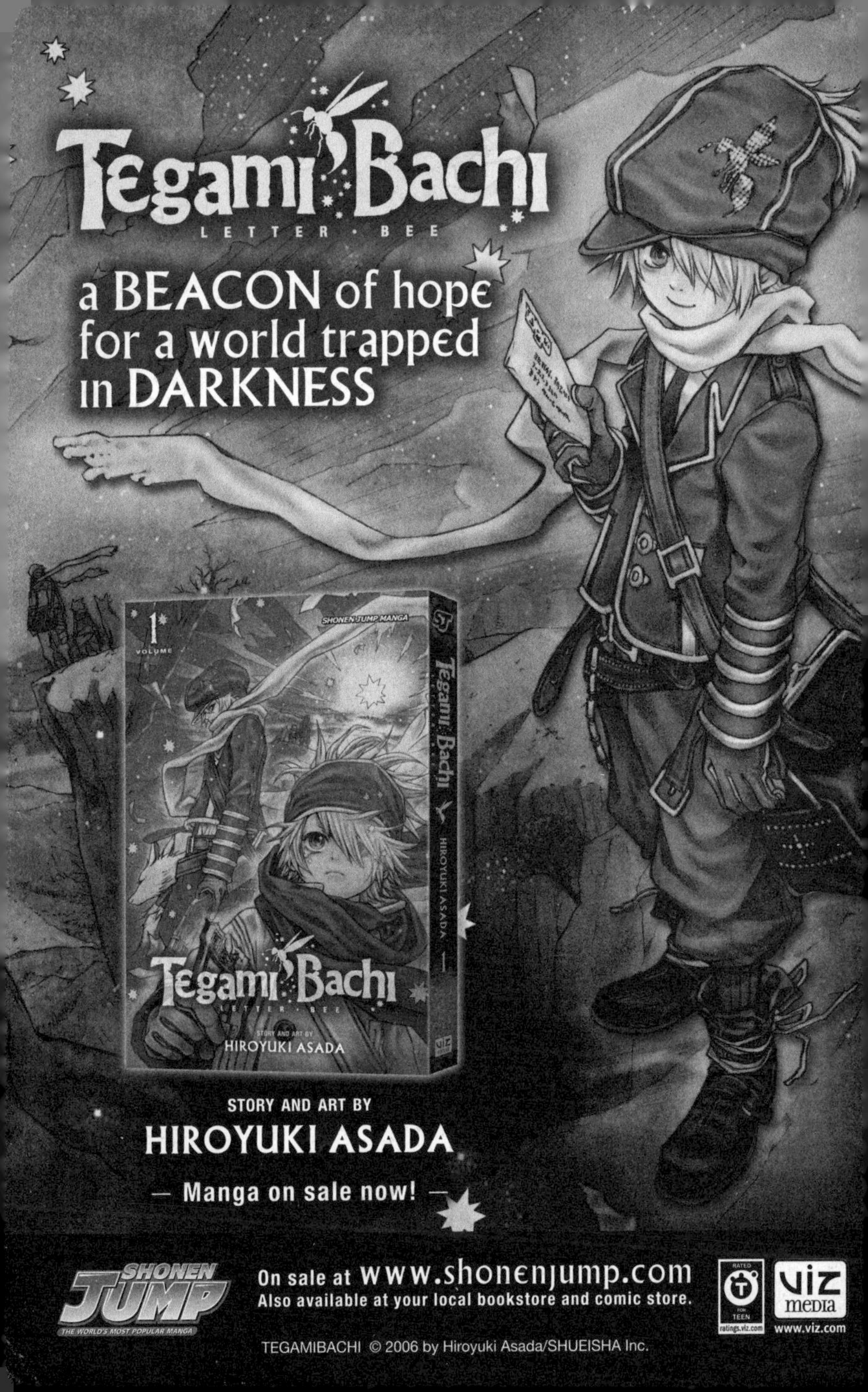
TEGAMI BACHI
LETTER · BEE
a BEACON of hope for a world trapped in DARKNESS
1 VOLUME
SHONEN JUMP MANGA
TEGAMI BACHI
LETTER · BEE
STORY AND ART BY
HIROYUKI ASADA
STORY AND ART BY
HIROYUKI ASADA
— Manga on sale now! —
SHONEN JUMP
THE WORLD'S MOST POPULAR MANGA
On sale at www.shonenjump.com
Also available at your local bookstore and comic store.
RATED T FOR TEEN
ratings.viz.com
VIZ media
www.viz.com
TEGAMIBACHI © 2006 by Hiroyuki Asada/SHUEISHA Inc.